A **Dictionary**
of Nonprofit
Terms and
Concepts

PHILANTHROPIC AND NONPROFIT STUDIES

Dwight F. Burlingame and David C. Hammack, editors

A
Dictionary
of Nonprofit
Terms and
Concepts

David Horton Smith,
Robert A. Stebbins,
and Michael A. Dover

INDIANA UNIVERSITY PRESS

Bloomington & Indianapolis

This book is a publication of

Indiana University Press
601 North Morton Street
Bloomington, IN 47404-3797 USA

http://iupress.indiana.edu

Telephone orders   800-842-6796
Fax orders   812-855-7931
Orders by e-mail   iuporder@indiana.edu

The paper used in this publication meets the minimum requirements of
American National Standard for Information Sciences—Permanence of
Paper for Printed Library Materials, ANSI Z39.48-1984.

MANUFACTURED IN THE UNITED STATES OF AMERICA

Library of Congress Cataloging-in-Publication Data

Smith, David Horton.
A dictionary of nonprofit terms and concepts / David Horton Smith,
Robert A. Stebbins, and Michael A. Dover.
p. cm.—(Philanthropic and nonprofit studies)
Includes bibliographical references.
ISBN 0-253-34783-1 (cloth : alk. paper)   1. Nonprofit
organizations—Terminology—Dictionaries.   2. Voluntarism—
Terminology—Dictionaries.   3. Charities—Terminology—
Dictionaries.   4. Social action—Terminology—Dictionaries.   5. Social
participation—Terminology—Dictionaries.   6. Political participation—
Terminology—Dictionaries.   7. Leisure—Social aspects—Terminology—
Dictionaries.   I. Stebbins, Robert A., date   II. Dover, Michael
A.   III. Title.   IV. Series.
HD2769.15.S63 2006
361.003—dc22
2006005271

1 2 3 5 11 10 09 08 07 06

For Catherine
D. H. S.

à Alain et Josée Bertrand
R. A. S.

Contents

Preface

The roots of this book go back over thirty years to when the senior author was founding and building the international, interprofessional, interdisciplinary organization now named the Association for Research on Nonprofit Organizations and Voluntary Action (ARNOVA) (see Smith 1999; Smith 2003). It was clear to him that part of the task of bringing together the parts of some thirty different fields, disciplines, and professions into a new field and association would involve identifying the terms most frequently used in those existing fields for the common phenomena of associations, volunteering, the nonprofit sector, and voluntary action broadly conceived.

To this end, Smith compiled a list of terms and concepts used in thirty fields he identified as relevant to nonprofit and voluntary action research and listed them, without definitions, in the first article of the first regular issue of the *Journal of Voluntary Action Research*, the forerunner of the current ARNOVA journal *Nonprofit and Voluntary Sector Quarterly* (Smith 1972b). Many of those terms listed are now defined in this dictionary, along with hundreds of others, many of which are more recent in origin.

Later in the 1970s, Smith worked on founding and building a more clearly international association focused on nonprofit and voluntary action research, since the Association of Voluntary Action Scholars (renamed ARNOVA in 1990) was largely North American in composition. In the process of this second association-building effort (Smith 2003:470–471) that resulted in the now defunct International Voluntary Action and Voluntary Organization Research Organization (IVAR-VOIR), Smith collaborated with several scholars from other nations in creating a list of seventy-five key nonprofit organization and voluntary action terms in American English and, to the extent possible, their equivalents in various other languages. Although the project was never funded or completed, an initial paper based on it (Smith et al. 1992) was presented in March 1992 at the Third International Conference of Research on Voluntary and Nonprofit Organizations, held in Indianapolis, Indiana, and organized by the Center on Philanthropy of Indiana University at Indianapolis. The languages included were American English, British English, Dutch, Italian, French, and German. The last section of the paper consisted of a glossary of thirty-nine of the terms defined by the senior author—perhaps the first attempt at such an endeavor as well as being a forerunner of this book.

The seventy-five terms and concepts from the foregoing effort formed the core of a subsequent effort by Smith (1996a) to define more than two hundred nonprofit/voluntary sector terms as an aid to writing his book *Grassroots Associations* (Smith 2000). This paper was unsuitable for a journal article and too small for a book and was therefore never published. While developing for Smith a Procite database of his references for the 2000 book, Dover shared with Smith copies of his two glossaries of nearly a thousand terms (less than a hundred used in this dictionary), compiled as part of his preparation for his Status and Power preliminary examination in sociology and his Older Adult Volunteer Participation preliminary examination in social work, both at the Doctoral Program in Social Work and Social Science at the University of Michigan. Plans were made at that time to prepare a co-authored volume, cited in the 2000 book as forthcoming under the title *Concepts and Terminology for Nonprofit and Voluntary Sector Studies*. However, preparation of this volume was delayed by Dover's dissertation research (Dover 2003). In 2003, Smith invited Robert A. Stebbins (University of Calgary) to join as second author in completing a dictionary of nonprofit terms and concepts, which became the present book. Terms were added from the index of Smith (2000) and other sources. These sources included some entries based on Dover's glossaries, which were originally envisioned to be approximately one-third of a 350-entry volume. The author team prepared a book proposal and circulated it to a few publishers known for books in the nonprofit field. Indiana University Press responded with a contract. As preparation of the volume continued, the number of entries more than tripled to 1,212 (with an additional 555 separate-entry cross-references), primarily the result of further work by Smith and Stebbins.

Stebbins's principal contribution to this dictionary rests on his extensive work in the interdisciplinary field of leisure studies, work dating to 1973 when he began exploratory research on amateurs in art, science, and sport (Stebbins 1979). Some of the interviewees in the study referred to their amateur involvements as hobbies, others as volunteering. Stebbins recognized that, theoretically, the three types of activity were different, even while they shared considerable common ground. A conceptual framework setting out their similarities and difference as forms of serious leisure, which was, in turn, contrasted with casual leisure, was published in 1982 (Stebbins 1982). A more detailed statement on volunteering as serious leisure appeared later (Stebbins 1996c), and research on volunteering using that framework has been published subsequently (e.g., Stebbins 1998; Stebbins and Graham 2004). Much of serious and casual leisure, we argue in this dictionary, can be conceived of as part of the nonprofit sector, and that includes, of course, leisure classifiable as volunteering.

Smith wrote the introduction and defined directly over six hundred of the basic terms and concepts and defined indirectly many more through his book (Smith 2000), and was especially active in the last quarter of 2004 and early 2005, although uninvolved earlier in 2004. Stebbins spearheaded completion of the book during this period, in collaboration with Dover in its later stages. In particular he added to Smith's and Dover's lists several hundred more terms found principally in Smith (2000) and to lesser extent in the social work dictionary written by Barker (2003) and in the nonprofit sector literature in general. Dover was involved early on in compiling references for the 2000 book, many of which were used by Smith as part of his definitions for this book. After completing his dissertation and the first year of his current academic appointment, he became re-involved in contributing references based upon his glossaries, as well as in assisting with preparation of the final manuscript. In all, the book has been a team effort.

Acknowledgments

The senior author is grateful for bibliographic help by Catherine Clinton McIntyre in the late stages of book preparation. He also wishes to thank his friends for moral support during periods of intensive work on the book. And most of all, he expresses his deep gratitude to Robert Stebbins, his co-author, without whom this particular scholarly dream would never have become a reality. Finally, all three authors wish to thank Sarah Brown, copy editor assigned to this project, for her most careful work on the manuscript. We would also like to thank Emily Tofte, MSW candidate at the University of Michigan, for her assistance to Michael Dover in the preparation of the index and in final corrections to the citations and bibliography. This book has been substantially improved thanks to their efforts.

Lexicographic Note

This dictionary contains terms and concepts, both of which sometimes appear as phrases or expressions rather than as single words. Furthermore, some terms and concepts have multiple meanings, with each being identified numerically as 1, 2, and so on. In most instances the meanings presented relate to the nonprofit sector, but occasionally more general usage is noted as well, primarily to show how technical usage varies from common sense and thereby place the term or concept in broader linguistic context.

We have strived to provide at least one reference for each entry, and have occasionally used a citation from the *Shorter Oxford English Dictionary* or a website. Moreover, we have tried to cite not only the broader reference but also the relevant page numbers within it. Still, many cited works deal largely or wholly with the defined term or concept, a situation noted here by the use of "passim," in lieu of page numbers. "Ibid." refers the reader to the preceding citation. "Cf." suggests the reader compare or see the following citation(s). An asterisk (*) signals that the word or phrase so marked is treated elsewhere in the dictionary in a separate entry. Likewise for reference entries preceded with *see* or *see also*.

On technical matters of style, particularly hyphenation, we have been guided by the eleventh edition of *Merriam Webster's Collegiate Dictionary* and the fifteenth edition of *The Chicago Manual of Style*. Spelling and punctuation conform to standard American practice. Following the other dictionaries in the social sciences with which we are familiar, we decided not to label as nouns, adjectives, and so on each term and concept. The handful of terms and concepts where there may be confusion in this regard are explicitly defined according to the appropriate part of speech.

Lexicographic Note

Finally, we have tried to note when a term or concept is informal or colloquial. Such a label is our judgment, however, since nearly all these words are not found in standard dictionaries, which could have otherwise offered lexicographic aid on this question. In fact most of the informal language of the nonprofit sector comes in the form of acronyms, which here are first presented and then spelled out.

A **Dictionary**
of Nonprofit
Terms and
Concepts

Introduction: Defining Nonprofit/Voluntary Sector Terms and Concepts

We need a general theory of the nonprofit sector. It is a critical weakness of this field. One way to launch this important project is, first, to concentrate on the terms and concepts that have been found useful in past research and theory. Next, it is necessary to give them clear, consistent definitions using other defined terms and "primitive terms," or simple words whose definitions are taken as given in the language used. In this regard Salamon and Anheier (1992) have made a start by defining some of the key terms related to the nonprofit/voluntary sector. And the present dictionary builds on their contribution by providing definitions of about 1,200 pertinent terms and concepts, accompanied by several hundred cross-references.

What we have undertaken here is, broadly conceived, a definition of the interdisciplinary, interprofessional field of nonprofit and voluntary action studies by indicating its usual conceptual contents and terms. The entries found here reflect the importance of associations, volunteering, citizen participation, philanthropy, voluntary action, nonprofit management, volunteer administration, leisure, and political activities of nonprofits, all being major aspects of the nonprofit sector, as defined here. But the entries also reflect a concern for the wider range of useful general concepts in theory and research that bear on the nonprofit sector and its manifestations in the United States and elsewhere.

Although our definitions are presented in alphabetic order, as a glossary or dictionary, note that they can also be clustered into meaningful sets. One such set consists of *general concepts* relevant to any researcher in the field, of which the following thirty-four terms are a sample, chosen purposely, based on our judgment of general relevance. Because of their special importance,

1

these terms are cited in many more references than usual in our dictionary entries (at least ten and often twenty or more references).

- Altruism
- Association
- Association management
- Church
- Citizen participation
- Civil society
- Community organizing
- Denomination
- Deviant nonprofit group
- Foundation
- Fund-raising
- Grassroots association
- Interest group
- Leisure activity
- New religion
- Nonprofit agency
- Nonprofit group

- Nonprofit management
- Nonprofit organization
- Nonprofit sector
- Philanthropy
- Pluralism, political
- Pluralism, religious
- Political party
- Sect
- Self-help group
- Social movement
- Union
- Voluntarism
- Voluntary action
- Volunteer
- Volunteer administration
- Volunteer program
- Volunteerism

A second main set of concepts relates to *nonprofit political activity,* the following being a sample of thirty-five terms of this cluster, chosen purposely, based on our judgment of specific relevance:

- Activist
- Advocacy group
- Agitator
- *Animateur*
- Citizen advisory board
- Citizen group
- Citizen involvement
- Citizen militia
- Citizen participation
- Community organizer
- Community organizing
- Corporatism
- Coup
- Demonstration
- Dissent
- Empowerment
- Freedom of dissent
- Interest group

- Intergovernmental organization
- Lobbying
- Mandated citizen participation
- Neocorporatism
- New social movement
- Organizer
- Political participation
- Political party
- Political pluralism
- Public interest group
- Rebellion
- Revolution
- Riot
- Social movement
- Social movement group
- Social protest activity
- Special interest group

A third set deals with *associations*. It includes the following thirty-four terms as a sample, chosen purposely, based on our judgment of specific relevance:

- Association
- Association management
- Associational activity
- Associational form of organization
- Associational volunteer
- Chapter
- Citizen group
- Club
- Common interest association
- Community group
- Community involvement
- Dues
- Freedom of assembly
- Freedom of association
- Grassroots association
- Member
- Member, analytic
- Member benefit
- Member benefit nonprofit group
- Member benefit organization
- Member eligibility
- Membership
- Monomorphic nonprofit group
- Mutual aid group
- National association
- Neighborhood association
- Nonprofit leader
- Participation
- Polymorphic nonprofit group
- Self-help group
- State association
- Transnational association
- Volunteer group
- Volunteer nonprofit group

The fourth set of concepts centers on *volunteers* and includes the following sample of twenty-seven terms, chosen purposely, based on our judgment of specific relevance:

- Association volunteer
- Board volunteer
- Episodic volunteer
- Imputed value of volunteer work
- Informal service volunteer
- Marginal volunteering
- Program volunteer
- Quasi-volunteer
- Service volunteer
- Traditional service volunteer
- Voluntary action
- Volunteer
- Volunteer center
- Volunteer department
- Volunteer exploitation
- Volunteer, habitual
- Volunteer, key
- Volunteer leadership
- Volunteer program
- Volunteer, pure
- Volunteer role
- Volunteer satisfaction
- Volunteer time
- Volunteer tourism
- Volunteer work
- Volunteering
- Volunteerism

The fifth set of terms relates to *philanthropy* and includes the following sample of thirty-one terms, chosen purposely, based on our judgment of specific relevance:

A Dictionary of Nonprofit Terms and Concepts

- Capital campaign
- Challenge grant
- Charity
- Company-sponsored foundation
- Donated goods
- Donation
- Donor
- Donor fatigue
- e-philanthropy
- Family foundation
- Flow-through funds
- Foundation
- General operational support
- Gift
- Giving
- Grant

- Grant proposal
- Grantee financial report
- Independent foundation
- In-kind contribution
- Letter of inquiry
- Matching grant
- Operating foundation
- Payout requirement
- Philanthropic foundation
- Philanthropy
- Public foundation
- Request for proposal
- Site visit
- Venture philanthropy
- Virtual foundation

The sixth set of terms refers to *nonprofit management* and includes the following sample of twenty-three terms, chosen purposely, based on our judgment of specific relevance:

- Alliance of nonprofits
- Board of directors in nonprofits
- Career in nonprofits
- Commercialization of nonprofits
- Communication in nonprofits
- Contracted services in nonprofits
- Ethics in nonprofit management
- Executive director in nonprofits
- Financial management in nonprofits
- Formation of a nonprofit
- Fund-raising in nonprofits
- Innovation in nonprofits
- Marketing in nonprofits

- Morale in nonprofits
- Nonprofit management
- Nonprofit management profession
- Power structure of nonprofits
- Privatization
- Professional/volunteer tensions in nonprofits
- Profits of nonprofits
- Risk management in nonprofits
- Strategic management in nonprofits
- Strategic planning in nonprofits

The seventh set of terms refers to *volunteer administration* and includes the following sample of eighteen terms, chosen purposely, based on our judgment of specific relevance:

- Accountability of volunteers/members
- Building paid staff-volunteer/member relationships

- Development of volunteers/members
- Formation of a volunteer program/association

- Job creation for volunteers/members
- Motivating volunteers/members
- Orientation of volunteers/members
- Personnel practices for volunteers/members
- Placement of volunteers/members
- Recognition of volunteers/members
- Recruitment of volunteers/members
- Retention of volunteers/members
- Risk management and liability for volunteers/members
- Screening of volunteers/members
- Supervision of volunteers/members
- Training of volunteers/members
- Volunteer administration
- Volunteer administrator

The eighth set of terms refers to *leisure* and includes the following sample of twenty-seven terms, chosen purposely, based on our judgment of specific relevance:

- Amateur
- Amateur group
- Amateur league
- Amateur team
- Casual leisure
- Casual volunteering
- Formal leisure activity
- Hobby
- Hobby group
- Hobbyist
- Informal cultural activity
- Informal interpersonal activity
- Informal leisure activity
- Informal mass media activity
- Informal resting inactivity
- Informal sports and outdoor recreational activity
- Leisure/leisure time
- Leisure activity
- Leisure class
- Leisure group
- Leisure society
- Project-based leisure
- Recreation/recreational activity
- Recreational group
- Serious leisure
- Volunteering as leisure
- Volunteering as unpaid work

The ninth set of terms concerns *religion* and includes the following sample of thirty-one terms, chosen purposely, based on our judgment of specific relevance:

- Church
- Church congregation
- Civil religion
- Clergy
- Confraternity
- Convent
- Conversion, religious
- Denomination
- Ecumenism
- Faith-based service
- Freedom of religion
- Fundamentalism
- Heresy
- Monastery
- Morality
- Mosque
- New religion
- Priest

- Proselytizing
- Religion
- Religiosity
- Religious functionary
- Religious nonprofit group
- Religious order
- Religious philanthropy
- Religious right
- Religious tolerance
- Ritual
- Secularization
- Stewardship
- Synagogue

The tenth set of terms concerns the *law* and includes the following sample of thirty-one terms, chosen purposely, based on our judgment of specific relevance:

- Bequest
- By-law
- Charitable federal tax exemption requirements
- Charitable remainder trust
- Charitable solicitation regulation
- Charitable trust
- Charity (sense 2)
- Commerciality doctrine
- Corporation, charitable
- *Cy pres* doctrine
- Dissolution and distribution of assets of nonprofit organization
- Donative intent
- Donor intent
- Excise tax on foundations
- Expulsion of association member
- Fiduciary obligation of board of directors
- Freedom of association
- Grant-making foundation
- Involuntary dissolution of non-profit organization
- Law and nonprofits/charity
- Lawful purpose of nonprofit corporation
- Limitations on charity lobbying and political campaign activity
- Nondistribution constraint
- Nonprofit corporation
- Operating foundation
- Private foundation
- Qualified donee for tax-deductible contribution
- State and local tax exemption, charitable
- Statute of Charitable Uses
- Tax-exempt organizations registered with the Internal Revenue Service
- Unrelated business income tax

As might be expected, these ten sets are not mutually exclusive. Some terms and concepts find a place in two or more clusters, especially the first cluster and some other cluster, since the first cluster is "stacked" above the other nine. Scholars with different interests could undoubtedly add more terms to these sets (and we have not exhausted the terms in our dictionary that might fit into each set) and possibly even add an additional set or two of their own. We welcome such contributions for future editions of this dictionary. Note, however, that we have avoided defining nonprofit accounting terms entirely, because several other authors have already accomplished this (e.g., M. J. Gross, Richard F. Larkin, and John H. McCarthy, *Financial* *and Accounting Guide for Nonprofit Organizations*, 6th ed. 2000; R. Hussey [ed.], *A Dictionary of Accounting*, 2nd ed. 1999). We have also been sparing in defining legal terms, which are myriad and already defined in Hopkins's (1994) *Nonprofit Law Dictionary* and in his *The Law of Tax-Exempt Organizations*, 8th ed. (2004). We have purposely defined only certain major relevant organizations: ARNOVA, ISTR, and INDEPENDENT SECTOR—all included because of their special relevance to research on nonprofits and the voluntary sector. We believe this dictionary should define terms and concepts rather than names of organizations. Additional relevant organizations are mentioned in the entry *nonprofit sector, infrastructure organizations, and are described in such other sources as Abramson and McCarthy (2002), Burlingame (2004), and Levy and Cherry (1996). We have defined many terms relevant to philanthropy and fund-raising, but more are to be found in Burlingame (2004:533–541 and passim) and in Levy and Cherry (1996). We have also defined many terms related to religion, but many more are to be found in Bowker (1997), Livingstone and Cross (1997) and Taylor (1998), among other sources.

Concerning the glossary itself, we have tried to keep it to manageable size, making it a useful manual that includes extensive cross-referencing of synonymous and related terms. Our approach is distinctive, even while, in its core definitions, it builds on previous literature. For instance, *nonprofit group* is defined as being either formal or informal. This differs from Salamon and Anheier's (1992a:135) definition, while nevertheless incorporating their point that nonprofit groups must have "some institutional reality," which can be demonstrated "by having regular meetings, officers or rules of procedure or some degree of organizational permanence." For us this level of institutional reality is achieved by social entities called "groups" (Smith 1967). This approach allows into the category of nonprofit group millions of groups in the United States alone that would otherwise be ignored (cf. Smith 1992a, 1994b, 2000; Wuthnow 1994).

Our approach also distinguishes nonprofit groups from household and family groups by noting absence in the first of the depth of personal attachment that is so characteristic of people in the second (Smith 1991). Our treatment of the self-governing, or autonomous, aspect of nonprofit groups is somewhat softer than that of Salamon and Anheier (1992a:135). This is based on Smith's (1994b) research, which shows that local affiliate (polymorphic) groups of higher level nonprofits (usually associations) tend to perceive themselves as quite autonomous, contrary to what might be assumed from their official structural position. Furthermore, we emphasize "significant autonomy," where Salamon and Anheier (1992a:135) seem to ask for complete autonomy ("not controlled by outside entities"). We also include as nonprofits both public (nonmember) benefit *and* private member benefit groups, as Salamon and Anheier (1992a:135) seem to do (though Salamon alone [1992:7] writes during the same year that nonprofit groups are only public benefit). We also argue that nonprofit groups reflect or manifest a "voluntary spirit" (O'Connell 1983)—a set of attitudes and values fostering participation in the nonprofit sector referred to these days in less ideologically loaded terms as "voluntary altruism" (Smith 2000:18–24).

Although disagreement is possible on all these special facets of our definition, they do have their merits as well as their drawbacks. The primary merits of our definition are the greater inclusiveness of the category of nonprofit group and attachment of such groups to a special compliance/motivational reward structure. This structure helps account for why people mainly volunteer in such groups in society and why wages for paid employees are generally lower there (cf. Smith 1994b; Steinberg 1990). Nonprofit organizations are seen here as nonprofits that are more formalized in structure, a narrower category than nonprofit groups. In turn, groups are more organized than collectivities, which are more organized than social categories.

We define the nonprofit sector more broadly in this dictionary than Salamon and Anheier (1992a:130) do. First, as noted above, the definition of nonprofit group is more inclusive. Second, we include not only nonprofit groups (organizations, in their terms) in the sector but also solitary individual voluntary action such as informal service volunteering, political participation, religious activity, and informal interpersonal activity because they are usually motivated by voluntary altruism. It could be argued that informal service volunteering is a traditional part of the nonprofit sector (along with volunteering in group contexts and program volunteering, associational activity, and board volunteering).

However, if we are serious about the parallelism in definition between organized and informal contexts of service volunteering, as in organized volunteer programs and informal service volunteering, then we should also be consistent and embrace that parallelism by accepting informal political participation, the latter corresponding to organized political nonprofits. Likewise, we should also accept informal religious activity corresponding to church and other religious groups and informal interpersonal activity corresponding to formal social clubs and fraternal groups. On the same grounds, we include in individual voluntary action three other types of informal activity: informal economic support activity, informal social innovation activity, and informal social esthetics activity. Informal leisure activity such as recreation, cultural activity, mass media exposure, and resting/relaxing is not included in these comparisons, however, for it falls outside the ten areas just described and is seen as lacking voluntary altruistic motivation (cf. Quarrick 1989). And possibly other activities should be excluded as well.

But when we too narrowly restrict the nonprofit sector to traditional social service oriented and philanthropic activities of individuals and groups (cf. Hodgkinson et al. 1992), we run into problems of exclusion. That is, the narrow approach ignores well over a hundred million people in America who, in their free time, participate for various reasons, including especially voluntary altruism, both in associations and in other nonprofits, including churches (cf. Smith 1994b, 2000). Accepting the relevance of member benefit groups in definitions of nonprofit group and nonprofit sector brings with it, in our view, the obligation to include as well certain informal activities. These activities correspond to such groups, and like them, they are motivated mainly by nonservice goals but also by such broad social purposes as citizenship, socioreligious interests, sociability, and other important humane core values. This orientation has also led us to include a number of definitions of relevant concepts from the field of leisure studies, primarily as they relate to the perspective of casual/serious/project-based leisure.

Our view states that public service is *one*, but only one, important value in the nonprofit sector. For instance, political nonprofits also play an important role in developing and maintaining participatory democracy in civil society. Without the latter, the service side of the nonprofit sector is unlikely to exist to any significant extent. The political nonprofits, we contend, ultimately drive the service nonprofits, not vice versa (doing so through influence on government and the larger political system). Moreover, the service nonprofits are often themselves directly involved in political nonprofit associations (e.g., associations of hospitals, colleges), which are interest groups working for the good of their members and clients. Briefly, to ignore member benefit nonprofits and their parallel forms of informal voluntary action is to omit most of the nonprofit sector (cf. Smith 1994b, 2000).

In sum, we see the nonprofit sector as one of four major sectors of society. It focuses on:

1. individual voluntary action (a) in formal nonprofit groups (associational and service volunteering broadly defined); or (b) in informal individual activity, such as informal service volunteering, solitary political participation, solitary individual religious activity, informal interpersonal activity, economic support activity (but not paid work), social esthetics activity, and social innovation activity; or (c) in both;
2. employed individual activity in nonprofits;
3. group voluntary action by nonprofits and the property or goods they own.

Roughly speaking, then, the nonprofit sector is all aspects of all nonprofit groups in a society, in addition to individual voluntary action of people acting informally out of voluntary altruism.

In this definition we differ from Salamon and Anheier (1992a:130), primarily by including people acting alone in individual voluntary action. We hold that, after all, groups and organizations are essentially in people's minds—all so-called group or organizational activity is, at bottom, sets of people acting *as if* there were a group or an organization and *as if* they were members who should therefore act in certain ways. Nonetheless, groups are "real" and have important consequences. In other words, when all is said and done, people acting in groups are not so different from people acting alone. Hence we should avoid dismissing as unimportant individual solitary voluntary action, or helping behavior.

Finally, of the three most important concepts in our list, *voluntary action* is the most controversial. Smith and colleagues (1972) originally defined it from an individual perspective as action a person is neither made nor paid to perform, essentially rephrasing Etzioni's (1961) idea of normative compliance structure (he applied it mainly to nonprofits), and then generalized it to people acting alone outside group contexts. Our position today is that voluntary action should be redefined as action of groups (i.e., people acting as or for a group) or action of individuals that is, in its essence, an expression of voluntary altruism. Within groups such voluntary altruism still refers to their normative compliance structure (cf. Etzioni 1961). But, by extension, this approach also has implications for individuals motivated by voluntary altruism.

This happens when they reach beyond their personal, often selfish, interests and goals to act according to one or a combination of service, sociability, citizenship, socioreligious, economic system support, social innovation, or social esthetics values. These values focus directly on benefits for people other than oneself (although possibly rewarding oneself as well; Smith 1981) or one's family. In broadest terms these are "social values" or, in our terms, "humane core values," growing out of a nation's cultural or subcultural values, if not both (Bellah et al. 1985). Societies vary in their voluntary altruism and voluntary action, in that some of these values overlap with or differ from those of other societies (Anheier 1987). Expression of such concern is framed in a nation's history, legal system, and socioeconomic development, among other conditions (Salamon and Anheier 1992a; Smith and Shen 2002).

People operating in the business and government sectors use mainly an economic calculus (utilitarian compliance structure; Etzioni 1961), but when they operate in the nonprofit sector, they act mainly using a social value calculus, broadly conceived of. This latter calculus involves seeing, as a social value, service, citizenship, socioreligious interests, sociability, and other desiderata that lead to benefits for people other than oneself (or possibly as well as oneself). In the household/family sector, people also tend to use a social value calculus, but one narrowly conceived of in the sense that altruism and other social values are applied chiefly to other household/family members and not outside the family. The kind of altruism in the two sectors, nonprofit and household/family, is similar, but its scope of application in social values differs markedly. This difference in scope leads some observers to see the values of the two sectors as highly different, whereas we prefer to stress the similarity of values while noting that the scope clearly differs.

The following list of terms and concepts serves as a glossary designed to help us move toward commonly held definitions in nonprofit sector research within and across nations and languages. With but a few exceptions, each entry is linked by way of at least one reference to the relevant literature or to one or more websites, be it to the origin of the term or concept or to illustrative theory, research, or practice bearing on it. Many of these references will be familiar to social scientists who have been working with or contributing to current nonprofit and voluntary action research. As for the definitions themselves, they are our own, even if some are similar to or draw on definitions of other scholars, reflecting thereby a common understanding of the meanings of the terms and concepts in question.

A

absolute monarchy. *See* dictatorship; monarchy

accommodation: process or outcome of a combination of adaptation, adjustment, and compromise among two or more parties concerning a contentious *issue. Accommodation resolves critical *conflict in and between *nonprofit groups, thereby enabling the parties involved to move forward with pursuit of their shared *goals. Simmel (1955:114–116) wrote a short but classic discussion of accommodation under the heading of compromise.

accountability of volunteers/members: capacity of *volunteers or *members to explain their volunteer actions. A major administrative function in *nonprofit groups and *volunteer programs is to provide regular evaluation of volunteers' accountability, based on supervision and work reports. When repeated corrective comments to a volunteer fail to result in appropriate changes in *volunteer work, that person may be terminated for the good of the *program and larger *organization. Connors (1995:176–178), Fisher and Cole (1993, chap. 8), and McCurley and Vineyard (1997, passim) offer practical advice on accountability and evaluation of volunteers. Battle (1988, chap. 6) deals briefly with member accountability in associations, which is very informal most of the time, and generally done by the *officers and *board of directors. Smith (2000: 141) states that termination of membership in *grassroots associations is usually voluntary—rarely is someone ejected against their will for misdeeds or failure to perform.

accounting in nonprofits: system of keeping records (usually in computers these days) of and analyzing the flow of money in a nonprofit, including credits and debits from all sources (Anthony and Young 1994; Engstrom and Copley 2004; Garner 1991; Gross, Larkin, and McCarthy 2000; Ruppel 2002). Can play an important role in nonprofit management, insofar as managers need certain financial information in order to make wise decisions (Anthony and Young 2004). Can be terribly complex in large, paid-staff nonprofits, but as simple as a checking account register in a small grassroots association.

action norm, distinctive: shared expectation held by members of a *nonprofit group about the strategies and tactics they should use to achieve their *goals. An action norm is distinctive when it is characteristic of that group. Smith (2000:139) discusses the distinctive action norms of *grassroots associations.

action planning: process of creating work programs, or specific means, that are designed to implement strategic plans. Considered an important part of *strategic planning (Bryson 1994:154, 173).

action repertoire: strategies and tactics regularly used in a *nonprofit group to help achieve its *goals. Smith (2000:139) discusses the action repertoires of grassroots associations. Tilly (1978:151–166) presented an early use of action repertoire in dealing with social movements.

action, social. *See* social action

action, voluntary. *See* voluntary action

active-effective character pattern: part of the larger *general activity model, which states that *volunteer action and other socioculturally valued discretionary time activity are likely to be greater where an individual has elements of the active-effective character set of socioculturally preferred traits and attitudes. These include higher verbal and social intelligence capacities, certain personality traits (extraversion, ego strength, emotional stability, intimacy, assertiveness, efficacy, etc.), certain values, certain general attitudes, certain specific attitudes, certain expectations, certain intentions, greater relevant retained information, and effectively functioning psychological processes (for further details see Smith et al. 1980:466–470). Smith (1975:255–258; 1994a:250–252, 255) reviews research evidence supporting the active-effective character pattern.

active member. *See* member, analytic

activism: 1. a form of *volunteering that, according to Ellis and Noyes (1990: 8), is oriented toward reform. 2. a form of individual activity within a *social movement group, which is either unpaid or paid. As social movement organizations grow in size, such activity is increasingly professionalized (McCarthy and Zald 1977). *See also* checkbook activism; citizen volunteer

activist: person especially active in one or a combination of *citizen participation, *political participation, *social movements, social protest (*activity, protest), or social change. Butler (2003, passim) wrote an autoethnography of his responsibilities as an activist, communications scholar, and member of the lesbian-gay-bisexual community as these considerations bore on his attempt to persuade the municipal council in his city to add protection for gays and lesbians. Verba, Schlozman, and Brady (1995, chaps. 4, 5) use national sample survey data from the United States to study the motivation of political activists (and their opposite, inactive people) and how they are recruited. Lichterman (1996, passim) writes of American activists reinventing *community, contrary to the negative conclusions of Bellah et al. (1985, passim) about the decline of community. Shaw (2001, passim) has written an activist's practical manual or handbook.

activity goal in program evaluation: expected results from a particular activity in a program of a *nonprofit group, which are commonly the focus of *program evaluation. Such a goal is concrete; it is reached when staff effectively implement the program. In program evaluation activity goals are contrasted with the more abstract *outcome goals of the program (Thomas 1994:347–348).

activity level in nonprofits: number and rate of events occurring in the name of a particular *nonprofit group or *organization. Levels may, for example, be low, medium, high, regular, or intermittent (Smith 2000:130).

activity, protest: individual or collective action undertaken in opposition to certain existing or proposed social policies or arrangements that are considered threatening or unfair. Usually involves unconventional means or goals in a society, hence causing irritation to authorities and often public condemnation, as contrasted with *political voluntary action that is more conventional and socially accepted (Gamson 1990, passim). Frey, Dietz, and Kalof (1992, passim) found that displacement and factionalism in protest groups are major predictors of success/failure in their protest activities. Powers et al. (1997, passim) have compiled an encyclopedia of instances, cases, and aspects of *nonviolent action protest activity. *See also* political voluntary action

activity theory: the proposition that there is a long-standing predisposition to see a positive relationship between activity per se and life *satisfaction (Turner 1992: 43–44). Higher levels of activity are assumed to produce greater life satisfaction, whereas lower levels of activity are assumed to produce the converse. Thus loss of social roles and attendant activities is thought to diminish life satisfaction. In the first systematic presentation of the theory, activity was seen as providing role support for participants, thus reaffirming their self-concepts. A positive self-concept is necessary for high satisfaction in one's activity and *volunteering is often capable of generating just such a view of oneself (Lemon, Bengtson, and Peterson 1972).

activity timing in nonprofits: time of day, week, month, or year during which a *nonprofit group or *organization holds its activities. In non-profit groups the *needs and interests of *members often dictate the timing of activities (on activity timing in *grassroots associations, see Smith 2000:127–128).

adhocracy: form of administrative organization having minimal hierarchy and *bureaucratization and thereby believed to enable greater flexibility in creating and delivering programs. Adhocracy is particularly common in *grassroots associations and equivalent entities. Skrtic (1991, passim) proposes adhocracy as an alternative structure for educating children with disabilities, in that it stresses collaboration and active problem solving. According to Morgan (1986:57), the term was coined by Warren Bennis to describe *organizations designed to be temporary but yet highly suited for performing complex, uncertain tasks in a turbulent environment (*turbulent field as environment). Waterman (1990, passim) wrote a book supporting the value of adhocracy, though only in a business context (*nonprofit sector is unimportant flat-earth paradigm).

admission/exclusion of association member: *associations generally have the right to select whom they will admit to membership, providing that they follow their own correct procedure and are not acting contrary to public policy, usually upholding free association (Fishman and Schwarz 2000:941, 966–998). But courts have prohibited gender and racial discrimination in selection of members as against public policy (ibid.).

adult learning theory of volunteering: a set of propositions explaining the variety of types of learning that volunteers engage in (Ilsley 1990): instrumental/didactic, social/expressive, critical reflection. Depending upon the object of *commitment, learning interests may differ. Volunteer-centered volunteers tend to prefer social expressive learning, organization-centered volunteers favor instrumental/didactic, and client-centered volunteers favor reflection on the work with clients. Social-vision centered volunteers value critical reflection, which raises their consciousness.

advisor. *See* mentor

advisory board: set of experts who provide, on request from a *community or a *nonprofit group, opinion, information, or recommendations bearing on the community's or group's *goals and *programs. Barker (2003: 11) observes that members of such boards, who may be hired, elected, or recruited as *volunteers, may be consulted individually or as a group. An advisory board may include one or more members of the group's *board of directors. Sterk (1999, passim) recommends that an advisory board be part of any *community development program designed to deal with hard-to-reach populations such as prostitutes and drug users.

advocacy: act of pleading, speaking, or interceding for a *cause supported by a person or group. O'Neill (1989:109) holds that *advocacy groups are the most antiestablishment and free-wheeling part of the *independent sector. Checkoway (1995) viewed public advocacy as a strategy in which legislative and administrative advocates, advocacy planners, and advocacy groups advocate for the relatively powerless and in which representatives of the traditionally excluded also advocate for themselves. For a history of advocacy within one *profession (social work) and more developed definition, see Lester and Schneider (2001).

advocacy group: a type of *political nonprofit group engaged in *advocacy; one that seeks or resists change in society through *political voluntary action. Advocacy groups using *social protest are *social movement groups. Gamson's concept "challenging group" is roughly synonymous with advocacy group as defined here (Gamson 1990, chap. 2).

advocacy in nonprofits: the process through which a *nonprofit group engages in *advocacy for its own political interests and public agenda at one or another level of government, both through grassroots advocacy mobilizing its membership or other affiliates, through *lobbying efforts, and through joining relevant *coalitions or *alliances (Avner 2002; Smucker 2004; Wilbur 2000, chap. 9). There are legal limits on the amount of lobbying that charitable nonprofits can engage in (Smucker 2004:237), but few limits on other forms of advocacy.

advocate. *See* activist

affiliate of a nonprofit group. *See* nonprofit group affiliate

affiliated volunteer. *See* disaster volunteer

age-grading group: *association of young boys of similar age in a preliterate society, who live, work, and play together, sometimes while residing in a special hut or domicile until accepted as adults in their society. Also known as "age-set" or "age-grade association' (cf. Ross 1976:56–57, where he mentions these associations as lifelong age cohorts). For further discussion of this form of social organization, see Ember and Ember (2004:187–189). One form of *sodality in preliterate societies. Stewart (1977) gives a classic statement on age-group systems in preliterate societies.

agency. *See* nonprofit agency

agency, alternative service: *nonprofit group that offers, in a new and different way, particular services related to health or well-being and intended to help a particular category of client (cf. Perlmutter 1988b, passim). Such agencies tend to spring up when traditional agencies are unable, or unwilling, to deliver the needed services. These alternative entities, say Miller and Phillip (1983:779), eventually stir change and innovation in the discipline of social work and the field of social welfare.

agency, governmental: *See* governmental agency

agency, social service: *agency that provides a *social service (sense 2) (mentioned in Chambers 1963).

agenda control in evaluation: a manipulative strategy, or game, played by people whose organization is being evaluated. It attempts to direct the *evaluation along the lines of criteria they judge as the most important. Murray and Tassie (1994:316) observe that such criteria are usually those on which the evaluation is likely to produce positive results.

age-set. *See* age-grading group

agitator: *activist whose activities are particularly annoying to people who support the status quo. The pejorative sense of agitator was evident in the hostile intellectual reception to Thorstein Veblen's critiques of capitalism that he made during World War I (Capozzola 1999, passim).

Alinsky-style nonprofit group participation: personal involvement in a paid-staff or autonomous community *nonprofit group that functions according to principles set out by Saul Alinsky. For example, an Alinsky-style group takes its direction from the practical goals of ordinary *members, with the group becoming their medium for expressing and achieving those goals (Alinsky 1969:196). Through Alinsky's Industrial Areas Foundation (IAF), his confrontational approach to *community organizing has become a prototype that has been widely and rather successfully replicated in America over the past half-century. The basic idea of Alinsky was to develop mass political organizations (*associations) that were rooted in neighborhoods and embraced local concerns, and then to use these organizations to fight for change (Lancourt 1979, passim; Reitzes and Reitzes 1984, passim; Robinson and Hanna 1994, passim). The IAF style was initially confrontational for many years, but in recent decades has been more collaborative, seeking to build effective local coalitions (Chrislip and Larson 1994:57).

alliance of nonprofits: *group of two or more nonprofits that have agreed to work together for one or more common *goals they believe they can achieve more readily in intergroup collaboration (*collaboration in nonprofits) than in intergroup competition (Arsenault 1998; Bailey and Koney 2000; McLaughlin 1998). An alliance may have strategic importance for a *nonprofit group (see Yankey and Willen 2004), or it may be only a nominal relationship of modest value (e.g., for the many nonprofits that are members of *INDEPENDENT SECTOR). Although these groups of nonprofits sometimes include *governmental agencies or *for-profits, usually they do not. Alternative terms for an alliance are *"coalition" and *"federation."

all-volunteer group: *volunteer entity where 95 percent or more of cumulative, group-related hours put in by *members are devoted to *volunteering (Smith 2000:25).

alternative community. *See* commune

alternative federated fund. *See* federated fund, alternative

alternative institution. *See* institution, alternative

alternative service agency. *See* agency, alternative service

altruism: an attitude of disinterested concern for the *welfare (sense 1) of others outside an individual's family, expressed by this person, or by a *nonprofit group, in giving money, *goods, time, or other property to increase the welfare of those others. Altruism is often expressed at some *sacrifice to the giver or *donor. Briefly put, altruism is an attitude that disposes a person to help others, because of concern for their welfare or *satisfaction or both. *Philanthropy is the behavioral expression of this attitude. Gintis and colleagues (2003, passim) present experimental evidence that strong *reciprocity can help predict altruism in human beings as well as explain this disposition. Many authors have written books or articles exploring altruism from the perspective of fields like psychology, sociology, anthropology, theology, neurology, evolutionary biology, and history (e.g., Allahyari 2000; Batson 1991; Kohn 1990; Kottler 2000; Margolis 1982; Monroe 1996; Oliner, Oliner, and Baron 1992; Ozinga 1999; Post et al. 2002; Puka 1994; Seaton 1996; Wolfe 2001). Titmuss (1971, passim) gives one classic statement on altruism in the context of gift-giving, as does Mauss (1925/1990) earlier. Research makes clear that there is a self-serving, self-helping aspect to altruism generally—it is relative altruism (*altruism, relative), so pure, other-serving altruism (*altruism, pure) is very rare (Smith 1981, passim; Kottler 2000, passim). *See also* altruism, volunteer; altruism, voluntary; altruism, nonvoluntary; altruism, quasi-volunteer; prosocial behavior

altruism, absolute. *See* altruism, pure

altruism, nonvoluntary: *altruism so substantially diluted by self-interested ends that it becomes a means to those ends rather than, as in absolute altruism (*altruism, pure), an end in itself. This type, which is common in industry and government, was first proposed by O'Neill and Young (1988:4). The concept fits well with Smith's (2000:17) statement that altruism can be found in all four sectors of society, not solely the non-profit sector.

altruism, pure: an ideal form of *altruism, very rarely achieved in imperfect humans, in which the altruistic person is totally focused on helping and satisfying another person, *group, or other *target of benefits, without any sense of self-satisfaction (*satisfaction) from the altruistic act. Sometimes referred to as "absolute altruism." Normally, the altruist gains some self-satisfaction from an altruistic act (e.g., feeling good about being altruistic, as a socially valued trait/act, and enjoying the satisfaction of the person helped) as well as helping the target of benefits gain some satisfaction from the act (Smith 1981, passim; 2000:16–18). Altruism, thus, is usually a reciprocal process with some satisfaction for both the altruist (see *self-interest) and his/her target of benefits.

altruism, quasi-volunteer: one of two types of *voluntary altruism (the other being volunteer altruism [*altruism]). The quasi-volunteer type is expressed in underremunerated activity. Whether activity is *underre-munerated* or fairly remunerated is determined by labor market prices for the service rendered. The term was coined by Smith (2000:24). *See also* quasi-volunteer; quasi-volunteer action

altruism, relative: the usual form of *altruism in which altruistic people, based on significant self-interest, gain self-satisfaction (*satisfaction) from the altruistic act (a) by feeling good (satisfied) about being altruistic (a socially valued trait); (b) by enjoying the satisfaction of the person, *group, or other *target of benefits being helped (if the *helpee seems to feel satisfied by the altruistic act); and sometimes (c) by enjoying the gratitude expressed by the target of benefits or a representative of it (if a group or collectivity). Thus, all normal altruism has a self-satisfying component as well as an other-satisfying intention (Smith 1981, passim; 2000:16–18) and is relative (Smith 2000:228) rather than pure altruism. But relative altruism is nonetheless probably much better for society and the altruist than more purely selfish (*selfishness) actions that ignore helping others and the satisfaction of others (Wolfe 2001, passim).

altruism, secondary. *See* altruism, nonvoluntary

altruism, self-serving: one of the two main facets of *voluntary altruism, the other being other-serving altruism. Carr (1975:83) was among the first to observe that altruism is never truly pure but rather is composed of both self-interested *and* other-interested motives.

altruism, voluntary. *See* voluntary altruism

altruism, volunteer: one of two types of *voluntary altruism (the other being *quasi-volunteer altruism). The volunteer type is expressed in *un*remunerated activity. The term was coined by Smith (2000:24).

altruistic organization: *formal group whose purpose and *goals attempt to optimize *satisfaction of nonmembers without expectation that they are obligated to contribute anything in return to the organization or its *members. Smith (1981) looked at *altruism not only at the level of the individual but at the level of the organization as well.

altruistic paradox: the reality that even the most *altruistic organization has organizational maintenance and organizational enhancement functions. Furthermore, Smith (1981) has pointed out the following paradox: an organization can be more altruistic than its *members and vice versa.

amateur: one of three types of participant in *serious leisure distinguished (a) by a special relationship with the *professionals in the same activity and with the *public (sense 2) interested in that activity, and (b) by a distinctive set of attitudes, notably confidence, perseverance, *commitment, preparedness, and self-conception. In general, professionals hold these attitudes more strongly than amateurs, while the latter hold them more strongly than dabblers or dilettantes, who only play disinterestedly at the activity (Stebbins 1992:38–46, 48–55). Stebbins (1979, passim) gives a classic discussion of amateurs.

amateur activity: a pursuit in art, science, sport, and entertainment undertaken on an *amateur basis. Stebbins (1979, passim) studied the amateur activities of theater, baseball, and astronomy. As with other *leisure activities, amateur activities, if they are to be considered part of the *nonprofit sector, must be motivated by *voluntary altruism. *See also* formal leisure activity; informal leisure activity

amateur group: formal or informal *collectivity of *amateurs pursuing a field of art, science, sport, or entertainment. Local chapters of the Society of American Magicians, known as "assemblies," are amateur groups, since their *membership is largely, if not entirely, amateur (Stebbins 1993b:15–16).

amateur league: an organization of *amateur teams in a particular sport, established to promote interteam competition for a championship. Guttmann (2000:253) writes that sports leagues were created to rationalize competition and provide, thus, a way to substantiate claims of being best team of the season.

amateur team: group of amateurs (*amateur group) in a particular sport playing together on one side of a game. A team may compete against other teams in an *amateur league. Stebbins (1993a, passim) examined two Canadian amateur football teams, one at the junior level, the other at the university level.

ambulance corps, volunteer: a *volunteer in a *grassroots association that runs an ambulance service. Perlstadt (1975) studied volunteer and non-volunteer ambulance corps in Michigan.

American Judaism: the American versions of the Jewish faith (cf. Glazer 1972, passim; Sarna 2004, passim).

American Protestantism: the American versions of Protestant Christianity (cf. Balmer and Winner 2002, passim; Donald Miller 1997, passim).

American religion: one of the many religions ever extant in America (cf. Finke and Stark 2005, passim; Gaustad and Schmidt 2002, passim; Marty 1980, passim; Mather and Nichols 1993, passim; Mead and Hill 1995, passim; Melton 1993, passim).

American Roman Catholicism: the American version of the Roman Catholic faith (cf. Gillis 1999, passim; Gleason 1987, passim).

analytic member of a group. *See* member, analytic

analytic type classification of nonprofit group. *See* classification of nonprofit groups

anarchy: a form of *government in a society or smaller territory in which there are no operative laws or effective government leaders. Total lack of *government in a territory. Often occurs during *revolution or *civil war. *Nonprofits are typically weak in anarchies, as are other types of *organizations. John Cage (2001, passim), a leading apologist for anarchy, sets out his case in a short book by this title.

angelic nonprofit groups flat-earth paradigm: *nonprofit sector model stating that the nonprofit sector is composed only of conventional, mainstream, wholly nondeviant groups. Discussed by Smith (2000:5, 138, 229–330). The validity of this *paradigm is challenged by the existence of such entities as *deviant nonprofit groups.

animateur: applied to the nonprofit sphere, *l'animateur* is the French term for one who either organizes or facilitates the course of an activity. Although no true direct translation to the English exists, the translator of Meister's (1984) book on participation in volunteer groups rendered the term as "animator," enclosing it in quotation marks. Besnard (1980, passim) and Poujol (1989, passim) give classic discussions of the *animateur*.

annual revenue. *See* revenue

anonymous group. *See* twelve-step group

antiauthoritarianism of grassroots associations: tendency for *nonprofit groups, and especially *grassroots associations, to be democratic and reject authoritarian arrangements (Harrison 1960, passim; Smith 2000: 170).

anticipatory reciprocity: a form of *reciprocity in which a person engaging in *giving or *volunteering in the interests of an *organization or *cause believes there is some probability that there will be a direct or indirect personal *benefit some time in the future. Anticipatory reciprocity is evident in one of Stebbins's (2001:5) six types of marginal volunteering: the exploratory type where, by volunteering, people hope to eventually find paid employment in the same line of activity. *See also* reciprocity; concurrent reciprocity; lateral reciprocity; retrospective reciprocity; altruism, self-serving; altruism, relative

antihistoricism flat-earth paradigm: the *nonprofit sector model stating that the histories of nonprofit sector phenomena are essentially irrelevant, that phenomena back in time are too distant and different to be worth examining in the present (Smith 2000:233–234).

antivoluntary nonprofit sector flat-earth paradigm. *See* nonprofit sector is unimportant flat-earth paradigm

antivolunteerism: attitude that employees (some of them *professional) in a *paid-staff nonprofit organization may hold toward *volunteers. It is commonly expressed in such evaluations as the latter should be allowed to fill only low-level posts in the organization, whatever their post they do inferior work, and they are unreliable. Pearce (1993:152) observed antivolunteerism in her study, and Ilsely (1990:4) discusses it in the field of social work vis-à-vis *professionalism there. This attitude can pose difficult personnel problems for *volunteer administration. *See also* volunteer unreliability; professionalization of volunteers and volunteerism

apostasy. *See* deconversion, religious

area planning council: a *group of local residents, often intended to be a cross section of the local area, that attempts to plan housing and *social services for that area. May be a *nonprofit group or the *volunteer department of a *governmental agency. Schmid (2001, passim) describes neighborhood self-management groups, which can be viewed as area planning councils, although he does not use this term.

ARNOVA. *See* Association for Research on Nonprofit Organizations and Voluntary Action

articles of incorporation. *See* articles of organization

articles of organization: document that creates a *nonprofit group. (a) In incorporated groups referred to as "articles of incorporation." (b) In unincorporated groups referred to as "constitution," if present. (c) In trusts, referred to as "trust agreement" or "declaration of trust" (Hopkins 2001:315).

asset in nonprofits: an item of property belonging to a *nonprofit group. Most such groups have financial assets generated from *revenues (often modest, Smith 2000:119) and rather few, if any, fixed assets such as land, buildings, or large machinery. *See also* resource

association: a relatively formally structured *nonprofit group that depends mainly on *volunteer *members for *participation and activity and that primarily seeks *member benefits, even if it may also seek some *public benefits. This type of association, frequently referred to as a "voluntary association" (see classic discussion in Smith and Freedman 1972), is the most common nonprofit in the United States (Smith 2000:41–42). The term "common interest association" is sometimes used to underscore the twin facts that associations form around the shared *interests of *members and tend mainly to serve those interests. Scott (1991, passim) presents an extensive history of women's associations in America. Knoke (1993, passim) explores the political economies of a sample of national associations in America. Schwartz and Pharr (2003, passim) examine and describe associations in Japan. Blair (1994, passim) reviews the history of women's amateur arts associations in America, 1890–1930. Ross (1976, passim) describes voluntary associations in history, from preliterate societies through modern times. See also books on many other types of associations or on associations generally, such as Aldrich (1995), Barrett (1999), Carter (1961), Charles (1993), Clarke (1993), Couto (1999), Delgado (1986), Ferree and Martin (1995), Fisher (1994), Gamwell (1984), Halpern and Levin (1996), Jones (1999), Kaufman (2002), Kloppenborg and Wilson (1996), Krause (1996), Macleod (1983), McKenzie (1994), Ornstein (1913/1963), Pennock and Chapman (1969), Pugliese (1986), Putnam (2000), Rauch (1995), Robertson (1966), Rosenblum (1998), Ross and Wheeler (1971), Sanyal (1980), Scott (1991), Sills (1957), Smith and Freedman (1972), Smith (1973, 1974), Smith and Elkin (1981), Van Deth (1997), and Wuthnow (1994, 1998). Nonprofit researchers who study associations but neglect other types of nonprofit groups are reflecting the *volunteer and membership flat-earth paradigm (Smith 2000:224–225). *See also* national voluntary association; state association; grassroots association; transnational association

Association for Research on Nonprofit Organizations and Voluntary Action (ARNOVA): an independent *nonprofit organization devoted to research and its application in the areas of *philanthropy, *nonprofit groups, *citizen participation, and *voluntary action. It was founded in 1971 by David Horton Smith, who also served as its first president and, more recently, has provided a short history of the organization (Smith 2003). Website: http://www.arnova.org.

associational activity: 1. individual participation in *associations; a form of *voluntary action that contrasts with activity by *program volunteers and other *traditional service volunteers (e.g., Smith 2000:51–52). 2. meetings or other collective events of an *association or its subgroups such as its *board, *committees, and the like, along with the actions of *officers and other formal leaders of the association playing these formal representative roles. Smith (2000:130) discusses the roots and impacts of internal activity levels of *grassroots associations. *See also* associational volunteering

associational form of organization: manner of operating a *group that usually involves having *official members who are mostly *volunteers, some elected *formal nonprofit leaders, often a *board of directors with *policy control, financial support mainly from annual *dues (but may also include *fees and *grants), often one or more *committees as part of the *leadership, and regular face-to-face meetings attended by *official members and informal participants. Form used in *associations, *transnational associations, *national voluntary associations, *state associations, and *grassroots associations (Smith 2000, passim; Battle 1988, passim; Flanagan 1984, passim).

associational management: 1. *management of a large, usually national, *paid-staff nonprofit *association. The American Society of Association Executives (ASAE) publishes a monthly magazine, *Association Management*, and various books on this topic, along with other publishers (e.g., ASAE 1988, 1994, 2001, 2002; Bethel 1993; Blanken and Liff 1999; Cox 1997; Dunlop 1989; Eadie and Daily 1994; Ernstthal and Jones 2001; Jacobs 2002; Kastner 1998; Schaw 2002; Shapiro 1987; Tecker and Fidler 1993). 2. *volunteer nonprofit group management. *See* nonprofit management; volunteer nonprofit group management

associational member. *See* member

associational network. *See* network of groups

associational officer. *See* officer in nonprofits

associational subsector. *See* subsector, nonprofit

associational volunteer: active *member (*member, analytical) or *leader of an *association, whether it has *member benefit or *nonmember benefit *goals. Smith (2000:48–53) cites survey data and extrapolations showing that this type of *volunteering is at least as important in America as *program volunteering. *See also* volunteer

associational volunteering: the activity of *associational volunteers in and for their respective *associations (Smith 2000:48–53). *See also* volunteering

associationalism: the practice of building *voluntary associations within *civil society. Seen by Toqueville as necessary for checking the growth of government and countering political apathy (Kaufman 1999).

astrophysical dark matter metaphor. *See* metaphor, dark matter astrophysical

atheneum: a scientific or literary *association, usually with classical aspirations or pretensions. Infrequent now, but more common in the 1800s and early 1900s in the United States. Pratt (2001, passim) reports on the discovery in the walls of the renovated Nantucket Atheneum of a set of pamphlets bearing on the abolition movement (*social movement) in the early nineteenth century.

authority: institutionalized power, or the power associated with a formal position (Hunter 1953:161). Positions in a *bureaucracy carry a certain measure of authority. *See also* influence

autocracy: *See* dictatorship

autonomy: the capacity of an individual or a *nonprofit group to function independently. Sometimes referred to as "rule from oneself" (Martin 1998, passim), autonomy is a matter of degree. In the case of groups, they may operate under little or no horizontal or vertical control or affiliation, thus having the greatest autonomy, with those operating under extensive, if not complete, control of another group having the least. A group also gains some autonomy by avoiding major funding and its limiting conditions, as established by an external granting organization (Smith 2000:79–81). *See also* heteronomy

B

---

background community: local and supralocal *interorganizational field in which a *nonprofit group may be embedded. Such a group may be a subunit of a larger *network of *organizations, an interorganizational system, or a residential community. This term was coined by Milofsky and Hunter (1994:1).

balance of informality and formalization: question of kind, amount, and interrelationship of formal and informal procedure and structure in a *nonprofit group. Harrison (1960:236) holds that the question of balance of informality and formalization is endemic to nonprofit groups. *See also* formalization; informal group style of operation

balanced volunteer/paid-staff group: question of optimal kind and amount of volunteer and paid-staff activity as well as optimal interrelationship among these two types of staff working in a *nonprofit group (Smith 2000:244–245). The balanced volunteer/paid-staff group is usually one where the two types of staff are in rough balance in terms of person-hours of work devoted to the group (*See also* Dunlop 1989).

balancing member and nonmember benefit goals: question of optimal distribution of such benefits as services and activities to *members and nonmembers of a *nonprofit group. Harris (1998a:148–149) says nonprofit groups are distinguished by the requirement that they try to balance member and nonmember benefit goals and activities. *See also* member benefit nonprofit group; nonmember benefit nonprofit group

barn raising: informal, temporary *group of friends and neighbors who come together to build a barn in a day or two for someone in their community. Characteristic of 1800s and earlier in the United States but still practiced by certain sects like the Amish. Gougler (1972, passim) describes an Amish barn raising in modern times.

barrier and limitation to voluntary action: two of several different kinds of obstacles to engaging in *voluntary action. Maria Smith (1989) developed a list of barriers to volunteering stemming from a multivolume study of the future of *volunteering conducted by the Red Cross. These include language barriers, cultural barriers, economic barriers (including hidden costs to *volunteers), physical barriers, barriers of time, and the like. Israel (1988) developed a typology of such barriers and limitations to access to community-based network interventions that can be adapted to use in the area of volunteer *participation: (a) individual characteristics that present barriers and limitations, (b) network-related barriers and limitations, (c) organization-related barriers and limitations, (d) sociopolitical barriers and limitations.

benefactor. *See* donor

benefactory: an organized *network of social relations, with an authentic organizational identity and set of identifiable *beneficiaries. Classified as one of three types: intrinsic benefactories (such as *self-help groups and other *member benefit organizations), extrinsic benefactories (*organizations whose beneficiaries are primarily external to the organizations), and mixed benefactories (organizations with a mix of intrinsic and extrinsic benefactions, such as most religious *congregations) (Lohmann 2001:170–171).

beneficiary. *See* donee; target of benefits

benefit: 1. an advantage, a *good. 2. an allowance or other advantage to which a person is entitled under a social insurance scheme, as *member of a *member benefit nonprofit group (*club, society), or as *target of benefits of a *public benefit nonprofit. Jeannotte (2003, passim) concludes from her analysis of Canadian General Social Survey data that collective benefits accrue from investments in cultural capital and that these benefits contribute significantly to social cohesion. *See also* service

benevolence: 1. disposition to do good, to be kind, generous, or charitable toward humankind. 2. act of doing good, of being kind, generous, or charitable toward someone or toward a group. Stonebraker (2003, passim) found that the proportion of overall benevolence payments sent to synodical and national Protestant church bodies in the United States is falling. *See also* altruism

bequest: *gift made available through a will upon a *donor's death. Pammer (2000, passim), using a sample of wills, studied bequest patterns in eighteenth-century central Europe to find, for example, that testators usually select as recipients of their bequest either their spouse or their children, but not both.

black church in America: the African-American church and religious experience in America (cf. Frazier and Lincoln 1974, passim; Johnstone 1992, chap. 12; Lincoln and Mamiya 1990, passim; Raboteau 1995, passim).

black power: *social movement of African-Americans in the 1960s and 1970s that was more radical in its *goals and means than the rest of the civil rights *movement in the United States at the time (cf. Ture and Hamilton 1967). Resisted integration and *cooperation with whites in its activities. Oppenheimer (2004, passim) examines the failure of the black power movement's internal colonialism theory to promulgate strategies of resistance (*resistance movement) for ethnic minority groups.

Black United Fund: philanthropic institution that amasses money for Black American growth, change, and opportunity (cf. Rabinowitz 1990, passim). The National Black United Fund raises funds for and provides technical assistance to Black organizations that provide needed services to Black Americans. Website: http://www.nbuf.org. *See also* United Way

block association: neighborhood *group or *organization founded to enhance neighborhood support systems, facilitate exercise of political skills relative to *community problems, and thereby improve quality of the local living environment (Unger and Wandersman 1983:291–292).

board chair: head of the *board of directors of a *nonprofit group. Typically the first or second most powerful person in the group (the other being the *executive director, if there is one). Zander (1993:53–63) offers a range of suggestions for board chair to facilitate discussion at meetings.

board member: *member of a *board of directors or *board of trustees. Bright (2001, passim) examined the relationship between board member *commitment and two outcome variables particularly relevant to members themselves: overall board performance and organizational citizenship behavior.

board of directors in nonprofits: highest *policy-making and administrative unit in American *nonprofit groups. It is believed to be central to nonprofit *effectiveness. Peter Hall (1997, passim) provides a history of nonprofit boards in the United States. Conrad and Glenn (1983, passim) offer an extended treatment of the effective *volunteer board of directors. There are many other books and chapters on how to develop an effective board of directors—some based on research, most based on practical experience (e.g., Axelrod 1994; Carver 1990; Carver and Carver 1997; Chait, Ryan, and Taylor 2005; Duca 1996; Houle 1989; Howe 1995; Pointer and Orlikoff 2002; Scott 2000; Wilbur 2000, chap. 2; Wolf 1991, chap. 2; Wood 1996). *See also* board volunteer

board of trustees: a *board of directors charged with advising, managing, and supervising a *trust (sense 1) or *charitable nonprofit. Emphasis here is on guardianship of *assets, mostly a concern of the larger, wealthier *nonprofit groups (e.g., *foundations, universities). See Hopkins (2001:16, 316) for further discussion of the idea of trust and the board of trustees. *See also* board volunteer

board volunteer: an individual serving as *volunteer *member of a *board of directors of a *nonprofit group. Board volunteers may be compensated for traveling expenses incurred for board-related activities. A type of volunteer often overlooked in *nonprofit sector studies. Zander (1993, passim) offers an extended treatment of the effective board volunteer.

board volunteer activity: the *volunteer work of a *board volunteer (cf. Conrad and Glenn 1983, passim).

boycott: type of *direct action protest, in which consumers or other potential buyers collaborate to withhold purchases as a *tactic for influencing the *group or business they are at loggerheads with. Garrow (1989, passim) has edited a collection of papers on the Montgomery bus boycott of 1955–1956.

brethren: an *association of men, usually with a religious purpose. One type of *brotherhood. Kraybill and Bowman (2001, passim) describe the Brethren of the Old Order Amish, Hutterites, and Mennonites and how they help sustain their religion's traditional ways in the modern world.

bridging goal in program evaluation: a *goal that helps link one or more *activity goals with their corresponding *outcome goals (Weiss 1972:48–49). A bridging goal is not an end in itself but a route to reaching an outcome goal (Thomas 1994:348). Bridging goals may also become the focus of a *program evaluation.

bright matter of the nonprofit sector: collective term for the most publicly visible *nonprofit groups in the *nonprofit sector such as *paid-staff nonprofits (Smith 2000:12). O'Neill (2002, passim) examines the scope of and trends in the principal types of paid-staff nonprofits in the United States. Pearce (1993, passim) conducted a comparative study of a sample of British paid-staff and volunteer-staffed nonprofits.

broad definition of nonprofit sector: refers to all *voluntary altruism, all *voluntary action, all *volunteers, and all *volunteer groups (i.e., the *narrow nonprofit sector) as well as all quasi-voluntary altruism, all *quasi-voluntary action, all *quasi-volunteers, and all *quasi-volunteer groups (Smith 2000:27). *See also* narrow definition of nonprofit sector

broader nonprofit group. *See* nonprofit group

brotherhood: an *association of men (and more recently sometimes including women) formed for a religious, economic (as in some unions), social, or other purpose. Traditional usage now rare. Summers (2003, passim) argues, using biographical data, that certain brotherhoods in the United States in the 1930s served as sites for formation of a gendered diasporic identity among immigrant blacks. *See also* brethren

budget: periodic, often annual, estimate of the revenue and expenses of a *nonprofit group, especially as these relate to its *programs and personnel costs; an account or statement of this estimate. Young (1994:472) notes that the budgeting process accepts the group's programs as given, focusing attention instead on how to finance them.

building association/tenant organization/tenant association: *grassroots association formed by and for renters in an apartment complex for the purpose of communicating to, and if necessary, pressuring the landlord or public housing authority to take such actions as lowering the rent (or refraining from raising it), improving living conditions, and providing certain services (Lawson 1983:372). Lawson studied the tenants' strike as one means of forcefully persuading reluctant landlords to accede to the demands of renters, a tactic made possible and effective when the renters formed a building association. *See also* tenant management

building paid staff-volunteer/member relationships: major administrative function in *nonprofit groups and *volunteer programs that involves developing smooth working ties and mutual respect between paid staff of the larger *organization and participants in the volunteer program. Friction between *paid staff and *volunteers can arise easily and needs to be actively combatted by the *volunteer administrator and management of the larger organization. Connors (1995, chap. 10), Fisher and Cole (1993, passim), and Scheier (1993, passim) give guidance on building healthy paid staff-volunteer relationships. This problem does not arise in most *grassroots associations, which usually lack any paid staff (Smith 2000:108). The problem can arise, however, in larger *associations that have one or more paid staff and needs to be attended to by the *board of directors and officers (*officer in nonprofits) of the association.

bureaucracy: Hall (1996:50) summarizes Weber's (1947) definition of bureaucracy as an *organization that includes such elements as "a hierarchy of *authority, limited authority, division of labor, technically competent participants, procedures for work, rules for incumbents, and differential rewards." Weber (1958:196–244) pioneered the scientific definition and description of the concept of bureaucracy. Bureaucracy and its central elements continue to play a major conceptual role in contemporary research on organizations, as reviewed, for instance, by Hall (1996, chap. 3).

bureaucratization: process by which the administrative part of a *formal nonprofit group is transformed into a *bureaucracy. In a bureaucracy governance of the group occurs, in significant part, according to formalized special functions, adherence to fixed rules, and a hierarchy of *authority. Smith (2000:168) notes that, in *nonprofit groups, bureaucratization has been measured by the number of levels of hierarchy found there. *See also* complexity; formalization

burnout: physical and emotional exhaustion stemming from long-term stress, frustration, and excessive *obligation in a *volunteer role. Stebbins (1998:34) argues that, under these conditions, the leisure character of *volunteering undergoes a metamorphosis, turning into overbearing obligation and taking on a work-like quality too unpleasant to bear in an activity once pursued for either pleasure or *satisfaction.

business: a *for-profit enterprise. Usually incorporated as a *for-profit organization or *corporation. Danes and Lee (2004, passim) examine various tensions generated by business in a sample of farm business-owning couples.

business association: a *member benefit association of (usually retail) business owners or managers that operates primarily to protect and enhance commerce/business in its community or larger territory (O'Neill 2002: 214). The Chamber of Commerce and Business and Professional Women's Association are examples at both the local and national levels in the United States. *Trade associations also fall into this category but tend to be supralocal in territorial scope (state, national, or international) and often include manufacturing or wholesale businesses. *See* trade association

business sector. *See* sector of society

business sector and nonprofits: the broad relationship between these two sectors of society. Aside from the *commercialization of nonprofits, which puts *nonprofit and *for-profit groups in more direct, and some say unfair, competition (Bennett and DiLorenzo 1989; Peterson 1988), there are various ways in which nonprofits collaborate with for-profits (Wymer and Samu 2003). This happens, for instance, through creating social enterprises, developing cause-related marketing, establishing sponsorships, and the like. The approach of *social economy is relevant here as well. Hammack and Young (1993a) consider several aspects of the relationship of nonprofits to the economy and businesses.

buying pool: a *collectivity whose participants purchase large quantities of a *good at a more favorable price than is available to individual buyers. Hunt and Satterlee (1986, passim), in their study of English pubs, observed that, to keep prices low, patrons engaged in pool buying of beer and other commodities, a practice the authors related to the social class of the patrons. *See also* economic activity, informal

buzz grouping: procedure for stimulating participation by all individuals in a large group, effected by dividing the group into units small enough for face-to-face interaction to be possible (Barker 2003:54). Buzz groups (sometimes called "huddle groups") typically choose one in their number to report their deliberations to the larger group when it reconvenes.

by-law: rule created for and adopted by a *nonprofit group primarily for governance of its *members and regulation of its affairs. Hopkins (2001: 15–16) lists the usual provisions that incorporated *nonprofits groups normally have in their set of by-laws or, as occasionally referred to, "code of regulations."

C

capital, bonding: social capital (*capital, social) that generates solidarity within *groups, including *nonprofit groups. Such capital tends to be inward looking and exclusive of outsiders. It tends to reinforce exclusive identities and group homogeneity (Putnam 2000:22–24). Compare with *capital, bridging.

capital, bridging: social capital (*capital, social) that generates community-wide ties between *groups, including *nonprofit groups. Such capital tends to be outward looking and inclusive of outsiders. It tends to re-inforce broad identities and reciprocity spanning some of the usual social divisions (Putnam 2000:22–24). Compare with *capital, bonding.

capital campaign: *fund-raising by a *nonprofit group for a building or similar major project (e.g., repair, endowment). Walker (2005, passim) provides a helpful manual for successfully organizing and conducting capital campaigns in the *nonprofit sector.

capital, cultural: familiarity with traditional high-cultural forms (e.g., music, art, dance) as a defining quality of people occupying high-status positions in society. Jeannotte (2003, passim) observes that investments in cultural capital, as in acquiring and learning about high culture, are linked to the propensity to *volunteer. The term is associated with the work of Pierre Bourdieu (1977).

capital, financial. *See* resources

capital gain property donation: a *donor can, subject to *percentage limitations on charitable donations, give appreciated long-term gain property (e.g., stocks, real estate) as a donation to a *qualified donee and deduct the fair market value of the donation, even if the property was acquired for a much lower price (Fishman and Schwarz 2000:911). This usually results in significant tax savings over the giving of cash or non-long-term gain property.

capital, human: ensemble of skills, knowledge, and experience of an individual or set of individuals and its value for an *organization or a society (cf. Samuelson and Nordhaus 1995:223). Smith (2000:58) explores the implications of the idea of human capital, originally developed for application to the sphere of work, for the *nonprofit sector, observing that the real assets of *nonprofit groups are their active *volunteers and *leaders.

capital, negative social: *social capital used to facilitate the interests of *deviant nonprofit groups. Discussed further by Putnam (2000:21–22).

capital, positive social: expressive, friendly, interpersonal interactions and relationships that are undertaken for their own sake and that, at the same time, contribute to sense of community and to social integration (Duck 1992:90–93).

capital, psychosocial leadership: ability of a *leader to generate *commitment and activity from *members of a *nonprofit group to give expression to certain important beliefs and values held by both the leader and the members (Smith 2000:58).

capital, social: connections among individuals, as manifested in social networks, trustworthiness, acts motivated by the norm of *reciprocity, and the like. Used by analogy to the concepts of *human capital and physical capital (e.g., natural resources, *financial resources) to emphasize that human groups of all kinds also benefit from and advance their interests according to the salutary interconnectivity of their members. Putnam (2000:18–24) provides a history of the concept of social capital, while relating it to the *nonprofit sector. Portes (1998, passim) also reviewed the origins and application of the concept of social capital. Putnam (1993, passim) studied how social capital affected *civic engagement in different regions of Italy. In his more recent book (Putnam 2000, passim), he relates social capital measures for the states of America to a variety of societal outcome measures.

care. *See* informal care

career in nonprofits: the search for or the fact of a career in a *nonprofit group, usually a *paid-staff nonprofit. Many books now describe the range of careers in nonprofits and how to enter them, including the important prerequisite of getting appropriate education in *nonprofit management or administration (Cohen and Young 1989; King 2000; Lowell 2000; McAdam 1991; O'Neill and Fletcher 1998; Slesinger 2004). Daniels (1988) describes the invisible careers of women who are very active in many *grassroots associations. *See also* career volunteering

career volunteer: one who engages in *career volunteering (Stebbins 1992: 15–17).

career volunteering: volunteering as *serious leisure (as opposed to *casual leisure), where *career volunteers find (nonwork) careers in the acquisition of special skills, knowledge, or training and, at times, two or three of these, as they relate to a volunteer role or a set of such roles (Stebbins 1992:15–17).

caregiver (carer): someone, either a *professional or *nonprofessional, who looks after the social, physical, and emotional needs of a dependent child, invalid, elderly person, and the like. Most nonprofessional caregivers are relatives of the person cared for. Thus Ingersoll-Dayton and colleagues (2003, passim) describe the distribution of care-giving responsibilities among a sample of siblings caring for their parents. *See also* caring; informal caring; caring society; compassion

caring: process of assuming personal responsibility for others' *welfare, by acknowledging their needs and acting responsively toward them. Defined broadly by Oliner and Oliner (1995) to include both people and the natural environment. The authors argue that caring is a social process, which includes both "attaching" processes (bonding, empathizing, learning caring norms, assuming personal responsibility) and "including" processes (diversifying one's interaction to include those unlike oneself, networking, resolving conflict and linking the local with the global). *See also* informal caring; caring society; caregiver; compassion

caring society: a compassionate society that has been transformed such that caring is evident in all major social institutions, including the family, schools, workplace, and religion (Oliner and Oliner 1995). The authors argue that care should penetrate these institutions but replace other functions there. *See also* informal caring; caregiver; compassion

casual leisure: immediately intrinsically rewarding, relatively short-lived pleasurable activity requiring little or no special training to enjoy it. It is fundamentally hedonic, being pursued for its significant level of pure enjoyment. The term was coined by Robert A. Stebbins (1982:255) in a conceptual statement about *serious leisure in which the casual form was described as a counterpart to it. Among the several types of casual leisure is *casual volunteering, or helping with such tasks as stuffing envelopes, handing out flyers, and directing traffic in a large parking lot (Stebbins 2003b:45).

casual volunteering: *volunteering done as *casual leisure (Stebbins 2003d: 541).

caucus: 1. committee composed of *members of a political party who meet regularly to determine *policy, select candidates, and so on. 2. a group or secret meeting of such group comprised of certain members of a

larger organization. Caucus in this sense frequently has derogatory connotations. As an illustration of sense 2, Devinatz (2001, passim) describes
the emergence, politics, and activities of the New Left union caucus, the
Workers' Voice Committee, which developed in 1970 in Local 61 of the
United Auto Workers.

causality in program evaluation: an objective in outcome evaluation, which
is to find evidence of causality or lack thereof. That is, does the program
being evaluated produce the desired changes (Thomas 1994:356)?

cause: in the *nonprofit sector, the side of a question or controversy espoused by an individual, party, *social movement, or *nonprofit group.
Roue (2003, passim) examined the ambiguity inherent in the mediator
and spokesperson role that *nongovernmental organizations feel in de-
fending the cause of indigenous peoples, in her research on the Cree of
James Bay in Quebec.

cause-oriented organization: a *nonprofit organization espousing a *cause.
Laville (2003, passim) studied American women's *associations, which
were especially active in efforts by the United States to counter the Soviet
"Peace Offensive" mounted after World War II.

centralization: process of concentration of decision making in a *nonprofit
group. Smith (2000:168) notes that centralization is high when all major
decisions are made by the president alone, whereas it is low when such
decisions are significantly shaped by all main hierarchies of the group.
Using a sample of fifty-three protest groups, Gamson (1990, chap. 7)
studied their degree of centralization of power as achieved by bureaucratic organization. *See also* complexity in nonprofits

century of information/service society: the 1900s, during which there was
a dramatic rise in the service sector (see *sector of society) and increase
in the availability of and reliance on information (facts, knowledge com-
municated on a particular subject). Discussed by Smith (2000:260) with
reference to the 2000s, the voluntary century (see *century, voluntary).

century of voluntary society. *See* century, voluntary

century, voluntary: the 2000s, during which, Smith (2000:260) predicts, people will participate much more than previously in voluntary and nonprofit roles, groups, choices, and activities in spatially diffuse, nonprofit
communities of their choice. Volunteering will grow significantly. Smith
believes, further, that volunteers in the voluntary century will tend to
develop and retain their individuality. Beck (2000:150–155) sketches a
similar transformation to occur in the growth of *civil labor. *See also*
homo voluntas

challenge grant: a *grant made to a *nonprofit group contingent on other
*fund-raising, either on a matching basis (*matching grant) or other
ratio. Often the fund-raising must be completed within a designated
period of time. The aim is to stimulate additional fund-raising. Peters
(1988, passim) describes how the journal *Zygon* used a Gift Subscription

Challenge Grant from the Fund for the Enhancement of the Human Spirit to put it on a firm financial base.

change agent: person or group, *professional or *nonprofessional, who tries to effect or actually effects change in a *nonprofit group or, more particularly, in the group's goals, programs, procedures, and the like. Buchanan and Bedham (1999, passim) describe the lived experience of organizational politics from the perspective of five senior managers with major responsibilities for implementing change.

channeling of volunteering. *See* volunteering, channeling of

chapter: local *group of an *association with a larger territorial base or catchment area, such as a *regional association or *national association. Reger (2004, passim) investigated the role emotions play in *social movements, using as a case study the New York City chapter of the National Organization for Women. She found that consciousness-raising in the chapter served to transform personal emotions into a collectively defined sense of injustice and enhance chapter *activism.

charismatic incentive: a type of *incentive rooted in the appeal to *members of the *charismatic leader of a *nonprofit group. Melton (1986:29–30) describes the charismatic qualities of Joseph Smith, Jr., founder of the Church of Jesus Christ of Latter Day Saints (popularly known as the Mormon Church). *See also* incentive type

charismatic leader: as used in the social sciences, someone seen by followers as having extraordinary (even superhuman or supernatural) abilities and advantages that inspire devotion and enthusiasm. Most research on charismatic leaders has been carried out on those driving a *social movement group (e.g., Burwell 1995).

charitable choice: title of a federal government provision in the United States permitting faith-based providers (*faith-based organization) of *social services to apply for public *funding for the work they do for the general public. Ebaugh and colleagues (2003, passim) found in a survey of faith-based and secular providers that 80 percent of the former use religious imagery of some kind in their public documents.

charitable contribution tax deduction: if a *donation is made with *donative intent to a *qualified donee, it is usually eligible for a tax deduction if the donor itemizes deductions on an annual federal income tax return (Fishman and Schwarz 2000:867). This deduction originated in 1917 with the income tax in America (Fishman and Schwarz 2000:849).

charitable donation. *See* donation

charitable exchange. *See* exchange, philanthropic

charitable federal tax-exemption requirements: series of tests that an organization must pass in order to become a tax-exempt IRS 501(c)(3) charitable nonprofit, including (a) be a *nonprofit group, organization, or corporation; (b) have a charitable purpose; (c) have a *nondistribution constraint; (d) do no substantial lobbying (none at all if a private foundation); (e) avoid involvement in any political campaign of a candidate for public office; (f) be in accord with established public policy and not illegal (cf. Fishman and Schwarz 2000:351–356, 383–384).

charitable foundation. *See* foundation

charitable gambling: organized, legal wagering on games of chance (e.g., bingos, raffles, casino games), a proportion of the proceeds from which goes to educational, religious, cultural, or other charitable *causes. Such games are typically conducted by one or more *charitable nonprofits. G. Smith (1994, passim) describes charitable gambling in Canada, where private enterprise is legally barred from operating games of chance.

charitable gift: *See* philanthropy

charitable giving. *See* philanthropy

charitable immunity and liability: legal status of a *nonprofit group, by which it is free from being held liable for harm it has caused. Traditional charitable immunity for nonprofits in the United States virtually disappeared in the 1940s, having been replaced with, depending on the state, a form of limited *liability (Tremper 1994:488). Furthermore, driven in part by the malaise created by 11 September 2001, nonprofit groups now face significantly higher payments for liability insurance (for a view of this situation in Canada, see the Voluntary Sector Forum's report on its website: http://www.vsf-fsbc.ca/eng. *See also* risk management; risk management and liability for volunteers/members; risk management in nonprofits

charitable mission: a central task assumed by a *nonprofit group, execution of which results in a public *gift or other *good. Rose-Ackerman (1990, passim) examines some of the conditions under which nonprofit groups abandon their charitable missions.

charitable nonprofit. *See* charity

charitable purpose of nonprofit organization: purpose of a *nonprofit organization to promote the general welfare and *public interest in some way not in violation of law and public policy (cf. Hopkins 1998:5.1–5.3; Fishman and Schwarz 2000:87–105).

charitable remainder trust: along with a simple *bequest, this form of trust is a very common vehicle of *planned giving; involves a *donor making a *donation to a *qualified donee of property in trust, which the donor retains an interest in for him-/herself or other beneficiaries for life or some period of years (Fishman and Schwarz 2000:929–930).

charitable sector. *See* nonprofit sector; philanthropic sector

charitable solicitation regulation: state laws regulating charitable solicitation by mandating disclosure of financial and operational information, by prohibiting fraudulent solicitation, and, less successfully, by trying to control the percentage of costs of solicitation and administration (Fishman and Schwarz 2000:278–279).

charitable tax-exempt nonprofit: tax-exempt nonprofit that falls into IRS tax-exempt category 501(c)(3) (see *tax-exempt nonprofit organizations registered with the IRS); such organizations serve the *public interest (Fishman and Schwarz 2000:325).

charitable transfer. *See* exchange, philanthropic

charitable trust: legal and financial arrangement wherein a person assigns a *charitable gift to a *charity or *foundation to be used for charitable beneficiaries with donor intent of realizing a deduction in income or estate tax, if not both (Hopkins 1998, passim). Barker (2003:65) notes that, until death, the *donor usually retains certain rights to the gift. Differs from private trusts in benefiting the *public interest rather than merely private individuals (Fishman and Schwarz 2000:62).

charity: 1. disposition to think favorably of others, of their thoughts and actions, and to make allowance for their shortcomings. 2. *nonprofit group, usually formally organized, that provides one or more *public benefits and receives a significant amount of its *revenue from *donations. In the United States, usually registered as a 501 (c)(3) group with the IRS, if registered there at all, and qualified under IRS Section 509(a); a *public charity. Eligible to receive tax-deductible charitable *gifts. Bowen and colleagues (1994, passim) discuss in detail the public charities. *See also* economy, philanthropic; philanthropy; nonprofit sector

charter: 1. written document authorized by the monarch or legislature that grants privileges, recognizes rights, or creates an organizational entity such as a *nonprofit group or company. Often synonymous with *articles of organization. 2. publicly conceded right or permission, a privilege, often authorized in the form of a license. (Both senses adapted from the *Shorter Oxford English Dictionary*, 5th ed. 2002:384.)

checkbook activism: donation of money to a *nonprofit group without accompanying dedication of volunteer work, because the *donor lacks time, opportunity, or inclination to become actively involved with that group (Barker 2003:65).

Christian base community: a *nonprofit group established by ordinary Roman Catholics in Latin America, and especially Brazil, that meets regularly to deepen *members' knowledge of the Gospel, consider community needs and their solutions, spread the word of God, and in the Eucharist, celebrate victories and share defeats (Hewitt 1986:17). These groups are known in Portuguese as *communidades eclesiais de base* (CEBs).

church: 1. *nonprofit group, usually local and formal in structure, whose central interest lies in practicing a kind of *religion (e.g., Islam, Christianity, Judaism) widely accepted by the society in which it operates (cf. Harris 1998b:214); a *church congregation. 2. a *denomination. 3. a formal *nonprofit group of international scope, whose central interest lies in a kind of *religion (e.g., Islam, Christianity, Judaism) widely accepted by the various societies in which it operates. Yinger (1970:256–

280), building on Ernest Troeltsch's famous typology, labels this church (sense 3) the "universal church" (see the more detailed definition of a state church in Johnstone 1992:86). There are thousands of books on churches, including state churches (e.g., Armstrong 2002; Chadwick 1993; Dominguez 1994b; Kitagawa 1989; Liebman and Don-Yiha 1983; Lopez 2001; Peters 2004; Prusak 2004; Reat 1994; Ware 1993). There is even a dictionary of the Christian church (Livingstone and Cross 1997) and a book on critical terms for religious studies (Taylor 1998), which obviates the need for defining here many church-related terms. *See also* sect, new religion

church attendance: common form of *religious activity, in which a person attends a worship service at a *church or equivalent. Blau, Land, and Redding (1992, passim) use the extension of religious affiliation in the United States to explain growth of church attendance there.

church congregation: body of believers (a set of *analytic members) organized as a nonprofit church, synagogue, mosque, or other religious body. More precisely a church congregation is either an evanescent religious gathering, a religious service for instance, or an enduring religious community, a *nonprofit group. Jeavons and Cnaan (1997, passim) examined the transitions these groups make to become viable, self-sustaining entities. A special supplementary issue of *Nonprofit and Voluntary Sector Quarterly* (vol. 26, 1997) contains several articles on *church congregations as nonprofits. Harris (1998b, passim) examines church and synagogue congregations in Britain, based on four case studies. Queen (2000, passim) provides a handbook on human service activities by church congregations and other *religious nonprofit groups. Cnaan and Boddie (2002, passim) have written a similar book on congregations only. Wilson (1983) has discussed how to mobilize church volunteers. Chaves (2004, passim) has written an extensive empirical study of American congregations. Nonprofit researchers who fail to include and study church congregations and *church-related nonprofit groups in their study of the *nonprofit sector are reflecting the *secularist focus flat-earth paradigm (Smith 2000:235–236), which was formerly widespread (Smith 1984, passim).

church, local: local religious *congregation or *group that may be affiliated with a *church or *religious organization having a larger territorial base or catchment area. Stonebraker (2003, passim) studied the impact on both local and national (*church, national) churches of shrinking *congregations and hence availability of funds. He found that, these days, the former are sending less and less money to the latter.

church membership. *See* membership

church, national: a *religious organization with affiliated *local churches in two or more states or provinces of a nation. Stonebraker (2003, passim) studied the impact on both local (*church, local) and national churches of shrinking *congregations and hence availability of funds. He found that, these days, the former are sending less and less money to the latter.

church-related nonprofit group: *nonprofit group organized substantially around the ideology of the *church with which it is affiliated. Examples include couples clubs, Bible study groups, and groups devoted to the interests of women and youth (Smith 2000:93).

church school: a *nonprofit school affiliated with a *church or other *religious organization (e.g., a *religious order). Francis and Brown (1991, passim) found, in their study of adolescents in Liverpool, England, that *church attendance is more important in shaping their practice of private prayer than attendance at a church school.

church volunteer: *volunteer who works for a church, usually for a church congregation. Common church volunteer roles include ushering, singing in the choir, teaching Sunday school, assisting with services, and running a food pantry. Cionca (1999) describes recruitment of church volunteers, as does Wilson (1983).

citizen action: *See* citizen participation

citizen advisory board: 1. a *group of local residents, often intended to be a cross section of the local community, that functions as a *volunteer department of a *government agency or program or a larger *nonprofit organization. 2. the local *volunteer group specifically affiliated with the U.S. Model Cities Program as advisors.

citizen advocacy group. *See* advocacy group

citizen engagement. *See* civic engagement

citizen group: *nonprofit group at the local, *grassroots level that seeks to influence political, economic, or other action on a local, regional, or national level. Sometimes refers to all *grassroots associations, though the present definition is preferred. Livojevic and Cornelius (1998, passim) studied for eighteen months the *effectiveness of a small citizen group that was attempting to influence local *social policy on juvenile detention.

citizen involvement. *See* citizen participation

citizen militia: *paramilitary group, usually based in a small geographical locale, who function as a *grassroots association of citizens armed and ready to do battle for their *civil liberties or other perceived freedoms and *rights. Usually, in the contemporary United States, politically conservative but antigovernmental, with ideological (*ideology) tendencies toward *anarchy. The group's *mission is often to prepare for armed defense of its geographic territory against a specified enemy (e.g., Communists, a certain ethnic group, invasive *government) or to survive a thermonuclear war. Zellner (1995:47–75) describes several widely different survivalist groups. A broader review of citizen militias can be found in Corcoran (1995, passim), Halpern and Levin (1996, passim), and Karl (1995). Snow (1999, passim) views citizen militias today as a terrorist threat. *See also* militia

citizen participation: individual *participation in a *citizen group or in other
local *political voluntary action, whether group or individual, conventional or deviant. In general, local *political participation. Conway (1991,
passim) examines political participation in the United States. Checkoway
(1995) views citizen participation in a very specific way, as a reference
to formal citizen involvement in government *organizations. Many
books in the 1970s and 1980s and more recently study citizen participation. Spiegel (1968, passim) edited an important early overview of
American citizen participation. Boyte (1980, passim) wrote on citizen
advocacy (*citizen participation) in the late 1970s, suggesting that such
participation was having a widespread positive impact. Gittell (1980, passim) examined government *mandated citizen participation programs
and resulting community organizations (sense 3), concluding that these
approaches to citizen participation did not work well, agreeing with
Moynihan (1970, passim) earlier. Hutcheson and Steggart (1979, passim)
review the citizen participation literature and some case studies on both
federally mandated and voluntary citizen-initiated citizen groups (see
also Buchbinder and Stevens 1974; Cole 1974; DeSario and Langton
1987). More recent books on voluntaristic citizen groups and citizen
participation see more generally positive effects (e.g., Beierle and Cayford
2002; Berry, Portney, and Thomson 1993; Couto 1999; Herring et al.
1998; Lappé and DuBois 1994, pt. 3; Rimmerman 2001; Naples 1998;
Sanoff 2000; Simonsen and Robbins 2000), writing of a new citizenship,
new citizen empowerment, and the rebirth of urban democracy. Citizen
participation is broader than *civic engagement, in that, unlike the latter,
the former is not centered strictly on duty, responsibility, or obligation.
Citizen participation is narrower than *community involvement, however, since the second also refers to nonpolitical action while it, too, is
not confined to matters of duty or responsibility.

citizen volunteer: early conception of *volunteering, which located volunteering in the larger role of citizen. The volunteer was seen as a form of
*citizen participation. Moise S. Cahn (writing in the preface to Cohen
1960:vii) defined the citizen volunteer as one who assumes voluntarily
and without pay his obligations of citizenship, including roles as *service
volunteer, policy-making volunteer (such as member of public and nonprofit boards and commissions), and social action volunteer.

citizenship: a personal political status rooted in a set of universal rights that
are enforceable by claims on the state and, historically, founded on the
legal necessities of capitalist society and its government (Somers 1993:
588). The core components of citizenship are seen as *membership,
*participation, *association, inclusion/exclusion, national identity, and
the rule of law (Somers 1993:594).

civic association: a form of *voluntary association that engages in nonpar-
tisan education and *advocacy around issues of common *community
or municipal concern (as distinguished from a *civic service nonprofit

group). However, Kaufman (1999) pointed out that civic associations were often formed to influence public policy in a way that is consistent with the perceived economic interests of those forming the association.

civic engagement: act or result of performing, using socially acceptable means, a felt civic duty, responsibility, or obligation (*see* civic obligation/responsibility) fulfilled by working toward amelioration of a *community concern. The noun "engagement" is etymologically related to the French verb *engager,* meaning to bind or commit. For this reason related terms like "civic participation" and "community participation" are, etymologically speaking, erroneously used as synonyms for civic engagement, while such terms as "citizen engagement" and "civil engagement" are, at bottom, synonymous with it. Norris (2001, passim) examines, on an international scale, the effects on civic engagement of lack of information and the role of the Internet in this situation. Putnam (1993) wrote an important empirical study of civic engagement in Italy. *See also* community involvement; citizen participation

civic engagement value. *See* humane core value

civic involvement. *See* community involvement

civic obligation/responsibility: duty or *obligation felt by citizens to participate (*participation) through some sort of *civic engagement or *civil labor in the *civil society in which they live. Kerber (1997, passim) argues that, at the national level, active, nonexclusionary *citizenship involving civic obligation is the most effective form. Verba, Schlozman, and Brady (1995:117–120) explore civic responsibility and civic gratifications in relation to different forms of political activity (*political voluntary action), including *protest activity and *nonprofit group participation.

civic participation. *See* citizen participation; political participation

civic renewal movement: a *social movement that emerged in America in the 1990s and that attempts to harness *political voluntary action by urban citizens. They use the arts of self-reliance, common problem solving, and democratic self-government in an attempt to make cities better serve *public needs (Siriani and Friedland 2001, chap. 6).

civic responsibility. *See* civic obligation

civic service: an organized period of substantial engagement leading to a recognized and valued contribution to the local, national, or international *community. Civic service is *formal volunteering, though *participants performing it receive minimal monetary compensation (McBride and Sherraden 2004:3S). *See also* civic service nonprofit group

civic service nonprofit group: *nonprofit group whose *mission includes provision of a public good or service. Most local service clubs (e.g., Lions, Rotary International) provide one or more *civic services, as do some men's and women's *lodges. Such groups are also formed for reasons other than provision of service; they include *member sociality, business connections, and fringe benefits such as life insurance (Smith 2000:101).

civic society. *See* civil society

civil disobedience: kind of *political voluntary action that involves disobeying a particular law or rule felt to be unjust, with the aim of having that law or rule changed. Henry David Thoreau (1849/1960) was an early exponent of this *tactic.

civil engagement. *See* civic engagement

civil involvement. *See* community involvement

civil labor: sphere of human activity devoted to unpaid renewal and expansion of *social capital (Rojek 2002:21). Beck (2000:125) says that civil labor comprises housework, family work, club work, and *volunteer work. An extremely broad concept, encompassing much of what is considered at the activity level under the headings of family/household sector and third sector (*see* sectors of society). Rojek (2002:26–27) argues that, for the most part, civil labor is the *serious leisure of *amateurs, *hobbyists, and *career volunteers. *See also* civil society; community involvement; civic engagement

civil liberty: a basic human right that is supported by law and permits a variety of important activities necessary for a *civil society. Sometimes referred to as a "civil right." These activities include the freedoms of assembly, association, dissent, and speech as well as rights like due process and privacy. "Civil right," a near synonym of civil liberty, differs only in its emphasis on equality. Aliabadi (2000, passim) examines the relevance of the concept of civil liberty in contemporary Iranian society. Many authors have written on civil liberties in general, especially those in America (e.g., Abraham and Perry 1998; Barth and Clayton 1983; Irons 2005; Leone 2003; McWhirter 1994).

civil participation. *See* citizen participation; political participation

civil religion: the public side of religion, which includes national beliefs, symbols, and rituals (term coined by Bellah 1975, passim). Demerath III and Williams (1985:154) further describe civil religion as the religion of a nation, as a nonsectarian faith whose symbols are those of the polity and the nation's history.

civil right. *See* civil liberty

civil rights organization: *nonprofit group formed for a specified category of citizen (e.g., Afro-Americans, Hispanic-Americans) to work toward establishing, for them, the routine availability of the *civil liberties of their society. American civil rights groups include the National Association for the Advancement of Colored People, American Council of the Blind, and American Civil Liberties Union. Bullard (1993, passim) has written a history of the civil rights movement in the United States.

civil society: 1. a national society with a well-developed, diverse, free, and actively functioning *nonprofit sector serving as a counterbalance to its governmental and business sectors (*see* sector of society). It is the democratic opposite of *dictatorship and involves extensive *citizen participation (O'Connell 1999:5). Moreover, as Beck (2000:3–5) argues, civil society, which is sometimes known as "voluntary society," runs parallel to a nation's work society. 2. another name for the nonprofit sector itself (see Naidoo and Tandon 1999:2), with special emphasis on the role of voluntary associations and freedom of association in contributing to a healthy public life (*the public interest). The nonprofit sector is seen as a political concept (ibid.:8). A strong and healthy civil society is seen as having a dense and diverse associational life (sometimes termed "institutional pluralism"; ibid.:10), structural and functional specialization and differentiation at local, regional, and national levels (ibid.), and a normative or values dimension emphasizing civic norms, values, democratic practices, and social capital (ibid.:11). Civil society has become a very popular concept in the last decade or two, with many books examining the subject at length using one or the other of the above senses of the term (e.g., C. Armstrong 2002; Eberly 2000; Eberly and Streeter 2002; Edwards 2004; Fullinwider 1999; Gellner 1994; Ginsberg 2003; Hann 1996; Howard 2003; Hudock 1999; Kaldor 2003; Keane 2003; Ndegwa 1996; Oxhorn, Tulchin, and Seles 2004; Sajoo 2002; Salamon et al. 1999; Schuler and Day 2004; Schwartz and Pharr 2003; Seligman 1992; Van Til 2000; Wiarda 1993). The origins of the term "civil society" reach back centuries to philosophers such as Thomas Hobbes, John Locke, and Jean Jacques Rousseau (Tester 1992, passim). *See also* participatory democracy; civil labor; civic obligation

civil society sector. *See* nonprofit sector

civil war: a war between two geographical areas or political factions of a nation. Moran and Pitcher (2004, passim) examine civil strife in Liberia and Mozambique and the ways women's groups in the two countries differentially affect war and peace and distribution of postwar aid.

classification of nonprofit groups: systematic distribution or arrangement of classes or categories of *nonprofit groups. Smith (2000:232–233) has identified two classificatory schemes in the field of nonprofit groups and voluntary action: (a) purposive type classification, which is by far the more common of the two, consists of categories of nonprofits established according to sector or institution of the society in which they operate (e.g., health, education, environment)—this approach reflects the *purposive type flat-earth paradigm; (b) analytic type classification, by contrast, proceeds from one or more theoretically important dimensions or concepts, such as whether staff are paid or whether groups are of the *grassroots association variety.

clergy: 1. Christian *religious functionaries such as priests, ministers, or pastors (cf. Harris 1998b:214). 2. less commonly, religious functionaries in any religion.

client. *See* target of benefits

closed shop union: a *union local in which all workers of a certain type in a company are required to join the *union as a condition of employment. Hanson (1982, passim) and Haggard (1977, passim) studied closed shop unions in America and Europe. *See also* open shop union

club: 1. nonprofit association (*nonprofit group), whose principal *goal is to foster social relations and *sociability, but which pursues as significant secondary goals either *service or *leisure, if not both. Sometimes known as "service clubs." Charles (1993, passim) studied a sample of them in the United States, as represented by Rotary, Kiwanis, and the Lions. 2. an *association, usually locally based, that has sociability (fellowship and friendly social relations) as its primary purpose. It is a social club. Many *associations ostensibly formed for other purposes (e.g., veterans' associations, civic service clubs, hobby or garden clubs, ethnic or nationality associations) are in fact mainly social clubs (sense 2). An early discussion of English clubs may be found in Timbs (1865, passim), but the concept goes back centuries earlier (Ross 1976, chaps. 4 and 5).

club good. *See* good, club

coalition: a set of two or more *groups formally cooperating (*cooperation) over a period of time in search of one or more common *goals. Harcourt and Waal (1992, passim) have edited a collection of papers on coalitions and alliances among humans and other animals. *See also* collaboration

coercive economy. *See* economy, coercive

coercive exchange. *See* exchange, coercive

coercive isomorphism. *See* isomorphism, coercive

coercive transfer. *See* exchange, coercive

co-housing. *See* intentional community

collaboration in nonprofits: joint cooperative (*cooperation) work in a set of *nonprofit groups that increases effectiveness of the *coalition they have formed. Kaplan (1986, passim) observes that, among these groups, collaboration occurs in degrees. High collaboration consists of numerous bilateral and multilateral relationships, while at the other end of the spectrum lie isolated groups with no working ties whatsoever. Horizontal collaboration is collaboration with other groups at the same territorial level, while vertical collaboration is collaboration with other groups at a higher or lower territorial level. Nonprofit researchers who study nonprofit groups without taking account of their collaboration activities are reflecting the *isolated nonprofit flat-earth paradigm. Hula (1999) describes *interest group coalitions that do *lobbying together on an issue of common interest—an increasingly common technique of *influence. Other recent books on nonprofit collaboration include Bailey and Koney (2000), Linden (2002), Warren (1997), and Wymer and Samu (2003). *See also* cooperation

collective: 1. (n.) a *commune or other collective entity. 2. (adj.) of or pertaining to a *group, *collective, or group-like activity, to individuals taken or acting together (adapted from the *Shorter Oxford English Dictionary,* 5th ed. 2002:448).

collective action: the purposive mobilization of forces within a *community to implement a *plan using pre-existing problem-solving and *decision-making mechanisms. Seen as the fourth of six steps through which *community-based initiatives are seen as traveling (Eng 1988:46). May also be seen as a mix of one or more of the types of *community-based initiatives defined by Checkoway (1995).

collective behavior: sociological term referring to a *collectivity in change-oriented, disorderly, violent, or otherwise unconventional action, such as in a *mob, *riot, *rebellion, and the like. 1. in its elementary form, spontaneous, emotional action of an aggregate of people whose thinking and behavior are more or less unstructured and, in some instances, impulsive (Lofland 1990, chap. 14). Miller (1985:5) traces the concept of collective behavior back to Gustave Le Bon's 1895 book on *The Crowd* and the use of the term "collective behavior" in an introductory sociology text in 1921 by Robert Park and Ernest Burgess. 2. collective behavior as a *social movement that is rather more structured, more of a collectivity (Zurcher and Snow 1990, chap. 15).

collective good. *See* good

collective settlement. *See* intentional community

collectiveness index: device for measuring the level at which a *nonprofit group provides goods or services to the public (high collectiveness) as opposed to providing them to members only (low collectiveness). Also called "publicness index." Both terms were coined by Weisbrod (1988: 75–76), who saw it as (a) a measure for describing types of nonprofit groups and (b) a basis for designing for such groups' *social policy that will enhance pursuit of the benefits they offer.

collectivist organization: *nonprofit group in which social values such as *voluntary altruism prevail over values like utilitarianism or coerciveness (the term was coined by Rothschild-Whitt 1979, passim). *Grassroots associations tend to be more collectivist than paid-staff nonprofits, which, as work organizations tend to be more bureaucratic and utilitarian (Smith 2000:78).

collectivity: a set of two or more individuals with a sense of collective identity and an effective level of intercommunication among themselves. In its bare bones form, a simple collectivity is a loose social unit that falls just short of being a group, because it lacks a shared goal with associated normative strength (Smith 2000:77). However, a collectivity is more cohesive than a mere *social category because of its significant intercommunication among participants. Collectivities with additional structural characteristics (see the relevant definitions in this dictionary) may also be *groups, *organizations, *social movements, *associations, and the like. A crowd, mob, or community is a simple collectivity. *See also* group; informal group; social category; primary group; secondary group

co-member service incentive: type of *service incentive that involves *satisfaction from serving other *members (co-members) of one's own *association or one's own other *nonprofit group. The type of *service incentive prevalent in *member benefit nonprofits (Smith 2000:98–99). *See also* incentive type

commercial purpose of nonprofit organization: a *nonprofit organization can operate commercial, profit-seeking ventures (which are not tax exempt; *see* unrelated business income tax), but organizations may not distribute any profit made to private individuals (*nondistribution constraint) (Fishman and Schwarz 2000:78–83).

commerciality doctrine: legal doctrine that an IRS 501(c)(3) charitable organization does not lose its tax exemption simply by engaging in business (commercial) activities unless the latter become the primary purpose of the organization (Fishman and Schwarz 2000:463–464).

commercialization of nonprofits: process of realizing financial return from goods or services, said by Starkweather (1993) to be a growing practice among *nonprofit groups. Crimmins and Keil (1983, passim) provide an early overview discussion of "enterprise in the nonprofit sector." Weisbrod (1998, passim) presents many essays on the commercial transformation of the nonprofit sector. Bennett and DiLorenzo (1989, passim) refer to the "profits" of nonprofits as an example of unfair competition with for-profits. Brody (1996, passim) sees an economic convergence of nonprofit and for-profit organizational forms. Tuckman (1996, passim) examines competition among nonprofits and between nonprofits and for-profits. Massarsky (1994, passim) argues for the value of profit-seeking enterprise strategies in *paid-staff nonprofit organizations. Hammack and Young (1993b, passim) treat commercialization and other economic issues regarding nonprofits. Kluger, Baker, and Garval (1998, passim) discuss how to commercialize a nonprofit. *See* contracted service in nonprofits

commitment: a set of attitudes or motivations that sustain *participation in an activity and provide impetus for investing effort in such activity regardless of its short-term cost and benefits (Mannell 1993:128) and despite the *voluntary nature of the activity. This is not to say, however, that long-term benefits of committed participation are inexistent. For instance, Mannell (1993:129) argued that participation in leisure activities can produce *status recognition and counter the detrimental effects on well-being of unemployment, retirement, or lack of job satisfaction. Kanter (1972, chap. 3) gives a major discussion of commitment and commitment-building mechanisms in the context of communes.

committee: small subgroup within a *nonprofit group (usually an *association), which has been officially assigned, and has accepted, the task of working on *planning or implementing some facet of the nonprofit's activity (Connors 1988a). Committees are important for nonprofit group *effectiveness. R. Khari Brown and Brown (2003, passim) found in their research that involvement of blacks in *church committees helped develop significantly their civic skills.

common good (the). *See* public interest (the) (sense 1)

common interest association. *See* association

common pool resources: 1. system of natural and human-made *resources of varied ownership, from which it is costly to exclude users ("difficulty of exclusion") and usage of which by some reduces usage by others ("subtractability") (Ostrom et al. 1999:278). 2. type of resource in which market-generated resource allocation is inefficient at ensuring that individual users are responsible for full cost of any negative externalities generated and at ensuring that individual users are sufficiently rewarded for generating positive externalities (Stiglitz 1986:88).

commons (the): 1. a pasture open to all, which carries with it the tragic potential for overgrazing and the enclosure of which infringes upon pre-existing conceptions of liberty (Hardin 1968). This conceptualization has given rise to both pessimistic conclusions about the potential for human *cooperation, which contend that *common pool resources must either be centrally regulated or privatized, and optimistic outlooks of more recent origin, which contend that new approaches to protecting the commons exist (Ostrom et al. 1999). 2. social, political, and economic space external to households, markets, and government in which there are associative communities or organizations (*benefactories) characterized by all five prerequisites for *koinonia that provide intrinsic and extrinsic *benefits (Lohmann 2001:170–171). 3. public realms that are spatially defined, are often put to multiple uses, and where a variety of entrepreneurial, community, political, religious, civic, educational, and recreational types of activity help increase opportunities for social interaction (Blau 2000). 4. post-industrial districts of public, nonprofit, and religious property containing governmental, educational, cultural, healthcare, musical, sports, entertainment, recreational, religious, and other facilities (Dover 2003:21), which may generate agglomeration economies similar to those theorized by Marshall for industrial districts (Marshall 1930: 287).

communal house: a major building in a *commune used to house many or all of its members. Endres (2001, passim) observes that the local communal house (*dinh*) in the villages of Northern Vietnam was, before the revolution, the center of male power and the place where the local status hierarchy was ritually reproduced. With the revolution this house became a main target of socialist ritual reform.

communal settlement. *See* commune

communal society. *See* commune

communal utopia. *See* commune

commune: residential *nonprofit group living and working together while sharing an *ideology, often reformist or utopian, about communal life; usually share finances and common ownership of land and buildings. Sometimes known as "voluntary community" (cf. Smith, Reddy, and Baldwin 1972:177). The shared tasks are, at the least, domestic, but may also include occupational duties. Since many communes are religious, *members may also worship together. Sosis and Bressler (2003, passim) studied nineteenth-century American communes to test the hypothesis that *rituals and taboos can promote intragroup *cooperation. Kanter (1972, passim) wrote a classic book on commitment mechanisms in nineteenth-century American communes, with some discussion of the problems of contemporary communes. Zablocki (1981, passim) analyzed contemporary communes of the 1960s and 1970s mainly, while Roberts (1971, passim) earlier described various types of 1960s communes in America. Pitzer's (1997, passim) book has chapters by various authors on communes across the span of American history, a list of "communal utopias" founded by 1965, and a useful bibliographical essay.

communication in nonprofits: the sharing of in-person and mediated informational and emotional messages to further the *mission of a *nonprofit group, both within it and across its boundaries to outsiders (Bonk, Griggs, and Tynes 1999; Radtke 1998; Salzman 1998). Internal communications occur both through *meetings and through information technology (Wilbur 2000, chap. 11). Communications directed toward nonmembers often tend to fall into the category of public relations— reaching a broader audience regarding the group's mission and activities (Wilbur 2000, chap. 8). And public relations, these days, tend to be seen as part of an overall marketing strategy for the nonprofit (*marketing in nonprofits).

communitarian movement: 1. the *social movement in society, especially in the United States during the 1800s, that promoted the formation of *communes, *utopias, and *intentional communities (cf. Kanter 1972, especially chap. 2). 2. a *commune (loosely). Lehman (2000, passim) has edited an interdisciplinary collection of papers critically examining the intellectual merit of the communitarian thought of the 1960s. Communitarian thinking at this time was largely in response to the dominant emphasis on individual rights and reduced social responsibility.

communitarianism: 1. belief and value system that promotes living in *communes or other *intentional communities. 2. Etzioni (2004, passim) writes that globalization has given birth to "soft communitarianism," defined as an integration of Western concerns for individual rights and political equality and Eastern concerns for social order and authoritarianism (cf. also Etzioni 1993, chap. 1). He presents several examples of Eastern societies that are slowly adopting aspects of the Western political tradition.

community: 1.*collectivity of people interacting in networks, *organizations, and *small groups within a more or less definable geographic area where the people carry out most of their daily activities accompanied by a sense of belonging to the collectivity. 2. Cohen (1985:118) has described as "symbolic" those collectivities that fail to meet the geographic criterion but that *members still see as an existing entity to which they belong. Bellah et al. (1985) note a loss of feeling of community (both senses) in America recently, which has been replaced with heightened emphasis on individualism.

community action: an attempt by poor communities to use the social and economic resources at hand to develop alternative ways to conquer the forces that perpetuate poverty. A form of *community involvement. The federal government of the United States helped foster community action through its Community Action Program, founded in 1965 as part of the Office of Economic Opportunity (Barker 2003:83–84).

community action group. *See* citizen group

community agency. *See* nonprofit agency

community association. *See* community organization; neighborhood non-profit group

community associational structure: the set of *associations in a community and the power, prestige, service, economic, and other relationships found among them. Warner and Lunt (1941, passim) were the first researchers to give an extensive portrait of a community associational structure. Stebbins (1994, chap. 6) described the community associational structure of the Calgary francophone community, a linguistic minority in a pre-dominantly anglophone city.

community-based initiative: a process in which activities or formalized structures are created to help people engage in *collective action leading to *policies, *programs, *plans, and *services for improving certain social conditions (Checkoway 1988a). Checkoway defined five models for such initiatives, including community *planning, community *advocacy, *community action, community education, and community services development (Checkoway 1988b).

community-based organization (CBO): a relatively recent term denoting a *nonprofit group that has substantial relations with its local *community and that serves this community in a significant way, often having several community representatives on its *board of directors. Moctezuma (2001, passim) describes how local *nonprofit groups as CBOs in Mexico City joined forces with students and *professionals in a stint of participative *planning to implement numerous new projects in health, culture, and education.

community center: both a building and an organization devoted to a com-munity's recreational or *social services, if not both. May be run by a *nonprofit or *governmental agency. Sterne (2000, passim) describes the role of the church parish as community center for three of the largest Catholic working-class communities operating at the turn of the nineteenth century in Providence, Rhode Island.

Community Chest: forerunner in the United States of local *United Way organizations, which are *nonprofit *fund-raising intermediaries that conduct annual community-wide fund-raising campaigns and subsequently distribute most of the proceeds to community charities. Brilliant (1990, chap. 2) describes the origins of Community Chests (p. 23) and the transition from Community Chests to United Ways in America. Website: http://www.national.unitedway.org. *See also* United Way; fund-raising intermediary

community club: *See* community association

community competence: quality of a community characterized by increased coping among its members, whereby they attempt to reduce the level of social isolation in the area (Eng 1988:46). It is seen as an outcome goal toward which a *community-based initiative may be directed (Eng 1988: 46), rather than directing efforts at solving a specific social problem without addressing the community as a unit of solution.

community control: a situation in which a cross section of a local community, usually through a *nonprofit or *volunteer department, has significant influence over a particular *governmental agency or *nonprofit program affecting that community. Spiegel (1974, passim) reprints many classic discussions of community control in different service areas. Wellock (1997, passim) presents a case study in which a broad-based, cross-ideological citizens' coalition substantially influenced experts and government on the matter of constructing a nuclear power plant near a California town.

community development: 1. process and product of reviving decaying or blighted urban neighborhoods by bringing in new jobs and businesses, new government funding, new or renovated housing, and new or reinvigorated *neighborhood nonprofit groups (Von Hoffman 2003, passim). In America, it often involves the formation and successful operation of a Community Development Corporation and/or a Community Development Financial Institution (CDFI; see Burlingame 2004:90). According to Green and Haines (2002, Part II), involves development of *human, *social, physical, financial, and environmental capital to create community sustainability. This process is aided by successful community building in the sense of creating new community social ties (Mattesich and Monsey 1997, passim). 2. improving living conditions and quality of life in a rural area or less developed nation (*Third World nation). Fisher (1993, passim) reports on successful community development by *grassroots associations and grassroots support organizations in Third World nations. The process in a rural area needs to involve all the elements mentioned above by Green and Haines (2002, pt. 2) in sense 1.

Professionals in community development often belong to the Community Development Society (http://www.comm-dev.org).

community embeddedness. *See* embededdness of nonprofit groups in communities

community engagement. *See* civic engagement

community foundation: local *nonprofit organization established to grant money to other, usually local or regional, service-producing *nonprofit groups (O'Neill 1989:139–140). Often lacks any substantial *endowment, but raises money through *donations and *grants. Serves *donors who do not wish to bother with establishing an independent *foundation. Walkenhorst et al. (2001, passim) and Magat (1989a, passim) review the world of community foundations. Wittstock and Williams (1998, passim) assess the diversity efforts of twenty community foundations. Loomis (1962, passim) describes the history of an early community foundation—the Chicago Community Trust. *See also* foundation

community fund: organized annual *fund-raising *program that uses *funds collected from the public to support local *nonprofit agencies. Goodman (1996, passim) recommends forming a community fund to secure the infrastructure of the Jewish *community in Liverpool, England, which in the mid-1990s was suffering population decline. *See also* Community Chest; United Way

community group. *See* nonprofit group; neighborhood nonprofit group

community involvement: local *voluntary action, where *members of a local *community participate together in *nonprofit groups or in other community activities. Often the *goal here is to improve community life. This concept, which is synonymous with those of civic, civil, citizen, and grassroots involvement, is broader than that of *citizen participation, in that it includes both local *political voluntary action and nonpolitical voluntary action. Sullivan (2004, passim) studied reentry of previously incarcerated youth in the United States, which he found enhanced by increased community involvement. Herring et al. (1998, passim) describe the *empowerment (sense 1) brought about by community involvement. *See also* civic engagement; citizen participation; political participation; community action; social action

community leadership: the ensemble of individuals in a community (ethnic, neighborhood, municipal) who are recognized for their ability to guide its members in action or opinion. For some *leaders this ability stems substantially from the exceptional power and influence they have there (Rose 1967:298–355). *See also* insider, societal

community meeting: a *meeting, usually occasional rather than regular, open to all residents of a community and usually focused on a local *issue, decision, *problem, and the like. Kim (1990, passim) suggests that community meetings can help ameliorate interracial conflicts by fostering greater understanding and sensitivity among the parties assembled.

community organization: 1. small, voluntaristic, loosely organized, heavily democratic *nonprofit group that represents residents of a particular geographic sector of a city, town, or rural area. Milofsky (1988:3) says that this group might be a block *club, free school, *cooperative, ethnic cultural *association, or disabled rights lobbying group (*lobby), among others. 2. the *network of *groups and *organizations, not all necessarily being nonprofits, present in a *community. 3. a local nonprofit group that has been formed by governmental mandate and that advises a governmental *agency or *program according to formal governmental rules or law (Gittell 1980, passim).

community organizational structure: the set of *organizations (governmental, *for-profit, and *nonprofit) in a community and the power, prestige, service, economic, and other relationships among them. Vidich and Bensman (1968, chap. 1) described the organizational structure of Springdale (pseudonym), a small town in upper New York state studied to explore its relationship with mass, urban society,

community organizer: a person, usually a full-time or part-time paid worker, who leads and manages *community organizing, developing local *nonprofit groups and local *participation in them aimed at social change and advocacy for community improvement. Ecklein's (1984, passim) book presents many case studies of community organizers at work. Mondros and Wilson (1994, chap. 2) discuss organizers in community organizing. Stroecker (1999, passim) examined the role of an academic in participatory research and subsequently as community organizer. Sen and Klein (2003, passim) give practical guidelines for community organizers.

community organizing: a style of activating *citizen participation in a locality, which often involves a *community organizer founding a *grassroots association or *nonprofit agency as an *advocacy group. Such groups may engage in *protest activities (Delgado 1986, passim), but in recent decades they more often do collaborative work in *nonprofit *coalitions using a more accommodative, conventional *political voluntary action style (*consensus organizing). Siriani and Friedland (2001, passim) describe such newer community organizing in the United States. The earlier government *mandated citizen participation and community organizing of the 1960s and 1970s in America was unsuccessful (Gittell 1980, passim), although independent community organizing in this period was moderately successful (Boyte 1980, passim), especially that organizing based on *Alinsky-style nonprofit group participation (Reitzes and Reitzes 1984, passim). Staples (1984, passim) provided a manual for community organizing. There are many books analyzing community organizing, such as those by Couto (2000), Fisher (1994), Fisher and Kling (1993), Gittell and Vidal (1998), Lichterman (1996), Mondros and Wilson (1994), Naples (1998), Sen and Klein (2003), and Smock (2004). *See also* neighborhood nonprofit group

community participation. *See* citizen participation; political participation

community patrol: an *association or *volunteer department of a larger *organization that attempts to provide protection and service to a community by regular movement within and observation of (especially during dark hours of the day) its physical environment, either as individual participants or small *groups who are members of the community patrol. Community patrols are sometimes termed "community policing" or "community police forces." Reisig and Parks (2004, passim) found that community policing helps bridge the gap between the town's police force and disadvantaged neighborhoods, because the latter are often substantially alienated from the former.

community policing/police force. *See* community patrol

community service: organized efforts by individuals mobilized by a *formal nonprofit organization or a *grassroots association to collectively provide services or tangible assistance to individuals, families, and communities or to maintain or improve the natural or built environment. Early usage of the term was associated with *social agencies organized to provide a wide variety of *social services (e.g., the Community Service Society in New York City). However, in recent decades, community service has become synonymous with involuntary and semi-voluntary community service hours delivered as part of a *community service sentence or *mandatory community service. Schools at different grade levels may have voluntary or required community service as part of *service-learning programs. In line with this more recent definition, McLellan and Youniss (2003, passim) found, in a study of two high schools, that students in the school that integrated community service in its curriculum were more likely to pursue, later, service that engaged them emotionally and cognitively compared with students in the school that left choice of service to the individual. *See also* service learning

community service sentence: court-mandated punishment requiring a convicted criminal, in lieu of incarceration, to undertake a specified number of hours of *community service. Some criminals serving these sentences do so by carrying out tasks otherwise done by *volunteers. The philosophy behind this form of punishment is that of reparation, of "making amends" to the community or the victim for harm done (Griffiths and Verdun-Jones 1994:541). *See also* marginal volunteering; mandatory community service

community social work. *See* community work

community work: practice of professional social work or *volunteer service, which consists of helping people in a *community with *community organizing or, less frequently, with *social services. Taylor and Roberts (1985, passim) have written a textbook on this subject.

company-sponsored foundation: corporate *nonprofit organization established to grant money to *nonprofit groups whose interests harmonize with those of the *foundation and its parent company (O'Neill 1989: 140–143). Obtains its *funds from the parent company. *See also* foundation

compassion: sympathy originating in feeling another person's suffering and resulting in an inclination to show mercy for or give aid to that person. Wuthnow (1991a, passim) examines the role of compassion in *caring and a *caring society.

compensation: anything of monetary value that a *nonprofit group provides its paid staff, including in the main, wages, benefits, and incentives (*incentive in nonprofits). Day (1994:557–590) discusses the design and management of compensation and benefit programs in the nonprofit sphere.

compensatory theory of volunteering: perspective arguing that people choose an activity such as *volunteering because it compensates for something missing in their other activities. Thus, if a volunteer assignment involves physical activity or social activity missing from other parts of a person's life, compensatory theory may help explain choice of volunteer activity. One of three theories Henderson (1984) cited as helping to explain choices of forms of recreation and to explain volunteering. One is the compensatory theory, its opposite is *familiarity theory, and the third theory is social community theory.

complexity: character of a complex *nonprofit group that has a comparatively large number of internal organizational divisions and substantial *bureaucracy. Nonprofit groups vary according to their complexity, running from those that are most informal (see *informal groups) and simple in structure to those that are highly formal (see *formal groups) and complex in structure (Smith 2000:20). *See also* bureaucratization; formalization

compliance structure: the set of reasons why *analytic members of a *nonprofit group stay involved in it and adhere to its rules for activity (Etzioni 1975:8–14). Compliance structures are also found in business, government, and household/family groups. Etzioni (ibid.:14) identifies three main types of compliance structures—normative (most frequent in *nonprofit groups, especially in *volunteer nonprofit groups), utilitarian (most frequent in businesses and government agencies), and coercive (most frequent in prisons, jails, concentration camps).

compromise. *See* accommodation

concurrent reciprocity: A form of *reciprocity in which a person who engages in *giving or *volunteering in interest of an *organization or *cause does so in part because that person is currently receiving some direct or indirect *benefit from the existence of that organization or cause. Concurrent reciprocity is evident in one of Stebbins's (2001:4–5) six types of marginal volunteering: volunteering rewarded by temporal-monetary credits to be used to "purchase" the volunteer services of someone else. No money changes hands in these "time-money schemes." *Also see* reciprocity; anticipatory reciprocity; lateral reciprocity; retrospective reciprocity; altruism, self-serving; altruism, relative

confederation. *See* federation

conference: large meeting, often occurring annually or biennially, of *nonprofit group affiliates of a particular kind (Union of International Associations 1994a, passim).

conflict: in the *nonprofit sector a fight between two or more opposing individuals, groups, or parties over *goals, principles, *strategies, *resources, and the like. Charles Cooley (1965, passim) wrote one of the classic statements about social conflict.

conflict induction: introduction at a meeting of a contentious issue or value intended to stimulate active debate, confrontation, and coalition building. Used when, to the detriment of its *goals, a *nonprofit group is avoiding conflict and the discomfort this can bring (Barker 2003:90).

confraternity: usually refers to an official (church-recognized), lay, male, Roman Catholic *association with *philanthropic purposes. The Knights of Columbus is a well-known current example, but confraternities reach back historically to medieval times (Barnes 1991, passim; Henderson 1997, passim).

congregation. *See* church congregation

congress: major *conference of a *transnational association (Union of International Associations 1994a, passim).

consensus: agreement or unity in a collectivity or *nonprofit group or among parties concerning a particular opinion, testimony, point of view, and the like (adapted from the *Shorter Oxford English Dictionary,* 5th ed. 2002:491).

consensus organizing: an approach to *community organizing used in recent decades that has emphasized building *coalitions and *collaboration among *groups, rather than confrontation and *protest activity. Gittell and Vidal (1998:2) describe a national demonstration *program in three urban areas that used this approach to community organizing. Can be contrasted to the traditional *Alinsky-style nonprofit group participation, which was confrontational (Lancourt 1979), although the Industrial Areas Foundation founded by Alinsky has been changing in recent years toward more consensus-based organizing.

conspiracy: a usually informal *group, sometimes a *nonprofit, that conspires secretly to reach an illegal *goal. A conspiracy may exist within any kind of larger *organization or may exist independently of any such organization. One kind of *deviant group. Pipes (1999, passim) explores the nature and origins of the paranoid style of conspiracy.

constitution. *See* articles of organization

constitutional monarchy. *See* monarchy

consultant use by nonprofits: process in a *nonprofit group of seeking and using outside consultants or consulting firms when there is a special internal *problem or *issue requiring expertise not presently or otherwise available to the group (Wilbur 2000, chap. 15). Practice limited to larger, *paid-staff nonprofit organizations who can afford a consultant; virtually never seen in *grassroots associations, where there tends to be low leader *professionalism (Smith 2000:153–154) and indeed "proud amateurism" among many leaders, in addition to scarce financial *resources (Smith 2000:119–122).

consumer cooperative: a *cooperative whose *members have as their main *goal consumption of certain kinds of goods (e.g., fresh produce, fresh meat, groceries in general) or services (e.g., child care, babysitting). Cooperatives, compared with regular enterprises, tend to have lower prices and higher quality goods or services. Often function in many ways as ordinary *associations, though ones with a consumptive purpose. Sommer, Hess, and Nelson (1985, passim) found in a study of members of a funeral cooperative that they joined it, among other reasons, to have an inexpensive ceremony and reduce responsibilities for survivors. Neptune (1977, passim) reviews the history of consumer cooperatives in California since 1935.

consumer group: a *nonprofit group of people concerned with consumer rights, treatment, and services, and/or with prices or quality of consumer goods in a specific territory. Anderson and Engledow (1977, passim) conducted a comparative study of members of two consumer groups— Consumers Union (United States) and Stiftung Warentest (Germany)— who had purchased a durable product. The authors, who wanted to learn about the information they used in making their purchase, found that the two samples, for the most part, sought much the same information.

contingency approach to leadership. *See* leadership, contingency approach to

continuous-service volunteer: a *volunteer committed to working a long time in a volunteer role, usually six months to a year or more (Macduff 1995:188). Contrasts with *episodic volunteer, who is only committed to more short-term work. *See also* regular volunteer; volunteer, habitual

contract: formal agreement for allocation of money, *goods, or other property, usually flowing from a governmental *agency or business firm (more rarely a nonprofit) to a *nonprofit group in return for *services to be performed by the latter and its affiliates (*nonprofit group affiliates). Contracts, as Kramer and colleagues (1993, passim) observe, play a crucial role in privatization and the "purchase of services."

contracted service in nonprofits: *service provided by a *nonprofit group under *contract to some other organization, usually a governmental *agency but sometimes a *foundation, other nonprofit, or business firm (Bernstein 1991). Such contracted services by a nonprofit require special management (Smith 2005) and usually are seen as resulting from *privatization of government services (Smith and Lipsky 1993).

contract failure theory: a set of propositions centering on the observation that *nonprofit groups emerge to correct information gaps between consumers and providers of particular services (e.g., the Consumers Union) (cf. Hansmann 1980). *See also* public goods theory; voluntary failure theory

contradictory formal position of volunteers: the feeling of uncertainty among *volunteers about their relationship with the *organization, a sentiment rooted in a multiplicity of implicit and explicit roles (Pearce 1993). If volunteers are also *members, they have a sense of ownership in the organization, but as direct service volunteers they are also workers within that same organization and are subject to supervision in that role. Volunteers may also be clients or former clients of the same organization as well. Finally, volunteers can be indirect clients, in the sense that they are not formal clients, but their participation serves intrinsic or intangible needs. These organizational roles have unique behavioral expectations, according to Pearce. Volunteers often combine them in idiosyncratic ways or deemphasize one or the other. Such contradictions can be lessened by explicit discussion, heightened sensitivity to those who have such contradictory roles, and active management of conflict among roles. Just as unionization can institutionalize conflict between paid staff and management, it has been suggested that volunteers need their own version of a union within an organization (Dover 1997).

contribution. *See* gift; giving

convent: 1. a building or buildings for the residence, religious activity, and work of a female *religious order. 2. a female religious *commune inhabiting such a building(s). Eckenstein (1963, passim), Monson (1995), and N. Warren (2001, passim) study early convents. O'Brien (2003, passim) studied the emotional experience of attending a convent (sense 2) secondary school in Ireland, as this varied by social class and gendered identity of the female students.

convention: synonymous with *conference, with, however, special emphasis on its infrequency and general nature. *National and *transnational associations often hold annual conventions or *congresses (Union of International Associations 1994b, passim).

conventional nonprofit group: group whose *leaders and *members respect the norms of the society of which the group is a part (Smith 2000:86–87). Examples include a local Elks Club, a local Episcopal church, and a neighborhood association. A conventional nonprofit group is not fundamentally deviant (*deviant nonprofit group).

conventional political voluntary action. *See* political voluntary action

conversion from a nonprofit to for-profit entity: nonprofits (usually financially successful ones like some hospitals, health maintenance organizations, Blue Cross/Blue Shield organizations, etc.) can legally reincorporate as for-profits, dropping the *nondistribution constraint (Fishman and Schwarz 2000:134–141). There are various ways to structure the conversion transaction (ibid.).

fort, giving up family and other activities, and financial sacrifices), solidary (cost through interpersonal conflict, negative social support, and concern about lack of participation by others, such as *free riders), and purposive, such as dissatisfaction with evolving activities and *goals of *organizations associated with participation and with scheduling and communication failure (Prestby et al. 1990, passim). Stebbins (1996c: 217–218) argues that committed *serious leisure participants, including certain kinds of *volunteers, find that the rewards of their leisure activity substantially outweigh such costs.

counterculture: either a *social movement or a set of *deviant nonprofit groups that has developed a subculture that is contrary to the mainstream culture of the larger society (Zellner 1995:vii). Roughly equivalent to the concept of deviant nonprofit, but with emphasis on the cultural side and its opposition to aspects of the mainstream culture. The counterculture of the 1960s and 1970s is discussed in Braunstein and Doyle (2002, passim), Hamilton (1997, passim), and in the classic statement of the concept by Roszak (1969, passim).

counter-terrorism: activities, usually by governmental authorities at a territorial level, aimed at stopping *terrorism and apprehending or killing the *terrorists involved. Holms and Burke (1994:212–246) discuss counter-terrorism in terms of discovery and detection, prevention technology, and engaging the enemy. Netanyahu (1995, passim) discusses recent terrorist history and how to defeat terrorists.

coup (coup d'état): violent or illegal change in a government organized by a substantial number of people engaged chiefly as *volunteers in *political voluntary action. They use force or threat of it against people or property or both to replace top *leadership of an existing government. Coups are not always successful. Moreover, they are usually short-lived, lasting only a few days or weeks. Farcau (1994, passim) has written a lengthy analysis of the coup. Malaparte (1932) wrote an early classic treatment of the coup as a revolutionary technique.

court-appointed special advocate (CASA): program found in many state courts, which uses qualified *volunteers to advocate on behalf of individuals, often young people. These volunteers advocate strictly for their clients, providing thus a degree of continuity not possible from others involved in the case. A study conducted by Leung (1996, passim) revealed that, in five-stage child protection court proceedings, CASA involvement was most effective in shortening the third and fourth placement periods.

craft union. *See* union

craze: a form of unusual willful behavior that, for a relatively short time, becomes frequent in a society or smaller territory. Lofland (1990: 441–442) classifies the craze (along with fad and fashion) as a type of mass joy, giving further weight to the observation that *collective behavior is neither always frightful nor destructive. Smelser (1962, passim) gave an early analytic treatment of the craze.

cross-national volunteering: a type of *volunteering that involves *volunteers traveling from one country to another to perform *volunteer work in the latter (Smith, Ellis, and Brewis 2005:64). *See also* volunteer tourism

crowding-out hypotheses: a series of important hypotheses stating, in general, that growth of one *sector of society or form of social *participation crowds out another sector or form. Drawing on Charles Henderson's theory that there may be cycles of public sector and voluntary sector predominance (Henderson 1895), Angell observed that new forms of *service clubs crowd out earlier *fraternal orders (Angell 1941). Lynd and Lynd, who found a shift in dominance from mutual aid groups (*see* mutual benefit group) to secular, nonmembership social *agencies, argued that these agencies also crowd out *volunteering (Lynd and Lynd 1929). More recently it was hypothesized that growth in government funding of social welfare and education sectors may reduce opportunities for volunteer participation (Menchik and Weisbrod 1987). David Horton Smith (1997a) expressed concern that growth of formal *program volunteering may occur at the expense of *grassroots voluntary association activity.

crusade: 1. an intensive campaign of *collective activity, often focused on eliminating something, accomplishing socio-legal change, or spreading religious evangelism. Wilson (2002, passim) examines the eugenics crusade to control the "socially inadequate" in the Progressive Era in the United States, with an eye to the lessons it holds for application of research from the modern Human Genome Project. 2. any of the military expeditions undertaken by European Christians from 1096–1271 to recover control of the Holy Land from the Muslims (cf. Oldenbourg 1966, passim; Riley-Smith 1995, passim).

cult. *See* new religion

cultural pluralism. *See* pluralism, ethnic

cutback: a reduction in *funding, *services, or *resources caused by such conditions as a decline in demand, funding, or availability of qualified personnel. Sink (1992, passim) provides a summary of research on how American *nonprofit agencies have dealt with cutbacks in federal funding during the 1980s and early 1990s. *See also* retrenchment in nonprofit groups

***cy pres* doctrine:** legal doctrine that when a charitable trust cannot fulfill its charitable purpose, the court can substitute another charitable purpose for the trust funds as close as possible (*si près possible* in French) to the original purpose (Fishman and Schwarz 2000:116–117).

D

damned nonprofit groups flat-earth paradigm: nonprofit sector model that the *nonprofit sector is composed primarily of deviant, corrupt, selfish, or worthless *nonprofit groups. Smith (2000:230–231) argues that this type of "muckraking" perspective tends to overemphasize, and even sensationalize, the negative sides of some groups while ignoring the positive sides of many others.

dark matter astrophysical metaphor. *See* metaphor, astrophysical dark matter

dark matter of the nonprofit sector: the various *nonprofit groups (especially *grassroots associations) not commonly counted or observed in research and official statistics as compared with those, usually *paid-staff nonprofits, that are routinely counted and observed (Smith 1997c, passim). Smith (2000:34–35) estimates that, in the United States, dark-matter groups may outnumber paid-staff groups by as much as ten to one.

dark side of the nonprofit sector: sum total across the *nonprofit sector (in some countries) of societal *deviance by *nonprofit groups, their *formal leaders, or other *analytic members acting in and for a particular *nonprofit group. Smith (2000:229–230) discusses the dark side of voluntarism in the context of the *angelic nonprofit groups flat-earth paradigm, which ignores deviance in and by nonprofits, especially the activities of *fundamentally *deviant nonprofit groups such as political radical groups, outlaw motorcycle gangs, the Ku Klux Klan, extremist cults, and the like. Smith (1995b:100) was one of the first to draw attention to the dark side of voluntarism as a general phenomenon. *See also* deviant nonprofit groups

dark side of voluntarism. *See* dark side of the nonprofit sector

dark territories of the nonprofit sector: metaphoric reference to that which is missing in the usual flat-earth conceptual and empirical maps of the *nonprofit sector (*map of nonprofit sector). What is missing is a focus on and analysis of *grassroots associations, *associational volunteers, and their place in the *nonprofit sector (Smith 2000:14).

decentralization: a collective effort or process of creating "operational units close to the grass roots that are capable of decision making concerning policy and/or administrative actions and that provide opportunities for broadening the base of citizen participation" (Spiegel 1974:4). There are two main types of decentralization—administrative and political. "Administrative decentralization usually refers to the delegation of some managerial functions from a central authority to its lower echelons, its field offices or to a wider circle of functionaries within its institutional framework" (ibid.:5). "Political decentralization . . . usually refers to sharing, granting, surrendering, or otherwise establishing power to actors (individual or institution) outside its usual institutional framework or jurisdiction" (ibid.:5). A multitude of *nonprofit groups have recently benefited from this second type. Decentralization is part of a continuum whose other pole is centralization, and it may vary from informal to formal in participatory style (ibid.:9). *Citizen participation is greater when political decentralization is greater in a territory. Spiegel (1974, passim) has edited a volume with many chapters on different aspects of decentralization, such as in the Model Cities Program, in schools, on the job, and in the neighborhood. Oxhorn et al. (2004, passim) present chapters by various authors on decentralization in *Third World nations. Meyer (1998, passim) offers a recent overview and critique of decentralization. *See also* privatization

decision making: the process in a *nonprofit group of setting priorities and deciding on which to pursue. Zander (1993:38–43) discusses effective decision making in nonprofit *boards of directors. *See also* leader; leadership

deconversion, religious: sudden or gradual rejection of the belief system of a religion and its social life (cf. Jacobs 1987, passim; Richardson 1978, passim; Johnstone 1992:78–82). Neutral term for apostasy, which connotes that deconversion is the act of a religious turncoat or infidel (cf. Bromley 1988).

deferred giving. *See* planned giving

delinquent gang: *grassroots *group of youth (usually teenagers) formed for the pursuit of *leisure, *sociability, and mutual protection. The juvenile *gang is discussed at length by Covey, Menard, and Franzese (1992, passim). Asbury (1927, passim) wrote an early book on New York gangs, including delinquent gangs in the 1800s. Bellamy (1973, passim) discusses delinquent gangs in England in the Middle Ages, though these were mainly aimed at material gain.

demagogue: *leader, often also an orator, who, to further personal interests, appeals to popular fears, desires, or prejudices. Darsey (1995, passim), in using the literary genre of fantasy, attempts to explain the demagoguery of Joe McCarthy. *See also* charismatic leader

democracy: a form of *government of a society or other territory or group in which the citizens/members have, by law and practice, a significant influence on important decision making and enjoy *civil rights and *civil liberties, including equal treatment under the law. Major decisions are made by simple majority rule or sometimes a larger majority (e.g., two-thirds of all voters). A wide variety of issues and aspects of democracy, including its history, are discussed in Lipset (1995)—*The Encyclopedia of Democracy.* In *direct democracy,* major decisions are made directly by those governed, as in a New England town meeting. In *representative democracy,* major decisions are made by representatives elected by those governed. *Nonprofits, and especially *associations, flourish in democracies. Barber (1984:148, 150–155) examines different types of democracy and advocates "strong democracy," which is participative, populist in institutional bias, values activity, and has an active centralizing citizen posture and an active decentralizing governmental posture. Lipset et al. (1956, passim) provide an early study of the factors promoting democracy in a nonprofit, in this case a craft union.

democracy in nonprofit groups: government of the group by *members, who exercise power either directly or through their elected representatives. Smith (2000:112–113) notes that democracy in *nonprofit groups, especially *grassroots associations, involves participative decision making, high turnover in *leadership (and hence less *oligarchy), and low hierarchy.

democratic personality: a set of personality traits that tends to promote *volunteering, *associational activity, *political participation, and other forms of *individual voluntary action in democratic societies. It is also, in part, a result of such *nonprofit sector activities. The most central traits of this personality type are self-confidence (ego strength) and sense of competence (felt efficacy or internal locus of control). Other important traits include sociability (extraversion), flexibility (low authoritarianism), optimism (low cynicism/alienation), assertiveness, and emotional stability (cf. Lasswell 1951, passim; Smith 1995a, passim). *See also* psychological factors in volunteering

demonstration: either a *symbolic or a *direct action form of *social protest that involves massing people, usually in the street, but sometimes in buildings, to express collective opposition to a particular person, group, action, situation, *policy, or *issue (Carter 1973, passim; Sharp 1973, passim). Missingham (2002, passim) describes the strategic use of space and the construction of place by the Assembly of the Poor for their demonstration in Thailand in 1997. Etzioni's (1970) book is a classic discussion and empirical study of demonstrations.

demonstration grant: a *grant made to a *nonprofit group to test a new *project, *program, or approach, which, if successful, is likely to be copied by other nonprofits. An example can be found online at the website of the Illinois Environmental Protection Agency (http://www.epa.state.il.us/green-illinois/green-communities).

denomination: 1. a *religion. 2. a firmly established nonprofit religious organization (*nonprofit organization) with an identifiable *membership operating in a multireligious society (cf. Mead and Hill 1995, passim). Denominations lie in an intermediate position conceptually between a state *church (sense 3) and a *sect. Prelinger (1992, passim) explored the situation of Episcopal women in one of the mainline denominations in the United States. Niebuhr (1929/1957, passim) gives a classic statement on the social sources of *denominationalism in America (cf. Richey 1977, passim). Johnstone (1992, chap. 13) discusses the American denominational society and Finke and Stark (2005, passim) wrote a history of it (see also Littell 1962, passim; Williams 2002, passim), but Greeley (1972, passim) wrote the first book entitled *The Denominational Society*. Lincoln and Mamiya (1990, passim) examine African-American denominations and the black church in America. Goldstein (2002, passim) describes an emerging Buddhist denomination for America. Morris (1997, passim) gives the history of the Catholics in America as a denomination. Stark and Bainbridge (1985, chap. 4) map major American denominations, as does Marty (1980, passim). *See also* pluralism, religious

denominationalism: societal structure, as in America, in which there is a diverse multiplicity of *denominations, all of which have more or less equal standing and no state church (*church, sense 3) (Greeley 1972, passim; Johnstone 1992, chap. 13; Richey 1977).

designated fund: type of *restricted fund, in which the fund *beneficiaries are specified by the *grantors (the Cleveland Foundation Glossary of Terms: http://www.clevelandfoundation.org/page1691.cfm).

developed world flat-earth paradigm: the model that *nonprofit groups are roughly the same the world over—like those of the industrialized world—no matter what their level of socioeconomic development (Smith 2000:162–163). This paradigm is, for the most part, invalid.

developmental incentive: a type of *incentive rooted in an interest in personal growth made possible by *membership in a *nonprofit group. Wuthnow (1994:84) observed that this incentive was the most common reason for joining the small social support groups he studied. *See also* incentive type

development of volunteers/members: 1. major administrative function in *nonprofit groups and *volunteer programs that involves providing volunteers with opportunities for personal growth as part of their *volunteer work and experiences. 2. process of developing oneself. 3. fact of having developed oneself. Both 2 and 3 are commonly rewarding in themselves, leading, at times, to the further reward (*extrinsic satisfaction) of preparing *volunteers for other paid work, thereby increasing their *human capital. Connors (1995:99–100), Fisher and Cole (1993, chap. 6), and Ilsley (1990, passim) discuss development of volunteers. Battle (1988:64–66) discusses personal improvement of *members in *associations, a form of development. *See also* self-fulfillment; satisfaction

deviance in nonprofit groups: behavior enacted in the name of a *nonprofit group that violates one or more of the moral norms (Stebbins 1996b:3) of the society in which the group is embedded. Smith (2000:87) notes that nonprofits may be "partly deviant," as when a leader temporarily rejects a moral norm regarding group goals or means, or "fundamentally deviant," as when a nonprofit group is formed to pursue deviant goals or use deviant means to pursue conventional goals. *See also* deviant group; deviant nonprofit group; moral standard

deviant association. *See* deviant group

deviant collective action: action by a *collectivity that has a socially deviant *goal or means. According to Hartnagel (2004:127) vandalism, a form of nonutilitarian crime, is perpetrated by deviant *collectivities in an effort by individual *members to assert independence and enhance self-esteem in each other's eyes.

deviant group: *group in any sector (business, government, household/family, nonprofit) that has at least one internal norm, accepted by at least half the group's *analytic members, specifying that members should deviate from one or more of the society's moral norms. Best and Luckenbill (1982, passim) provide one of the first extensive treatments of deviant groups generally. Stewart and Spille (1988, passim) examine "diploma mills," so-called higher educational institutions that sell worthless degrees that involve no classes or learning. Balsamo and Carpozi (1999, passim) describe the first hundred years of the American Mafia: "Crime Incorporated" (see also Davis 1993). Ermann and Lundman (2002, passim) present chapters by various authors on corporate and governmental deviance (see also Simon 2002; Tonry and Reiss 1997). Rummel (1994, passim) reviews evidence on death by government—megamurders under Stalin, Mao Tse-tung, Hitler, and other dictators. Daniels (1993, passim) writes of American and Canadian concentration camps during World War II for people of Japanese ancestry in America, most of them American citizens who had committed no crime. Constantine and Constantine report on the deviant household phenomenon of contemporary group marriage (1973, passim), and Hollenbach (2004, passim) gives a personal account of life in a group marriage commune. *Deviant nonprofit groups also abound. *See also* deviant nonprofit group; fundamentally deviant group

deviant nonprofit group: a *nonprofit group that deviates significantly from certain moral norms of the society. In an early classic, Sagarin (1969, passim) explored *associations of deviants in America, including various *twelve-step groups, homosexual groups, and little-people groups. Bennett and DiLorenzo (1994, passim) examine fraudulent *charities in the United States. Anthropologist Daniel Wolf (1991, passim) studied the Rebels, an Edmonton, Canada, motorcycle gang and deviant nonprofit group. Zack (2003, passim) examined financial fraud and abuse in *paid-staff nonprofits. Many other books describe various deviant nonprofits, such as Adam (1995), Adler (1986), Alexander et al. (2001), Appel (1983), Breault and King (1993), Dawley (1982), George and Wilcox (1996), Golden and McConnell (1986), Holmes and Burke (1994), Kamen (1998), Kaplan and Marshall (1996), Karl (1995), Lambert (1992), Lavigne (1993), McAdam (1982), McCaghy et al. (2002), Moore (1977/1994), Partridge (2004), Reavis (1995), Robbins (2004), Scarboro et al. (1994), Sims (1997), Singer (1995), Spergel (1995), Tucker (1991), Wolf (1991), and Zakin (1995).

deviant voluntary group. *See* deviant nonprofit group

devolution: opposite of evolution; the passing on or delegating of *authority to another person or group, especially one with initially less authority. Slyke and Roch (2004, passim) note that governmental devolution of the provision of *services to contracted *nonprofit groups has left many citizens wondering about the *accountability of the latter. The authors' study suggests that citizens are more likely to misidentify nonprofit service providers (see *service) as *governmental agencies when they are less satisfied with the services they have received. *See also* privatization; decentralization

devotional activity: a type of *religious practice that is typically informal and private, such as private prayer, religious reading (e.g., of the Bible), informal hymn singing, religious meditation, and so forth (cf. Johnstone 1992:67; Stark and Glock 1968:15 and chap. 5).

dictatorship: a form of *government of a society or other territory in which one person (or family) holds essentially absolute power and unlimited authority over all people in the society or territory; autocracy. Absolute *monarchy or divine right monarchy is a traditional form of dictatorship. In a dictatorship, *nonprofits are usually either prevented, eliminated, or controlled by the dictator and his or her allies in *government. For an overview of the history and theory of dictatorship, see Cobban (1971, passim). Lipset (1995) contains useful entries on dictatorship, monarchy, and related topics. *See also* monarchy

diffuseness vs. specificity of goals: dimension expressing the number and breadth of goals animating a *nonprofit group. Smith (2000:85) observes that, earlier in history, such groups typically had several broad goals (high diffuseness), whereas more recently they have tended to develop specialized missions (high specificity). Simpson and Gulley (1962, passim) made an early study of goal diffuseness vs. specificity in associations.

dimensions of grassroots associations, basic/analytic: criteria for defining *grassroots associations. Smith (2000:107–108) listed three: they have a small locality base (e.g., metropolitan area or smaller), conduct mainly *volunteer work, and are, in effect, autonomous.

direct action protest: *social protest that takes irritating, unconventional *political voluntary action to where the holders of power are located (Carter 1974, passim). This is usually a factory or an office building but may be found elsewhere, such as a *church (pray-in), eating establishment (*sit-in), or school or university (teach-in). Direct action protest is nonviolent in intent, although it can escalate into violence, especially when met with violence at the hands of the police of other authority. Heunks (1991, passim) explored in three countries direct action protest, among other kinds of social protest, to determine the characteristics of its *activists and initiators.

direct giving: providing, without organizational mediation, financial or other assistance to needy people living outside the household of the *donor. In 1995 in the United States, 53.8 percent of the national adult sample surveyed directly gave such assistance to needy relatives or friends living outside the donor's household (INDEPENDENT SECTOR 1996:4–102).

direct mail fund-raising: raising funds for a *nonprofit through mailed letters of appeal (often with brochures and usually with a return envelope). This effective fund-raising strategy, which has a long history (cf. Cutlip 1965:4), has been perfected in recent decades (cf. Lister 2001).

director. *See* board member

direct/primary satisfaction: *satisfaction (senses 1 and 2) that comes directly from a particular experience that does not, however, necessarily increase someone else's satisfaction (Smith 2000:20). *See also* indirect satisfaction; psychic benefit

disaster volunteer: a *volunteer affiliated with a disaster relief *nonprofit group (e.g., the Red Cross), who is trained in this specialty and who, on a moment's notice, is ready to go to disaster sites. Britton (1991, passim) has written on the role of the permanent disaster volunteer.

discretionary activity. *See* leisure activity

discretionary time. *See* leisure/leisure time

discretionary time activity. *See* leisure activity

dissent: disagreement that may remain unexpressed, be expressed individually, or take the form of public opinion. Dissent sometimes occurs in *nonprofit groups but is at least as likely to be observed at the governmental level vis-à-vis a particular *policy *issue. The latter is a form of *political voluntary action. Historically, an important form of dissent has been religious dissent, often called "heresy" by the dominant church (Moore 1977/1994, passim). The alternative view of religious dissent is that it is the source of all *new religions and *sects, and if one goes back in time far enough, of all *denominations and even state *churches (sense 3). Moser (2003, passim) considers theater as a creative, "positive" vehicle for grassroots dissent. Woliver (1993, passim) considers several instances of dissent by *grassroots associations. Commager (1959, passim) wrote on dissent generally, while Keniston (1971, passim) wrote on dissent and youth in the 1960s and 1970s. Streitmatter (2001, passim) discusses the dissident press in America. *See also* protest activity; social movement

dissolution and distribution of assets of a nonprofit organization: upon dissolution forced by insolvency or voluntarily by board decision, a *mutual benefit organization may distribute assets to its members, but a *public charity must direct those assets to charitable uses (Fishman and Schwarz 2000:113). To qualify for Internal Revenue Service category 501(c)(3), a *nonprofit organization must provide for the *public interest/benefit type of distribution of assets upon dissolution (ibid.). *See also* involuntary dissolution of a nonprofit organization

distinctive action norms. *See* action norms

distinctive nationalist focus flat-earth paradigm: nonprofit sector model stating that *nonprofit group activity in a particular nation is essentially unique, markedly unlike such activity in other countries (Smith 2000: 163). This paradigm is generally invalid.

divine right monarchy. *See* monarchy

do-gooder: colloquial term for someone (e.g., a *volunteer, a social worker) who tries to help other people, which turns derisive when such action is seen by others as unrealistic or officious. The derisiveness of the term is evident in Schevitz's (1967, passim) examination of the do-gooder as status striver.

dominant status model: model for predicting *associational or *program volunteering (*see also* participation), initially suggested by Lemon et al. (1972, passim). It explains the direction of relationships of many sociodemographic predictor variables leading to higher participation. In expanded form by Smith (1983:86) the model states that "participation is generally greater for individuals who are characterized by a more dominant [sociocultural system-valued/preferred] set of social positions and roles, both ascribed and achieved." Examples of dominant statuses include "male gender, middle age, . . . married, parent of [a few] legitimate children, parents of children who are mainly in the age range of about five to fifteen years, friend of several persons of both sexes, . . . member of several *formal voluntary groups, nonsick, nonimpaired, . . . long-term residents, . . . high in income and wealth, . . . employed in paid work, . . . high in occupational prestige, [and] high in formal educational level" (Smith 1983:86–87). Many of these suggested relationships have been confirmed in research (e.g., Smith 1975:254, 1994a:246–250, 254, 256; Kirsch et al. 1999:106, 121, and passim). Nonprofit researchers who study only sociodemographic predictors of volunteering are reflecting the *sociodemographic participation predictors flat-earth paradigm, ignoring such dynamic variables as those in the *active-effective character pattern.

donated goods: objects or goods defined as a *gift or *donation, often to a *nonprofit group.

donation: *gift of money, *goods, or other property (e.g., land, a painting, a bodily organ) from an individual or a group to a *nonprofit group without expectation of direct, immediate economic benefit. Donations—*philanthropy applied to nonprofits as *target of benefits—are a central source of *revenue for *charities. Strictly speaking a donation is a non-labor contribution, implying that *volunteer time cannot be labeled such. Many donations qualify for *charitable contribution tax deduction. Caille (2001) explores the philosophical differences and similarities between gift and donation.

donative intent: motivation to give a *donation without adequate consideration, meaning return benefit expected from or given by the *donee. The donation must exceed the fair market value of any goods or services received in return (Fishman and Schwarz 2000:881). Charities are now expected to inform *donors of the tax-deductible portion of donations (Fishman and Schwarz 2000:900).

donee: recipient of a *donation. Kutner (1970, passim) proposed a due process of human transplants for donees, involving their informed consent and knowledge of the risks proportionate to the potential medical *benefits. *See also* target of benefits

donor: person or group making a *donation. In the eyes of the person or group receiving the donor's donation, the latter is a benefactor. Howell (2002, passim) describes how donor *agencies have begun to harness the concept of *civil society to promote a model of economic development, an idea once linked only to democratization. Dowie (1988, passim) wrote about organ donors, while Magat (1989b, passim) wrote about philanthropic donors more generally.

donor constituency: The ensemble of contributors of funds and other resources to a *nonprofit group. Individual and collective contributors may try to exert direct or indirect influence on the *goals, *values, and *programs of the group (Barker 2003:128).

donor fatigue: reluctance of a *donor to give money to a *charity, because excessive financial demands on the donor by that cause, and possibly others, have generated a loss of interest in making donations. Donors suffering from such fatigue have made one or more previous donations, but in this regard, have subsequently reached their monetary limit. Eisemon and Davis (1997, passim) found that donor fatigue was one of several factors leading to decreased quality and quantity of postgraduate training and research in Kenya. Donor fatigue differs from *volunteer *burnout.

donor intent: 1. the *donor's personal preferences for how a *nonprofit should use a specific *gift or *donation. 2. legally, the restrictions placed by a donor at the time of giving on how a gift or donation should be used by a nonprofit. Bork and Nielsen (1993, passim) have written a classic book on donor intent.

donor renewal: a practice engaged in by fund-raisers of attracting return donors to a cause. Donor renewal is believed to require significantly less effort than trying to attract new donors (Nichols 2001:345).

doubly dark continent of the nonprofit sector: further metaphoric reference to missing components of the usual flat-earth conceptual and empirical maps of the *nonprofit sector (*map of nonprofit sector). The flat-earth paradigm is not only lacking focus on and analysis of *grassroots associations and their place in the nonprofit sector but is also lacking focus on and analysis of *deviant nonprofit groups (Smith 2000:230).

drop-by/occasional volunteering: volunteer activity done within settings that actively seek *volunteers who are not required to commit themselves to specific amounts, times, or hours of volunteering. Fischer, Mueller, and Cooper (1991) contrasted regular volunteering (involving a time commitment) with occasional volunteering. Recent trends are to promote *volunteerism among young professionals by enabling drop-by volunteerism in groups such as Chicago Cares. *See also* episodic volunteer

dues: usually annual payment to a *nonprofit group, normally an *association, for rights of *membership in the *group. Dues are usually the main source of *revenue for *national associations (Knoke 1990:92), and especially for *grassroots associations (Smith 2000:58).

E

ecology group. *See* environmental group

economic activity, informal: a concept, not often precisely defined, that goes by various names (e.g., grey, *informal, underground, parallel economy) and that was developed in economics to refer to both formal and informal and legal and illegal *volunteering and *exchange. Carson (1984, passim) provides an introduction to the topic of underground economy. Smith (2000:45) observes that informal economic activity may be conducted either in groups or by individuals on their own. *See also* buying pool

economic goal. *See* goal

economic incentive. *See* utilitarian incentive

economic measure of nonprofit groups. *See* measure, economic

economic nonprofit group. *See* economic support system

economic resource: umbrella term used by Smith (2000:119) to subsume financial and personnel resources. Can be seen more broadly as an economic (scarce) *good (cf. Samuelson and Nordhaus 1995:4). *See also* resource

economic scale of nonprofit group: level of monetary outlay needed to run a *nonprofit group. A group's economic scale may be low or high, with the hiring of paid staff pushing the outlay toward the high end of this dimension (Smith 2000:76).

economic support system: a *nonprofit group that provides financial support for a particular constituency or the larger economy. Smith (2000: 100) says such groups include labor unions, professional associations, businesspeople's groups, and the like.

economic support system value. *See* value, humane core

economic transfer: allocation of money, *goods, or other property or *service to another person or group with the direct, high probability of reciprocal (*reciprocity) transfer (*exchange) of money, goods, or other property or service. This exchange results in little or no change in total net worth of the exchanging parties, whether individuals or groups. Examples of economic transfer include renting, investing, lending, buying, selling, and employment (Boulding 1973, passim). *See also* grant transfer; coercive transfer

economic utility model: a method of ascertaining the marginal utility achieved from individual *volunteer activity. Smith (1981:26) cited research using this model, which found that volunteer *satisfaction stems from "intrinsic rewards (some of which may be altruistic) and from extrinsic rewards (none of which are altruistic)." *See* utilitarian incentive

économie sociale. *See* economy, social

economy, coercive: economy based on transfer of goods or services of unequal value, where the transaction is perceived by the disadvantaged party as forced, possibly even threatening (Boulding 1973:107); taxation and theft are examples.

economy, market: economy based on transfer of goods or services of equal value, where the transaction is perceived by both parties as undertaken without coercion (Boulding 1973:107).

economy, philanthropic: economy of "love" based on charitable transfer of *goods or *services of unequal value, where the *donor, or giver, loses material wealth while a recipient or *donee receives material wealth (Boulding 1973:107). Smith (2000:11) expanded the idea of philanthropic economy to include *gifts of volunteer time in the *nonprofit sector.

economy, social: in the United States refers to ways the business sector can be made more conscious of *public service, *philanthropy, and *altruism, including such business activities as workplace *democracy, employee stock ownership, *cooperatives, socially conscious investing, worker *participation, *credit associations/credit unions, and the like. In France, this is *économie sociale.* Bruyn (1977, passim) presented one of the earliest monographic analyses of this concept.

ecumenism: the process and movement in the twentieth century, mainly, toward better cooperation and understanding among different Christian denominations, and more broadly among different world religions, with some hope of mergers and eventual world religious unity or at least Christian unity (Johnstone 1992:212–216). Books abound on ecumenism (e.g., Kung 1969; Lambert 1967; Rusch 1985; Wainwright 1997).

educational incentive. *See* informational incentive

educational program in nonprofits: although some *nonprofit groups have education as a central mission (e.g., nonprofit schools and universities), nearly every nonprofit can have a need at times for an educational *program or *project of some sort (Wilbur 2000, chap. 6). One frequent educational program need is for training new *paid staff. Another frequent need is for public education ("consciousness raising") regarding the *mission and accomplishments of the nonprofit, and the larger *problem or *issue in society addressed by the nonprofit (e.g., global warming; homelessness; child abuse; drug addiction). A third possible educational need is paid-staff training for forthcoming organizational changes. *See also* training of volunteers/members

effectiveness: how well *nonprofit groups accomplish the *impact they want to bring about using their structure and operations (Smith 2000:195). Weiss (1972, passim) wrote an important book on evaluating program effectiveness.

effectiveness evaluation: investigation, by any of a variety of methods, designed to measure the level of *effectiveness of a *nonprofit group. Murray and Tassie (1994:306–309) describe some of the common models of *organizational effectiveness evaluation.

efficiency. *See* effectiveness

elected leadership. *See* leadership

eleemosynary: synonym for the adjective charitable; something relating to or supported by charity. A literature review revealed that the term is now largely outmoded. One must go back to at least the 1970s to find it used in the professional journals (e.g., Herbst 1972, passim).

elite. *See* insider, societal

embeddedness of nonprofit groups in communities: the set of horizontal and vertical relationships with other *groups and *organizations in the *community in which a *nonprofit group is situated (Milofsky and Hunter 1994, passim). *See also* polymorphic vs. monomorphic nonprofit group

employee in nonprofit group: one remunerated for full- or part-time work in a *nonprofit group. In the *nonprofit sector employees are part of *paid staff. Hodgkinson and Weitzman (1996:44) reported that, in 1994 in the United States, the *nonprofit sector employed 10.3 million full- or part-time workers. *See also* full-time equivalent of paid-staff work

employee matching grant: *donation by an employee to a *nonprofit group, where the employer matches the amount of the *donation with a grant of its own to the same nonprofit. For an example, see the IBM Employee Matching Grants website (http://www.ibm.com/ibmgives/grant/giving/match.shtml). *See also* matching grant

employee volunteer program. *See* corporate volunteer program

employment-based volunteering: *volunteering at the request of the *volunteer's employer, which may be an agreeable assignment for the volunteer (experienced as *leisure) or a disagreeable one (experienced as disagreeable *obligation) (Thompson 1997, passim). One of six types of *marginal volunteering. *See also* corporate (employee) volunteer program

empowerment: 1. helping residents or citizens to take control of and responsibility for their own lives, *organizations, or *communities, often with outside help of a *community organizer or governmental program (e.g., Herring et al. 1998, passim). 2. psychic empowerment as a feeling and belief that one can make a difference or have an impact in one's community and the larger society, particularly through exercising *nonprofit group power (Ahlbrandt 1984, passim; Zimmerman 1995, passim). Empowerment is thus a multilevel process (Prestby et al 1990; Checkoway 1995; Minkler 1998): individual as well as organizational and community-based. At the individual level, Kiefer (1984) viewed empowerment as a developmental process, as a transition from an alienated state of perceived powerlessness to a more insightful and politically capable state of *participatory competence,* and Zimmerman (1995) posited a *psychological empowerment impact. At the organizational level, Zimmerman (1995) distinguished between empowering and empowered organizations. The first provides an organizational environment empowering to members; it enables people to gain control over their lives. Empowered organizations are effective at mobilizing resources influencing *social policy or providing *social services. Zimmerman (1995) defined an *empowered community* as one actively working for *community competence and enhanced quality of life as well as providing significant opportunities for *civic engagement. The term became widely used in the early 1970s (Solomon 1976). Smith (2000:201) examines psychological empowerment as one kind of internal *impact of *grassroots associations.

empowerment metaphor: analogy for the *organizational environment of *volunteering (seen as opposite of the *workplace metaphor): managers of volunteers realize they can reach their goals by ceding control to volunteers and permitting them to achieve self-sufficiency in terms of shaping their volunteer environment (Ilsley 190:112).

encounter group: a small *group whose aim is for *members to become more sensitive and emotionally vulnerable to other *members, with the ultimate goal of becoming open and frank about one's feelings and attitudes in relating to others in general. Back (1988, passim) interprets the encounter group, a form much less used today than in the past, as an innovative *social movement with scientific content, which in its day met an emotional need.

endogenous phenomena: 1. something originating within a body (Barker 2003:143). 2. groups, processes, situations, and the like that exist or occur within a *nonprofit group and that have a cause or origin internal to it.

endowment in nonprofits: an endowment consists of monies given to a *nonprofit group by *donors, who typically intend that the fund's principal be held for a long period of time, if not permanently, and that earnings from investments of the principal be used to cover operating expenses (Anthony and Young 1994:408) including grant making, if a foundation. Endowments, whose principals are not to be used, are usually invested in some way, the interest from which helps further the *mission of the *organization, sometimes in restricted ways (Schumacher 2003). Because it is a relatively sure source of funding, an endowment greatly aids financial *planning in nonprofits fortunate enough to have one. Very common in *independent foundations and nonprofit universities, but rarely large in most *paid-staff nonprofit organizations, and nonexistent in nearly all *grassroots associations. The most favored source of nonprofit income. *See also* restricted fund

entitlement: 1. governmental *program providing *benefits to *members of a specified group or category. 2. funds supporting such a program. 3. right to such benefits, especially as specified by law or contract. Salamon (1994:86–87) writes that during periods of retrenchment the U.S. government broadened some of its entitlements for the needy to include significant portions of the middle class.

environment affecting nonprofits: organizational environment (*environment, organizational) of a *nonprofit group. Although a truism that *nonprofit groups, as other *organizations and *groups, are embedded in and affected by their social and physical environments, successful *nonprofit management is careful to pay attention to changes in the group's environment (*see* environment, organizational) that might affect the nonprofit's plans or operations (O'Leary et al. 1999). The environment of *paid-staff nonprofit organizations is usually more important to the group than is the environment of *grassroots associations (GAs) (Smith 2000:163–164), especially because of relationships of the former to businesses, governmental *agencies, and other nonprofits. But even GAs have a variety of environmental dependencies (ibid.).

environment, organizational: set of virtually all influences impinging on a *nonprofit group from outside its boundaries. Every institution in society can potentially affect the functioning of a given organization. The idea of organizational environment was pioneered by Lawrence and Lorsch (1967, passim). *See also* interorganizational field; population ecology of organizations approach

environmental clean-up campaign: a *group effort to clean up a specified territory or portion of the environment, usually sponsored by a *nonprofit or a *governmental agency. Sylves (1998, passim) describes how the Exxon Valdez oil spill off Alaska triggered adoption of a range of industrial and governmental controls, thereby boosting the marine wing of America's environmental clean-up campaign.

environmental group: a *nonprofit group centrally concerned with preserving, protecting, or improving a specified territory or portion of the environment, sometimes with a focus on particular flora or fauna there. Usually seen as part of the larger environmental (*social) movement (cf. Burlingame 2004:132–138). Driedger and Eyles (2001, passim) explore the scientific evidence on the use of chlorine and breast cancer by examining the *goals and claims of the environmental group Greenpeace and its opponents.

e-philanthropy: Internet-facilitated *philanthropy through websites that represent *charities, accept *donations, and provide information on the *nonprofit group or groups falling within their scope (cf. Johnston 1999, passim). Some e-commerce sites give a portion of their profits to *charity. Discussed in greater detail on the website of ePhilanthropy-Foundation.Org: http://www.ephilanthropy.org. This organization is devoted to promoting secure, private, ethical online philanthropy.

episodic volunteer: a *volunteer committed to working only for a short time, usually a number of days or weeks, rather than committed to working for, say, six months to a year or longer (Macduff 1991, 1995: 188). Episodic volunteers may do the same short-term volunteer work on a regular annual basis, or may do it only once. Contrasts with *continuous-service volunteer, who is committed to working for six months to a year or longer. *See also* sporadic volunteer

erosion of social trust: decline in *trust among people. Putnam (1995) argued that, along with the decline in associational and family life and in neighborly interaction, there has been erosion of social trust, which he feared can lead to reduced *participation, *democracy, and *tolerance (cf. also Putnam 2000, chap. 8). Putnam saw social trust as an important component of *social capital. He cited research showing that levels of social trust and *civic engagement in thirty-five countries are highly correlated.

essence of nonprofit sector. *See* voluntary altruism

established federated fund. *See* federated fund, established

established sect. *See* sect, established

ethical investing. *See* socially responsible investing

ethic of care: the proposition that women, because of their broad *commitment to caring activity, are uniquely motivated to volunteer. Such a proposition is plausible given the disproportionate involvement of women in the labor of caring, a function of male power over women's market, domestic, reproductive, and caring labor (Orloff 1993). However, Gallagher (1994) found in his study of older men and women and their caring and volunteer activities that gender played little or no role in shaping the patterns of help older people give through formal volunteerism, not even in formal volunteerism aimed at people in need outside circles of family or friends. He also found no difference in ethic of care between male and female volunteers.

ethics: as relates to the *nonprofit sector, the set of moral principles by which *volunteers and *paid staff are guided and, more specifically, the rules of conduct recognized in a given *nonprofit group (INDEPEN-DENT SECTOR 1991, passim; Jeavons 1994:187). *See also* moral standards

ethics in nonprofit management: set of moral principles (*ethics) guiding *nonprofit management. Ethical behavior, not just ethical rules and rhetoric, is crucial in *nonprofit groups and in *nonprofit management, especially for charitable nonprofits (*charity) that are held to higher standards than, say, *member benefit *grassroots associations. Trust and integrity are called for and can only exist, according to Jeavons (2004: 206–207), where an organizational culture has been created "in which key ethical ideals and expectations are incorporated in the *organization's 'core values' . . . and thus permeate its operations" and in which there is "modeling of the core values in the behavior of key individuals in the organization and reinforcement of those values through the organization's structures and reward systems."

ethnic pluralism. *See* pluralism, ethnic

evaluation of nonprofit associations: the process or outcome of assessing (often regularly) the *effectiveness (efficiency), *impact (outcomes), or activities of a *nonprofit association. *Grassroots associations (GAs) rarely do formal evaluations on themselves, although social science researchers have focused on GAs to study internal impact and external impact (see review of literature by Smith 1997a, 2000, chap. 9). Larger, paid-staff based associations do formal evaluations, similar to those done by other nonprofit organizations. *See also* program evaluation; volunteer evaluation

evaluation of nonprofit groups/volunteer programs: the process or outcome of assessing (often regularly) the *effectiveness (efficiency), *impact (outcomes), or activities of a *nonprofit group or *volunteer program, which may be done informally or more scientifically through some extensive study and research, either (a) by some *analytic members such as the *board of directors, an evaluation *project, or the *executive director, (b) by some outside expert consultant or evaluation research organization (Flynn and Hodgkinson 2002; Murray 2004; Poister 2003; Schmaedick 1993; Thomas 2004; Wolf 1999, chap. 11), or (c) by collaboration of the two approaches. Patton (1986, passim) argues for "utilization-focused evaluation," which puts less emphasis on scientific objectivity and more emphasis on balance of qualitative and quantitative approaches, and also type (c) above. Evaluation may be done in various ways, but includes especially *process evaluation (formative evaluation), and *outcome evaluation (summative evaluation), among other approaches (Thomas 1994:346, 362–364). The larger and wealthier the nonprofit or volunteer program, the more extensive and scientific evaluations tend to be, although most nonprofits and volunteer programs never do a scientific evaluation (among other reasons because of the cost of such evaluations). Connors (1995:81 and passim), Fisher and Cole (1993, chap. 8), Vineyard (1988, passim), and McCurley and Vineyard (1997, passim) discuss volunteer program evaluation. *See also* volunteer evaluation

e-volunteering. *See* virtual volunteering

excess revenue: for *nonprofit groups, this is money that would be called "profit (or loss)" by business firms. It is, roughly, the difference between total gross income from exempt functions (*gifts, *fees, *dues, *grants, investment income, etc.) and total expenditures for such functions for a given period, usually a fiscal year (Connors 1988b:414; Smith 2000: 231). *See also* revenue

exchange: act of reciprocal giving and receiving of a *good or *service. Boulding (1973:107) discusses several types of exchange that take place in the *nonprofit sector.

exchange, charitable. *See* exchange, philanthropic

exchange, coercive: transfer of *goods (including money) or *services of unequal value, where the exchange is perceived by the disadvantaged party as forced, possibly even threatening (Boulding 1973:107). The net worth of the party making the coercive allocation is significantly reduced, while the net worth of the recipient is increased. Robbery and payment of taxes are examples. *See also* economic transfer; grant transfer

exchange, market: transfer of *goods (including money) or *services of equal value, where the exchange is perceived by both parties as undertaken without coercion (Boulding 1973:107).

exchange, philanthropic: charitable transfer of *goods (including money) or *services of unequal value, where the *donor or giver loses material wealth while a recipient or *donee receives material wealth (Boulding 1973:107). The *donor is usually motivated significantly by *voluntary altruism. Smith (2000:11) expanded the idea of philanthropic exchange to include *gifts of volunteer time in the *nonprofit sector.

excise tax: 1. annual 1 or 2 percent tax (depending on technical circumstances; Fishman and Schwarz 2000:627–629, 672–674) on net investment income paid by independent *foundations to the Internal Revenue Service in America (cf. Burlingame 2004:154). 2. internal tax levied on manufacture, consumption, or sale of a commodity. Gould (1996, passim) observed that such tax provoked *resistance leading to the Whiskey Rebellion of 1874 in western Pennsylvania.

exclusion/inclusion. *See* inclusion/exclusion

exclusion of association member. *See* admission/exclusion of association member

executive committee: official subcommittee of the *board of directors of a *nonprofit group, which, between board meetings is charged with making and implementing *policy (cf. Connors 1988:10.2; Wilbur 2000:41–42). Executive *committees are common in large boards of directors (e.g., those with fifteen or more *members). Siciliano (1997, passim) found, nevertheless, that better performing boards assigned responsibility for *planning to a *strategic planning subcommittee rather than to the executive committee or an outside consultant.

executive director in nonprofits: chief managerial *officer in larger *nonprofit groups, especially in *paid-staff nonprofit organizations. This person, who is usually remunerated, is appointed by and responsible to the *board of directors. Executive directors help develop board *policy, carry out board-approved *policy, and manage the daily affairs and activities of the *nonprofit group. This position is rare in *associations, especially *grassroots groups, where it is seen as unnecessary and unaffordable. Herman and Heimovics (1991, passim) examine the role and process of executive *leadership in nonprofit organizations. Carlson (2003) and Herman and Heimovics (2004) have written recently about the role of executive director.

exempt organization: 1. classification of the U.S. Internal Revenue Service (IRS) of qualified *nonprofit groups as immune from taxation on their income, justified in part by the fact that private shareholders or individual members receive no *benefits from the net earnings (*excess revenue) of such groups and that the groups serve the *public interest. Includes IRS categories 501(c)(1)–(21), 501(d)–(f), 501(k), 501(n), 521, 527–529 (O'Neill 2002:4–5). O'Neill (1998:2) observes that exempt status is the most common way of defining *third-sector organizations. Certain nonprofits, particularly those classified as *public charities in IRS category 501(c)(3), are doubly exempt, with donations to them being tax-deductible to donors. 2. more broadly, any *nonprofit, whether registered with the IRS or not, that observes the *nondistribution constraint and serves either the *public interest or *member interests, while operating generally in accord with established public policy and law. *See also* tax-exempt status of nonprofits

ex-officio member: one who is a *member of a *nonprofit group or subgroup by virtue of the office that person holds in the nonprofit group or subgroup (Barker 2003:149). For example, the president of the group might be an ex-officio member of its volunteer recruitment committee.

exogenous phenomena: 1. something that originates outside a body, but that affects a person emotionally or physically (Barker 2003:150). 2. groups, processes, situations, and the like that exist or occur outside a *nonprofit group and that have a cause or origin external to it.

expense reimbursement of volunteers/members: 1. occasional administrative function in *nonprofit groups and *volunteer programs that involves paying certain (e.g., poor) or all *volunteers for their travel expenses to or parking expenses at their *volunteer work site (Connors 1995:66, 78), or paying out-of-town board volunteers for their travel expenses to *board of directors meetings. 2. the money paid as reimbursement.

experiential knowledge. *See* knowledge

experimental community. *See* intentional community

expressive goal/group: the focus of a *goal or *nonprofit group activity that is intrinsically rewarding ("consummatory"), that is not directed toward accomplishing an external goal ("instrumental"). It is an early term, now largely subsumed under the idea of *member-benefit goal/ group (e.g., Smith 1993, passim). *See also* instrumental goal/group

expressive management. *See* management

expressive structure. *See* structural forms of nonprofit groups

expressive vs. instrumental nonprofit group. *See* expressive goal/group; instrumental goal/group

expulsion of association member: *associations of all types generally have the right to expel *members if this is done in a procedurally correct manner, following group *by-laws, *articles of incorporation, and other requirements or rules (Fishman and Schwarz 2000:949–965).

external environment. *See* environment, organizational

external funding. *See* funding

external impact. *See* impact of nonprofit groups

external linkage. *See* linkage of nonprofit groups

external power. *See* power of nonprofit groups

extraordinary group: an unusual or unconventional *group; a *deviant nonprofit group. Kephart and Zellner (1994, passim) consider an array of extraordinary groups in American society. George and Wilcox (1996, passim) describe an even more extreme and deviant set of *nonprofit groups.

extrinsic satisfaction: *satisfaction engendered by something external to an activity itself. Originally a component in measuring job satisfaction, as in pay, working conditions, and quality of supervision, but can also be applied to *volunteer and *quasi-volunteer activity (Lawler 1973, passim). Aryee and Debrah (1997, passim) found in their study of *union participation in Singapore that it was negatively related to level of extrinsic satisfaction. *See also* intrinsic satisfaction; fulfillment; direct satisfaction; indirect satisfaction; psychic benefit

F

---

failure of nonprofits: the demise or cessation of operations of a *nonprofit group (owing to lack of success in reaching its *goals), often a result of inadequate *leadership (Wolf 1999, chap. 10). Block (2004, passim) describes and analyzes a variety of obstacles to nonprofit organization success and sustainability, such as "fundphobia" and "founder's syndrome" (*see* founder choice). There may be failure to successfully lobby government, meet market demand (Smith 2000:72), or recruit enough new *analytic members. Formal *nonprofit organizations tend to have a lower death rate per thousand (Bowen et al. 1994, passim) than do more informal *grassroots associations (Smith 2000, passim).

faith-based organization. *See* religious nonprofit group

faith-based service: service, usually by a *religious nonprofit group (or, alternatively, by an individual religious person acting alone as a *service volunteer), that is directed at meeting human needs and serving the *public interest (cf. Jeavons 1994, passim; Queen 2000, passim; Solomon 2003, passim; Wuthnow 2004, passim).

fallacy of disaggregation: failure by some researchers, analysts, and *community *leaders to see or understand the nature and meaning of *grassroots associations and what they can accomplish collectively and cumulatively, seeing them in isolation as small, poor, and weak (Smith 2000:35).

fallacy of small group size: failure by some researchers, analysts, and *community *leaders to recognize the collective importance of small *grass-roots associations, because of the usual diminutive size of their *membership (Smith 2000:35).

familiarity theory of volunteering: a theory that explains *volunteering by arguing that such activity is consistent with a person's other activities or parallels those other activities (Henderson 1984). Thus, people involved in informal helping might also want to be involved in formal helping, people who do paid work as *quasi-volunteers might also engage in pure *volunteering, and so on. The opposite of the *compensatory theory of volunteering and part of a trio of theories including *social community theory cited by Henderson (1984).

family foundation: *foundation whose *funds come from members of a certain family, typically with at least one family member being on the foundation's *board of directors/trustees and playing a significant role in governing the foundation. Most common kind of foundation in America. Among the many family foundations in the United States are the Henry J. Kaiser Family Foundation (http://www.kff.org) and the Rockefeller Foundation (http://www.rockfound.org).

family sector. *See* sector of society

farm laborers' association: a *member benefit association whose aim is to serve farm laborers. The United Farm Workers operates as both a *farm labor union and a farm laborers' association. In the latter capacity it offers a pension plan, credit union, and health benefit scheme (http://www.ufw.org).

farm labor union: a *union formed to benefit farm laborers (e.g., United Farm Workers in the United States). Majka and Majka (1992, passim) examine the decline during the 1980s of the farm labor movement (*social movement) in California, one of the causes of which was an internal crisis in the United Farm Workers union.

farmers' association: a *member benefit association whose aim is to serve farm owners, especially owners of small farms and family farms. American examples include the Grange and the American Farm Bureau at both local and national levels. Heinze and Voelzkow (1993, passim) studied resistance by the German Farmers Association (DBV) to changing consumer interests and increased demand for environmental protection, a stance that eventually caused economic hardship for the small farmer.

fascist corporatism: economic approach of a corporate state that integrates both managers and workers into the process of government (Heywood 2002:80), as in Fascist Italy in the late 1930s and early 1940s when that nation was a *dictatorship. Fascist corporatism (ibid.:189) "is based on the belief that business and labour are bound together in an organic and spiritually unified whole."

feasibility study of nonprofits: formal, systematic analysis centering on one or more *issues critical to success of a *nonprofit group. Such analysis is conducted to learn whether the group can succeed at the level required by its principals (Massarsky 1994:394).

federated fund. *See* federated fund, alternative; federated fund, established

federated fund, alternative: a *fund-raising intermediary *nonprofit organization that attempts to be a viable alternative (especially in charitable giving through payroll deduction; cf. National Committee for Responsive Philanthropy 1987) to the larger, well-established federated fund-raising intermediaries like the *United Way, Catholic Charities USA, and the Combined Federal Campaign. The alternative federated funds are usually distinctive in focusing on a coherent set or "package" of *charities and *nonprofit groups as the ultimate recipients of the money raised, such as health charities, international aid/development charities, women's nonprofits, Afro-American nonprofits (e.g., *Black United Fund and the nonprofits they support), environmental nonprofits, and the like (Perlmutter 1988a, passim). Many alternative federated funds are social change oriented (cf. Rabinowitz 1990). Brilliant (1990, passim, especially pp. 89–99) discusses the "Alternative fund movement" at some length. The United Way of America strongly resists alternative federated funds competing for charitable giving through corporate and government payroll deductions (Brilliant 1990, passim; Smith 1978, passim).

federated fund, established: a long-existing, mainstream *fund-raising intermediary *nonprofit organization, like the *United Way, the Combined Federal Campaign, or Catholic Charities USA, that provides funding generally to conventional *nonprofit agencies within their usual set of parameters for giving (e.g., religious affiliation parameters in the third example). The United Way (Brilliant 1990, passim) is the most widespread federated fund in America and Canada and raises collectively the most total *funds annually of all federated funds—about eighteen times the amount alternative federated funds raise (Burlingame 2004:152). It has been sharply criticized for some of its *policies and *leadership (Brilliant 1990, passim; Smith 1978, passim).

federated fund-raising: amassing money for *charities and *nonprofit groups using fund-raising organizations linked together regionally or nationally in a *federation of such organizations (e.g., *United Way, *Community Chest, *Black United Fund) (cf. Burlingame 2004:149–153). Smith (2000:131) notes that *grassroots associations are unlikely to receive money from federated sources, which typically support *paid-staff nonprofits.

federation in nonprofit sector: a formal, enduring *coalition of largely independent *nonprofit groups established to realize such advantages as coordination of activities, development of collective strategies, and sharing of facilities or *resources (Smith 2000:143). A federation is itself an *organization, with a clear *membership, *leadership structure, and unique name. To achieve greater collective strength, some federations absorb previously unaffiliated nonprofits, albeit at the price of local non-profit autonomy for the latter. Andrews (1991, passim) and Matson (1990, passim) provide studies of two federations in the United States, namely, the American Federation of Labor and the organized movement (*social movement) for the blind. *See also* collaboration; alliance

fee: payment for *nonprofit group services made by a *target of benefits or that person's or group's agent or representative. Chetkovich and Frumkin (2003, passim) propose a framework for meeting competition in the *nonprofit sector that should help it meet both organizational *needs and demands from the *public there and that involves collecting both fees and *donations.

fellowship: 1. a *group, often but not necessarily having religious *goals (Balmer and Winner 2002, passim; Washington 1986, passim). 2. the positive, informal, interpersonal relations that take place in *groups, especially in *grassroots associations. The term is not gender specific. 3. a monetary grant to an individual for some specific purpose, usually involving study of some kind (cf. Princenthal and Dowley 2001, passim).

feminist-style nonprofit group participation: involvement in usually *autonomous, female-dominated *nonprofit groups, where emphasis is on, among other arrangements, low hierarchy and consensual *decision making (Iannello 1992).

fiduciary obligations of board of directors: a *nonprofit's *board of directors occupy a relationship of trust to the organization, its purposes, and resources, including the duty of care or good faith diligence (Fishman and Schwarz 2000:152–155), the duty of loyalty or not harming the organization (pp. 190–193), the duty of obedience to the articles of incorporation (pp. 230–232), the duty of investment responsibility (pp. 232–233), and the duty of reasonable executive compensation (pp. 246–248). Enforcement is by record keeping and filing reports, by the state attorney general, by the trustees/directors, by donors, by members, and by beneficiaries and special interests (pp. 252–272).

financial management in nonprofits: *management of the income and expenses of a *nonprofit group in such a manner as to attempt to accomplish its *mission with optimal *effectiveness and *impact (Anthony and Young 2004; Bryce 2000; Blazek 1996; Garner 1991; Gronbjerg 1993; Gross et al. 2000; Hankin et al. 1998; Mayers 2004; McKinney 2004; McLaughlin 1985; Dropkin and Hayden 2001; Randall and Palmer 2002; Shim and Siegel 1997; Wilbur 2000, chap. 12). A complex matter in large, *paid-staff nonprofit organizations, financial management is very simple in *grassroots associations because they seldom have much money to manage (Battle 1988, chap. 7; Smith 2000:119–122).

financial resource. *See* resource

firm. *See* for-profit enterprise

501(c)(3): the section of the American federal (Internal Revenue Service) tax code that defines *nonprofit, *charitable, *tax-exempt organizations; 501(c)(3) *organizations are further defined as *public charities, private *operating foundations, and private *independent (nonoperating) foundations (adapted from the Foundation Center Glossary: http://www.fdncenter.org/learn/ufg/glossary.html).

509(a): the section of the American federal (Internal Revenue Service [IRS]) tax code that defines *public charities, which pass the *public support test contained herein, as contrasted with *private foundations, the rest of IRS 501(c)(3) organizations, which fail the public support test (ibid.).

five-sector model of society. *See* model of society

fixed asset. *See* asset

flat-earth map of nonprofit sector. *See* map of nonprofit sector

flat-earth nonprofit sector metaphor. *See* metaphor, flat-earth nonprofit sector

Flat-Earth Research Society International (International Flat-Earth Society): world organization whose mission is "to carefully observe, think freely, rediscover forgotten fact, and oppose theoretical dogmatic assumptions. To help establish the United States . . . of the world on this flat earth. Replace the science religion . . . with SANITY" [ellipses in original] (taken from the society's website: http://www.skepticfiles.org/aj/flaterth.htm).

flow-through funds: *donations to a *foundation (especially a *company-sponsored foundation or a certain *community foundation) used for direct *grants to *nonprofit groups rather than building foundation *endowment. In the Calgary Foundation (http://www.thecalgary foundation.org), such funds are generally distributed to registered *charities in the year received. Such funds appeal to *donors wanting to make an immediate impact.

Form 990/Form 990PF: the Internal Revenue Service (IRS) reporting forms filed annually by *public charities/*private foundations to indicate their assets, revenues, expenses, and so forth. The form for private foundations also lists grants made during the year. The data are used by the IRS to ensure compliance with the law and by researchers to study larger registered nonprofits. Only nonprofits with $25,000 or greater revenues are required to file these forms (Hopkins 1998, passim).

formal group: *group (usually an *organization) having a proper and unique name, clear boundaries (updated, complete list of *analytic members), and clear *leadership structure (widely accepted means of making binding group decisions) (cf. Smith 1972a, passim). Incorporation is not a requirement of formality in the *nonprofit sector, however, nor, contrary to Salamon and Anheier (1992:130), is listing with the Internal Revenue Service. Nonprofit researchers like the latter, who over-emphasize formal nonprofit groups to the neglect of *informal groups and *collectivities, especially *grassroots associations, are guided by the

*formalized group flat-earth paradigm. *See also* complexity; informal group

formal leisure activity: *free time activity pursued within a formal *program of leisure or under the aegis of a leisure *service offered by a *formal group that has been established to provide such service. Stebbins (2002: 47–62) examines the nature and types of *volunteer and leisure service groups. *See also* informal leisure activity

formal member. *See* official member; membership eligibility criteria in nonprofit groups

formal nonprofit group: *formal group or *organization with a nonprofit structure (*structural form of nonprofit groups) and *mission (Smith, Reddy, and Baldwin 1972:176).

formal nonprofit organization. *See* formal nonprofit group

formal social innovation activity. *See* social innovation activity

formal voluntary action: *voluntary action undertaken in or by a *formal nonprofit group or organization (cf. Smith 2000:24).

formal voluntary group. *See* formal nonprofit group

formal volunteer: *volunteer serving in a formal *nonprofit group or *volunteer department that sponsors or directs the individual's *volunteer action (Smith 2000:25). Examples include volunteers in a *volunteer program or an *association.

formal volunteer group. *See* volunteer nonprofit group

formal volunteer time. *See* volunteer time

formal volunteering: activity of *formal volunteers (Smith 2000:25).

formalization in nonprofits: process of transforming a nonprofit *informal group into a *formal group, accomplished by creating, for example, clearly articulated and written *goals, rules, and regulations as well as rights and duties. Tsouderos (1955, passim) presented a classic empirical study of formalization in nonprofits, mostly associations. As Smith (2000:20) notes, the services offered by *nonprofit groups vary by degree of formalization, running from highly informal to highly formal. *See also* complexity

formalized groups flat-earth paradigm: nonprofit sector model stating that only *formal nonprofit groups should be studied as part of the *nonprofit sector (described in Smith 2000:234–235). Invalid approach.

formation of a nonprofit organization: initial process of organizing and incorporating a formal *nonprofit organization in a state or province, which usually includes seeking appropriate *tax-exempt status, in the United States from the Internal Revenue Service or, elsewhere, from its equivalent (Hopkins 2001; Hummel 1996; Mancuso 2004). Far more complicated, legalistic, and expensive than forming a *grassroots association (Smith 2000, chap. 3). *See also* formation of a volunteer program/association

formation of a volunteer program/association: initial process of organizing and starting a *volunteer program (Connors 1995, chap. 3; Fisher and Cole 1993, pt. 1) or an *association. Smith (2000, chap. 3) reviews the choices that the *founder(s) of a *grassroots association have to make in setting up a new group. Battle (1988, chap. 3) discusses *planning for an association already in existence but his points could apply to planning to start an association as well.

formative evaluation. *See* process evaluation

for-profit: 1. (n.) business enterprise whose principal *goal is to make a profit. James (2003, passim) argues that, because of growing commercialism among *paid-staff nonprofits, the boundaries separating them from for-profits are becoming increasingly blurred. This seldom holds for *grassroots associations (Smith 2000:57–58), however, which are rarely commercial in their activities. 2. (adj.) profit-seeking. *See also* for-profit enterprise; for-profit group; for-profit organization

for-profit enterprise: an individual or *group mainly seeking a profit from certain activities; often termed a "firm" by economists (cf. Samuelson and Nordhaus 1995:101). Van Til (1988:138–141) explores today's fuzzy boundaries separating *nonprofit corporations and for-profit enterprise, setting out some of the ways in which *business and *volunteering are often linked.

for-profit group: a *for-profit enterprise that involves a group, usually a partnership or corporation. James (2003, passim) argues that, because of growing commercialism among *nonprofit groups, the boundaries separating them from for-profits are becoming increasingly blurred. The distinction between for-profit group and "not-for-profit" group is the language of economics (see Keating and Keating 1980, passim). The latter term, though a synonym for nonprofit, is nonetheless held by some in that field to be the more accurate descriptor. Still it is only occasionally found in the larger contemporary literature, most often in the fields of accounting and economics. *See also* for-profit organization

for-profit in disguise: apparent *nonprofit group that, through its *operative goals, pursues the private, usually economic, for-profit *interests of its managers or *board of directors, if not both. The disguised for-profit can be conceived of as a form of *deviant nonprofit. James (2003, passim) argues that, because of growing commercialism among nonprofits, the boundaries separating them from *for-profit groups are becoming increasingly blurred. Hammack and Young (1993b, passim) provide readings that explore the relation of nonprofits to for-profit activities.

for-profit organization: a large, formally structured, usually incorporated *for-profit group that seeks profit as its central *goal. Van Til (1988: 138–141) explores today's fuzzy boundaries separating *nonprofit corporations and for-profit organizations, setting out some of the ways in which *business and *volunteering are often connected.

foundation: 1.*nonprofit group usually having a substantial *endowment and, in the United States, a special tax status as a private foundation (cf. Freeman 1991, passim)—Internal Revenue Service category 501(c)(3) but not 509(a), which makes philanthropic (*philanthropy) *grants to individuals or nonprofits or both. *Independent, nonoperating, or grant-making private foundations have a long history in the United States (e.g., Kiger 2000; Sealander 1997) and elsewhere (Cizakca 2000; Stromberg 1968) and exist in many countries (Anheier and Toepler 1995; Lagemann 1999). There are studies of large foundations generally (e.g., Nielsen 1972) and of specific, usually large endowment, foundations (e.g., Isaacs and Knickman 1997). Ostrander (1995) studied a social change oriented foundation. There are also practical guides to managing a foundation (e.g., Ellsworth and Lumarda 2003; Freeman 1981). Lenkowsky (2002, chap. 11) examines the foundation and corporate philanthropy in the United States. 2. *nonprofit group that is an *operating foundation, spending 85 percent or more of its annual expenses on it own charitable program (Fishman and Schwarz 2000:326). 3. nonprofit group that raises money and makes philanthropic *grants to individuals or nonprofit groups or both, as does a *community foundation (cf. Magat 1989a). 4. a *company-sponsored foundation. Freeman (1991, passim) has written a classic book on private foundations of all kinds. *See also* independent foundation; company-sponsored foundation; community foundation; operating foundation

foundation giving: process by which a *foundation donates money to a *charity. Anheier and Cunningham (1994:107–108) describe the nature and scope of international foundation giving in the United States and Canada.

foundation payout: the money paid out in a given fiscal year by a *private foundation for grants and relevant administrative expenses; required to be at least 5 percent of net (average) investment assets according to the current U.S. Internal Revenue Code (Hopkins 1998, chap. 11).

founder attitude: fixed way of thinking or feeling held by a *founder of a *nonprofit group about any conceivable aspect of that group (e.g., its size, *goals, nature, structure). Thus, Sidjanski (1974:118–121) observed that Swiss founders of such groups were likely to avoid forming those that engage in protest, because in their society, protest is generally scorned.

founder choice: decision made early in the formation of a *nonprofit group by one or more of its *founders to give it a certain structure (*structure of nonprofit group) or operate according to a certain procedure (Smith 2000, chap. 3).

founder of nonprofit group: one who institutes or helps institute a *nonprofit group (Rock 1988, passim).

four-sector model of society. *See* model of society

fourth sector: historically correct ordinal sectoral label for *nonprofit sector (Smith 2000:222). *See also* nonprofit sector

Fourth World: 1. the more weakly developed segment of the *Third World—a distinction necessitated by the fact that some *Third World nations are substantially less developed than other nations usually classified as Third World (cf. Ebata and Neufeld 2000, passim; Smith 2000:244). 2. Dispossessed or disenfranchised minorities within larger states, a situation sometimes traced to language loss in the minority group (Rigsby 1987: passim).

franchise nonprofit group: local *nonprofit group licensed to use the name, logo, and trademark of the supralocal, often national, *association with which it is affiliated. Young (1989, passim) is possibly the first to describe as franchised such nonprofit groups.

fraternal association: a *member benefit association whose primary aim is sociability and *fellowship among the *members and that publicly recognizes this aim as primary. In earlier times, and to some extent currently, such associations offered a kind of health, accident, unemployment, and life insurance. Ross (1976, chap. 4) discusses the religious origins of fraternities as English associations several centuries ago. Picardie (1988, passim) reveals the workings of the Oddfellows, a British secret society of long standing. Beito (2000, passim) explores how fraternal *associations have innovated *social services in the period 1890–1967 in America (see also Kaufman 2002, passim). *See also* confraternity

fraternal group. *See* fraternal association

fraternity: male social *club, commonly one specially established for undergraduate students at a college or university. Often, in the United States, it is named with three Greek letters. Scott (1965, passim) wrote a classic empirical study of college fraternities and sororities. Drout and Corsoro (2003, passim) studied the differences among Greek (fraternity) and non-Greek students in their perception of hazing conducted in fraternities.

free clinic: a medical or dental clinic operated as or by a *nonprofit group without charge to patients. Fairly common in the United States in the 1960s and 1970s. Indeed, Kaseman's (1995, passim) analysis led her to believe that, at this time, these clinics were successful where more mainline health-care centers tended to fail.

free rider: one who benefits from *membership in or services of a *nonprofit group at the expense of the group or without the usual cost or effort of being a *member. Olson (1965, passim) presented an early theoretical discussion of the free rider problem in nonprofits. Kilbane and Beck (1990, passim) found more free riders in the large nonprofits they studied than in the small ones.

free school: a school operated as or by a *nonprofit group without charge to students. Fairly common in the United States in the 1960s and 1970s (cf. Graubard 1972, passim). Walter (1996, passim) points out that Jean-Jacques Rousseau's treatise on education, *Emile,* though often viewed as the foundation for school reform and the free school movement (*social movement), was actually considerably more conservative than modern free school practice.

free time: time left over after work and other, nonleisure *obligations have been met. Some scholars treat free time as synonymous with *leisure time. Others, however, distinguish it from leisure time, noting that boredom can occur in the former but not, by definition, in the latter (Stebbins 2003a, passim). Szalai (1972, passim) and colleagues present a classic report on the use of time in many countries, including free time activities. *See also* leisure time

free university: 1. a small college or university operated as or by a *nonprofit group without charge to students. Fairly common in the United States during the 1960s and 1970s (cf. Kerr 1967, passim). 2. any university that tries to contain influence of the reigning ideologies of the day by maintaining a policy of freedom of scholarly thought. Rhoads and Mina (2001, passim) consider the ramifications of the 1999 student strike at the National Autonomous University of Mexico, a free university. The students, who were of diverse political persuasions, were attempting to institute cultural change, sometimes without regard for various marginalized groups in their midst.

free will: proposition that in the *nonprofit sector people can freely choose, without remuneration or coercion, *voluntary action over other possible activities. Although debate over free will has a long history in philosophy (e.g., Mele 2003, chap. 6), it is of little concern in psychology.

freedom of assembly: basic human *civil liberty supported by law and allowing for any set of people in a society to meet and talk together publicly, indoors or outdoors, in a peaceable manner, without interference from authorities. King (1997) and McWhirter (1994) examine freedom of assembly and its importance to *civil society (sense 2).

freedom of association: basic human *civil liberty supported by law and allowing for widespread opportunity for people in a society to freely participate in, form, or dissolve *associations of their choice and to freely join or leave them. Bresler (2004, passim) and Gutman (1998, passim) discuss freedom of association and its importance for *civil society (sense 2).

freedom of dissent: basic human *civil liberty supported by law and allowing for widespread opportunity for people in a society to engage in peaceful *dissent or *social protest (technically called "petitioning the government for redress of grievances") against *policies or practices of government at any level. Sherr (1989) and Gora and Master (1991) treat freedom of dissent or protest and its importance for *civil society (sense 2).

freedom of protest. *See* freedom of dissent

freedom of religion: a basic *civil liberty, usually found in a *democracy, that permits people to choose their own *religion or *denomination, or to have no religion at all. Fundamental aspect of *freedom of association, because a *church is an *association generally. Hammond (1998) and Lynn et al. (1995) review freedom of religion and its importance for *religious pluralism and *civil society (sense 2).

freedom of speech: basic human *civil liberty supported by law and allowing for widespread opportunity for people in a society to speak or publish ideas and words, providing they are not a clear and present danger to others. This freedom is, for *nonprofit groups in a free society, basic to the process of attracting *resources, including people. Eastland (2000) and McWhirter (1994) assess freedom of speech and its importance for *civil society (sense 1).

friendly society: a type of *mutual benefit association, common in Europe especially in the nineteenth century, that assisted members and their families financially in times of sickness, unemployment, retirement, or death of the breadwinner. Similar to *fraternal associations in the United States (see Beito 2000, passim). Gosden (1961, passim) wrote a classic book on English friendly societies in the 1800s.

FTE. *See* full-time equivalent of paid-staff work

fulfillment/self-fulfillment. 1. realizing, or fact of having realized, to the fullest one's gifts and character, one's potential. 2. contentment from having satisfied a particular need or want (*see* satisfaction, sense 1). Stebbins (2004a, passim) discusses the fulfilling properties of *serious leisure and the "devotee occupations," as part of the common ground shared by the fields of work and leisure.

full-time equivalent of paid-staff work (FTE): in the *nonprofit sector, an estimate of the number of hours put in by *volunteers for a *nonprofit group as an equivalent of the value of full-time employment by *paid staff of the group. Weitzman and colleagues (2002:73, table 3.12) report that, excluding *informal volunteering, FTE employment of volunteers in 1998 in the United States stood at 9.3 million people. An FTE year is usually considered the equivalent of 1,700 work hours (ibid.).

function of nonprofits. *See* impact of nonprofits

functional analysis: assessment of the social and personal motivations satisfied, goals reached, needs met, and functions served by individual actions and beliefs associated with *volunteering. Clary, Snyder, and Ridge (1992:333) conducted a functional analysis, which also helped them devise their *volunteer functions inventory.

fund. *See* resource

fundamentalism, Christian: approach and movement of conservative Christians in America, which, beginning late in the nineteenth century, began to oppose *secularization, liberal theology, and the social (service) gospel by stating several fundamental principles to which they adhered (Gasper 1963; Johnstone 1992:144–145). Chief among these principles were the inerrancy of the Bible and various aspects of the deity of Jesus Christ and his role on earth and the Second Coming (ibid.). The movement has had its ups and downs in the twentieth century, and recently has seen a revival in the new *religious right (Brown 2002, passim; Johnstone 1992:146–153).

fundamentally deviant group: *group in any *sector of society formed to pursue deviant *goals or use deviant means to pursue conventional goals (cf. the Gambino Mafia crime family, as described by Davis 1993, passim). Stebbins (1996b:1–2) observes that individual and group deviance have emerged at all times in human history where people controvert local moral norms. Smith (1996b) devised a university course on deviant groups whose description has been published.

fundamentally deviant nonprofit group: *nonprofit group formed to pursue deviant *goals or use deviant means to pursue conventional goals. Cults, nudist resorts, witches' covens, and delinquent gangs number among today's fundamentally deviant nonprofit groups (Smith 2000:87).

funding in nonprofits: act of supplying a *nonprofit group over a specified period of time with a particular amount of money for carrying out its *program (Barker 2003:171). Internal funding refers to money raised by *dues, *donations, *fees, and the like from members. External funding refers to money raised by *grants, *contracts, nonmember donations, fees, and *fund-raising events in which nonmembers participate as *donors or buyers.

fund-raising event: in the *nonprofit sector a special, planned occurrence such as an auction, concert, raffle, or bake sale the *goal of which is to bring in money for a *charity. Shaw and Taylor (1995, passim) and Burlingame and Hulse (1991, passim) explore the complex world of fund-raising. *See also* special events fund-raising

fund-raising event monopoly: a usually local arrangement in which one *nonprofit group has, in effect, a monopoly on use of a particular *fund-raising event, such as a craft fair or pancake breakfast, or over a particular procedure, such as payroll deduction of *donations (e.g., United Way). Smith (2000:132, 185) terms these "trademark events." *See also* fund-raising in nonprofits

fund-raising in nonprofits: one or more methods of *funding, or providing *revenue for, a *nonprofit group. They include soliciting *donations, charging *fees/*dues, holding *fund-raising events, deducting donations from payroll, and seeking *grants or *contracts. Nonprofit researchers or practitioners who overemphasize fund-raising to the neglect of *voluntary altruism and *volunteering are reflecting the *"money is the key" flat-earth paradigm. The complex world of nonprofit fund-raising is explored by numerous authors, attesting to the crucial place this practice holds in *nonprofit management and nonprofit operations, especially for *paid-staff nonprofits (e.g., Armstrong 2001; Burlingame and Hulse 1991; Dove 2000, 2001; Fine 1992; Flanagan 2002; Freedman and Feldman 1998; Fogel 2004; Gilpatrick 1989; Greenfield 2001; Herron 1997; Klein 1988; Lauffer 1997; McLeish 1995; Mixer 1993; Nichols 1999; Robinson 2002; Rosso 1991; Schaff and Schaff 1999; Shaw and Taylor 1995; Sturtevant 1998; Warwick and Hitchcock 2002; Warwick et al. 2002; Weeden 1998; Wendroff 2004; Wilbur 2000, chaps. 4, 5; Young et al. 2002). *See also* fund-raising event monopoly; grant seeking by nonprofits; fund-raising intermediary; funding in nonprofits

fund-raising intermediary: *nonprofit group specialized in raising funds (*resource) from the *public (sense 1) used to make philanthropic (*philanthropy) *grants to other nonprofits. Examples include the *United Way, Combined Federal Campaign, Catholic Charities USA, and *alternative funds. Brilliant (1990, passim) provides a lengthy overview of the rise and contemporary operations of the United Way. *See also* intermediary

future of nonprofit sector/associations/volunteering: prediction, forecast, projection, or speculation about the future of the *nonprofit sector or its component elements. Some forecasting is essential for proper *planning by *nonprofit groups and *volunteer programs (Kluger et al. 1998). Hodgkinson and Lyman (1989, passim) edited a volume of papers on the future of the nonprofit sector. The Wolfenden Committee (1978) in the United Kingdom titled their report "The Future of Voluntary Organizations." Naisbitt (1982, passim) predicted trends for the 1980s and thereafter that included more *voluntary action—increasing *self-help, *decentralization, and participatory democracy (*civil society). More recently, Naisbitt and Aburdene (1990, passim) predicted for the 1990s and beyond a religious revival (*church; *religious nonprofit group) and the triumph of the individual, so people can "build community, the free association of individuals" (p. 324). Vineyard (1993, passim) made predictions about the future of *volunteerism and *volunteer programs, and Allen (1981, passim) has also examined this future. R. Herman (2005) discusses the future of nonprofit management. Weisbrod (1997, passim) sees the future of the nonprofit sector as involving its greater intertwining with the business and governmental sector. Smith (2000:254–259) predicts an expansion of voluntary role choices, including more *grassroots associations and variety of these groups. He also predicts (pp. 259–261) that the 2000s will be the "voluntary century," the beginning of the "volunteer millennium," with the rise of *Homo Voluntas—the volunteer person.

G

gang: an *association, usually small, with deviant or illegal *goals or means
of achieving them. 1. a *delinquent gang* or *youth gang* is an *association
composed mainly of adolescents who have committed one or more illegal acts, often as a *group, and who spend their *leisure time together
(e.g., Covey et al. 1997, passim; Dawley 1992, passim; Spergel 1995,
passim). 2. a *motorcycle gang,* or *club,* is an *association of people, sometimes called "bikers" or "outlaws," who enjoy riding motorcycles together in their leisure time and usually who have committed one or
more illegal acts, often as a *deviant group (e.g., Wolf 1991, passim;
Lavigne 1993, passim). 3. a *criminal gang* is a group of criminals who
have banded together to make more profit from their illegal activities.
Because profit, broadly conceived, is the aim, a criminal gang is not a
*nonprofit group, unlike most youth and motorcycle gangs, but is a
business. Examples of studies of criminal gangs include Balsamo and
Carpozi (1991, passim), Davis (1993, passim) on Mafia gangs, and English (1990, passim) on the Irish mob (gang) in New York City. Moreover some motorcycle gangs in the United States and Canada have become criminal gangs.

gatekeeper: one who facilitates or obstructs communication or movement
between groups. Barker (2003:174) writes that gatekeepers are, typically,
natural, indigenous *leaders in a *community capable of controlling access to target populations sought by outsiders.

general activity model: model for understanding socioculturally valued *leisure activities, including *volunteer action, that postulates "positive intercorrelations among socioculturally valued *discretionary time activities like *volunteer participation and friendship, neighboring, political activity, and *recreation" to mention only a few major types of such activities. The model also postulates the predictive value of the *active-effective character pattern. Although little studied directly (but see Smith 1969, 1973/2001), substantial research evidence supports the clustering of discretionary activities suggested by this model (e.g., Kirsch et al. 1999:121; Smith 1975:260–261, 1994:255, 257; Smith and Macauley 1980, chap. 19 and passim; Smith and Theberge 1987, passim).

general activity pattern: positive interrelationships of an individual's *leisure time roles, positions, and *participation in that person's society (Smith 1980a:21–29. 1980b:462). This pattern develops over time, and its components (roles, activities, etc.) tend to be positively and significantly correlated, even if this correlation is limited by various constraints on amount and depth of individual participation.

general long-term welfare. *See* welfare (sense 2)

general operating support (fund): *grant to a *nonprofit group to support its general operations (*operating expense) rather than being made for a specific *project or other purpose. The Evangelical Lutheran Church in America (http://www.elca.org) says its general operating fund supports all business activity of a *congregation, by accounting for and accumulating all income except restricted *gifts and payments.

general welfare. *See* public interest

gift: that which is given in the course of *giving something to an individual or a *group. In the *nonprofit sector the two main types of gift are the *donation and the act of *volunteer work, both the result of giving money, property, or time as an expression of *voluntary altruism or desire to provide public *benefit. Van Loo (1990, passim) examines the process of "gift exchange" (*exchange, philanthropic). Mauss (1925/1990, passim) and Titmuss (1971, passim) have written classic books on the gift relationship. Jas (2000, passim) explores the gift relationship in charitable giving. *See also* exchange, philanthropic; philanthropy

gift in kind, business: *gift other than money made by a corporation or other business to a *charity. Typical in-kind gifts consist of *goods or commodities. Since such gifts go unreported as charitable contributions, systematically collected data on the extent to which they are made are unavailable (Weitzman et al. 2002:83–84).

gift matching by a corporation: *donation of a sum of money (*gift) by a corporation to a *charity in or near the amount given by an *employee to that charity. In 1998 in the United States, grants made by corporations amounted to 3.4 percent of all *foundation giving that year, a figure that included scholarships and employee matching gifts (Weitzman et al. 2002:84, table 3.17).

gild. *See* guild (standard spelling)

giving: process of allocating money, *goods, other property, or *service (time) to an individual or *group, without expecting any direct, high probability, reciprocal transfer (*exchange, philanthropic) of money, goods, other property, or service in return. In giving something the net worth of the giver (*donor) is (at least temporarily) reduced, while the net worth of the recipient (*target of benefits) is increased. Giving within the family is not philanthropic (*philanthropy), whereas giving outside it may be philanthropic if *altruism or public *service is the *goal (cf. Magat 1989b, passim). Smith, Shue, and Villarreal (1992, passim) studied philanthropic giving among Asian- and Hispanic-Americans. Bremner (1996, passim) provides a history of charitable giving. Kirsch et al. (1999, passim) report on a national survey of giving in America.

goal: in the *nonprofit sector, what a *nonprofit group or altruistic (*altruism) individual is trying to achieve, like a certain change in society, a particular *member benefit, or a special *service for a targeted clientele. Such a goal might be, for example, political, economic, or domestic (family/household). Smith (1991, passim) observes that a nonprofit may have *operative goals aimed at benefiting *members or nonmembers or both. *See also* goal, official; goal, operative; goal, unofficial

goal achievement model of organizational effectiveness evaluation: evaluation based on assessment of how well an *organization is achieving its *goals. One weakness of this model is the fact that considerable disagreement may exist over what an organization's goals are, or should be (Murray and Tassie 1994:307).

goal diffuseness vs. specificity. *See* diffuseness vs. specificity of goals

goal displacement in nonprofits: tendency for *nonprofit groups to stray over time from their official goals (*goal, official) to seek the unofficial goals (*goal, unofficial) of maintaining nonprofit structure (*structure of nonprofit groups), personnel, and procedures. Perrow (1961, passim) wrote the classic analysis of this process. *See also* goal displacement

goal limitations in nonprofits: the *goals a *nonprofit group finds extremely difficult, if not impossible, to achieve. Such groups are capable of seeking and even achieving many goals, but significant exceptions exist. For instance, most (especially *grassroots associations) have difficulty raising much money, and none can collect taxes (Smith 2000:85).

goal, official: a *goal that a *nonprofit group claims in its formal, or official, statements (e.g., its *articles of organization) (Perrow 1961, passim; Smith 2000:74). *See also* goal, operative; goal, unofficial

goal, operative: a *goal that a *nonprofit group tends to seek in actuality, in its everyday operations (Perrow 1961, passim; Smith 2000:74). *See also* goal, official; goal, unofficial

goal succession: change in one or more of a *nonprofit group's basic goals (cf. Sills 1957:254–264), sometimes because the original goals have been achieved or rendered irrelevant by the environment. Smith (2000:186) notes goal succession becomes ever likelier as the group ages. *See also* goal displacement

goal, unofficial: in nonprofit groups an unstated, secret, or hidden *goal that is nonetheless operative (*goal, operative) in being implicitly sought through actual operating policies of the group. Often identified only through social scientific research using interviews with insiders or inferences from expenditures of *resources such as time and money (Smith 2000:74). Perrow (1961, passim) wrote the classic analysis of the pursuit of unofficial goals. *See also* goal, official; goal displacement in nonprofits

goal-appropriateness: logical consistency of a *nonprofit group's *goals and *ideology or the goals and ideology of its larger supralocal association. Thus, Woycke (2003:251–264) concludes that changes in the ideology of Canadian nudism have found expression in the emergence of new groups in tune with these changes.

good: 1. something advancing *community well-being or prosperity and shared indivisibly in consumption among a population; a "collective good" or "public good" (e.g., clean air, national defense; cf. Samuelson and Nordhaus 1995:347). 2. something scarce having individual economic utility or satisfying an economic want; an economic good. Such a good is not shared indivisibly among people; it is a "private good" or "personal good" consumable separately by an individual (cf. Samuelson and Nordhaus 1995:347). 3. something benefiting members of a *nonprofit group, a "club good" (Cornes and Sandler 1996, pt. 4; Smith 2000: 98). According to economists goods in the first and third senses—labeled "collective goods" or "club goods"—are often produced by *nonprofit groups, government and business having failed to provide them (cf. Weisbrod 1988, passim). *See also* benefit

good, collective. *See* good

good, private. *See* good

good, public. *See* good

good work. *See* charitable act

governance group: *group commonly found in residential settings (e.g., prisons, psychiatric hospitals, boarding schools), established to involve residents in the daily running of the institution (Barker 2003:182). Such groups help facilitate its smooth operation as well as help mediate intergroup conflict that can emerge there.

governance of nonprofits. *See* nonprofit governance

governing board. *See* board of directors

governing committee. *See* board of directors

governing instrument in nonprofits: a formal legal document that serves as a guide to managing a *nonprofit group. A group's *articles of organization constitute a governing instrument (Hopkins 2001:315), as do its *by-laws.

government: a person or *group that is the controlling political administration of a territory. Usually has taxation and police powers, among others. For an overview of government as a form of sociopolitical organization, see McFall (2002, passim). The Aspen Institute (2002, passim) clarifies the relationship between government and the *nonprofit sector.

government and nonprofit relations: the numerous interchanges that *nonprofit groups, especially *paid-staff nonprofit organizations, have with government at one territorial level or another. These links can lead to *tax-exempt status, governmental *contracted service in *nonprofit groups, and attempts to influence the political process through *lobbying and grassroots public education, to mention only a few (Smith 2000: 164). Many authors have examined in recent years the interactions of government and paid-staff nonprofits (e.g., Banting and Brock 2002; Berry and Arons 2003; Brock 2003; Burlingame 2004:199–204; Gidron et al. 1992; Glenn 2000; Salamon 1995). By contrast, *grassroots associations are much less affected by relations with government (Smith 2000:163–164). *See also* environment affecting nonprofits

government mandated citizen participation: *citizen participation in a particular *governmental agency or *program required by law or governmental regulation (e.g., in the War on Poverty Model Cities Program of the 1960s). Gittell (1980, passim) concluded that this type of citizen participation was ineffective, usually being dominated by governmental leaders. Moynihan (1970, passim) also found such mandated participation to be ineffective. *See also* mandated nonprofit group participation

governmental agency: a subgroup of a *government (cf. Millspaugh 1949, passim). Jones-Johnson and Johnson (1992, passim) examined the effects of subjective underemployment on psychosocial stress among employees of a public utility governmental agency. They found that supervisor support, though not social support, was positively related to this type of stress.

governmental failure: one reason given for the presence of *nonprofit groups is that government fails to provide all the collective *goods that people in the society need or want. Thus nonprofits emerge to fill the gap. This process is also referred to at times as "governmental market failure" (e.g., Salamon 1987, passim). *See also* private market failure

governmental organization: 1. an *organization that operates as a *government or a *governmental agency (cf. Gilbert 1983). 2. how a government is organized (cf. Blondel 1982; Millspaugh 1949).

governmental sector. *See* sector of society

governmental volunteer program: volunteer *program organized and operated by a governmental *agency to perform internal governmental work. Brudney (1990, passim) provides an in-depth analysis of these programs.

grant: allocation of money, *goods, or other property (but not *service, labor, or time) to an individual or group (usually *nonprofit), without any expectation of direct, high probability, reciprocal return of similar allocation to the *donor and without coercion of the donor to make the grant; often made by a foundation or government agency (cf. Orosz 2000, passim; Weaver 1967, passim). A grant made for altruistic (*altruism) or public service purposes is known as a philanthropic grant (*philanthropy). The complexity of making grants to *grantees, a process known as "grant making," has given rise to Grantmakers for Effective Organizations Affinity Group, an *organization for *grantors (Abramson and McCarthy 2002:347). *See also* matching grant

grant application. *See* grant proposal

grant economy: that part of a society's economy, broadly conceived of, concerning transfers in *grants, *giving, and contributions (cf. Boulding 1973, passim). Galaskiewicz (1985, passim) examined the social organization of an urban grants economy.

grantee: person or *nonprofit group to whom a *grant is made by a *grantor. O'Brien and colleagues (1995, passim) studied, as an exemplary model for serving mobile, at-risk populations, the East Coast Migrant Head Start Project, a federal grantee providing quality Head Start services to migrant families in the eastern states. The federal government was the grantor.

grantee financial report: a report by a *grantee describing how all *grant funds were used by a given *nonprofit group, often including a general accounting/financial report on the nonprofit. The website—http://www.writewinningproposals.com—includes a section on the grantee financial report.

grant making: process of making a *grant to a *grantee; usually done by a foundation or government agency to a nonprofit or private individual (see Council on Foundations 1986, passim; Orosz 2000, passim).

grant-making foundation. *See* foundation (sense 1)

grantor: person or *organization who makes a *grant to a *grantee. *See* grantee for a research illustration of the grantor-grantee relationship.

grant proposal: an extensive written application to a *foundation, *government agency, or *corporate philanthropy program by a *nonprofit group or individual seeking a *grant. Usually follows positive response by a funder to a *letter of inquiry. The art of writing such proposals is set out in detail in, for example, Danis and Burke (1996, passim) and Garris and Lettner (1996, passim).

grant seeking: process in which an entity, usually a *nonprofit but sometimes a private individual, explores the possibility of obtaining a *grant from a *foundation or *government agency, often employing a *grant proposal in the latter stages (see Brown and Brown 2001, passim; Golden 1997, passim).

grant seeking by nonprofits: attempt by a *nonprofit group to obtain a *grant to help pursuit of a collective *goal, as by approaching a *foundation, *government agency, or corporation of some kind. This is an important source of income for larger, *paid-staff nonprofit organizations (Gilpatrick 1989; Golden 1997; Lauffer 1997). By contrast, *grassroots associations (GAs) rarely seek or receive grants (Smith 2000, p. 131). Indeed, Smith (ibid.:251) recommends that foundations not make operating fund grants to such associations, because healthy GAs can sustain themselves by *dues, *fees, or *donations.

grant transfer: the giving of a *grant to a *grantee. May be done by a *philanthropic foundation. Boulding (1973:1–5) stresses the one-way nature of grant giving, contrasting it with the two-way nature of *exchange, or the traditional explanation that economists give for the distribution of *goods and *services in society.

grass roots: in the *nonprofit sector, the ordinary people as representative of a basic point of view, or more particularly in politics, the voters in a constituency. Thus Kenney (2003, passim) argues that, to know how norms change vis-à-vis women's *issues, feminist scholars must broaden their scope beyond political elites (*insider, societal) and *interest groups to include *social movements and newly politicized grassroots *activists. *See also* grassroots association/group

grassroots action. *See* community involvement; civic engagement; citizen participation

grassroots association/group: locally based, significantly autonomous, volunteer-run *formal or *informal nonprofit group that manifests substantial *voluntary altruism as a group and uses the *associational form of organization. Thus grassroots associations (GAs) have an official *membership of volunteers who perform most, and often all, of the work/activity done in and by these nonprofits (Smith 2000:8). Such groups may be local chapters or branches of supralocal *associations, often *state associations or *national associations, in which case they are *polymorphic nonprofit groups. Or GAs may be essentially unique and unaffiliated with any supralocal association, in which case they are *monomorphic nonprofit groups (Smith 2000:80–81). GAs, both in present and in earlier times, form a web of social ties through memberships and participation in most communities and neighborhoods in America (Von Hoffman 1994, chap. 5). GAs are also found frequently elsewhere in developed nations (Smith 2000:44) and developing nations (Fisher 1993, 1998). Smith (2000, pt. 2) gives an overview of research on GAs and their distinctive nature as contrasted with *paid-staff nonprofits. Smith (1997c, passim) argues that most mainstream nonprofit scholars have ignored GAs as the "dark matter" of the nonprofit sector. Putnam (2000, passim) reviews data that show a decline in traditional GA membership in recent decades in America. Clifton and Dahms (1993) provide a resource book on grassroots organizations. Many studies have been done of GAs of various types, including Alexander et al. (2001), Berry et al. (1993), Bestor (1985), Blair (1994), Charles (1993), Clarke (1993), Dawley (1982), Esman and Uphoff (1984), Ferree and Martin (1995), J. Fisher (1993, 1998), R. Fisher (1994), Gora and Nemerowicz (1985), Kaplan and Marshall (1996), Karl (1995), Kaufman (2002), Lane (1976), McGerr (1986/2000), McKenzie (1994), Osigweh (1983), Pearce (1993), Scarboro et al. (1994), Scott (1992), Siriani and Friedland (2001), Stepan-Norris and Zeitlin (1996), Von Hoffman (1994), Wellman (1995), and Wuthnow (1998). Smith and Freedman (1972, passim) wrote a classic research literature review on voluntary associations more generally. *See also* grass roots

grassroots association, participation in: being an *official member, especially an active member (*member, analytic) of one or more *grassroots associations (GAs), but technically also including *paper members who are usually *members only by virtue of paying annual *dues (Smith 2000:7, 49, 181). Studies of predictors of *participation in GAs include, for example, Curtis et al. (1992), Hirschman (1970), Hausknecht (1962), Palisi and Korn (1989), Pearce (1993, pt. 2), Ross and Wheeler (1981), Smith (1975, 1994a), Smith and Van Til (1983, pt. 3), Verba et al. (1978; 1995, chap. 3, pts. 2 and 3), Verba and Nie (1972, pt. 1). *See also* general activity pattern; active-effective character pattern; sociodemographic participation predictors flat-earth paradigm

grassroots association, social movement: *grassroots association whose goals are to realize the aims of a *social movement. The distinctive *goals and *values of a social movement give *membership in its grassroots associations special meaning, since membership is accompanied by a particular identity based on shared "weness" and "groupness" that comes with participation there (Beaford, Gongaware, and Valadez 2000:2721). *See also* grass roots

grassroots fund-raising: *fund-raising from the general *public, usually in the local *community of a nonprofit group and especially from the affiliates or constituents of that nonprofit. There is a monthly electronic journal devoted to this subject entitled *Grassroots Fundraising Journal E-newsletter.*

grassroots lobbying. *See* lobbying

grassroots mobilization. *See* community involvement; civic engagement; citizen participation

grassroots organizing: process of bringing together and directing people to participate in the activities and *programs of a *grassroots association. Kahn (1982, passim) has written a guide for grassroots organizers. *See also* grass roots; community organizing

grassroots participation. *See* community involvement; civic engagement; citizen participation

"great man" theory of leadership: original version of *trait approach to *leadership in *groups, which specified that a "great person" with out-standing leadership traits and skills (e.g., high intelligence, high asser-tiveness, high sociability/friendliness, high confidence, etc.) was neces-sary to have good leadership in a group—and especially to found the group (cf. Bryson 1996, passim; Stogdill 1948, passim). Winston Chur-chill exemplifies well the great man theory of leadership (for a literary portrait of him, see Payne 1974, passim).

group: set of two or more individuals sharing one or more *goals with associated normative strength, having a sense of common identity as distinct from other groups and the population at large, and having a relatively dense intercommunicational structure based on various rules and roles (cf. Smith 1967, passim). Groups are qualified in social science as "small" when all *members can at the very least be known to each other. Large groups lack this quality, as seen in some *associations and *organizations. Groups, small and large, formal and informal, comprise a main part of the *nonprofit sector (Smith 2000:25–26). *See also* formal group; informal group; primary group; secondary group; volunteer non-profit group; group subculture; collectivity

group action: action performed essentially by or on behalf of a *group acting collectively, such as a *meeting, committee meeting, *fund-raising event, *conference, *project, or *program. Greenfield and Connor's (2001, pas-sim) handbook on fund-raising contains numerous sections on how to organize fund-raising projects and events in *nonprofit groups.

group, formal. *See* formal group

group, informal. *See* informal group

group marriage: informal marriage relationship with three or more individ-uals participating; sometimes found in communes. Constantine and Constantine (1973, passim) analyze contemporary group marriage as a deviant household phenomenon.

group subculture: distinctive configuration of values, norms, beliefs, arti-facts, and patterns of behavior that, together, constitute a special way of life for *members of a *group. Fine (1998:169–179) describes several aspects of the subculture of the amateur mycological society that he studied.

group voluntary action: *voluntary action performed essentially by a *non-profit group acting collectively; a form of *group action. *See also* group action

group, volunteer. *See* volunteer nonprofit group

guidance system in nonprofits: those aspects of a *nonprofit *group's sub-culture that guide *members in thoughts, motives, feelings, and actions acceptable and appropriate to that group (Smith 2000:91). The guidance system has two main parts: the group's ideology and its *incentive system (cf. Knoke 1990, chaps. 6 and 7; Smith 2000, chap. 4; Wilson 1974, chap. 3).

guild: association of people formed for mutual aid and protection of members or for promotion of similar interests or pursuits; in particular, a medieval group of merchants or craftsmen established for these purposes (cf. Gross 1890, passim; Hartson 1911, passim). For example, Ross (1976:106) notes that the guilds usually offered funeral and burial payments to spouses of deceased *members. Epstein (1991, passim) examines at length the relationship of guilds to wage labor in medieval Europe.

H

habitual volunteer. *See* volunteer, habitual

halfway house: a house or residential building, usually run on a *nonprofit basis or as a *program of a larger *nonprofit group, for recovering alcoholics, addicts, former prisoners, former mental patients, and the like (cf. Golomb and Kocsis 1988, passim; Raush and Raush 1968, passim). The house provides a somewhat sheltered environment halfway between institutionalization and the condition of being a normal member of society. May involve some special norms or activities aimed at dealing with the problem that previously led to institutionalization of the participants. Jensen (2001, passim) compares the perceptions and attitudes of offenders and staff toward two community-based correctional programs: a community-based corrections facility using a therapeutic community approach and a traditional halfway house. The results suggest that residents and staff can create different correctional environments, to which they then respond differently.

hate group: a *nonprofit group, often small and informal, the *mission of which is to disseminate (usually) written or visual material intended to psychologically injure a target group or *social category; sometimes also engage in hate crimes and violence. Hamm (1994, passim), studying American "skinheads," presents one of the first criminological analyses of organized hate crime violence. Donelan (2004, passim) studied the websites of hate groups and *citizen militias in South Dakota. She found that the first concentrated on race or citizenship or both, while the second were concerned with such matters as strict interpretation of the Constitution, fundamentalist religious beliefs, and protection of or from the *government.

helpee. *See* target of benefits

helper-therapy principle: principle basic to *self-help groups and, to a lesser extent, other *support groups, namely that people who have experienced a given problem, challenge, or addiction are often best able to help the recovery of others with a similar condition *and* in this helping process the helper himself or herself is further aided in various therapeutic ways (e.g., by being vividly reminded of the causes and effects of the problem in its untreated, pre-recovery, or early recovery state). Gartner and Riessman (1977:99) state the principle briefly as, "those who help are helped the most." *Twelve-step groups have as their twelfth step the helping of other untreated or recovering victims of their specific problem, challenge, or addiction (e.g., Rudy 1986:40–42).

helping/helping behavior: act of personally giving time, *goods, money, or other property to people or groups. Helping behavior is often motivated by *altruism (Batson 1991, passim). *See also* prosocial behavior

helping network: *network made up of any or all of the following types of components: individuals, *groups, *organizations (governmental, nongovernmental), social service agencies (*nonprofit agency), and the like. These components operate individually or in combinations to provide an individual with support, information, resources, and other means needed to solve a particular *problem or meet a particular *need. Vinton (1992), in a study of helping networks among the elderly in Florida, found that only two of twenty-five battered women's shelters in her sample offered services to this age group. That is, elderly female Floridians do not commonly have such shelters as part of their helping networks.

heresy: 1. a religious belief that is contrary to the orthodox (accepted) beliefs of the dominant church or state *church (sense 3). Brown (1998, passim) reviews heresies and orthodoxy in the history of the Catholic Church. 2. the (usually nonprofit) *group of people who are fostering a new form or aspect of religious belief or practice (*new religion; *sect). Moore (1977/1994, passim) discusses the history of such heresies in late medieval Europe, as does Lambert (1992, passim).

heteronomy: Martin (1998, passim) defines it as "rule from another," or rule from sources outside the individual or *nonprofit group; opposite of *autonomy. He examines the role of heteronomy in classical sociological thought.

hierarchy of volunteer role engagement: a ranking of different combinations of various forms of volunteer activity. Perlmutter and Cnaan (1993) contend that such a hierarchy exists within human service organizations, based upon the typology of *volunteer roles, which they identified and developed into a Guttman scale. Working from a typology developed by Lauffer and Gorodezky (1977), Perlmutter and Cnaan constructed a scale of eight combinations of roles. The most frequent (in Guttman scale order) were direct practice and administrative support (24%); direct practice, administration, and advocacy (35%); and direct practice, administration, and advocacy, and policy (36%). Higher levels of education were associated with roles higher in this hierarchy, as was volunteering in more than one human service organization. Sex, age, ethnicity, religion, marital status, and income were unrelated.

hiring paid staff for nonprofits. *See* recruitment of nonprofit group paid staff; staffing

history of philanthropy: the long-term history of philanthropy and public service giving, beginning in ancient times (see, for instance, Burlingame 2004: 234–243; Cavallo 1995; Constantelos 1991; Kiger 2000; Weaver 1967).

history of volunteering/nonprofits: the long-term account of the rise of *nonprofit groups and *volunteering. Smith (1997b, passim) presents a bibliographical essay tracing the international history of nonprofit groups, particularly *grassroots associations, from their origins about 27,000 years ago (Anderson 1973:10) through the present. Ross (1976, passim) reviews the history of *associations from their origins. Ellis and Noyes (1990) sketch an informal history of Americans as *volunteers, and Hall (1987) offers a more scholarly overview of nonprofits in America. Hammack (1998, passim) edited a historical reader on the making of the *nonprofit sector in America. O'Neill (1989, passim) presents a historical account of the origins of various purposive types of American nonprofit groups. There are many histories of specific *nonprofit groups (e.g., Smith 2003, passim) or types of nonprofit groups in various nations (e.g., Pelling 1963, passim, for British trade *unions; Finke and Stark 2005, for American churches). The worldwide historical literature on nonprofits, including associations, is vast, as Smith (1997b) indicates, showing the tip of the iceberg, whereas the history of *volunteers and volunteering per se is a much thinner literature. Despite the wealth of historical literature on volunteering and nonprofits, ignorance of this history by most nonprofit researchers reflects the *antihistoricism flat-earth paradigm (Smith 2000:233–234).

hobby (hobbyist activity): a systematic, enduring pursuit of a reasonably evolved and specialized *free-time activity having no *professional counterpart (Stebbins 2003c, passim). Such *leisure leads to acquisition of substantial skill, knowledge, or experience, or a combination of these. Although *hobbyists differ from *amateurs in that they lack a professional reference point, they sometimes have commercial equivalents and often have small publics (sense 2) who take an interest in what they do. Many hobbies are pursued alone, although just as many seem to be enjoyed in *nonprofit groups of various sizes. As with other *leisure activities, hobbies, if they are to be considered part of the *nonprofit sector, must be motivated by *voluntary altruism. Gelber (1999:passim) has conducted the most comprehensive study of hobbies in the United States. *See also* formal leisure activity; informal leisure activity

hobby group: a *grassroots association whose central purpose is to practice and share a hobby like quilting, kayaking, coin collecting, and model railroading. Stebbins (1996a, passim) studied male and female barbershop singers in Calgary, who were organized as quartets or as choruses. These hobby groups became major points of interest in the leisure lifestyles of the respondents in the study.

hobbyist: someone who pursues a *hobby. King (2001, passim) studied hobbyist quilters in Texas, some of whom worked alone but many of whom joined local *clubs.

home church. *See* house church

homeowners association: a *member benefit association whose *members own homes in a particular community housing development or condominium/cooperative and that operates to protect, serve, and enhance the homes and *community where it is located. Often involve deed restrictions on properties whose owners are *members. McKenzie (1994, passim) explores the rise of common interest housing developments in recent decades and describes the functions and impact of their governing associations, which he terms "residential private governments." The roughly 150,000 of these homeowner associations in 1992 (ibid.:11) affected the lives of over thirty million residents in America.

homo faber: translated from Latin as the human species as maker of tools or, more generally, "man the maker" (Tilgher 1977, passim).

homo ludens: translated from Latin as the human species as player or, in Huizinga's (1955:ix) terms, "man the player."

homo voluntas: translated from Latin as the human species regarded as volunteer or, in Smith's (2000:260) terms, "man the volunteer."

homogeneity, sociodemographic: similarity along lines of such population variables as age, sex, education, race/ethnicity, and marital status. McPherson and Rotolo (1996, passim) found that some *nonprofit groups (specifically *associations) tend toward considerable sociodemographic homogeneity.

horizontal collaboration in nonprofits. *See* collaboration

hospice: facility for or *program of physical and emotional palliative care for the terminally ill who want no further remedial medical assistance. Many hospices are small *paid-staff nonprofit groups that, even though they have a *formal group structure, tend to avoid bureaucratic practices (*bureaucracy) (Gummer 1988, passim).

hotline: a telephone line and number available twenty-four hours a day seven days a week that offers information or help to callers on some specific *issue or *problem. Hotlines are usually operated by *nonprofit groups but are sometimes operated by *governmental agencies. Some examples are suicide prevention hotlines, AIDS hotlines, and abuse hotlines. Cuadrado (1999, passim) studied a hotline in Florida for problem gamblers to determine differences and similarities along demographic lines and in rate of use between Caucasians and non-Caucasians

house church: a small *congregation that meets in someone's dwelling or house (Hadaway et al. 1987, passim). Usually informal, with an emphasis on *fellowship of worshipers and shared *leadership responsibility. Banks (1980, passim) discusses house churches in early Christianity. McDaniel (2002, passim) explores how people involved in house churches attempt to create spiritual *communities and negotiate everyday difficulties in an unconventional religious setting.

household/family goal. *See* goal

household/family sector. *See* sector of society

human capital. *See* capital, human

human resource effectiveness model of organizational effectiveness evaluation: assessment of *employee beliefs, attitudes, and performance relative to a particular *organization, including all organizational *policy and practice that shapes these criteria (Murray and Tassie 1994:308).

human resource management in nonprofits: the *management of the *paid and *volunteer staff or workers of a *nonprofit group for optimal attainment of the group's *mission (Pynes 1997; Wilbur 2000, chap. 13; Wolf 1999, chap. 4). Involves *recruitment of nonprofit group *paid staff and, initially, recruitment of *volunteers and, possibly, *members. Such management also requires proper supervision of people working according to group-established personnel *policies and procedures in a positive work environment that will bring out the best contribution of each worker.

human right. *See* civil liberties

human services. *See* social services

humane caring for others. *See* caring

humane core value. *See* value, humane core

hybrid nonprofit: *nonprofit group classifiable in two or more of the five *sectors of society. Some hybrids are formed and mainly funded by government (e.g., the RAND Corporation—B. Smith 1966, passim; the Urban Institute), some by business (e.g., trade associations, corporate foundations, Enterprise Development Corporation), and some by households (e.g., *communes—Kanter 1972, passim). Hyde (2000, passim), however, works with a different definition of hybrid nonprofit. She analyzed six feminist *social movement organizations according to their places along the continuum between two types of *nonprofit organization: bureaucratic and grassroots. She concluded that the groups were "hybrid"; they fell between the two poles.

hybrid organization. *See* hybrid nonprofit

I

ICNPO. *See* international classification of nonprofit organizations

idealistic community. *See* intentional community

ideology: a logically loose system of ideas and *values serving to justify use of power to achieve special *interests. Smith (2000:92) observes that most *nonprofit groups are guided by some sort of ideology, though not typically an elaborate one.

IGO. *See* intergovernmental organization

immigrant grassroots association: *grassroots association founded to serve the *interests of a certain category of immigrant. Those interests may be sociable or practical or both, and the group may include *members who are not themselves immigrants. Owusu (2000, passim) examined these functions in the Ghanaian immigrant associations of Toronto. Soysal (1994, chap. 6) examines local and national migrant associations in Europe.

immunity, charitable. *See* charitable immunity and liability

impact of nonprofits/nonprofit sector: a cumulative consequence of *nonprofit group activity on *analytic members, on the *targets of benefits, and on the larger society. Impact on *analytic members is labeled internal impact, while impact on *targets of benefits who are not analytic members and impact on the larger society are labeled external impact. Smith (1997a, 2000:196–206) examines the literature on internal and external impacts of *grassroots associations. In an earlier work, various authors in Clotfelter's (1992, passim) anthology examine aspects of who benefits from the *nonprofit sector. Smith (1973/2001) gives an overview of the impact of the voluntary, *nonprofit sector on society, as does Diaz (2002). Flynn and Hodgkinson (2002) give a broader view of measuring the impact of the nonprofit sector. *See also* effectiveness

imputed value of donated goods: estimated monetary value of *donated goods given to a *nonprofit group. Usually based on fair market value considering the condition of the goods (e.g., new, used, in working order). The Salvation Army accepts donated property of various kinds, using its experts, sometimes in conjunction with those of the *donor, to establish the monetary value of the *gift or *donation (see its website and then click on a particular country: http://www.salvationarmy.org).

imputed value of volunteer time: *See* imputed value of volunteer work

imputed value of volunteer work: monetary value assigned to hours of *volunteer work, so as to assess better its economic significance. Wolozin (1975) was one of the first to perform such imputation. The bases for such assessment include minimum wage, average service wage, and wage rate foregone by each *volunteer. Weisbrod (1988, chap. 7) discusses further the question of imputed monetary worth of *volunteer work.

incentive in nonprofits: a single inducement found either among many kinds of inducements or in a system of mixed inducements, either of which encourages *voluntary action. Smith (1981) and Tomeh (1981) cited the typology of Clark and Wilson (1961), which divided incentives into solidary incentives (intangible and consummatory and not related to organizational goals, also known as the *sociability incentive), material incentives (tangible, concrete and utilitarian rewards, also known as the *utilitarian incentive), and *purposive incentives (intangible but also related to a defined end). Smith (2000, chap. 4) reviewed nine types of incentives in grassroots associations that have applicability to all nonprofits. He viewed the most important ones to be sociability, purposive, and service incentives, with utilitarian incentives much weaker. The latter would be stronger for *quasi-volunteers in *paid-staff nonprofits. Prestby et al. (1990) argued that organizations should recognize that mixed incentives rather than pure incentives are more likely to appeal to a broader number of people, and called attention to what might be thought of as the opposite of incentives, the *costs of volunteer participation. *See also* charismatic incentive; co-member service incentive; developmental incentive; economic incentive; incentive system in nonprofits; incentive type in nonprofits; informational incentive; lobbying incentive; material incentive; motivation; nonmember service incentive; normative incentive in nonprofit groups; personal growth incentive; prestige incentive; purposive incentive; service incentive; sociability incentive; solidary incentive; utilitarian incentive

incentive system in nonprofits: a *nonprofit group's set of rewards and punishments for *members, which to attain its *goals using accepted group means, the group manipulates from to time (Knoke 1990:55; Smith 2000:91).

incentive type in nonprofits: class of *incentive in *nonprofit groups. Smith (2000:96–102) sets out a nine-fold typology of incentives that motivate *members of nonprofits groups: *sociability, *purposive, *service, *informational, *developmental, *utilitarian, *charismatic, *lobbying, and *prestige. This typology builds on Clark and Wilson (1961, passim) and Knoke (1990, chaps. 6 and 7).

incidence of nonprofits. *See* nonprofit group incidence

inclusion/exclusion: in *nonprofit groups the process, intentional or not, of welcoming (inclusion) or barring (exclusion) one or more categories of humankind. All groups are at least minimally exclusive in that, at the very least, *members must profess an interest in a group's *mission and *goals. Exclusion may become problematic when people are denied entry to the group based on questionable criteria such as sex, age, race, religion, and occupation. Shokeid (2001, passim) studied the problems of exclusion from organizational power faced by women trying to assume *leadership positions in a formerly male-dominated gay/lesbian synagogue.

incorporation of a nonprofit corporation: process of obtaining legal recognition of a *nonprofit group in a particular state as a corporate body with limited liability for its directors/officers (Fishman and Schwarz 2000:66–67). Requires articles of incorporation and by-laws, plus an initial meeting (ibid.).

independent foundation: private, nonoperating, grant-making *foundation. In the United States such foundations constitute the largest proportion of all foundations, as determined by number, asset size, and *grants made (Weitzman et al 2002:75).

independent sector: 1. usually a synonym for *nonprofit sector, although 2. the organization *INDEPENDENT SECTOR has unsuccessfully tried to give the term a somewhat narrower meaning, including only groups with formal Internal Revenue Service designations as 501(c)(3) and 501(c)(4), ignoring other tax-exempt and nonregistered nonprofits (cf. Hodgkinson et al. 1992:15). *See* nonprofit sector

INDEPENDENT SECTOR: a national *coalition of *organizations that share a commitment to preserving and expanding *voluntary action, *philanthropy, and other aspects of private initiative for the *public good (O'Connell 1997, book jacket). Established in 1980 with John W. Gardner as founding chairperson and Brian O'Connell as founding president, INDEPENDENT SECTOR is one of the major infrastructure *nonprofit organizations of and for the *nonprofit sector in America (O'Connell 1997, passim). It performs useful research on the nonprofit sector in

America, although overemphasizing *program volunteers, *program volunteering, *philanthropic giving, and *paid-staff nonprofits to the neglect of *grassroots associations, *associational volunteers generally, *social movements, and *deviant nonprofit groups. Such neglect seems to occur because the organization subscribes generally to the *paid-staff nonprofit group flat-earth paradigm, the *status quo/establishment flat-earth paradigm, the *traditional nonmember service flat-earth paradigm, the *angelic nonprofit groups flat-earth paradigm, and the *formalized group flat-earth paradigm (Smith 2000, chap. 10). INDEPENDENT SECTOR also engages in attempts at *lobbying on important sector issues, as well as holding biennially a research conference (website: http://www.independentsector.org).

indigenous group: a *group native to a given society or territory (cf. Anheier 1987, passim). *See also* indigenous nonprofit group

indigenous nonprofit group: an *indigenous group with nonprofit structure (*structure of nonprofit groups) native to the traditional culture and social structure of a particular country. Not a group recently imported from, imposed by, or based primarily in another nation (e.g., nonprofits dealing with transnational relief or developmental aid). Anheier (1987, passim) examines how indigenous *nonprofits and *voluntary associations in Africa affect development there. *See also* Third World development/aid nonprofit

indirect/secondary satisfaction: *satisfaction (senses 1 and 2) that comes indirectly from an experience, such as *volunteering, so-called because helping someone else increases the satisfaction of both that person and the *volunteer (Smith 2000:20). *See also* direct satisfaction; psychic benefit

individual voluntary action: *voluntary action performed by an individual, whether *volunteer action or *quasi-volunteer action. In addition to activity by the individual in formal *nonprofit group contexts (Smith 2000: 22–23), includes certain activity in informal (nongroup) contexts motivated by *voluntary altruism (e.g., *informal service volunteering, *informal economic support activity, *informal interpersonal activity, *informal political participation, *informal religious activity, *informal social innovation activity, and *informal social esthetics activity). Does not include *informal mass media activity, *informal sports and outdoor recreation activity, *informal study activity, *informal cultural activity, informal *hobby activity, or *informal resting inactivity because they have a less clear relationship to *humane core values and voluntary altruism. Smith, Reddy, and Baldwin (1972:160–165) presented an early definition of individual voluntary action, since revised to exclude nonaltruistic action.

industrial union. *See* union

inertia and organizational transformation: tendency for a *nonprofit group to remain unchanged, thereby stifling its transformation in such areas as investment in its physical plant and specialized personnel (Perlmutter and Gummer 1994:235–236).

influence in nonprofits: 1. the capacity of an individual to indirectly cause change in, for example, the conduct of another person or *nonprofit group or the conditions under which either entity operates. 2. influence is also defined as an act in which this capacity is expressed. Influence (both senses) is political when used in governmental settings. In his classic study of *community power, Hunter (1953:161–162) distinguished between (political) influence and *authority. *See also* nonprofit leader

informal action by board: one or more decisions made consensually (*consensus) by the *board of directors of a *nonprofit group that do not involve the formalized procedures (*see* formalization) established by that group. Smith (1992) studied fifty-nine mainly semiformal *grassroots associations in which informal board action was both common and acceptable.

informal amateur activity. *See* informal leisure activity

informal care: care of the *service variety, so-called because it consists of caring for someone as a kind of *informal volunteering as well as caring for someone *within* the family but not necessarily within the household (cf. Whittaker and Garbarino 1983, passim). It is contrasted with health care given by *professionals. Informal care also tends to be more emotionally, or expressively, involved with the *target of this benefit than its professional counterpart. Linsk and colleagues (1992, passim) address themselves to the matter of *compensation for family care of the elderly (*see* imputed value of volunteer work). *See also* informal volunteering; informal service volunteering

informal cultural activity: act of watching, listening, and otherwise consuming as *leisure any of a wide variety of cultural products (e.g., watching television, reading a magazine, attending a concert, watching a football game, going to an art gallery). Informal cultural activity may be done alone or in a *collectivity and, compared with *informal sports and outdoor recreational activity, is passive. It is, we should note, a broader idea than *informal mass media activity, for informal cultural activity also includes nonmass "high culture" (Gans 1974, passim). Such culture is not part of *individual voluntary action, however, because it is not normally motivated by *voluntary altruism. Rojek (2000, passim) critically examines the relationship between leisure and culture.

informal economic activity. *See* economic activity, informal

informal economic system support activity: an act, performed alone or in an *informal group, that supports a socioeconomic system. The act is nonetheless performed in accordance with socioeconomic system support *values, exemplified in advising a friend about a job possibility, discussing a strike with a neighbor who is a union member, and telling an acquaintance how she might improve her small business. Such activity is part of the *nonprofit sector, even though it also supports the business sector (*sector of society). Advising on business strategy on a *meeting of the local *cooperative can also be classified as *voluntary action (Pestoff 1979, passim). In each example social value (*value, humane core) is uppermost, rather than the value of acquiring money or making profit.

informal economy: the entire cash-and-barter-based economy that operates informally outside conventional economic institutions (banks, businesses, stores, etc.) and the national taxation system (e.g., the U.S. Internal Revenue Service) in a society or territory. Sometimes referred to as the underground economy (Carson 1984, passim). Smith (2000:45) says that informal economic activity may be conducted either in groups or by individuals on their own. *See also* economic activity, informal

informal eligibility criteria. *See* member eligibility

informal grassroots association. *See* informal nonprofit group

informal group: *group lacking the minimal properties of a *formal group (Smith, Reddy, and Baldwin 1972:175).

informal group style of operation: everyday functioning of a *nonprofit group, characterized in good part by frequent face-to-face interaction of *members who come to know each other while enacting group roles, which, however, are usually somewhat vague (cf. Smith 2000:77–79). As Kanter and Zurcher, Jr. (1973:387–388), demonstrate, the informal style works best in small *collectivities, where typically it is highly valued. Ianello (1992, passim) describes an important aspect of informal group operation: *decision making through modified *consensus, rather than through *leadership hierarchy.

informal hobby activity. *See* informal leisure activity

informal interpersonal activity: *sociability or *caring or both by an individual involving one or more people outside that person's family (e.g., with friends, neighbors, co-workers, co-religionists). Such activity may occur outside the organizational world. It intentionally provides, in accordance with sociability values (*value, humane core), *intrinsic satisfaction and *psychic benefits for both self and others. In short, as Salamon and Anheier (1992:135) conclude, informal interpersonal activity is *voluntary action and hence part of the *informal sector.

informal interpersonal relations. *See* informal interpersonal activity

informal leader. *See* leader, informal

informal leisure activity: *free-time activity conducted outside *formal group arrangements, as alone or in ephemeral *collectivities or *informal groups. Some *hobbies can be pursued informally, among them, hiking, reading, and making things (e.g., baked goods, furniture). It is likewise with some *amateur activities, including writing poetry, performing chamber music, and playing pick-up hockey. *Volunteering in an informal *self-help group is informal leisure activity (Stebbins 2002:45), as is the pursuit of allotment gardening (Crouch and Ward 1988, passim). Stands in contrast to *formal leisure activity. *See also* leisure activity

informal mass media activity: individual exposure to such mass, or popular (Gans 1974, passim), media as radio, television, movies, videos, other recorded media, the Internet, newspapers, magazines, newsletters, and the like as a primary focus of attention either alone, in a *collectivity, or in an *informal group. Not a part of *individual voluntary action, because it lacks *voluntary altruism. *See also* informal cultural activity

informal member. *See* member

informal nonprofit group: *nonprofit group lacking one or more of the following aspects of a *formal nonprofit: unique name, clear group boundaries (formal list of *analytic members), and clear *leadership structure (routinized *decision-making procedures) (Smith, Reddy, and Baldwin 1972:175).

informal organization: the patterns of informal relationships of power, prestige, friendship, and the like that exist in an *organization (cf. Blau and Scott 1962, chap. 4). Often more important than its formal authority or *power structure. Found in *nonprofit groups as well as in *for-profit organizations and *governmental organizations. Blau and Meyer (1987: 51–54) examine, in greater detail, the nature and role of informal organization in large-scale organizations. Davis (1953, passim) gave an early report on informal organization in a company. Smith (2000:109–112) discusses the tendency toward informal organization in grassroots associations.

informal political participation: *political participation carried out alone or in *informal groups that, in harmony with the relevant political *values, generates mainly *psychic benefits and *intrinsic satisfaction. Examples include voting, political discussion, writing letters to the editor, and contributing money to a candidate (cf. Verba and Nie 1972:31). Some analysts see informal political participation as *voluntary action and hence part of the *nonprofit sector. Others see it as part of the *informal sector (e.g., Salamon and Anheier 1992:135), and some contend that it is just more politics and thus of scant relevance to the nonprofit sector.

informal recruitment. *See* recruitment of members

informal religious activity: *religious activity performed alone or in informal groups, primarily for *intrinsic satisfaction or *psychic benefit and in accord with religious *values (e.g., individual prayer, individual reading of religious material, watching religious TV programs; cf. Stark and Glock 1968, passim). Some analysts see informal religious activity as *voluntary action and hence part of the *nonprofit sector. Others see it as part of the *informal sector (e.g., Salamon and Anheier 1992:135), and some contend that it is just more *religion and thus of little relevance to the nonprofit sector. *See also* devotional activity

informal resting inactivity: individual napping, sleeping, dozing, resting, loafing, and the like. Solitary *leisure activity (cf. Chambré 1987:86). Not part of *individual voluntary action, because it is not motivated by *voluntary altruism. Treated by Kleiber (2000, passim) under the rubric of "relaxation."

informal sector: broad view of the *household/family sector, which includes friendship, neighboring, co-worker relations, and other *informal interpersonal activity as found in cliques, neighbor groups, and co-worker groups. The concept of informal sector also includes *informal leisure activity, but only where the latter is carried out with others. Nonetheless, this conception is problematic, for by treating the area of household and family activities as part of the broader field of informal interpersonal activities, theorists tend to obscure the importance of the former (Van Til 1988:141–143).

informal service volunteer: *volunteer who, outside a *formal group context, provides *service, labor, or time to help others beyond the volunteer's family, doing so primarily for *intrinsic satisfaction or *psychic benefit in accord with service *values. The preferred label for "informal volunteer" (cf. Smith 2000:25). Some analysts see informal service volunteering as part of *voluntary action, broadly conceived of, and hence part of the *nonprofit sector. Others see it as part of the *informal sector (e.g., Salamon and Anheier 1992:135), and some contend that it is just more *leisure and thus not relevant to the nonprofit sector. Weitzman et al. (2002:75) report that *informal volunteering by Americans as a ratio of all types of *volunteering rose from 18.8 percent in 1987 to 24.4 percent in 1998.

informal service volunteering: activity of *informal service volunteers. The preferred label for "informal volunteering." Some analysts see informal service volunteering as part of *voluntary action, broadly conceived of, and hence part of the *nonprofit sector. Others see it as part of the *informal sector and some contend that it is just more *leisure and thus not relevant to the nonprofit sector (Van Til 1988:141).

informal social esthetics activity: individual activity performed outside a formal organizational context (*organization) centered on creating, presenting, or preserving particular stimuli that a certain *public (sense 2) is expected to find intrinsically satisfying. Such activity is performed mainly for *satisfaction (senses 1 and 2) of self and others (cf. Stebbins 2004a:1) rather than for remuneration of the artist. Examples include playing music for people at a party, telling a story to co-workers, producing and showing home videos, dancing or singing informally with others, and exhibiting one's doll collection. These are inherently social activities, even if earlier periods of creativity are usually intensely personal and nonsocial.

informal social innovation activity: *political participation aimed at reform or change of the social system or political system or both that may be carried out at any level of government in accord with social innovation *values. Such innovation—called *"sociopolitical innovation"—may occur formally or informally. Thus a person might contribute formally to a *social movement group as *member or informally as nonmember. Or a person might speak up informally for basic reform as an individual citizen at a public meeting, or serve formally as chair of the *meeting while encouraging those in attendance to express their views. Put otherwise, informal social innovation activity is the informal counterpart of formally organized social innovation, both being instances of *nonprofit sector activity. Rohracher (2003, passim) studied the intersection of formal and informal social innovation as users, producers, and intermediary actors dealt with each other on the question of adoption of two new environmental technologies.

informal socialization. *See* socialization

informal sports and outdoor recreational activity: individual activity performed alone, in a *collectivity, or in an *informal group that involves playing of active sports or games or engaging in other outdoor play activities like walking, jogging, swimming, hunting, fishing, and gardening (for pleasure). Is not part of *individual voluntary action, because it is not motivated by *voluntary altruism. Major (2001, passim on jogging), Bryan (1977, passim on trout fishing), and Crouch and Ward (1994, passim on allotment gardening), among others, have examined this kind of activity,

informal study activity: individual activity alone, in a *collectivity, or in an *informal group that involves centrally focused attention on learning, study, information absorption, education, and knowledge acquisition as *goals. Not part of *individual voluntary action, because it is not motivated by *voluntary altruism and some such activity may even be coerced (as in schoolwork). Stebbins (1993c:130) looked at informal study activity under the heading of "goal-oriented aloneness," where as an effective way to study or work on a complicated project, people try to momentarily isolate themselves.

informal tax-exempt status of nonprofits. *See* tax-exempt status

informal voluntary action. *See* individual voluntary action

informal voluntary group. *See* informal nonprofit group

informal volunteer. *See* informal service volunteer

informal volunteering. *See* informal service volunteering

informal volunteer time. *See* volunteer time

informal work group. *See* work group

informational incentive: a type of *incentive rooted in the desire to learn new information and *knowledge while participating in a *nonprofit group (cf. Knoke 1990:115; Smith 2000:99). *See also* incentive type

infrastructure organization of nonprofit sector. *See* nonprofit sector, infrastructure organization of

in-kind contribution: a contribution (*donation) to a *nonprofit group in the form of physical commodities or physical space/facilities (or sometimes special services). Connors and Wise (1988:35-12 to 35-13) list a variety of possible in-kind contributions businesses may make to nonprofit groups, including various kinds of space and facilities and various products and services. In-kind contributions are generally contrasted with monetary contributions but sometimes include (usually specialized, short-term) *service volunteering.

in-kind matching: business gift in-kind (*gift in-kind, business) of more or less equal value to in-kind gifts that a *nonprofit group has received from other sources. Since such *gifts go unreported as charitable contributions, systematically collected data on the extent to which they are made are unavailable (Weitzman et al. 2002:83–84).

innovation in nonprofits: the planned process of changing a *nonprofit group so it can better achieve its *mission, often based on evaluation (*evaluation of nonprofit groups) of prior group *effectiveness and *impacts (*see* impact of nonprofits/nonprofit sector) (Eadie 1997). Successful nonprofits, especially *paid-staff nonprofit organizations, tend to be continually reinventing themselves and changing consciously to deal with a changing environment, changing clientele, and changing staff characteristics (cf. Light 1998, passim).

inquiry letter. *See* letter of inquiry

in-service training in nonprofits: a job-related educational program provided by an employer (e.g., *paid-staff nonprofit), possibly through a supervisor or specialist, designed to increase work-role effectiveness of a particular group of employees (cf. Macduff 2005, passim). Such training is usually conducted on the job over a short period of time and centers on the latest administrative, scientific, or technological advances in the trainees' occupational area. Reilly and Peterson (1997, passim) describe the in-service training provided to child welfare workers in Nevada. *See also* staff development

insider, societal: the elite and established strata of a society. The most powerful and influential members of society, typically along the lines of a particular institutional sector. C. Wright Mills (1956, passim) studied the power elite as societal insiders in the United States.

insider vs. outsider orientation of nonprofit: 1. (insider orientation) the tendency for a *nonprofit group to direct its benefits to the elite and established strata of the society in which it is located. 2. (outsider orientation) the tendency for a *nonprofit group to direct its benefits to the poorer and less powerful members of the society in which it is located. Use of the term "outsider" (and its opposite, "insider") here expands on the usage introduced by Becker (1963, passim). Historically, nonprofit groups have tended to be insider oriented, but outsider orientation became more common after approximately 1800 (Smith 2000: 88).

institution, alternative: a radically different way, espoused by a minority of people in society, of perceiving, enacting, and experiencing such phenomena as *work, *leisure, *religion, family, politics, education as well as other basic relationships and life activities. Alternative institutions challenge their existing counterparts by calling into question operating assumptions in Western life and by proposing new complexes of *values (Kanter and Zurcher 1973:138).

institutional isomorphism: process that forces an *organization, including *nonprofits, to take on characteristics of other organizations facing the same set of environmental conditions. This process unfolds as all the organizations in question compete for political power and social legitimacy in the society in which they are operating (DiMaggio and Powell 1983:149).

institutionalized sect. *See* sect, established

instrumental goal/group: *goal or *nonprofit group centered on achievement of a condition or circumstance lying beyond the individuals involved, as in *helping outsiders or creating political change. Instrumental goals and groups are typically contrasted with *expressive goals and groups, where focus is principally on the *analytic members of the nonprofit group concerned and their needs and emotions (Gordon and Babchuk 1959, passim). Both concepts are now outmoded, for the most part, being largely subsumed under the twin ideas of *nonmember benefit (*public benefit) and *member benefit, respectively (e.g., Smith 1993, passim; 2000:115). *See also* expressive goal/group

insurrection. *See* rebellion

intensity of participation: the degree to which participation is reasoned or passionate or both as opposed to being ritualistic or routine or both (Kasperson and Breitbart 1974:4).

intensity of volunteer activity: a difficult to measure conceptualization of the *intensity of participation—because it relates to volunteer activity—a measure that goes beyond merely calculating hours of volunteering (Harootyan and Vorek 1994).

intentional community: a *nonprofit group who have chosen to reside in close proximity or in the same building complex and who share an ideology of everyday living, often reformist or utopian, that binds them together in special cooperative (*cooperation) relationships (cf. Bouvard 1975, passim). Although some of these groups share their work and hold their money, land, and buildings in common ownership, being thus *communes, most intentional communities in the United States are not, by strict definition, communes. Anonymous (2000, passim) is a directory of intentional communities in America. McCamant et al. (1994, passim) and Hanson (1996, passim) have written on co-housing (living in buildings in close proximity) as one approach to intentional community. Schehr (1997, passim) views, as a *new social movement, the recent founding of intentional communities in America.

Interdisciplinary Sequential Specificity Time Allocation Lifespan (ISSTAL) model: model devised by Smith et al. (1980, chap. 18, especially pp.

408–409) for explaining individual *leisure activity, including individual *volunteering and *individual voluntary action. It takes a dynamic life-span or longitudinal perspective on human behavior studied in terms of a *time budget/time diary method focusing on the daily allocation of time to various activities. The model also argues that any leisure activity can best be understood by the interdisciplinary combination of predictor variables starting from the more general historical and social contextual variables, then ranging through middle level sociodemographic variables, to more specific personality, intellectual capacities, attitudinal, and retained information variables, down to the most specific situational variables (Smith et al. 1980:414–415, 441). This latter pattern of increasing specificity of predictor variables is termed the "sequential specificity approach." Research on social and political activity (Smith and Macauley 1980, chap. 18 and passim), outdoor recreational activity (Smith and Theberge 1987, passim), and *volunteering (Smith 1994: 256) generally support this model. Support is strongest for the use of as many as possible of the different analytical types of predictors (Smith 1975:260, 1994:256).

interest: Three definitions of this concept bear directly on the *nonprofit sector, all adapted from the *Shorter Oxford English Dictionary*, 5th ed. (2002:1400). 1. the fact or relation of having a share or concern in, or a right to, something such as property or a right or a title. 2. a *benefit. 3. something of importance to an individual or a *nonprofit group. The latter definition is the most general of the three. "Interest" is a widely used commonsense term in the nonprofit sector literature that has never been carefully examined and elaborated and thereby transformed into a scientific concept.

interest group: *nonprofit group formed to influence by way of conventional *political voluntary action the political process and *decision making. Though distinct from social *protest, such groups may nevertheless use *intermediary nonprofits, particularly trade *associations. And though clearly not part of the *nonprofit sector, business firms sometimes act alone as interest groups. Wilson (1990, passim) provides an overview of the complex question of the interest group, as do Berry (1997, passim), Cigler and Loomis (2002), Clawson et al. (1992), Goldstein (1999), Hrebenar (1997), Hula (1999), Lowery and Brasher (2004), McCaghy et al. (2002), Richardson (1993), Thomas (2004), Van Deth (1997), and Wright and Oppenheimer (2003). Thomas and Hrebenar (1996, passim) review American interest groups at the state level. *See also* public interest group; special interest group; self-interest

intergovernmental association: 1. an *association of *governments of one territorial level or another (e.g., SEMCOG, Southeastern Michigan Council of Governments), 2. an *international governmental organization or *intergovernmental organization (IGO); that is, an intergovernmental association with representation from two or more separate national governments (Feld et al. 1994, passim).

intergovernmental organization (IGO): *nonprofit *coalition of national *governments like the United Nations organization (and its many agencies), the Organization of American States [nations], and the North Atlantic Treaty Organization (NATO) (Iriye 2002, passim; Feld et al. 1994; Hawdon 1996, passim; Jordan and Feld 2001; Muldoon 2004; Van de Fliert 1994, passim). The European Union is an IGO that is becoming a regional governmental federation, which organizationally speaking may in time be like the United States of America.

intergroup relations: 1. interaction by individuals representing two or more *groups, usually centered on particular concerns or *interests shared by those groups. Falomir-Pichastor and colleagues (2004, passim) analyzed the role of in-group threat in intergroup discrimination as well as the influence of in-group norms on such discrimination. 2. a term referring to interethnic or interracial relations, now often referred to as multicultural relations (Banks and McGee 1995, passim; Fromkin and Sherwood 1976, passim; Rose 1965, passim).

intermediary: a person or group who links the money and time of *donors with the needs that *nonprofit groups seek to meet (Van Til 1994:58). Furthermore, consultants, trainers, counselors, and program officers serve as intermediaries in the *nonprofit sector. They run their own companies as *intermediary nonprofit organizations or work for *foundations, support centers, *fund-raising firms, and the like. *See also* fund-raising intermediary; nonprofit sector, infrastructure organization of

intermediary nonprofit organization. *See* intermediary; intermediary organization

intermediary organization: general term referring to a *nonprofit group, especially an *association, that mediates between the individual citizen and government, or between other groups or *sectors of society (Van Deth 1997:2). Berger and Neuhaus (1977, passim) wrote a classic statement on the role of what they termed "mediating structures," which empower people in public *social arenas.

intern as volunteer: the proposition that, in internship *programs, the interns are, in fact, *volunteers, or the argument that they should be treated as such. Ellis discusses the pros and cons of this stance in Energize Volunteer Management Update (Nov. 2004) at website http:// www.energizeinc.com. *See also* marginal volunteering

internal activity level. *See* activity level

internal democracy. *See* democracy in nonprofit groups

internal dynamics of nonprofits. *See* processes of nonprofits

internal funding. *See* funding

internal guidance system. *See* guidance system

internal impact. *See* impact of nonprofit groups

internal organizational health. *See* organizational health

internal process. *See* process of nonprofit groups

Internal Revenue Service (IRS) registration of nonprofits: formal process of recognition of *nonprofit groups as tax exempt in the United States in IRS categories 501(c)(1)–(21), 501(d)–(f), 501(k), 501(n), 521, 527–529 (O'Neill 2002:4–5). Encompasses many different categories of *nonprofits, including all *foundations, most *paid-staff nonprofit organizations, but only a small proportion of existing *grassroots associations (Smith 2000:36; Toepler 2003).

internal structure. *See* structure of nonprofit groups

international association. *See* transnational association/nonprofit

international classification of nonprofit organizations (ICNPO): scheme that, based on economic activity, classifies *nonprofit organizations into twelve primary categories and twenty-four subcategories. Salamon and Anheier (1992b, passim), who developed the ICNPO, found that it scores high on five key evaluation criteria: significance, economy, rigor, organizing power, and richness. A partial test of the ICNPO reveals that it outperforms its competitors in terms of its ability to classify diverse types of nonprofit institutions. Smith (1996a) proposes several improvements for the ICNPO.

international governmental organization. *See* intergovernmental organization

international nongovernmental organization (INGO). *See* transnational association/nonprofit; nongovernmental association

international nonprofit. *See* transnational association/nonprofit

International Society for Third Sector Research (ISTR): international association promoting research and education in the fields of *philanthropy, *civil society, and the *nonprofit sector. It emphasizes especially *third sector research in developing countries (Third World) and nations of Central and Eastern Europe. The ISTR, which was founded in 1992, is based in Baltimore, Maryland (website: http://www.istr.org).

international volunteering. *See* cross-national volunteering

Internet activism: *activism carried out using the Internet. Such activism, which may be international in scope, is exemplified in Kahn and Kellner's (2004) article on the "Battle of Seattle" and the use of Web logs. *See also* virtual volunteering

Internet group: a loosely structured, usually *informal group or *collectivity that interacts on the Internet, rather than face-to-face, through chat rooms, bulletin boards, and interactive websites. Rheingold (1993, passim) wrote the first book-length treatment of this phenomenon under the title of *The Virtual Community*. More recently, Brainard and Brinkerhoff (2004) reported on two Internet groups (which they term "Cyber-Grassroots Organizations") that focused on the *problems of Afghanistan. The authors argue that such groups are a new, nonspatially confined, form of *grassroots association. In another study Van Aelst and Walgrave (2002, passim) describe the Internet group and its role in shaping the antiglobalization movement (*social movement). Schuler and Day (2004, passim) discuss the new role of civil society in cyberspace. *See also* online support group

interorganizational field: local and supralocal organizational context of a set of *nonprofit groups, where these groups constitute a recognized area of institutional life (DiMaggio and Powell 1983:148). Thus an interorganizational field consists of, for example, residential communities, interorganizational systems, and network organizations, as they influence the structure and process of the groups. The concept was introduced by Warren (1967, passim). *See also* environment, organizational; population ecology of organizations approach

interorganizational relations (IOR): relationships among a set of two or more *organizations, ranging in intensity from mutual recognition to active partnerships and formation of federations or even mergers (cf. Klonglan and Yep 1972, passim). Nicholls (2003, passim) studied the *problems of forging a new organizational infrastructure for the Los Angeles progressive *community. He identified several mechanisms that have nourished interorganizational relations in this community and made possible collective action.

intrinsic satisfaction: *satisfaction (sense 1) derived by the performer of an activity (e.g., job, *volunteering, other *voluntary action) from the activity in itself (Kelly 1996:23; Lawler 1973, passim). Contrasted with *extrinsic satisfaction, which is gained from conditions external to that activity. Volunteering is believed to give more intrinsic satisfaction than most paid work, in significant part because most people do the second for pay and the first for little or no pay (cf. Stebbins 2004a, chap. 6). *See also* fulfillment

introverted nonprofit group. *See* isolated nonprofit group

inurement prohibition: U.S. Treasury regulations prohibit Internal Revenue Service 501(c)(3) charitable organizations from having their net earnings (*excess revenues) go to insiders, such as funders, directors, and officers, though this is loosely enforced (Fishman and Schwarz 2000:494–495).

investment by nonprofits: 1. the transfer of a *nonprofit group's funds (*resource) not immediately needed for operations into investment vehicles, ranging from interest-bearing bank accounts, money market funds, and certificates of deposit to bonds, stocks, mutual funds, and other investment approaches, all intended to increase the value of idle money. 2. the presence of funds not immediately needed for operations, or not eligible for support of operations (e.g., restricted endowments), in investment vehicles of the kind mentioned in sense 1. Usually present at a minimum when a nonprofit has an *endowment, but is, in any event, part of good *financial management in nonprofits. Kolaric, Meglic-

Crnak, and Svetlik (1995, passim) argue that, in Slovenia, the state must change its *policy toward capital investment by nonprofits, since the current one is stifling their growth.

involuntary dissolution of a nonprofit organization: a *nonprofit organization can be legally forced to dissolve under a variety of circumstances, including abandonment of activity, fraudulent mismanagement, and failure to pay creditors (Fishman and Schwarz 2000:114). *See also* dissolution and distribution of assets of a nonprofit organization

iron cage of bureaucracy: metaphor for the rational side of *bureaucracy that enforces mechanism, depersonalization, oppressive routine, and, hence, suppression of personal freedom for the individual (Weber 1952: 181–182; Gerth and Mills 1958:50).

iron law of oligarchy: tendency, regardless of form of government, for power to become concentrated in the hands of a few individuals. The term was coined by Robert Michels (1915/1959:372–392). Van Til (1988:60–61) examines the validity of this "law" in the *nonprofit sector.

iron triangle, the: interlocking three-way relationship of mutual *influence and *accommodation pertaining among a well-financed *special interest group, the legislative *committee or subcommittee that makes laws in the area of the group's special interest (e.g., education, health, highways, etc.), and the *bureaucracy in Washington, D.C. (or at a state level) that applies these laws (White 1973:71–72; see also Hrebenar 1997:263–265). Thought to be common in America. Although initially applied at the national level, the iron triangle concept has been extended (e.g., by Hamm 1986, passim) to the state level. Often referred to as "subgovernment" (McCool 1990, passim), this approach is extemely important to *interest groups, because it presents "the most pervasive and effective channel for interest group impact on *policy and *program decisions" (Ripley and Franklin 1980:10).

isolated nonprofit group: *nonprofit group with no working ties whatsoever to other such groups or sponsors. Kaplan (1986:24) points out that nonprofit isolation can be reduced by establishing among groups *coalitions and mutual support arrangements that address common concerns through "power in numbers."

isolated nonprofit group flat-earth paradigm: analytic nonprofit model that omits consideration of the environment of *nonprofit groups and their place in the *community and the larger society (Smith 2000:237–238).

isomorphism, coercive: *institutional isomorphism resulting from formal and informal pressures exerted on a particular *organization by other organizations on which the first is dependent (DiMaggio and Powell 1983:150). Among the formal pressures are the obligatory practices set out and enforced by, for example, funding *agencies and *federations of nonprofit groups that require the groups within their jurisdiction to function according to similar annual budget cycles, audited financial reporting, standard operating procedures, and the like.

ISSTAL model. *See* Interdisciplinary Sequential Specificity Time Allocation Lifespan model

issue: a complex of *problems so poorly defined that no obvious solution is immediately evident (McWhinney 1992:62–64). Boris and Krehely (2002:312) discuss the issue of campaign finance reform, the solution to which will affect tax-exempt organizations (*tax-exempt status).

J

job creation for volunteers/members: major administrative function in *nonprofit groups and *volunteer programs that involves designing *volunteer roles and job descriptions that describe what a given *volunteer/ *member is to do, with whom, where, when, and with what expected results. Finding volunteer niches in a larger *paid-staff organization is something of an art, while volunteer roles in *associations tend to be more traditional (*officers, *board members, *committee *members; Battle 1988, chap. 6). Practices of job creation for volunteers are discussed by Connors (1995, chap. 3), Ellis (2002, chap. 2), Fisher and Cole (1993, chap. 2), Thomas and Thomas (1998, passim), and Wittich (2003a, passim).

joint funding: support of a *nonprofit group or *project by multiple *grants from multiple *donors, often *foundations. The website of Whizz-Kidz, the Movement for Non-Mobile Children in the United Kingdom (http:// www.whizz-kidz.org.uk) carries an example of joint funding of some of the services offered by this *charity.

juvenile gang. *See* gang

K

key volunteer. *See* volunteer, key

kibbutz: an Israeli *commune. Gavron (2000, passim) provides a portrait of ten veterans and youths presently living in Kibbutzim, including a look at their views on the future of this institution in a changing world. *See* commune

knowledge: state of being aware of or informed about certain facts, *problems, *issues, procedures, and the like. In the *nonprofit sector knowledge gained through *group experience (as opposed to lectures or written literature, for example) is referred to as "experiential knowledge" (Borkman 1976, passim). Smith (2000:199) notes research that shows most kinds of *grassroots associations provide some information or knowledge to their *members.

Koinonia: Ancient Greek term for a form of *commons that meets five prerequisites: (a) uncoerced *participation, (b) some degree and level of immediacy of common purpose, (c) associated *common pool resources, (d) a degree of mutuality among participants, and (e) social relations that are fair (Finley 1974, passim).

L

labor union. *See* union

Lady Bountiful: a patronizingly generous wealthy woman (originally a character in George Farquhar's play *The Beaux' Strategem*). Smith (2000:17) observes that usage of this term in the *nonprofit sector imbues the practice of *voluntary altruism with a sense of condescension. McCarthy (1990, passim) revisited the Lady Bountiful theme in her book on women and philanthropy. *See also* noblesse oblige

laissez-faire: 1. a doctrine opposing governmental interference in economic affairs beyond the minimum needed to maintain peace and property rights. 2. a philosophy and practice characterized, in the typical case, by an intentional abstention from directing or interfering with personal freedom of choice and action. Concerning sense 2, Ayman (2000:1565–1566) summarizes the research on laissez-faire *leadership vis-à-vis leadership that is democratic (*democracy) or autocratic (*see* dictatorship).

lapsed donor renewal. *See* donor renewal

lateral reciprocity: a form of *reciprocity in which a person engages in *giving or *volunteering in the interests of an *organization or *cause, doing so in part because a friend or family member of that person previously received direct or indirect *benefit through that organization or cause. This concept was suggested by the findings of Chambré (1987) that 24 percent of older adult volunteers had friends or family members who had previously received services from the organization for which they volunteered. *See also* reciprocity; anticipatory reciprocity; concurrent reciprocity; retrospective reciprocity

law and nonprofits/charity: the legal and regulatory aspects of starting and operating a *nonprofit group, which can be quite complex in large, *paid-staff nonprofit organizations (Hopkins 1998, 2001; Mancuso 2004; Silk 2004; Wilbur 2000, chap. 14) or very simple in most *grassroots associations (Smith 2000). Laws relating to charity have a long history, reaching back to the 1601 *Statute of Charitable Uses and earlier (Burlingame 2004:295–305; Luxton 2001, passim).

lawful purpose of *nonprofit corporation: a *nonprofit corporation can pursue any purpose not in violation of the law so long as it does not operate mainly for monetary profit and abides by the *nondistribution constraint (cf. Fishman and Schwarz 2000:72).

leader: 1. one who guides others in an action or an opinion. 2. one who takes the lead in a *social movement or *nonprofit group. Working from both definitions, Harris (1998a:151–152) observes that leaders of *nonprofit groups are often significantly limited by the fact that they direct or manage *volunteers, who can easily quit their group if they define the demands of the their leaders as too disagreeable.

leader, formal nonprofit: *leader occupying an official post or role in a *nonprofit group (e.g., elected officer, *board member, *committee chair). In such groups formal leaders are commonly called *volunteers, especially in *grassroots associations (Smith 2000:152).

leader, informal nonprofit: *one who is a *leader but who does not occupy in a *nonprofit group an official post or role from which to lead. Such people, many of whom are past *formal leaders not presently holding office, can in nonprofit groups, nonetheless, be quite influential (Smith 2000:152).

leader, social movement: one who takes the lead in a *social movement. Baker, Johnson, and Lavalette (2001:5–7) observe that movement leaders are both intellectual and practical with reference to what their movements can and should do and to urging on others the conclusions of their thinking.

leader, succession of: replacement of one *leader by another. Succession is often temporarily stalled in small *nonprofit groups, especially *associations, because finding leaders is typically problematic, and therefore, many incumbent leaders feel obliged to remain at their post until a successor can be found (Smith 2000:160).

leadership: 1. action of being a *leader (senses 1 and 2). Northouse (1997, passim) provides an excellent general coverage of types and theories of leadership with a pragmatic overall approach. Burns (1978, passim) is a classic treatment of leadership, with several chapters of special relevance to *nonprofit group leadership (chaps. 2, 7, 8, 9, 11, 12). Chrislip and Larson (1994, passim) assess collaborative leadership with special reference to civic and nonprofit groups. Bryson and Crosby (1992) discuss leadership for the common good in nonprofits. Light (1998, passim) discusses leadership for sustaining innovation. 2. the leaders of a *group considered together. Leadership appears to be more important in volunteer *nonprofit than in *paid-staff groups, in part because there is less rule-based guidance and more "social momentum" (Adler 1981:44–45) involved in keeping the first in operation. Leadership may be elected by group members or appointed by an existing leader (e.g., president, *executive director) or leadership group (e.g., *board of directors, *executive committee). The leadership of *associations consists generally of elected *officers, *board of directors members, and *committee chairs (Battle 1988, chap. 5; Flanagan 1984, chap. 10; Milligan and Milligan 1965, chap. 4).

leadership, contingency approach to: theoretical perspective centered on the proposition that *leadership (sense 1) emerges from interaction of the person with the situation (Bryman 1996:279; Northouse 1997, chap. 5).

leadership, situational approach to: theoretical perspective centered on the proposition that *leadership (sense 1) needs to be different in different situations, with both directive and supportive components (Hersey and Blanchard 1969, passim; Northouse 1997, chap. 4).

leadership, trait approach to: theoretical perspective centered on the proposition that *leadership (sense 1) emerges from special personality traits of individuals (cf. Northouse 1997. chap. 2; Stogdill 1948, passim). Although the psychological traits of *nonprofit *leaders have been little studied, Bryman (1996:277) found in research on leaders in work *organizations that they, compared with the rank and file, tend to have higher loadings on measures of intelligence, masculinity, and dominance.

leadership, transformational approach to: theoretical perspective centered on the proposition that *leadership (sense 1) is a process that changes and transforms individuals, building on followers needs and values; subsumes visionary and charismatic leadership (Burns 1978, passim; Downton 1973, passim; Northouse 1997, chap. 8). This form of leadership is most appropriate to value-based *nonprofits, including *social movements.

least-developing countries (less-developing countries): A United Nations term synonymous with *Fourth World. Estes (2000, passim), using various social indicators, charts the social development trends between 1970 and 1997 of several least-developing Middle Eastern countries.

least effort, principle of: the generalization that, in pursuing a *goal, a person or animal tends to follow a route requiring minimal effort. Zipf (1949, passim), who wrote a book on this principle, is widely cited in social science circles as having made the definitive statement on it.

legal aspects of nonprofits. *See* law and nonprofits/charity

legal status of nonprofit: 1. concern with whether a *nonprofit group is formally incorporated in a state, province, or nation (cf. Hopkins 1998, passim). 2. concern with whether a *nonprofit is formally tax exempt according to *Internal Revenue Service registration (United States) or its equivalent in other countries (Hopkins 1998, passim; Weisbrod 1992, passim). *Paid-staff nonprofits are nearly always legally constituted in both senses 1 and 2, whereas many *grassroots associations are not so constituted in sense 1 and only informally tax exempt (sense 2) (Smith 2000:109–110).

legislative advocacy by nonprofits. *See* lobbying; lobbyist, interest group

legitimacy, change in nonprofit's: occurs when a *nonprofit group ceases to be an *informal group and becomes one legitimized through a formal relationship with the state, a change usually accomplished by adopting a set of *articles of organization (Perlmutter and Gummer 1994:232).

leisure/leisure time: uncoerced activity undertaken within *free time (cf. Brightbill 1960:4). Uncoerced activity, including *volunteer action, is thus something people want to do and, at a personally satisfying (*satisfaction) level using their abilities and *resources, succeed in doing (Stebbins 2002). Further, as uncoerced activity, leisure is an antithesis to work as an economic function; a pleasant expectation and recollection; a minimum of involuntary obligations; a psychological perception of freedom; and a range of activity running from inconsequence and insignificance to weightiness and importance (Kaplan 1960:22–25). *See also* free time; tertiary time; leisure activity; noncoercion

leisure activity: what a person does in *leisure time, such as watch television, play tennis, or volunteer for the Red Cross (cf. Kelly 1996:19–20). Sometimes referred to as "discretionary activity." Godbey (1999:91–92) discusses several of the conditions that lead people to get involved in particular leisure activities. Though much of modern leisure can be considered part of the *nonprofit sector, free-time activities not motivated by *voluntary altruism, including most individual hedonic leisure (e.g., napping, strolling, daydreaming), lie outside that sector. Thus *voluntary action is typically a leisure activity, especially *pure volunteering. Kelly (1996, pt. 3) discusses the major forms of leisure activity as sports and exercise, outdoor recreation, leisure and the arts, popular culture and the arts, travel and tourism. Various other authors examine aspects of leisure activity at length (e.g., Csikzentmihalyi 1990; Kubey and Csikzentmihalyi 1990; Stebbins 1979, 1992, 1998, 2001, 2002, 2004a; Zolberg 1990; Kaplan 1960; Jackson and Burton 1999; Neulinger 1974; Roberts 1999; Parker 1976; Dumazedier 1988; Pronovost 1998; Kelly 1983, 1987; Kleiber and Mannell 1997; Rojek 2000; and Haworth 1997). *See also* casual leisure; project-based leisure; serious leisure; recreation/recreational activity; satisfaction

leisure class: a stratum of society whose members have income sufficient to enable them to pursue *leisure interests all or most of the time that other people spend working. Some members of the modern leisure class pursue their leisure as *volunteers. Veblen (1899, passim) coined the term and was the first to explore the area extensively.

leisure group: a *nonprofit group (*formal or *informal) devoted to organizing and providing a particular *leisure activity for *members or nonmembers, if not both. Stebbins (2002:17–62) has examined the motivational boost that comes from belonging to or patronizing such leisure entities as small groups, *grassroots associations, *nonprofit groups, and leisure service *organizations. *See also* recreational group

leisure nonprofit group. *See* leisure group

leisure society: a nation or society in which there is very substantial *leisure time and *leisure activity, as contrasted with *occupational activity and (other) *obligatory activity. Haworth (1984, passim) explored the idea of leisure society, setting out five national *policy objectives implied by commitment to building such a society. Subsequently, two books on the subject were published on both sides of the Atlantic (cf. Seabrook 1988; Neulinger 1989).

letter of inquiry: letter from a *nonprofit group to a *foundation or *government agency stating its activities, *programs, and *plans, and asking if the foundation or agency would be interested in a full proposal (*grant proposal) for *grant funds. The Foundation Center (http://www.fnd center.org/learn/faqs/html/letter.html) discusses the importance of this kind of letter and the difficulties in writing one.

letter of intent. *See* letter of inquiry

liability: condition of being liable, of being bound or obliged by law or equity. According to Axelrod (1994:120), *board members of *nonprofit groups in the United States are personally liable for any breach of the duties of care of as well as loyalty and obedience to their *organizations. *See also* charitable immunity and liability; fiduciary obligations of board of directors; risk management; risk management and liability for volunteers/members; risk management in nonprofits

liberal corporatism. *See* neocorporatism

life cycle of nonprofit groups: course, or history, of initiation, development, change, and, possibly, decline of a *nonprofit group. Smith (2000:167–194) examines many of the forces that influence the life cycles of *associations. Bowen et al. (1994, chap. 9) examine data on the life cycle of paid-staff nonprofits. Hall (1996, chap. 10) reviews research on the life cycle of organizations more generally.

life span of nonprofit groups: period of duration of a *nonprofit group, which among *grassroots associations, even if they are successful, tends to be relatively short (Smith 2000:77). Bowen et al. (1994, chap. 6) examine exit or death rates of nonprofits generally and find higher rates for younger organizations (p. 104)—a liability of newness.

limitations on board powers: condition that the board of directors in a nonprofit with a membership structure has restrictions on its powers such that the board is generally subject to control by the membership in major matters as well as in elections and removal of board members (Fishman and Schwarz 2000:147).

limitations on charity lobbying and political campaign activities: Internal Revenue Service (IRS) 501(c)(3) charitable organizations qualify for this tax exemption only if they do no substantial lobbying and participate in no political campaigns for or against any candidate for public office (private foundations can do no lobbying at all) (Fishman and Schwarz 2000:520–521). There is an alternative, complex 501(h) Expenditure Test Election that nonprofits can elect to fall under instead (Fishman and Schwarz 2000:544–552). IRS 501(c)(3) nonprofits can form 501(c)(4) nonprofits affiliated with and controlled by the former for lobbying and other political activities (Fishman and Schwarz 2000:568–569).

limited monarchy. *See* monarchy

limited-purpose foundation: a *foundation that gives *grants only in one or very few areas of activity, such as the environment or higher education (the Cleveland Foundation Glossary of Terms found on its website: http://www.clevelandfoundation.org).

linkage of nonprofit groups: formal tie, vertical or horizontal, connecting a *nonprofit to another group, be it a business, a governmental unit, or an *organization in the *nonprofit sector. Some linkages are nominal, which preserve the nonprofit's *autonomy, whereas others are heavily binding. The latter tend to limit that autonomy (Smith 2000:80). *See also* interorganizational relations

literature of the nonprofit sector: the research literature on the *nonprofit sector is vast, as can be inferred from the voluminous references in books by, for example, McAdam and Snow (1997) and Smith (2000) on major types of *nonprofit groups. Free-standing bibliographies of this literature give further evidence (e.g., Layton 1987; Pugliese 1986; Smith and Freedman 1972; various authors: *The Literature of the Nonprofit Sector: A Bibliography with Abstracts,* annual 1989–1996, New York: Foundation Center); and the online version of the last-mentioned source is even better evidence: Researching Philanthropy: Literature of the Nonprofit Sector; the Foundation Center's Online Catalog with Abstracts, available from 1995 from the Foundation Center in New York. N=22,953 full bibliographical citations, as noted on 8 November 2004 (http://www.lnps.fdn center.org). Searching the WorldCat online (mostly) book database from First Search reveals on the same day 1.20 million hits for the key word "church," 621,893 for the key word "union," 33,000 for the key word "volunteer," 29,643 for the key word "civil society," 18,965 for the key word "nonprofit," and so on. A search of articles on nonprofit sector topics would give even larger numbers by perhaps a factor of ten or more (estimate by Smith).

lobby. *See* interest group

lobbying: activity of *lobbyists. Smucker (1991, passim) provides a comprehensive guide for the nonprofit lobbyist, as does Dekieffer (1997, passim) for citizen lobbyists more generally. Hrebenar (1997, pts. 1 and 2) discusses *foundations, *strategies, and *tactics of lobbying (see also Wright and Oppenheimer 2003, passim). Goldstein (1999, passim) examines grassroots, or "outside," lobbying, which involves lobbying attempts to influence government (especially the federal government) by influencing the attitudes and behavior of the *public (sense 1).

lobbying incentive: a type of *nonprofit group *incentive rooted in the desire to wield political influence on public or governmental decision makers and administrators (Knoke 1990:115; Smith 2000:102). *See also* incentive type

lobbyist: someone who engages in *lobbying, usually as a paid, full-time advocate (*activist) of the *policies or *issues of a particular private group, be it a business, *political action committee, and the like or a *nonprofit group (cf. Berry 1997, chap. 5; Greenwald 1977, chap. 3). Lobbyists attempt to communicate with and influence in person legislators and other government officials. Gibelman and Kraft (1996, passim) have examined the many parameters of a lobbyist *program designed for voluntary human service *agencies. *See also* special interest group; public interest group; interest group

local exchange trading system (LETS). *See* time-money scheme

local union. *See* union, local

lodge: historically an adult male social *club (cf. Ferguson 1937, passim), though recently, some have begun to admit female *members. Bee (2002, passim) examined the change in focus of the Old Elm Tree Lodge in Britain (part of the Independent Order of Oddfellows), as it evolved from a preoccupation with organizational and legislative *issues to evaluation of the society's relevance to the community of which it was a part.

loneliness: the negative feeling component of a state of *social isolation (cf. Weiss 1973). Bernikow (1986, passim) and Pappano (2001, passim) have written on the increased prevalence of loneliness in America in recent times.

long-range planning in nonprofits: *planning done for an extended period such as five or ten years in a *nonprofit group. It often supplements the annual planning exercise. Shostak (1998, passim) highlights the importance of long-range planning for American labor *unions as well as the various approaches to achieve this.

lyceum: a scientific, literary, or musical *association, with classical aspirations or pretensions, that presents public readings, lectures, concerts, and similar events (Bode 1956, passim). Now both the term and the group are relatively uncommon, whereas both were used more frequently in the latter 1800s and first half of the 1900s. Ray (2002, passim) analyzes the impact of the appearance of Frederick Douglass, noted statesman, abolitionist, and journalist, on the lyceum circuit.

M

mainstream nonprofit group: *nonprofit group oriented toward preserving the status quo, which generally avoids *protest activities and fundamental deviance (*fundamentally deviant nonprofit group; Smith 2000:226–227). Such groups are dominated by *societal insiders. Brudney's (1990, passim) manual on mobilizing *volunteers in public agencies (*nonprofit agency) for *public service concentrates on mainstream nonprofit groups.

management: 1. action and manner of managing; application of skill or care in the use, treatment, manipulation, or control of things or people or in the conduct of an enterprise, operation, and the like (cf. Drucker 1974, 1995, passim). Mason (1984, passim) has attempted to identify the manifold features of *nonprofit group management. In another book, Mason (1996, passim) focuses on leading and managing the expressive or emotional aspects of nonprofit groups. 2. the set of individuals in an *organization responsible for managing it. *See also* nonprofit management

management control system: set of formal or informal organizational procedures that, at least in principle, works to ensure effective and efficient use of the *resources of a *nonprofit group (Young 1994:465–466).

manager. *See* nonprofit manager

mandated citizen participation. *See* government mandated citizen participation

mandated nonprofit group participation: *participation in a *program of a *paid-staff nonprofit group required of the participant by government (cf. Gittell 1980, passim) or by a secondary or higher educational institution (cf. Wade 1997, passim). In the first case the *nonprofit group itself is also typically government mandated. Smith's (2000:202) review of the literature on evaluation of this type of *organization reveals that it has generally failed to reach its *goals. However, *service learning in schools, even when mandated, tends to have positive effects (cf. Janoski et al. 1998, passim; Wade 1997, passim). *See also* community service sentence; government mandated citizen participation

mandatory community service: 1. synonymous with *community service sentence. 2. refers, more broadly, to feeling obligated to do such *service to gain social acceptance, or graduate from school (usually high school), as illustrated in the study by Janoski, Musick, and Wilson (1998, passim), who found that *volunteer work undertaken as mandatory community service in high school does generate long-term *benefits. *See also* marginal volunteering

map of nonprofit sector: metaphor used by Smith (2000:13–15) to describe and classify the various types of intellectual orientation toward the *nonprofit sector. He classified these orientations according to whether they fit the metaphor of "flat-earth" (*metaphor, flat-earth nonprofit sector) or "round-earth" (*metaphor, round-earth nonprofit sector).

mapping the nonprofit sector. *See* mental discovery of the nonprofit sector

march: social *protest activity in the form of first assembling and then walking together in a long file to a specified location, usually while carrying large signs bearing messages related to the *cause (Sharp 1973, passim). When the location is a site of power of those against whom the protest is directed, this is referred to as *direct action protest (Carter 1974, passim). Otherwise, it is *symbolic protest. Cowlishaw (2003, passim) discusses the march in 2000 by massive numbers of Australians protesting recent revelations of violence, disorder, and misery in Australian indigenous *communities.

marginal volunteering: *volunteering wherein the *volunteer feels significant moral coercion to agree to do it. Depending on the activity, a certain range of choice of activity is available to the *volunteer, but choice that is nonetheless guided substantially by extrinsic *interests or pressures, by influential forces lying outside the *volunteer activity itself. Stebbins (2001:4–6) discusses six types of marginal volunteering. *See also* volunteering as leisure; mandatory community service; community service sentence; intern as volunteer; obligation; anticipatory reciprocity; employment-based volunteering

market approach to nonprofit groups: analysis of *nonprofit groups according to their place in a *market economy. Hammack and Young (1993:3–4) hold that this approach must consider three questions: (a)

How do nonprofits acquire the *resources needed to survive and fulfill their *missions? (b) How are public *policies designed for profit-making businesses applied to nonprofits that operate in the marketplace? (c) How do we understand the interrelationship among nonprofits, for-profit organizations (*for-profit group), and government at all levels, running from regional to international? *See also* mixed-form market

market economy. *See* economy, market

market failure. *See* private market failure

market transfer. *See* exchange

marketing in nonprofits: 1. *nonprofit group fund-raising. 2. more broadly, the art of selling the general public and public-in-contact (*clients, *board, staff, *volunteers, *donors, *members, and other *nonprofit group affiliates) on the value and importance of a particular nonprofit so they will be disposed to donate to, work for, or use this group. This process is an expanded version of what used to be called "public relations" (Wilbur 2000, chap. 8). Several authors have written books or chapters on the subject (e.g., Andreason 1995; Fine 1992; Gainer and Moyer 2005; Herron 1997; Horvath 1995; McLeish 1995; Self and Wyman 1999; Wilbur 2000, chap. 3; Wolf 1999, chap. 5).

mass canvass: a *program of dwelling-to-dwelling, in-person communication covering a particular territory, usually carried out by a *nonprofit group with political, religious, or philanthropic *goals. Political candidate *organizations, some *charities, some *religious groups (e.g., Jehovah's Witnesses), and some other *nonprofits like Boy Scouts or Girl Scouts rely substantially on mass canvassing. Wielhouwer (2000, passim) studied political party canvassing in American federal elections running from 1952 to 1996 to learn that African-Americans are contacted this way much less than their proportional representation in the voting age public.

mass meeting. *See* community meeting

mass mobilization: the visible amassing of individuals around an *issue (Checkoway 1995). Mass mobilization can take many forms and does not require that organizational forms be inputs or outputs of the mobilization. It is, as a form of *empowerment, primarily oriented to individual involvement. Mass mobilizations are often temporary and can generate their own repression.

mass society (theory of): a set of propositions centered on the proposition that size, density, anonymity, and other characteristics of modern society have, together, suppressed the tendency for people to engage in *political participation and *associational activity (Kornhauser 1959, passim). This has led, in turn, to long-term decline in *participation in the *nonprofit sector and in *civil society. Lee (2002, passim) examines the relationship between the theory of mass society and current globalization theory.

matching grant: an arrangement by which *nonprofit groups raise money.

In this arrangement a nonprofit promises to raise or allocate funds equivalent to or as a percentage of the amount received over a specified period from an external matching source. By entering into a matching-grant arrangement with such a source, the nonprofit must normally identify particular *programs or *projects for funding that the source also wants funded. The precariousness of matching-grant arrangements is evident in Jones's (1982, passim) study of *funding village health workers in Senegal.

material benefit: a reward, or advantage, that can be acquired with money such as through trade or the marketplace. Uphoff (2000, passim) presents a case study from Sri Lanka showing how two forms of *social capital can produce substantial material benefits for a group of farmers. *See also* psychic benefit; utilitarian incentive

material incentive. *See* utilitarian incentive

meaning of volunteering and volunteer work. *See* voluntary altruism; satisfaction

means of achievement model of organizational effectiveness: evaluation based on assessment of how well various collective decisions (the means) have contributed to an *organization's success in reaching its *goals (Murray and Tassie 1994:307–308).

measure, economic: a monetary quantity that helps describe a *group and that is determined by employing a monetary measuring scale or instrument. Common economic measures of *nonprofit groups include amount of *revenue, size of *budget, and number and value of *assets (see Smith 2000:119–120).

mediating structure. *See* intermediary organization

meeting: 1. private or public gathering of people for such purposes as entertainment, discussion, legislation, or worship. 2. all the people attending a meeting. 3. the act of getting together in a meeting (*Shorter Oxford English Dictionary*, 5th ed. 2002:1737).

meeting in nonprofits: a planned in-person interaction for a specified collective purpose, ranging from small staff gatherings to large (e.g., annual or special event) *conferences with hundreds or thousands of attendees (Tropman 2003; Wilbur 2000, chap. 7). Meetings vary in the degree of formality and specificity of agenda, running from rigidly scheduled board (*board of directors, *board of trustees) meetings or conferences to essentially open *support group and *grassroots association meetings having a discussion topic but no agenda (e.g., Rudy 1986, passim).

member: one who belongs to or forms a *group or assembly (including a church congregation; Harris 1998a:215). Some members of *nonprofit groups are "active"; that is, they participate in some way in group affairs (cf. Smith 2000:51–52). The rest are qualified as "nominal," as "on-paper-only" members (ibid.:181). "Official members" are those listed on the group's *membership roll, those who, if required, have paid their membership *dues. But in nonprofit groups, some active members may belong informally; they are neither listed on the membership roll (if any) nor have they paid dues (if any) (cf. Smith 1992b, passim). Putnam (2000, passim) argued that, in the United States, there has been a decline in number of official members in nonprofit groups that require frequent, direct interaction with nonmembers who members know little or not at all. *See also* volunteer; paper member; analytic member

member analysis: study of *members of a *nonprofit group designed to reveal either inductively or by pre-established criteria certain member characteristics. Rothbart and John (1985, passim) examined the perceptions of intergroup contacts among a sample of students, using established scales to measure the traits the latter saw in outgroup members.

member, analytic: *member of a *nonprofit group who regularly provides *services that help meet the *operative goals of that group (Smith 2000: 7).

member benefit: something desirable that *members obtain by dint of belonging to a particular *nonprofit group. Smith (1993, passim) contrasts *member benefits with *public benefits.

member benefit association: a *member benefit nonprofit group organized as an *association (cf. Smith 2000:114–117). The labor union is a member benefit association. Stepan-Norris and Zeitlin (1996, passim) examined the rise of an *industrial union at an automotive plant in the United States. In particular they looked at the difficulties the organizers encountered as they strove to create a *collectivity that would effectively benefit its *members.

member benefit nonprofit group: *nonprofit group, often an *association, whose principal *goal is to benefit and serve its *members rather than nonmember outsiders. O'Neill (1994, passim) considers the philanthropic (*philanthropy) dimensions of member benefit *organizations.

member benefit organization: a formalized (*formal group) version of *member benefit nonprofit group (O'Neill 2002, chap. 11).

member benefit sector. *See* subsector

member eligibility: being entitled to or qualified for admission as *member of a *nonprofit group. Eligibility criteria for such groups, which may be formal, informal, or mixed, can range from extremely narrow to extremely wide (Smith 2000:83).

membership: 1. the condition of being *member of a particular *group or *collectivity; that is, having mere affiliation with a *group, *church, or *organization, formal or informal, voluntary or involuntary, as broadly defined by Ellis and Noyes (1990). May or may not involve *giving or *volunteering over and above the requirement of affiliation. 2. the total set of *members of a group.

membership association. *See* association

memorial gift: sum of money given, usually, to a *nonprofit organization by an individual or another organization in memory of a particular person. An important motive for memorial giving is to leave a permanent remembrance, using the donated funds to name a *program, building, scholarship, endowed chair, and the like in honor of the memorialized person (Brakeley Jr. 2001:746).

mental discovery of the nonprofit sector: process by which the *nonprofit sector is mapped, primarily through intellectual efforts such as survey, speculation, and library research, as opposed to directly experiencing this sector, as by *volunteering. Framing his observations in the imagery of Zerubavel's (1992:30–35) "mental discovery" of America, Smith (2000: 245) argues that such discovery of the nonprofit sector is still going on and is in its early stages.

mentor: an experienced and trusted advisor or guide. The *Shorter Oxford English Dictionary,* 5th ed. (2002:1747) indicates that the word, of Greek origin, was the name of the man who guided Telemachus, Odysseus's son, and was probably chosen for its relationship to words meaning to think, remember, counsel.

merger of nonprofits: coalescence of two or more pre-existing *nonprofit groups into one new nonprofit, with most of the *paid staff and *volunteers of the earlier groups being present in the combined new group, usually under a new or altered name (Bailey and Koney 2000, chap. 10; McLaughlin 1998). Mergers of nonprofits tend to spring from previous *collaborations and *alliances.

metaphor, astrophysical dark matter: figure of speech denoting, by analogy, those parts of the *nonprofit sector (e.g., *grassroots associations, *associational volunteers) that, at present, because they have been relatively little studied, are poorly understood (Smith 2000:12–13). The dark matter metaphor has been picked up in subsequent articles (e.g., Brainerd and Brinkerhoff 2004:32S).

metaphor, flat-earth nonprofit sector: figure of speech denoting, by analogy, those *paradigms bearing on the *nonprofit sector that omit consideration of some major part of it, overemphasize one part while giving inadequate attention to its opposite, or view as unimportant this entire sector (Smith 2000:13–14, 219–238). *See also* the following flat-earth paradigms: "nonprofit sector is unimportant"; three-sector model of society; paid-staff nonprofit group; status quo/establishment; social movement/protest; traditional nonmember service; modern, member benefit, self-help, and advocacy; angelic nonprofit groups; damned nonprofit groups; "money is the key"; distinctive nationalist focus; purposive type; antihistoricism; developed world; formalized groups; secularist focus; sociodemographic participation predictors; isolated nonprofit group

metaphor, round-earth nonprofit sector: figure of speech denoting, by analogy, the *paradigm bearing on the *nonprofit sector that was developed to correct the omissions and over- and underemphases of the flat-earth nonprofit sector paradigms (*paradigm, flat-earth nonprofit sector). Smith (2000:238–240) provides an extensive outline of the round-earth nonprofit sector paradigm as expressed through this metaphor.

militia: 1. a *citizen militia. Discussed by Corcoran (1995) and Karl (1995). 2. historically in the American colonies, a *volunteer military unit, called on only occasionally, whose purpose was to defend a *community or other territory from marauders, Native Americans, or foreign invasion (Shy 1976, passim). Donelan (2004, passim) studied the websites of *hate groups and citizen militias in South Dakota. She found that the first concentrated on race or citizenship or both, while the second were concerned with such matters as strict interpretation of the Constitution, fundamentalist religious beliefs, and protection of or from the *government.

mimetic process: imitation by a new *nonprofit group of the operation and organization of similar groups seen by the first as being successful in these two areas (DiMaggio and Powell 1983, passim; Smith 2000:173–174).

minister: a *religious functionary, usually in a Protestant church, although some use the term more broadly (Harris 1998b:215; Ranson et al. 1977, passim).

minority report: a statement of dissenting (*dissent) conclusions or opinion of a minority of *members of the *group or *committee, stating why they disagree with the majority of members. Creighton (1977, passim) analyzed the minority report that accompanied the majority Bullock Report on industrial democracy in the 1970s in Britain.

mission: central purpose for which a *nonprofit group is established (cf. Seiler 2001, passim). Salamon (1994:95) says that, in one sense, mission orientation is the basic distinguishing characteristic of *nonprofit groups. By contrast for-profit organizations (*for-profit group) have as their raison d'être the pursuit of profit.

mixed-form market: a market for a particular *good or * service simultaneously served by *nonprofit, *for-profit, and governmental groups (Marwell and McInerney 2005:7). *See also* market approach to nonprofit groups

mixed nonprofit group. *See* balanced volunteer/paid-staff group

mob: an unruly or disorderly informal *collectivity, usually bent on some form of mischief, destruction, or criminal activity (Miller 1985:238). Lofland (1990:429) classifies a mob as a hostile *crowd.

Model Nonprofit Corporation Act, revised: a model statute or act for use by states that sets forth the nature, types, conditions, and laws pertaining to nonprofits of all types (cf. Fishman and Schwarz 2000:liii and passim).

model of society: a theoretical and conceptual representation of society centered, in the case of research on the *nonprofit sector, on the number and kinds of sectors comprising it. Smith (2000:221–222, 244–245) presents four such models: two-, three-, four-, and five-sector (*see* sector of society).

modern, member benefit, self-help, and advocacy flat-earth paradigm: the *nonprofit sector model that tends to ignore traditional *nonmember benefit, *personal social service *nonprofit groups and their affiliated *volunteers, as though such groups were no longer of value (Smith 2000: 229).

monarchy: a form of *government of a society or other territory in which a king or queen (or both)—the monarch—holds substantial power and highest societal prestige. (a) In an *absolute monarchy* or *divine right monarchy*, the power held by the monarch is essentially absolute power and unlimited authority over all people in the society or territory (Lipset 1995, passim). This is the most traditional form of *dictatorship. (b) A *limited monarchy* or *constitutional monarchy* is a society in which the rule of a monarch (or other noble leader) is strictly limited by a constitution or charter, and, in the past two centuries, the main political power resides in a legislature or parliament, which is at least partially elected by the citizens of the country or territory (Lipset 1995, passim). *Nonprofits are relatively rare in absolute monarchies but quite common in limited monarchies, especially if they are industrial or post-industrial societies. Wittrock (2004, passim) examines the evolution of the Swedish monarchy in the making of the nation of Sweden. *See also* democracy; dictatorship

monastery: 1. a building or set of buildings for the residence, religious activities, and work of a male *religious order. 2. a male religious *commune inhabiting such a building(s) (Pennington 1983, passim). Sharma (1999, passim) studied credit practices and economic transactions occurring in early twentieth-century India between monasteries (sense 2) and two groups of artisans.

monasticism: the system or condition of residing in a monastery or convent, leading an ascetic life separate from the world and larger society (cf. N. Warren 2001); dates back nearly two thousand years in Christianity (Pennington 1983, passim).

money and property in the nonprofit sector: two economic resources that tend to be found in significant amounts only on the *paid-staff area of the *nonprofit sector (vis-à-vis *volunteer nonprofits). Glamorous as money and property are, Smith (2000:56) argues that this sector, as a whole, is nevertheless mainly about people's time, attitudes, emotions, *ideologies, and the like and not about matters like economic *resources, money, and property. That is, *voluntary altruism is the key underlying value.

"money is the key" flat-earth paradigm: nonprofit sector model that money is the most important *resource of *nonprofit groups, an approach that thereby ignores other resources of these groups such as the time, effort, and *voluntary altruism of their *members (Smith 2000:231).

monomorphic nonprofit group: unique *nonprofit group, or one not vertically affiliated at either the local or the supralocal level with any other larger, umbrella group or *organization (Smith 2000:80). *See also* polymorphic nonprofit group

moral standard: principle of human conduct that, relative to a given issue, sets out what is right and wrong, good and bad. Jeavons (1994:187–192) considers the role of *ethics and moral standards in *nonprofit management. Synonym for "moral norm," as used in discussing *deviance in nonprofits and *deviant groups. *See also* morality; ethics

morale in nonprofits: the mental and emotional outlook of a *volunteer in or *member of a *nonprofit group expressing that person's hope for, confidence in, and willingness to work toward any or all aspects of the group's *goals, *programs, and *mission. Morale can be a critical *problem for *nonprofit management, as Hohl (1996, passim) found in her study of flexible *volunteer service arrangements.

morality: 1. branch of knowledge dealing with right and wrong; ethics (Becker and Becker 1992, passim. 2. moral conduct, the moral side of human behavior. 3. quality of being moral, degree of conformity by a person to a *moral standard. Jeavons (1994:187–192) treats morality (senses 2 and 3) in *nonprofit groups, using the vehicle of *ethics to consider morality among *professionals. *See also* deviance in nonprofits; deviant group; ethics

mosque: 1. the local religious *congregation of the religion of Islam (Macaulay 2003, passim). 2. the building in which such a congregation meets (Frishman and Khan 1994, passim). Kahera (2002, passim), in a study of urban mosques (sense 1) in the United States, found that they both include and shape the ethnic, racial, and religious identities of their worshippers as well as communicate universal *values concerning humankind.

motivating volunteers/members: major administrative function in *nonprofit groups and *volunteer programs that involves providing rewards and *incentives, both formally and informally, to *volunteers so that they are inspired to perform well in their *volunteer role and to remain in the program. Whereas some of this *motivation comes from *recognition of volunteers and *members, this administrative function is broader, for it includes the general maintenance of volunteer *morale. Connors (1995, chaps. 2, 11), Fisher and Cole (1993, chap. 4), Ilsley (1990, passim), and Moore (1985, passim) offer practical advice on motivating and rewarding volunteers. Smith (2000, chap. 4) reviews research on *grassroots association *ideology and *incentive as motivating forces for members.

motivation: 1. act or action of motivating someone. 2. stimulus (conscious or unconscious), *incentive, motive, and the like for action toward a goal. 3. state and degree of being motivated, of having purpose and direction to behavior. Emmons (1997, passim) reviews recent literature and earlier history of the concept of motivation, consistent with these definitions. Brudney (1994:290) observes that effective *volunteer programs link client demands on *nonprofit groups with the various motivations (sense 2) that *volunteers have for contributing their time. *See also* motivating volunteers/members

motive talk: statements made by participants, when asked about why they engage in *voluntary action, or more narrowly, *volunteering. This simple-minded approach to psychology and *motivation assumes that people can analyze themselves accurately and completely and, moreover, are willing and able to communicate the results of this analysis to investigators (Smith 1994a:256–257).

motorcycle club. *See* gang

motorcycle gang. *See* gang

muckraking perspective in the nonprofit sector: view that omits the mainstream majority of *nonprofit groups, while overemphasizing and sometimes even sensationalizing the negative facets of some of them (Smith 2000:230–231). In part because they are more visible, *paid-staff nonprofits are more often subjected to such treatment than *grassroots associations.

multiculturalism. *See* pluralism, ethnic

mutual aid: 1. people in a locality helping each other from time to time in a neighborly way. 2. people in a *member benefit group helping each other from time to time with a life *problem. 3. the practice of people helping each other deal with a common problem. Kropotkin (1914) wrote the first major book on mutual aid among animals and humans. Humphreys (1998, passim) found that *self-help groups for drug addicts lowered demand for professional treatment, while in most instances still providing effective treatment.

mutual aid group: a *member benefit association whose central *goal is to arrange for *members to help each other with a life *problem like alcoholism, drug addiction, gambling, overeating, a handicap, or an illness (Lavoie et al. 1994, passim). Many mutual aid groups use the twelve-step approach (Beattie 1990:229–240). For example, Kurtz's (2002, passim) analysis of Alcoholics Anonymous and the disease concept of alcoholism reveals that this mutual aid group is mainly responsible for neither the origins nor the promulgation of the idea but rather for broadening it by emphasizing "the spiritual." *See* self-help group; twelve-step group; member benefit group

mutual benefit group. *See* member benefit group

mutual benefit organization (MBO): a formal *association whose central *goal is to encourage *members to help each other in specified ways or consider a particular life *issue or *problem, be it economic, social, health-related, or what have you. This is a very broad category, including *unions, *farmers' associations, *trade associations, *mutual aid groups, *fraternal associations, *homeowners associations, *support groups, and *self-help groups (O'Neill 2002:209). *See also* member benefit group

mutual obligation: shared sense of obligation toward each other felt among those who help and those who are helped. Mutual obligation is also expected between government and the *citizens who benefit from its *services, in that the first must provide and the second must make proper use of the provision (e.g., look for work while on unemployment insurance, follow medical advice while under care at a state-supported clinic). Popenoe (1996, passim) argued with reference to the federal Aid to Families with Dependent Children program that to place a cap on payments to families is to call for increased mutual obligation between state and citizen.

mutualistic community. *See* commune

N

narrow definition of nonprofit sector: sum of all *volunteer altruism, all *voluntary action, all *volunteers, and all *volunteer groups (Smith 2000:27). Compare with *broad definition of nonprofit sector.

national association. *See* national voluntary association

national conference: a *conference drawing *participants from many parts of a nation. Commonly held annually or biennially by *national voluntary associations. The vast majority of associations in the *nonprofit sector hold annual national conferences, which are described well in advance on their websites (e.g., http://www.arnova.org [*ARNOVA]; http://www.nrpa.org [National Recreation and Parks Association]).

national congress. *See* national conference

national meeting. *See* national conference

National Opinion Research Center's (NORC) classification of nonprofit groups: one of several purposive-type classification schemes for *nonprofit groups and, in this case, mainly associations. This scheme is used from time to time by NORC in its General Social Survey of the population of the United States (e.g., Verba and Nie 1972:42). Website: http://www.norc.uchicago.edu.

national service: the concept or *program requiring all citizens to serve their nation, usually during their late teens or early twenties, by doing a term (e.g., one or two years) in the armed services or, alternatively, by doing *social service work in, for example, a *nonprofit agency, an *association, or a special national service *stipended volunteer program like Americorps or the Peace Corps. Moskos (1986, passim) discusses national service for country and *community, as do Eyre (2003, passim) and Van Til (1995, passim). Dionne et al. (2003, passim) contains an up-to-date review by various authors of issues in national service, including whether it should be compulsory. Hackenberg (2003, passim) profiles the Peace Corps.

national studies of nonprofit sector. *See* nonprofit sector, national studies of

National Taxonomy of Exempt Entities (NTEE): one of several purposive type classification schemes of *nonprofit groups. The NTEE, which was developed by the Foundation Center and the National Center for Charitable Statistics at INDEPENDENT SECTOR and reported on by Hodgkinson and Toppe (1991, passim), classifies these groups according to their major purpose (e.g., arts, education, health, etc.) and structural type (e.g., alliance, professional society, research institute, public education, etc.). *See also* exempt organization

national voluntary association: *nonprofit *association serving or purporting to serve most or all of a nation. Compared with regional and local groups, national voluntary associations tend to rely more on *paid staff and have larger *memberships and numbers of *employees. They also tend to be older as well as richer in *revenue and equity (Smith 1992a, passim). Knoke (1990, passim) studied the internal dynamics of a sample of national associations. Delgado (1986, passim) described the origins and activities of ACORN (Association of Community Organizations for Reform Now), a national association. Carter (1961, passim) examined big national health associations in America. *See also* association

Native American religion: one or all of the *religions of Native Americans through their history (cf. Hirschfelder and Molin 2000, passim; Johnstone 1992:263–272).

natural helper: non-kin lay people turned to for advice and support. Natural helpers can be trained and mobilized into an effective *volunteer force to supplement kin support and existing formal support *services (Milligan et al. 1987).

need: the physical, psychological, economic, cultural, and social requirements for personal survival, well-being, and *fulfillment (Barker 2003: 291). *See also* public need

need assessment: systematic appraisal of a target category of nonmembers (*target of benefits) to learn about their *needs, in particular, their *problems, *resources, possible solutions, and obstacles to solving the problems. Such assessment is done with an eye to establishing priorities for action by an appropriate *nonprofit group. As McCurley (1994:513–515) notes, *nonprofit groups must determine how their *volunteers can be most effectively used to meet the needs identified in these assessments.

negative social capital. *See* capital, negative social

neighborhood association: 1. a *grassroots association whose *members are drawn from a given urban neighborhood. 2. a *grassroots association whose *members are drawn from a given urban neighborhood and that has as it primary *goal the maintenance, protection, and/or improvement of that neighborhood (Berry et al. 1993, passim). Dilger (1992, passim) reviews some of the literature on neighborhood associations. Austin (1991, passim), in a study of fifty-eight neighborhood associations in Oklahoma City, concluded that age, race, and socioeconomic status are positively correlated with level of *complexity of *organizational structure. *See also* homeowners association; neighborhood nonprofit group

neighborhood meeting: a *meeting to which all residents of a given urban neighborhood are invited. Usually held to discuss a particular neighborhood *issue or *problem. May be called by a *neighborhood association or other organizer(s). Blokland (2001) studied how the elderly in a neighborhood in Rotterdam, Netherlands, used their neighborhood meeting to generate new local networks and to develop a sense of localness rather than one of class (though there were class differences).

neighborhood nonprofit group: a *nonprofit group based in and serving a particular urban or rural neighborhood. These groups usually meet the criteria of *grassroots association (Smith 2000:8). McKenzie (1994, passim) examines *homeowners associations in America, concluding that they have basically selfish (*selfishness) rather than civic *public interest *goals and *impacts. However, Fisher (1994, passim) and Berry et al. (1993, passim) find quite positive features of *neighborhood associations as forms of *citizen participation and *political voluntary action. Schmid (2001, passim) reports on his action research with successful *community councils in Jerusalem, which are essentially neighborhood associations. He also reviews research on neighborhood self-management organizations (*neighborhood associations) in many other nations, including America (ibid., chap. 4). Neighborhood nonprofit groups exemplify *decentralization of municipal political authority when municipal *governments take seriously the wishes and opinions of such associations about neighborhood *issues, especially where, as in New York City (Lowe 1990, passim), these associations are formally recognized by city government.

neighborhood self-management organizations. *See* neighborhood nonprofit group

neocorporatism: tendency by *government in mature liberal democracies to give organized interests privileged and institutionalized access to formulation of *policy (Heywood 2002:275). Also called "liberal *corporatism" or "societal corporatism" (Keeler 1987, passim).

network: in the *nonprofit sector, an informal or formal chain or system of interconnected and intercommunicating people, *groups, or *organizations (nodes and links) (cf. Barabási 2002, passim). Bott (1957, passim) wrote an early work on family and social network. There is a journal dealing with this subject generally: *Social Networks*. Strain and Blandford (2003, passim) found that the personal care networks of older cognitively impaired adults were more evolved than those of older adults without such impairment. *See also* social network

network of groups: an informal *coalition of *groups organized along lines of a common *interest. Brunton (1988, passim) examined the relevance of this concept in his explanation of the institutional origins of the military-industrial complex in the United States.

network of nonprofits: a loose *collectivity of *nonprofit groups of some kind whose *members are linked to each other in a particular way (e.g., mutual recognition, shared *goal, shared network membership). May span a territory of any size. Composed of looser connections (links) than a *federation of *nonprofits. Banaszak-Holl and colleagues (1998, passim) studied a network of agencies (*nonprofit agency) serving people with disabilities, finding that for all types of agencies, except health maintenance, the network structure varies for administrative and client-centered activities.

networking: process of communicating and establishing relationships with other people in a *network, something often done for personal advantage of the networker. Herman and Heimovics (1994:143–144) discuss the need to develop at the executive level of *nonprofit leadership a successful informal information network.

new religion: a *religion recently introduced to a culture where, because it is unique and indigenous or comes from outside, it is considered new and therefore deviant (*deviant nonprofit group). Collective expression of the new religion is enacted in cults (Appel 1983, passim), which may be considered part of the *nonprofit sector. The more successful of these innovations sometimes go on to become *sects (Wilson 1970, passim). Note, too, that some so-called new religions may nevertheless be established religions in another culture (Hadden 2000:2366). Johnstone (1992:99–106), discusses cults, taking Jim Jones's People's Temple as an extended example. Many books describe or discuss at length the new religions, among them Bainbridge (1997, chaps. 6–9), Partridge (2004), Bromley and Hadden (1992), Mather and Nichols (1993), Singer and Lalich (1995), Stark and Bainbridge (1985, pt. 3), Wilson and Cresswell (1999), and Zellner and Petrowsky (1998). Other books focus on particular new religions or "cults," as they are commonly termed (Breault and King 1983; Kaplan and Marshall 1996; Mills 1979; Reavis 1995)

new social movement (NSM): a *social movement, especially in the past half-century or so, that focuses more on identity issues than on political, economic, and class *ideology (the latter exemplified by labor movements and new *political parties). According to Johnston et al. (1994:6–7), new social movements first "do not bear a clear relation to the structural [e.g., social class] roles of the participants." Second, "the ideological characteristics of NSMs stand in sharp contrast to the working-class movement" and to Marxist ideology. Third, "NSMs often involve the emergence of new and formerly weak dimensions of identity" (with "focus on cultural and symbolic issues . . . rather than on economic grievances"). "Fourth, the relation between the individual and the collective is blurred" (with individual citizen participation being important "rather than [actions] through or among mobilized groups"). "Fifth, NSMs often involve personal and intimate aspects of human life." Sixth, NSMs tend to use "radical mobilization tactics of disruption and resistance that differ from those practiced by the working-class movements" (especially *nonviolence and *civil disobedience). Seventh, the rise of NSMs is "related to the credibility crisis of the conventional channels for parties in Western democracies." Finally, "NSM organizations tend to be segmented, diffuse, and decentralized." Examples of NSMs include (ibid.: 3) "peace movements, student movements, the anti-nuclear energy protests, minority nationalism, gay rights, animal rights, alternative medicine, fundamentalist religious movements, and New Age and ecology movements" (see Adam 1995; Chatfield 1992; Ferree et al. 1997; Finsen and Finsen 1994; Josephy 1970; Price 1990; Scholsberg 1999). Authors analyzing NSMs more generally include Haynes (1997), Kenedy (2004), Kriesi and Koopmans (1995); Laraña et al. (1994); Melucci (1989); Schehr (1997); Scholsberg (1999); and Todd and Taylor (2004).

NGO. *See* nongovernmental organization

NGO sector. *See* nonprofit sector

niche position of nonprofit groups: metaphor modeled on population ecology and applied by McPherson (1983, passim) to competition among *nonprofit organizations (particularly *associations) for *members. In competing for members, a nonprofit exploits its special place, or role, in the *nonprofit sector. McPherson, in his study, used demographic dimensions to explain this competition but allowed that time, geography, attitude, and possibly other variables could also be incorporated into the niche position model.

noblesse oblige: dictum commonly translated from the French as "privilege entails responsibility." Smith (2000:17) observes that usage of this term in the *nonprofit sector imbues the practice of *voluntary altruism with a sense of condescension. *See also* Lady Bountiful

nominal member. *See* paper member

noncharitable tax-exempt nonprofits: tax-exempt nonprofits that fall into all Internal Revenue Service (IRS) tax-exempt categories except 501(c)(3) (see *tax-exempt nonprofit organizations registered with the IRS); such organizations serve the private interests of their members, generally, but are subject to the *nondistribution constraint (Fishman and Schwarz 2000:325).

noncoercion: principle, applied from time to time in the *nonprofit sector literature (e.g., Van Til 1988:9; Stebbins 2004:5; Smith 2000:19, 24), stating that *voluntary action is uncoerced, or unforced, behavior. *See also* leisure/leisure time; volunteering as leisure

nondependent volunteer: *volunteer who depends very little for vital everyday life *needs on the *volunteer organization in which that person serves. According to Pearce (1993:160–163), such workers do gain certain tangible rewards and *benefits from training and experience, but by being nondependent, they pose a problem for *nonprofit enterprise management, who must try to further motivate them without recourse to powerful rewards or sanctions. *See also* volunteer unreliability

nondistribution constraint: prohibition by legal fiat of distribution to *members of profits (*excess revenue) gained by *nonprofit groups— funds that must instead be retained and used strictly for financing further production of the *services that the group was founded to provide (Hansmann 1980:838).

nongovernmental organization (NGO): 1. *nonprofit group, particularly a *nonprofit organization or *association whose classification emphasizes the nongovernmental character of nonprofits (Salamon and Anheier 1992:129). 2. this is the preferred term by many who deal with international associations (*transnational association/nonprofit) or aid to developing countries (*Third World), including indigenous Third World nonprofits (Fisher 1998:2).

nonmarket activity: 1. voluntary action activities or transactions that fall outside the economic market system of a territory (Department of Commerce 1982, passim). *Volunteering, *voluntary action, and *nonprofit groups are, in a basic sense, nonmarket activities, since profit is not their *goal. In fact, in the strictest sense, nonmarket activities do not even involve exchanging money for *goods or *services transferred (e.g., *volunteering, pure; *informal care). 2. goods or services or both produced for personal use and consumption outside the formal market (*see* market economy), as in a household or nonprofit group. Examples include subsistence crops, gathered fuel and water, food preparation, informal *care for people, and *volunteer work. Women often engage in nonmarket activity (e.g., Floro 1995, passim). *See also* sector of society

nonmember: a person or group that is not a formal member of some *nonprofit group. In the *nonprofit sector an important subset of nonmembers is the *target of benefits of particular *nonmember benefit nonprofits, as seen in the study of a local Meals on Wheels *organization conducted by Bartholdi and colleagues (1983, passim).

nonmember benefit nonprofit group: *nonprofit group formed to provide certain benefits to a nonmember target group (*target of benefits), often called, more loosely, a *"public benefit group" (Smith 2000:114–117). Such a group is exemplified in a study conducted by Bartholdi and colleagues (1983, passim) on a local Meals on Wheels *organization.

nonmember benefit sector. *See* subsector

nonmember service incentive: type of *service incentive that involves *satisfaction from serving *nonmembers of one's own *nonprofit group or *volunteer program—satisfaction gained from serving *targets of benefits outside one's group or program. The traditional type of service incentive prevalent in *nonmember benefit nonprofits and volunteer programs (Smith 2000:98) and for *traditional service volunteers. *See* service incentive

nonmonetized form of contribution. *See* in-kind contribution

nonoperating foundation. *See* foundation (sense 1)

nonoperating fund: sum of money in a *nonprofit group set aside for purposes other than paying operating expenses. Examples include loan funds (for employees or clients) and pension funds (Anthony and Young 1994: 418).

nonprofessional: 1. *amateur (cf. Stebbins 1979, passim); the opposite of *professional (sense 1). 2. someone who is not paid to pursue an activity; the opposite of *professional (sense 2). 3. paid worker who falls outside the category of *professional (sense 1). A study by Price (2002) examines the retirement experience of professional (sense 1) and nonprofessional (sense 3) women.

nonprofit: *See* nonprofit group

nonprofit agency: *nonprofit organization providing a *public benefit. Such agencies usually operate with *paid staff, though some are small, *volunteer-run *nonprofit groups. Generally speaking, then, the nonprofit agency relies on staff to accomplish its *goals rather than *members or *service program volunteers. Note that the term "social agency" is sometimes also applied to *for-profit groups with *missions similar to nonprofit agencies; the former typically employ a number of *professionals and other *paid staff (Glenn 2000). In fact, the term "voluntary agency" is more commonly used, even if, for conceptual consistency, "nonprofit agency" is preferred. Both large and small agencies have a *board of directors. Billis (1993, passim) discusses public and voluntary (i.e., nonprofit) agencies. Stanton (1970) describes and analyzes how nonprofit agencies can become inauthentic, by not living up to stated goals. Lohmann (1992:132–133) provides a special but related definition of nonprofit agency as a part of the *commons. Most books on nonprofit agencies use the latter term as synonymous with *nonprofit organization (e.g., Bernstein 1991; Brown and Zahrly 1990; Clifton and Dahms 1993; Fine 1992; McKinney 2004; Savedoff 1998; Young et al. 1977).

nonprofit association. *See* association

nonprofit board. *See* board of directors

nonprofit commercialization. *See* commercialization of nonprofits

nonprofit corporation: *nonprofit organization, with a *charter and usually federal governmental Internal Revenue Service *tax-exempt status, that is legally established in a state (cf. Hopkins 1998, passim). Presence of the *nondistribution constraint is the key difference from a business corporation (Fishman and Schwarz 2000:63). Governing statutes are similar to state corporation law (ibid.). May have a *public benefit or *member benefit (mutual benefit) purpose (Fishman and Schwarz 2000: 68–70). Van Til (1988:138–141) explores today's fuzzy boundaries separating nonprofit corporations and *for-profit organizations, setting out some of the ways in which *business and *volunteering are often connected. *See also* corporation, charitable; corporation, ecclesiastical

nonprofit deviance: *deviance from a society's moral norms either by one or more *leaders in or by several *members of a *nonprofit group. Nonprofit deviance can occur even if no deviant norm exists in the group, whereas existence of such a norm is a requirement for deviance in *deviant nonprofit groups (Smith 2000:86–88). Milofsky and Blades (1991, passim) address themselves to nonprofit deviance in their treatment of accountability problems in *nonprofit organizations. *See also* moral standard

nonprofit enterprise management: following Mason (1984), action and manner of managing a *nonprofit group; application of skill or care in the use, treatment, manipulation, or control of things or people or in the conduct of a *nonprofit group, whether *paid staff or *volunteer nonprofit. Shapiro (1987) argues the same for associational management. *See also* nondependent worker; nonprofit management

nonprofit goal: goal of a *nonprofit group, which may be operative (*goal, operative) as well as official (*goal, official) or unofficial (*goal, unofficial) (cf. Perrow 1961, passim; Smith 2000:74).

nonprofit goal succession. *See* goal succession

nonprofit governance: 1. the activities and processes of top *policy *leadership (sense 2) or *management of a *nonprofit group, usually mainly the province of the *board of directors and, to a lesser extent, between board *meetings, the *executive director or president plus committees (cf. Burlingame 2004:191–199; Cornforth 2003, passim; Ott 2001, passim; Widmer and Houchin 1999, passim; Young et al. 1993, passim). 2. loosely, *nonprofit management generally.

nonprofit group: *formal or *informal group of people joined together to pursue a common not-for-profit *goal. That is, it is not the intention of the *group to distribute excess *revenue to *members or *leaders or to operate mainly according to personal attachment as to a household or family. Nor is a nonprofit group a government agency (*see* nonprofit agency). Such groups, which are sometimes referred to as "voluntary groups," do enjoy substantial levels of *autonomy and are usually inspired by a significant level of *voluntary spirit or, more broadly, *voluntary altruism (Smith 2000:24–26, 64). Further, nonprofit groups may offer one or more *public benefits (mainly classified in the United States as Internal Revenue Service (IRS) category 501[c][3]) or one or more *member benefits (classified in the United States as other tax-exempt IRS categories; cf. O'Neill 2002:210). There is dispute regarding whether IRS category 501(c)(4) organizations are member benefit or nonmember benefit organizations (ibid.). "Nonprofit group" is the broadest term for the *nonprofit sector groups, and nonprofit groups are present in all societies so far studied. The concept is extensively covered in discussions of the nonprofit sector (e.g., Edwards and Yankey 1998, passim; McCarthy et al. 1992, passim; O'Neill 2002, passim; Salamon 2002, passim). It is also mentioned in many of the practical guides to aspects of *nonprofit management (e.g., Horvath 1995; Mancuso 2004; Salzman 1998; Tropman 2003; Young et al. 2002). *See also* volunteer nonprofit group; nonprofit organization

nonprofit group affiliate: all people or groups or both having an established relationship of some sort with a particular *nonprofit group. These include the following: *donors, *volunteers, *board members, *paid staff, *targets of benefits, *official members, superordinate *organizations (e.g., *coalitions, *federations, central offices at a more inclusive territorial level), and suppliers (Smith 1972a, passim). *See also* analytic member

nonprofit group complexity. *See* complexity

nonprofit group cooperation/collaboration: *nonprofit groups helping each other and themselves by sharing information or other *resources, if not both, while striving to reach one or more common *goals. Higher level *cooperation occurs in *coalitions, *federations, and even mergers of nonprofits (Klonglan and Yep 1972, passim). Power (1993, passim) has published a collection of papers on cooperation among *organizations in a computer-supported *cooperative network. *See also* collaboration

nonprofit group incidence: the rate at which new *nonprofit groups arise in a particular geographic territory during a specified period of time. This rate is commonly expressed as the number of nonprofits per thousand population formed during a specified year (Knoke 1993:145).

nonprofit group participation: active involvement by *analytic members in a *nonprofit group or *nonprofit organization. Smith (2000:51–52) estimates the number of active *grassroots association members in America in 1991 to be at least ninety-eight million. *See also* participation

nonprofit group prevalence: the frequency of *nonprofit groups currently existing in a particular geographic territory during a specified period of time. This frequency is commonly expressed as the number of nonprofits per thousand population present during a specified year (Knoke 1993: 145), or as the raw prevalence rate (the number of *nonprofits in the territory at a given time; Smith and Shen 2002:95–96). The latter authors (ibid., passim) present and test successfully a model of *voluntary association prevalence for the larger nations of the world.

nonprofit leader: a *leader (sense 2) in a *nonprofit group, and therefore the person responsible for development, approval, and implementation of *policy, achieved in good part by working with other *analytic members of the group. The term generally refers to people holding official *leadership positions in *associations but is also used at times to refer to influential people (*see* influence) at any level in a nonprofit. Herman and Heimovics (1991, passim) examine executive leadership in *nonprofit organizations. Herman and Associates (2005, pt. 2) deals with key nonprofit leadership issues, mainly for paid-staff nonprofits. Smith (2000, chap. 7) deals with research on leadership in grassroots associations.

nonprofit leadership. *See* leadership; nonprofit leader

nonprofit management: 1. role activities of *nonprofit managers (e.g., Herman 1994, passim; Drucker 1992, passim; Anthony and Young 1984; Bordt 1997; Bryson and Crosby 1992; Burlingame 2004:344–351; Connors 2001; Cornforth 2003; Grobman 2005; *Harvard Business Review* 1999; Herman and Associates 1994, 2005; Herman and Heimovics 1991; Hummel 1996; Jinkins and Jinkins 1998; Knauft et al. 1991; Light 1998; Luke 1998; Lynch 1993; Mason 1984; Ott 2001; Werther and Berman 2001; Widmer and Houchin 1999; Wilbur 2000; Wolf and Carter 1999; Young et al. 1993). 2. occupation of managing *nonprofit groups, usually *associations and *organizations. The *nonprofit management profession. Shaiko (1997, passim), in studying a sample of professional *nonprofit associations in the United States, identified several internal organizational barriers that prevented women from working in nonprofit management (sense 2). *See also* volunteer administration

nonprofit management education: usually refers to formal, post-secondary education in the theory and practice of *nonprofit management. O'Neill and Young (1988, passim) wrote an early resource book in the field, and O'Neill and Fletcher (1998, passim) is a more recent one (see also Burlingame 2004:351–355).

nonprofit management profession: occupational classification of those whose livelihood is managing *nonprofit groups. Smith (2000:130) observes that *grassroots associations tend to be little interested in or involved with this *profession. Block (2001, passim) reviews the history of the field.

nonprofit manager: *nonprofit leader specialized in and responsible for *management of *paid staff in *paid-staff nonprofit organizations. Such managers are commonly found at higher organizational levels and are associated with a significant level of effective *leadership. Moyer (1984, passim) covers the complex subject of managing voluntary organizations (*nonprofit organizations). *See also* volunteer administrator; nonprofit management

nonprofit officer: 1. *nonprofit leader. 2. elected *officer of a *nonprofit group, usually an *association (cf. Connors 1988b, chap. 11).

nonprofit organization (NPO): *nonprofit group that has achieved formal status, that has become an *organization (Smith 1972a, passim). The term "nonprofit organization" serves poorly as an umbrella word for the groups comprising the *nonprofit sector, for it omits semiformal and informal nonprofits, many of which play an important role there (Smith 1992b, 1997b). Major books either examining a particular aspect of non-profit organizations or giving an overview of this subject include Block (2004), Bordt (1997), Bowen et al. (1994), Connors (1988), Galaskiewicz and Bielefeld (1998), Jinkins and Jinkins (1998), Knoke (1990), Light (2000), Mancuso (2004), O'Neill (2002), Powell and Steinberg (2006), Ruckle (1993), Salamon (2002), Sills (1957), Simon and Donovan (2001), and Zack (2003). DiMaggio and Anheier (1990, passim) review the literature and state of the art of research on NPOs. *See also* paid-staff nonprofit group; quasi-volunteer

nonprofit sector: 1. narrow definition: sum of all types of volunteer altruism (*altruism, volunteer), *volunteer action, *volunteers, and *volunteer groups. 2. broad definition: sum of the four components set out in sense 1 in addition to all types of quasi-volunteer altruism (*altruism, quasi-volunteer), *quasi-volunteer action, *quasi-volunteers, and *quasi-volunteer groups (Smith 2000:27). Generally put, the nonprofit sector en-compasses all aspects of all *nonprofit groups in a society, in addition to all *individual voluntary action found there (e.g., Anheier and Sala-mon 1998; Ben-Ner and Gui 1993; Commission on Private Philanthropy and Public Needs 1975; Evers and Laville 2004; Frumkin and Imber 2004; Grobman 2004; Hall 1992; Hammack 1998; INDEPENDENT SEC-TOR and Urban Institute 2002; Levitt 1973; Lohmann 1992; McCarthy et al. 1992; Nielsen 1979; O'Neill 2002; Ott 2001; Powell 1987; Salamon 2002, 2003; Salamon and Anheier 1994; Salamon et al. 1999; Silber 2001; Steinberg 2004; Van Til 1988; Smith with Dixon 1973; J. Smith et al. 1995; Weisbrod 1977, 1988; Wuthnow 1991). Some sort of nonprofit sector has been found in all societies studied so far. The terms *"vol-untary sector," *"independent sector," *"third sector," "civil society sec-tor," "tax-exempt sector," "not-for-profit sector," "the commons," *"philanthropic sector," "charitable sector," and others are sometimes used synonymously with either of these senses, though in the case of the last two, emphasis is on charitable nonprofits, such as those registered in the United States with the Internal Revenue Service (IRS) as 501(c)(3). Burlingame (2004:355–356) presents distinctions among the various near synonyms for the nonprofit sector. The nonprofit sector is one of the four *sectors of society (or five sectors, in one scheme) and definitely includes groups and organizations not listed or registered by the IRS (O'Neill 2002:7; Smith 2000, chap. 2; Toepler 2003, passim).

nonprofit sector, infrastructure organization of: *organization that sup-ports one or more *nonprofit groups and seeks to improve their *ef-fectiveness (Abramson and McCarthy 2002:331). There are many such organizations in the United States, only a few of which are covered further in this dictionary. They include the *Association for Research on Nonprofit Organizations and Voluntary Action, *International Society for Third Sector Research, National Center on Nonprofit Boards, National Center for Charitable Statistics, Nonprofit Academic Centers Council, Nonprofit Sector Support Fund (Aspen Institute), American Association of Fund-Raising Counsel, Association of Fundraising Professionals, Volunteer, Points of Light Foundation, Council on Foundations, Foundation Center, Association for Volunteer Administration, *INDEPENDENT SECTOR, Alliance for Nonprofit Management, and National Council of Nonprofit Associations. Many have descriptive entries in Burlingame (2004, passim). Energize, Inc., an international training, consulting, and publishing firm, maintains an interactive website (http://www.energizeinc.com) whose *mission is to help improve nonprofit effectiveness. *See also* intermediary

"nonprofit sector is unimportant" flat-earth paradigm: nonprofit sector model, held implicitly or explicitly, that the whole of the *nonprofit sector is unimportant, that only the *public (government) and *private (business) sectors in modern society merit careful scientific scrutiny (Smith 2000:219–220).

nonprofit sector, national studies of: research studies examining the *nonprofit sector in a particular nation, many of which have come about as a result of the Johns Hopkins Comparative Nonprofit Sector Project (Salamon et al. 1999:xvii and passim). The latter volume reports on national studies of the nonprofit sector in twenty-two nations. In addition, there are many book-length treatments of the nonprofit sector in various nations, which have grown out of that project (e.g., Kendall, Kendall, and Knapp 1996, on the United Kingdom; Gidron, Bar, and Kats 2004, on Israel; Yamamoto and Amenomori 1998, on Japan; Anheier and Seibel 2001, on Germany; Archambault 1997, on France; Kuti 1996, on Hungary; Barbetta 1997, on Italy; Lundstrom and Wijkstrom 1997, on Sweden; Lyons 2001, on Australia; Banting 1999, on Canada; Salamon 1999, on America; Landim, 1993, on Brazil; Sen 1993, on India; Atingdui 1995, on Ghana). Some national studies conducted independently also exist (e.g., Bútora and Fialová 1995, on Slovakia; Pongsapich and Kataleeradaphan 1997, on Thailand). And McCarthy et al. (1992) edited a compendium on the nonprofit sector as seen by authors from many nations.

nonprofit spirit. *See* voluntary spirit

nonprofit staff: *analytic members of a *nonprofit group, paid or not, who carry out its main responsibilities of *leadership and office work. In *grassroots associations *committees and elected *officers constitute the main staff. In *paid-staff nonprofit organizations, nearly all staff are remunerated. Smith (2000:120–122) discusses the personnel of nonprofit groups.

nonviolence: both a *policy and a *value of many nonprofit *leaders and *nonprofit groups, to the effect that, in most situations, social protest can work without violence (cf. Sharp 1973, passim). That is, *symbolic and *direct action protest are generally effective, whereas *violent protest tends to provoke more violence, causing harm to people and society. Gamson (1990, passim) discusses the different forms of social protest (*activity, protest).

nonviolent action: *political voluntary action by an individual or *collectivity (often a *nonprofit group) based on the principle of *nonviolence. McCarthy (1997, passim) compiled a comprehensive guide to cases of nonviolent action around the world, mostly in recent history. In his chapter 6 (ibid.), he reviews methods and dynamics of nonviolent action. Sharp (1973, passim) describes comprehensively the methods of nonviolent action. Epstein (1991, passim), using several case studies as examples, examines nonviolent *direct action protest in the 1970s and 1980s in America. Powers et al. (1997, passim) have compiled an encyclopedia of nonviolent action, in which they present groups, aspects, and instances of such protest leading to social change.

normative compliance structure: acquiescent, cooperative relations in a *nonprofit group, where the relations are based on the persuasive power of internalized norms as these bear on the group's *mission or *ideology or both (Etzioni 1975:8–14).

normative incentive in nonprofit groups. *See* purposive incentive

not-for-profit: 1. (n.) a synonym of *"nonprofit" referring to a kind of *group, usually an *organization (formal group). Much less frequently used than the term "nonprofit." Term preferred by some scholars (especially in accounting and economics) and practitioners as more technically correct, because it contrasts better with *for-profit groups/organizations. 2. (adj.) a synonym of *"nonprofit" referring to activities, groups, and so on characterized by *voluntary altruism, which is the essence of *nonprofit nature. Keating and Keating (1980, passim) examine, using the perspective of economics, the concept of not-for-profit.

not-for-profit group. *See* for-profit group; nonprofit group

not-for-profit sector. *See* nonprofit sector

O

objective. *See* goal

obligation: attitude or act of doing or refraining from doing something because the actor, though not coerced, still feels bound in this regard by
promise, convention, or circumstance (Stebbins 2000:152). Obligation,
which may be pleasant or unpleasant, is both a state of mind, an attitude—a person feels obligated—and a form of behavior—a person must
carry out a particular course of action. Personal care, child care, yard
care, housework, and shopping are common nonoccupational obligations, while one's paid occupation, if employed (or self-employed), is a
central work or occupational obligation. Pleasant obligations are sometimes part of *leisure, such as when a *volunteer is obliged to serve at
a certain time of day. *See also* obligatory activity; marginal volunteering

obligatory activity: 1. in the context of a twenty-four-hour daily time budget, one or all of the activities required by biological need or socio-
cultural compulsion such as sleep, eating, personal care, housework,
child care. Obligatory activity along with *occupational activity and occupation-related activity (e.g., commuting, work breaks) are contrasted
with *leisure time, in which much *voluntary action takes place, particularly *pure volunteering. Thus Stebbins (2000:154) notes that some
obligations can be "agreeable" and hence part of *leisure time. 2. in the
context of a twenty-four-hour daily time budget, *occupational activity
and occupation-related activity along with activities required by biological need or socio-cultural compulsion.

occasional volunteer. *See* drop-by/occasional volunteer; volunteer, habitual (sporadic type); episodic volunteer

occupation: a paid job or type of remunerated work. An occupation is one of the social roles most adults of working age play in society (Ritzer and Walczak 1986:2). If one performs two or more kinds of paid jobs, occupation usually refers to the main job, the one requiring the most time. *See also* occupational activity

occupational activity: activity that is part of an *occupation. Sanders (1995, passim) investigated the difficulties that emerge for one of the central occupational activities of veterinarians, which is to evaluate the health of family pets and, where warranted, euthanize them.

occupational association: a common kind of *association formed to further the interests of *members of a given *occupation. Abbott (1988:79–85) discusses the nature of professional associations, under the heading of "internal structure" of the professions. *See* farmers' association; farm laborers' association; union; professional association

officer in nonprofits: in the *nonprofit sector someone holding office and participating in the *management or direction of a *nonprofit group. President, secretary, and treasurer are the most common officers of such groups. Stebbins (1998:3–6) holds that these officers as well as certain other important participants in nonprofit groups can be considered *key volunteers.

official member: an individual or group or both who a *nonprofit group officially and legally defines as *member. *Associations always have official members, whereas *voluntary agencies usually do not. Many official members of associations tend to be *paper members (cf. Smith 1972a, passim). *See also* analytic member

official nonprofit goal. *See* goal, official

old-boys' network: mutual assistance, especially through preferment in employment, shown among old cronies who share a social background. One kind of *informal volunteer *collectivity. Gamba and Kleiner (2001, passim) found that an old-boys' network lacking women has emerged in the Internet *community of senior *managers of venture capital firms.

oligarchy: concentration of power in a *nonprofit group in the hands of a few *members (cf. Lipset 1995, passim). Vis-à-vis other nonprofits those that are larger, more formalized, and well-established tend to be more elitist (*elite) and oligarchic (Smith 2000:83). *See also* iron law of oligarchy

ombudsman. *See* ombudsperson

ombudsperson: noted in the *Shorter Oxford English Dictionary,* 5th ed. (2002:1994) as the gender-neutral expression of "ombudsman" as an English term (it is originally a Swedish word). Someone officially appointed as either *volunteer or *paid worker to investigate complaints by individuals against maladministration by governmental or organizational authorities. Filinson (2001), in a study of a long-term care ombudsperson program, learned that volunteer ombudspersons were more prevalent where complaints about the facilities were more frequent and serious. *See also* watchdog

online support group: set of people communicating over the Internet (e.g., using e-mail, chatrooms, listservs) to share advice, information, encouragement, and the like centered on a common interest or *problem. One kind of informal volunteer *collectivity (cf. Brainerd and Brinkerhoff 2004, passim). Meier (1997) tested the technical feasibility and appropriateness of a six-week online support group formed among a sample of master's-level social work students and designed to help social workers manage stress.

online volunteering. *See* virtual volunteering

open shop union: a *union local in which all workers of a certain type in a company are free to choose whether to join the relevant *union. Mihlar et al. (1999, passim) studied the global impact of right-to-work laws, which prescribe open shop unions. *See also* closed shop union

operating cost. *See* operating expense

operating expense: 1. a cost incurred in running a *nonprofit group, in supporting its general operations. 2. an expenditure made to cover such a cost (sense 1). The Evangelical Lutheran Church in America (http://www.elca.org) says its general operating fund supports all business activity of a *congregation, by accounting for and accumulating all income except restricted *gifts and payments. *See also* general operating support (fund)

operating foundation: *foundation, usually endowment-based, the main *goal of which is to fund its own *public benefit activities or charitable program (e.g., social science research funded by Russell Sage Foundation; promotion of art funded by J. Paul Getty Trust; cf. Dale 1997). Operating foundations in the United States are prohibited by law from giving more than 15 percent of their total income to other *nonprofits groups, as in *grant making (Fishman and Schwarz 2000:326; O'Neill 1989:138).

operating fund. *See* general operating support (fund)

operating support. *See* general operating support (fund)

operative nonprofit goal. *See* goal, operative

opportunity cost: "the value of the next best use (or opportunity) for an economic *good, or the value of the sacrificed alternative" (Samuelson and Nordhaus 1995:759). In nonprofit research, can be used to refer to foregone wages by *volunteers who, for instance, could have been doing equivalent or other paid work (see *imputed value of *volunteer work). Concept can also be used in valuing *public goods (*good, sense 1).

organization: *formal group; *group with a proper (unique) name, clear *membership boundaries, and clear *leadership structure. Organizations can be simple or complex in structure, the latter having three or more levels of *bureaucracy (Smith 1972a, passim). *See also* association; non-profit organization

organizational analysis (studies): the field of scientific examination of complex, or large-scale, *organizations. Hassard (1994, passim) discusses a new approach to organizational analysis, involving a blend of modernist and postmodernist thinking. Hall and Tolbert (2005), who have written several editions of a book that comprehensively reviews the mainstream organizational studies literature, ignore *nonprofit groups and thus embrace the *nonprofit sector is unimportant flat-earth paradigm (Smith 2000:219–221).

organizational change: 1. change in a *nonprofit group, particularly in its *process or *structure or both. 2. change in the structure or process of an *organization of any kind (cf. Hall 1996, chap. 10). Van Maanen (1998: pt. 3) offers several studies of organizational change in a variety of settings.

organizational chart: a diagram portraying the main *leaders and subgroups of an *organization and their formal *authority relationships. Biggart (1998:243) describes the organizational chart of the U.S. Post Office, one he observes that, in its rigidity, is poorly structured to deal with change.

organizational demography: description and explanation of organizational (*organization) phenomena using demographic variables. Stewman (1988:176) holds that this field breaks down theoretically into four areas: intraorganizational demography, interorganizational demography, careers, and organizational and external populations.

organizational development (OD) in nonprofits: a systems model—typically mathematic—created for identifying and applying the characteristics of *organizations recognized as indicators of their health (*organizational health) and *effectiveness (Gross and Etzioni 1985:27). OD is an expensive, albeit effective, way of improving a *nonprofit group, but nevertheless one that, because it requires professional application, can only be afforded by a few.

organizational effectiveness evaluation: *effectiveness evaluation undertaken on an *organization. Murray and Tassie (1994:306–309) describe some of the common models of organizational effectiveness evaluation.

organizational environment. *See* environment, organizational

organizational health: state of soundness and of collective well-being of a *nonprofit group. Smith (2000:130) identifies as a simple measure of such health in *associations the amount of internal activity per *member.

organizational objective: *goal pursued by a *nonprofit group. Pearce (1993:39) observes that the goals of nonprofit groups and those of their *members are by no means always commensurate.

organizational processes. *See* processes of nonprofits

organizational purpose. *See* mission

organizational revolution: the efflorescence of *organizations that accompanied the industrial revolution. The organizational revolution was manifested in increased size, number, and power of organizations of many kinds (including *nonprofit groups) from approximately 1850 (Boulding 1953:3–4).

organizational society: society, or nation, in which *organizations are a dominate feature (Boulding 1953:4) Also referred to as "organizational state" (Laumann and Knoke 1987, passim). The classic statement on the subject was penned by Robert Presthus (1978, passim).

organizational structure. *See* structure of nonprofits

organizational transformation: a fundamental change in a *nonprofit group such that its essence and operations are profoundly reshaped. Such change is not evolutionary, which is expected development. Nor is it so dramatic that the group loses sight of its *goals and unique *mission (Perlmutter and Gummer 1994:228–229).

organizer: person who works, usually full time, at recruiting people to new or existing *advocacy groups, *social movements, *social protest activities, and opportunities for *citizen participation or *community involvement. Ecklein (1984, passim) has written a basic text for community organizers.

orientation of nonprofit groups: the collective attitude of a *nonprofit group toward sociopolitical change. Smith (2000:226) writes that this orientation varies according to *paradigm (round-earth vs. flat-earth).

orientation of volunteers/members: major administrative function in *nonprofit groups and *volunteer programs carried out by providing general information on the *volunteer program and its role in the larger *organization (Connors 1995, chap. 4). May also be used as a screening technique. Battle (1988, chap. 6) discusses the orientation of new *members in an *association.

outcome evaluation for program evaluation: investigation, by any of a variety of methods, designed to measure the impact of a *nonprofit group's *program. Does the program result in the desired outcomes (Thomas 1994:356)? *See also* program evaluation; summative evaluation; outcome goal

outcome goal in program evaluation: final intended consequences of a *nonprofit group's *program, both for society and for target clientele (*target of benefit) of the program (Thomas 1994:347–348). *See also* program evaluation

outside lobbying. *See* lobbying

outsider, societal: the poorer, less powerful members of a society; those not part of its elite and established strata (*insider, societal). Use of the term "outsider" (and its opposite, "insider") here expands on the usage introduced by Becker (1963, passim). Smith (2000:249–250) notes that *grassroots associations can offer much to societal outsiders who are striving for political and socioeconomic equality. *See also* deviant group

P

PAC. *See* political action committee

paid staff: a remunerated, part- or full-time *employee of a *nonprofit group. Pearce (1993:141–147) examined the sometimes prickly relations between paid staff and *volunteers in six different nonprofit groups.

paid-staff nonprofit. *See* paid-staff nonprofit group; paid-staff nonprofit organization; quasi-volunteer group

paid-staff nonprofit group: a *nonprofit group with *paid staff. As Smith (2000:7) points out, no precise rule exists as to the proportion of a group's *membership that must be remunerated for it to qualify as a paid-staff entity. Smith (ibid.:7) suggests as a cutting point for *volunteer nonprofits (vis-à-vis paid-staff nonprofits) the point at which 50 percent or more of the total work done in and for the group is done by *volunteers. Nonprofit researchers who overemphasize this kind of nonprofit to the neglect of volunteer nonprofits are oriented by the *paid-staff nonprofit group flat-earth paradigm. *See also* management; sector of society

paid-staff nonprofit group flat-earth paradigm: *nonprofit sector model centering more or less exclusively on *paid-staff nonprofit groups, thereby neglecting in the nonprofit sector the more numerous *grassroots associations as well as supralocal volunteer groups (Smith 2000: 33–34).

paid-staff nonprofit organization (PSNPO): *nonprofit group with organizational structure (*organization) that, to accomplish its *goals, operates primarily with *paid staff (Smith 1981:28). Hula and Jackson-Elmoore (2000, passim) provide several chapters on a variety of urban PSNPOs. Stanton (1970) examined how paid-staff nonprofits sometimes operate such that clients come last in priority.

paid staff-volunteer relations. *See* building paid staff-volunteer relations

paper member. *official member of a *nonprofit group who does not regularly provide *services to it and is thus not an *analytic member. Paper members are inactive, with their only real link to the group being payment of *dues as a sort of *donation (cf. Smith 1972a, passim).

paradigm: scientific model or pattern composed of a set of basic assumptions, propositions, and findings that guides research and thought in a particular field of study. Kuhn (1962, passim) introduced the idea in social science circles.

paradigm, flat-earth nonprofit sector: nonprofit sector model that omits consideration of a major part of the *nonprofit sector. This is done by overemphasizing one part while giving inadequate attention to its opposite type or by holding as unimportant this entire sector (Smith 2000: 13–14, 219–238). Smith discusses nineteen flat-earth *paradigms in the aforementioned volume: angelic; antihistoricism; damned; developed world; distinctive nationalist focus; formalized group; isolated; modern, member benefit, self-help, and advocacy; money is key; nonprofit sector is unimportant; paid-staff nonprofit; purposive type; secularist focus; social movement/protest; sociodemographic participation predictors; status quo/establishment; three-sector model of society; traditional nonmember service; volunteer and membership nonprofit

paradigm, round-earth nonprofit sector: model of the *nonprofit sector developed to correct the omissions and over- and underemphases of the flat-earth nonprofit sector paradigms (*paradigm, flat-earth nonprofit sector). Smith (2000:238–240) provides an extensive outline of the round-earth nonprofit sector paradigm.

paramilitary group: 1. a *group, usually an *association, that performs or is prepared to perform martial activities (e.g., defense or combat against outsiders) without being formally part of a military *governmental agency (i.e., official armed services). 2. a *citizen militia. Broad reviews of citizen militias can be found in Corcoran (1995, passim), Halpern and Levin (1996, passim), and Karl (1995).

parish: local *congregation of the Roman Catholic or Episcopalian/Anglican *religions, which usually consists of one or more *congregations (Jackson 1974:152). Lummis (2004, passim), interested in the question of why men less frequently attend *church services than women, found that this discrepancy in the Episcopalian parishes he studied is not because men feel undervalued for their church *participation. Both sexes felt equally valued in this respect.

participant: a person who engages with others in an activity, especially in
*collective behavior or in a *group (*Shorter Oxford English Dictionary,*
5th ed. 2002:2107). May involve being a *member of a group.

participation: taking part or engaging in *voluntary action, usually with others. Smith, Macaulay, and Associates (1980, passim) have written at
length on *participation in social and political activities. Pateman (1970,
passim) theorized about participation and democracy. Nagel (1987, passim) wrote a primer on (political) participation. *See also* political participation

participatory action research (PAR): a collaborative data collection procedure involving both professionally trained researchers and *amateur
*participants (trained by the researchers and belonging to a *group,
*community, *organization, etc.). Together they study one or more ques-
tions of interest to the latter, using their insider understandings to identify the questions, gather the relevant data, interpret the results, and
thereby help solve key local *problems. Whyte (1990, passim) has assembled an influential collection of papers on PAR.

participatory democracy. *See* civil society

participatory government. *See* civil society

participatory (participative) management: an administrative strategy occasionally used in *nonprofit groups that involves in the *decision making
all who are likely to be affected by it, including group *members, target
clients (*target of benefits), and *sponsors. Anheier and Cunningham
(1994:113) note that participatory management emphasizes such processes as team building, *problem solving, facilitation skills, active listening skills, and conflict resolution (*conflict).

partly deviant nonprofit group: conventional *nonprofit group in which a
minority of *members or one or more *leaders deviate temporarily from
certain community norms related to group *goals or means or both
(Smith 2000:87).

passive resistance: nonviolent refusal by individuals or a *collectivity to
cooperate (*cooperation), especially with legal requirements (cf. Sharp
1973, passim); a form of *activism. The *boycott is a form of passive
resistance. Moland (2002, passim) examines the American passive resistance movement (*social movement) as an expression of civility in pursuit of justice as accorded by the Constitution and expressed in the
*value system of society.

pastor: top *religious functionary of a Christian *congregation (cf. Ranson
et al. 1977, passim).

payout requirement: annual minimum amount that an *independent foundation is required by law to spend on charitable *grants and *operating
expenses (in the United States, about 5 percent of average value of *assets) (see the Foundation Center Glossary at http://www.fdncenter.org/
learn/ufg/glossary.html).

peasant movement: a *social movement made up of peasants (small land-holders or farm workers on large farms), usually inspired by the *goal of improving the situation of peasants in a nation or territory (cf. Pereira 1997, passim). Wouters (2001, passim), who examined the black peasant movement against armed pressure groups in Columbia, found that *organizations representing the former are trying to use land entitlements as a tool to counter the violence inflicted by the latter.

peer pairing: conscious use of pairs of previously related or unrelated persons to facilitate the building of organizational *membership or various forms of *giving or *volunteering. Tomeh (1981) stressed the value of peer pairing to co-involve suburban *volunteers and volunteers of color from poor neighborhoods. Peer pairing is consistent with Kaplan's (1993) observation on the value of enabling intimate (rather than casual) contact between volunteers of different cultural backgrounds. Hunter and Linn (1980–1981) reported the conscious use of pairs of volunteers who were also patients. For Stevens (1991) peer pairing means recruiting people as natural pairs or match-made pairs. Conscious efforts to use diverse pairs instead of individual *members as the unit of membership has been seen as a method for developing diverse *social movement organizations (Dover 1991). The attaching and including processes (Oliner and Oliner 1995) involved in *caring may be enhanced by peer pairing within *organizations.

percentage limitation on charitable donation: complex Internal Revenue Service (IRS) limits on percentage of Adjusted Gross Income (AGI) that a *donor can give in one tax year. For most IRS 501(c)(3) *donees (*public charities), the limit is 50 percent of AGI, while for *private foundations the limit is 30 percent of AGI (Fishman and Schwarz 2000: 904). There are qualifications and technicalities that apply, so that the maximum in any given tax year is limited to 50 percent or 30 percent, respectively (ibid.).

performance. *See* effectiveness; impact of nonprofits

performance-based budgeting: administrative procedure designed to allocate *resources on the basis of predicted or observed results, rather than according to the *operating costs of maintaining existing *programs. Nelson, Robbins, and Simonsen (1998, passim) discuss the current preference of government for performance-based budgeting and its effect on the need to increase *citizen participation and decrease citizen distrust of government.

periphery volunteer. *See* core/periphery volunteer

personal good. *See* good (sense 2)

personal growth incentive. *See* developmental incentive

personal social service. *See* service, personal social

personal social service nonprofit group: *nonprofit group offering one or more *personal social services. More or less exclusive attention to such groups is a distinguishing feature of the *traditional nonmember service flat-earth paradigm (Smith 2000:227).

personal social service value. *See* value, humane core

personnel management in nonprofits. *See* human resource management in nonprofits

personnel practice for volunteers/members: arrangement or procedure for dealing with *volunteers in or *members of a *nonprofit group. Some of these practices promote member or volunteer retention and group or *program success. They include, in addition to ones mentioned in cross-references to *volunteer administration: *supervision, *leadership, communications, *morale maintenance, recognition, *incentives, reward systems, openness to feedback, regular personnel evaluation (*evaluation of nonprofits), volunteer *accountability, access to equipment and supplies, *expense reimbursement (where relevant), promotion and volunteer career ladders (*career in nonprofits), and good paid staff-volunteer/member relations (Smith 1985:249). Battle (1988, passim), Flanagan (1984, passim), and Milligan and Milligan (1965, passim) cover extensively the administrative and personnel practices for *volunteer nonprofits. *See also* volunteer administration; morale in nonprofits; nondependent volunteer; volunteer unreliability

personnel resource. *See* resource

philanthropic economy. *See* economy, philanthropic

philanthropic exchange. *See* exchange, philanthropic

philanthropic foundation: 1. a *foundation. 2. a *nonprofit organization with special tax-exempt status as a *private foundation (Internal Revenue Service category *501[c][3] but not designated *509[a]), usually operating with an *endowment, that regularly disburses *funds to individuals and *nonprofit groups for public *service, broadly conceived of (cf. Fishman and Schwarz 2000, chap. 6) and without receiving anything equivalent directly in return. Lenkowsky (2002, chap. 11) describes the world of American *foundations and corporate philanthropy (*philanthropy, corporate).

philanthropic gift. *See* philanthropy

philanthropic giving. *See* philanthropy

philanthropic grant. *See* grant

philanthropic grant transfer. *See* grant transfer

philanthropic interaction, traditional: described in simplified terms by Smith (2000:17) as charitable giving (*philanthropy), wherein an altruistic provider group (e.g., a *grassroots association) helps through direct social interaction a needy recipient (*target of benefits), who is not a *member of that group. The actual workings of traditional philanthropic interaction in the United States are described in detail by Bremner (1960, passim).

philanthropic sector: 1. usually a synonym for *nonprofit sector. 2. sometimes used to refer just to the charitable organizations and groups of the nonprofit sector, especially those public charities and private foundations registered with the Internal Revenue Service as category *501(c)(3). *See* nonprofit sector

philanthropic transfer. *See* exchange, philanthropic

philanthropy: allocation of one or more of the following to one or more individuals or *nonprofit groups outside the family: money, *goods, other property, or *services (time). Such allocations are for altruistic (*altruism) or public *service purposes and are given without expectation of high probability of similar *benefit in return. This is *charitable giving, as compared with general *giving, and that which is given is a *charitable gift. Philanthropy has a long history (Constantelos 1991, passim; Bremner 1996, passim), especially in England (Jordan 1959, passim), but also in America (Bremner 1988, passim; Curti 1963, passim; Friedman and McGarvie 2003, passim; Gray 1905/1967, passim; Sealander 1997, passim). A key general source on philanthropy is the 2004 encyclopedia on the subject edited by Burlingame (passim). Many authors analyze different aspects of philanthropy (e.g., Anheier and Toepler 1999; Cizakca 2000); Clotfelter and Ehrlich 1999; Colwell 1993; Dale 1997; Ellsworth and Lumarda 2003; Freeman 1981; Gaudiani 2003; Himmelstein 1997; Kiger 2000; Magat 1989b; McCarthy 1991; Nielsen 1972, 1996; Ostrower 1995; Van Til 1990; Walkenhorst 2001) and others provide practical advice on encouraging philanthropy/giving to a certain nonprofit (e.g., Wendroff and Grace 2001). Social change oriented philanthropy receives some special attention (e.g., Ostrander 1995; Rabinowitz 1990). Smith, Shue, and Villarreal (1992, passim) examined Asian and Hispanic philanthropy in the United States. A few authors critique philanthropy (Brown and Karoff 2004; Maren 1997). *See also* economy, philanthropic; gift; philanthropy, corporate; philanthropy, scientific; philanthropic foundation; fund-raising; grant

philanthropy, corporate: *philanthropy undertaken by a corporation and usually given to *nonprofit groups. King (2001, passim) discusses corporate philanthropy and *fund-raising for breast cancer in the United States. Picker (2001:620) writes that, for eventual success of a corporate solicitation program, *nonprofit group *leaders must understand, from the corporation's perspective, its rationale for philanthropic support. Himmelstein (1997, passim) examines the public relations value of corporate philanthropy. Zukowski (1998, passim) writes about being realistic in seeking corporate philanthropy. London (1991, passim) describes Japanese corporate philanthropy.

philanthropy, scientific: 1. *philanthropy the aim of which is to fund scientific research and intellectual inquiry. Bremner (1960:89–105) traces the rise of this sense of scientific philanthropy in the United States. 2. a *social movement as well as personal orientation in Europe and the

United States between 1870 and 1900 to use systematic, efficient procedures to identify the needy as well as raise private funds and coordinate efforts to aid them. Barker (2003:383) writes that the *volunteers and friendly visitors who subsequently used this approach set the stage for emergence of the profession of social work.

physical activity audit: assessment of the degree of physical activity involved in *volunteer assignments. Necessary for redesigning assignments to accommodate both those who seek opportunities for physical activity and those with mobility limitations or a need for mobility aids, if not both. For an example of research on physical activity, see a recent study on mall walking (Duncan, Travis, and McAuley 1995).

pioneering role of nonprofits/nonprofit sector: Smith (1973/2001:80) wrote that "one of the most central impacts of the *voluntary sector is to provide society with a large variety of partially tested social innovations, from which business, government, and other institutions can select and institutionalize those innovations that seem most promising. The *independent sector is thus the prototyping test bed of many, perhaps most new social forms and modes of human relations. . . . Nearly every function currently performed by governments at various levels was once a new social idea and the experiment of some *voluntary group, formal or informal—this is true of education, welfare, care for the aged, building roads, even fighting wars (volunteer *citizen militias)." This pioneering role is nowhere more evident than in the manifold activities of *social movements and *social movement groups (see the nearly two thousand references to such activities in the bibliography of McAdam and Snow 1997). What is especially striking is that the overall success rate of social movement challenging groups in getting new advantages has been about 50 percent, as estimated by Gamson (1990:37) from a random sample of such groups for the period 1800–1945 in America (p. 17). Social movements are especially good in bringing about social change and social innovation over time, though other forms of *nonprofit groups sometimes also innovate successfully. *Fraternal associations in America, for instance, innovated in *social services that subsequently were provided by businesses (e.g., insurance of various types) and government (the welfare state services), according to Beito (2000, passim). And hospice care, now supported by government Medicare and private health insurers, has its roots in the nonprofit hospice movement (Siebold 1992:139, 145, passim). *See also* advocacy group; protest activities; informal social innovation activity; social influence nonprofit group

placement of volunteers/members: major administrative function in *nonprofit groups and *volunteer programs that involves allocating *volunteers or *members to specific or general roles (*volunteer role) in the program or group. In *associations, role allocation is either by election of officers (*officer in nonprofits) and of *board members among the members (Milligan and Milligan 1965, chap. 9), or by appointment of chairs and members of *committees by the president or *board of directors (Milligan and Milligan 1965:114–116; see also Flanagan 1984, chap. 10). Other association members tend to be *rank and file. In volunteer programs, the *volunteer administrator makes role allocations of volunteers, after assessing program and organizational *needs, writing volunteer job descriptions, and screening candidates (Brudney 1990:102–106). However, volunteer programs are departments of larger *organizations in one or another *sector of society, and the *paid staff of the organization often have substantial resistance to volunteers, a *problem that must be dealt with directly and skillfully if volunteer role allocation and the entire volunteer program are to be at all successful (Brudney 1990, chap. 6; Smith 1985:228–231). Connors (1995:174–176) deals with placement of volunteers, while Battle (1988, chap. 6) treats member placement

planned giving program: any charitable *donation preceded by some kind of intentional preparation by the *donor, such as deciding when to donate the money or objects, how much to give, which legal arrangements to use, and how to present the *donation when calculating taxes (cf. White 1998, passim). The ultimate aims are to maximize potential benefit to donor and donee and minimize net cost (Burlingame 2004:380). Planned giving is often complicated, and the *charities receiving the donation are, in this regard, commonly in no position to fully advise their *benefactors. Thus, here, professional advice is usually recommended (White 2001:355).

planning: in *nonprofit groups, the attempt to identify future *goals, evaluate the means for reaching them, and choose appropriate courses of action with reference to the first two. Planning tends to be an annual activity. Axelrod (1994:122) argues that *boards of directors of nonprofits are remiss if they fail to devote some of their time and energy to planning. *See also* long-range planning

pluralism: 1. a concept or condition of the multiplicity of *groups or *social categories in a society and their effects on that society. 2. *ethnic pluralism. 3. *political pluralism. 4. *religious pluralism. See Baghramian and Ingram (2000, passim) for an overview of pluralism in general.

pluralism, ethnic: a concept or form of society in which ethnic, racial, cultural, nationality, and other distinct *social categories maintain some of their independent traditions, practices, and attitudes (see Soysal 1994, especially chap. 6 on migrant nationality *nonprofit groups in Europe). Effective ethnic pluralism rests, in significant part, on *tolerance throughout much of the overall society of existence of these diverse groups and their traditions, practices, and the like. Such pluralism is often expressed in nonprofit groups. Perlmutter (1992) examines the history of ethnic, racial, and religious prejudice in America—the opposite of ethnic pluralism as *tolerance. Recently termed "multiculturalism," ethnic pluralism, to flourish in a society, depends on *civil liberties such as *freedom of religion and *freedom of association (Kukathas 2003; Kymlicka 1993; Schweder and Minow 2002). Knobel (1996, passim) writes of the history of the nativist ("America for Americans") movement in the United States, showing that significant intolerance of ethnic pluralism has existed at different times. Schlesinger (1993, passim) argues that multiculturalism has led to "disuniting of America," a sentiment echoed by Wilkinson (1997, passim). Blank (2002), Gordon and Newfield (1996), Hing (1997), Wood (2003), and hundreds of other authors have written books on aspects of ethnic pluralism, especially in the United States, which is one of the most highly multicultural nations in the world. The concept overlaps with *religious pluralism to a significant extent, because different ethnic or nationality *social categories often adhere to different *religions.

pluralism, political: a theory advocating, in preference to monolithic state power, increased *devolution and *autonomy for individual *groups, including *nonprofit groups, and their functioning in the *social policy process; the condition of such variety of *nonprofit political activity by *nonprofits in a society. In addition, the concept or form of society usually includes the idea or fact that *groups with many different political perspectives compete in the political arenas of a nation, usually through *interest groups, and that the political outcome reflects these various inputs (see Dahl 1967; Greene 1984, passim). The concept has, for the past several decades, been sharply criticized, and its existence in America challenged (e.g., Kariel 1981; Kelso 1978; Schattschneider 1960). Jordan (1990:295) argues that, given the power of *societal insiders, political pluralism is more an ideal than a reality. Rauch (1995, passim) argues that "hyperpluralism" (too many *associations in America) is "the silent killer of American government" causing a *special interest group gridlock (ibid.:10). M. Smith (1990) and Jordan (1993) review the variety of theories or versions of political pluralism, finding great confusion and disagreement. *Corporatism is a clear alternative to political pluralism. Political pluralism overlaps to some extent with other forms of *pluralism (see *ethnic pluralism, *religious pluralism), as the groups or *social categories involved tend to form interest groups. Depends for its existence upon the presence of *civil liberties in society.

pluralism, religious: the theory or actuality of multiple *religions or *denominations present in a society, instead of a state church (*church, sense 3), with the added position that various religions or denominations have a right to exist and a right to equal treatment as guaranteed in America by the Bill of Rights of the Constitution (Evans 1997, passim; Monsma and Soper 1998, passim). Religious pluralism depends substantially on *freedom of religion and *freedom of association, as well as other *civil liberties (Robertson 1966, passim). Also referred to as "religious toleration," an idea whose history in the West is examined by Zagorin (2003, passim). Has led to America being labelled a "denominational society" (Greeley 1972, passim). The history of America as a multireligious, multidenominational society is explored in a multitude of books (e.g., Finke and Stark 2005; Hutchison 2003; Lippy 2000; Littell 1962; Robbins and Anthony 1981; Williams 2002). The problems of religious intolerance and discrimination are treated in Nye (2001, passim), Ghanea-Hercak (2003, passim), and Perlmutter (1992, passim). Religious pluralism overlaps significantly with *ethnic pluralism, because different ethnic, racial, or nationality *social categories often tend to have different religions or denominations. There is also some overlap with *political pluralism, as different religious groups or social categories may form different *interest groups.

policy: in the *nonprofit sector, a course of action or a principle adopted or proposed by an individual or a *nonprofit group or, from the outside, by government or business (adapted from the *Shorter Oxford English Dictionary*, 5th ed. 2002:2267). *See also* social policy

policy dilemma: a difficult choice between two *policy options concerning allocation of public or *nonprofit sector (*sector of society) *resources. For instance, with respect to mediating structures such as *voluntary associations and other *organizations that engage *volunteers, Moody (1988) raised what he called a "policy dilemma." He asked whether *social policy should favor strengthening existing *nonprofit groups, many of which are homogenous in makeup in terms of gender, race, and ethnicity, or promote development of publicly accessible, freestanding *volunteer programs (e.g., the Foster Grandparents Program).

policy volunteer: one who volunteers as a board or commission member (*board volunteer). Cahn (1960, passim) saw the policy volunteer as of one of three types of *citizen volunteers, the other two being *service volunteers and social action volunteers. Metzendorf and Cnaan (1992) distinguish between policy volunteer and service volunteer.

political action: action by individuals or *groups aimed at influencing political *decision making or the political process in a territory (cf. Verba et al. 1995:51). Public charities, classified as Internal Revenue Service (IRS) category 501(c)(3) and 509(a), are strictly limited in their political action; specifically, they cannot engage substantially in *lobbying nor intervene in any partisan political campaign (cf. Fishman and Schwarz 2000:520–580). *Private foundations, classified as IRS category 501(c)(3) but not 509(a), are even more limited and cannot do any political action at all (ibid.). Holmes (2004, passim) investigated the role of anger in motivating political action, in how people do politics. Her study explores the ways anger influences other people and is produced through relations with them. *See also* political participation

political action committee (PAC): an *interest group, sometimes a *non-profit group, that collects money from one (e.g., a single large corporation) or more contributors, pools it, and then makes campaign *donations to candidates intending to influence, in the long term, legislation and executive *decision making. Clawson et al. (1992, passim) examines in detail corporate PACs.

political goal. *See* goal

political influence: *group or individual attempt at or accomplishment of purposeful *influence on political *decision making or political process in a territory; the constrained exercise of social power (Goodin and Klingemann 1996:7–8). *See also* political participation

political involvement: 1. activity by a *nonprofit group intended to influence government. Smith (2000:133) notes that virtually every type of *grassroots association gets involved at one time or another in the political process. 2. synonym for the individual process, *political participation. *See also* impact of nonprofit groups; political nonprofit group

political nonprofit. *See* political nonprofit group

political nonprofit group: *nonprofit group concerned chiefly with *political voluntary action at any territorial level. Examples include *citizen groups, *interest groups, *political parties, and *social movement groups. Douglas (1987, passim) discusses the various theories that help explain political nonprofit groups.

political participation: individual *political voluntary action intended to affect governmental *social policy, policy implementation, and *decision making, whether at a local (i.e., *citizen participation), regional, national, or international level. Political participation ranges from voting to involvement in *political nonprofit groups. It may be motivated by selfish (*selfishness) or altruistic (*altruism) *goals, sometimes both. Political participation in the United States has been studied in depth by Conway (1991), Christy (1987), Dobratz and Buzzell (2002), Milbrath and Goel (1977), Nagel (1987), Norris (2002), Pateman (1970), Powers et al. (1993), Rosenstone and Hansen (1993), Smith et al. (1980), Smock (2004), Verba et al. (1978, 1995), and Verba and Nie (1972). *See also* political involvement; political party

political party: *association whose primary *goal is to select and help elect a slate of candidates for governmental office. Once in power, the party has, as additional goal, governance of the jurisdiction on which the election centered. Broadly, the goal of political parties is to gain and retain a monopoly on political power. The classic statement on political parties was written by Robert Michels (1915/1959, passim). Aldrich (1995, passim) describes the origin and transformation of political parties in America. Milkis (1999, passim) discusses the role of these groups in a constitutional *democracy (see also Ware 2001, passim). Disch (2002, passim) examines the "tyranny" of the two-party system in America, while Sifry (2003, passim) focuses on third-party politics in the United States. Bibby and Holbrook (1996) discuss American state political party activities. Witcover (2003, passim) wrote a history of the Democratic Party, and Gould (2003, passim) did the same for the Republicans. McGerr (1986/2000, passim) wrote of the decline of local political party identification and activity 1865–1892 in the American North. Chapter authors in Mair (1990, passim) discuss issues regarding West European political parties (see also Stammen 1981, passim). Chapter authors in Dominguez (1994, passim) discuss political parties in Latin America. *See also* power in nonprofit groups

political pluralism. *See* pluralism, political

political voluntary action: *voluntary action aimed at influencing governmental *social policy and practice. In particular, individual or group action intended to affect public opinion (*public, sense 2) or a combination of the structure, selection of members, *policies, or practices of government at any territorial level. Political voluntary action at the group level is often called *"interest group activity" and at the individual level *"political participation." Political action organized by business, *government, or families or households falls, since it lacks a *voluntary altruistic component, outside the field of political voluntary action. Political voluntary action is usually conventional or mainstream (widely accepted in a society), though it may be unconventional in varying degrees (deviates from societal norms). Conway (1991, passim) and Verba et al. (1995, passim) have studied political participation and voluntary action in the United States.

political voluntary group. *See* political nonprofit group

polymorphic nonprofit group: one of several *nonprofit groups, all of which are linked vertically to a larger, umbrella *organization (Smith 2000:80). *See also* monomorphic nonprofit group

population ecology of organizations approach: a theoretical perspective on organizational-environmental relations set out as a complement to the dominant adaptation perspective. Population ecology of *organizations emphasizes the strength of inertial pressures on organizational structure, both from internal structural arrangements (investment in plant and equipment, normative agreements) and environmental constraints (legal and fiscal barriers to entry into and exit from markets). It includes application of models based on competition and selection to populations of organizations (Hannan and Freeman 1977, passim). Although usually applied to business firms, this approach can also be applied to *nonprofit groups (see McPherson 1983). *See also* environment, organizational; interorganizational field

position statement/paper: a written declaration of the attitude or intentions of an individual or *nonprofit group toward a certain subject. Such declaration includes the rationale and documentation for the stance taken therein. Hunter (1997, passim) analyzes the pro-life movement's position statement "The America We Seek."

positive social capital. *See* capital, social

posse: a *volunteer group of men, usually armed, who may be authorized on a temporary basis by a sheriff to help keep law and order. Common in the American West prior to 1900 or so, but uncommon now. Full name is properly the Middle-Latin term *posse comitatus*. Pitcavage (2001, passim) likens the right-wing paramilitary groups of the 1990s in the United States to posses, especially in the conspiratorial antigovernmental spirit shared by both.

post-grant evaluation: assessment of results of a *grant received by a *nonprofit group to determine if its *goals were achieved (see the Cleveland Foundation Glossary of Terms at http://www.clevelandfoundation.org/page1691.cfm).

power elite. *See* insiders, societal

power of nonprofit groups: the capacity of *nonprofit groups to meet their *goals, even in the face of individual or collective resistance to these goals, internal or external to the *group (cf. Lasswell 1936, passim). Most *grassroots associations tend to be politically weak, especially those that are new, small, and informal (Smith 2000:134).

power structure of nonprofits: the relationships of power, formal and informal, in a *nonprofit group (cf. Hall 1996, chap. 5). In *formal nonprofits, often portrayed graphically in an *organizational chart, with the top *leader at the head of the diagram and lines of *authority running downward to other individuals or positions. One of the reasons why people in the upper ranks of this structure are, for volunteer groups, the most powerful is that they serve as *key volunteers. They number among the group's most skilled, knowledgeable, and hard-working *members in helping to reach its *goals (Stebbins 1998:3–6).

predictor of volunteer participation: indicator of the likelihood a person will volunteer. Smith (2000:240) argues that research in this area should use not only sociodemographic predictors but also psychological, situational, and environmental predictors, as reviewed in Smith (1994, passim). See Chambré (1987) for a national sample study of predictors of *volunteering among the aged. Kirsch, Hume, and Jalandoni (1999) and earlier editions of this regular volume also give predictors of *volunteer participation, particularly in *volunteer programs.

pressure group. *See* interest group

prestige incentive: type of *incentive rooted in the desire to gain esteem by dint of belonging to a renowned *nonprofit group (Smith 2000:102). *See also* incentive type

prestige of nonprofit groups: esteem with which *nonprofit groups are held by the general public, be this local, regional, or national (cf. Young and Larson 1965, passim). Most *grassroots associations have low to moderate prestige in their communities, with many of them being little known (Smith 2000:135).

prevalence of nonprofits. *See* nonprofit group prevalence

priest: 1. a Christian *religious functionary in the Roman Catholic, Eastern Orthodox, Anglican/Episcopal, or Mormon (Church of Jesus Christ of Latter-day Saints) churches (Ranson et al. 1977). 2. a *religious functionary in any of various Asian religions (e.g., Buddhism, Shintoism, Taoism).

primary group: small number of people who interact with each other long enough to form a *group (e.g., a family, friendship group). Some primary groups have clearly defined roles and *goals, while in all groups, *members recognize their *collectivity as a distinct entity. Cooley (1909, chap. 3) pioneered the idea of primary group. *See also* informal group; secondary group; collectivity; small group

primary satisfaction. *See* direct satisfaction

principle of human association: basis, or primary source, for human interaction and growth of *collectivities. Fuller (1969, passim) identifies two such principles: freely given shared *commitment and legal coercion. Boulding (1973:107) argues for a third, namely, market exchange (*exchange, market).

priority setting. *See* decision making

private foundation: term for Internal Revenue Service (IRS) 501(c)(3) nonprofits that do not qualify as *public charities under IRS designation 509(a), failing the *public support test; a *philanthropic foundation usually with an endowment of private wealth established for charitable purposes (Fishman and Schwarz 2000:602–603; Hopkins 1998, passim). Freeman (1991, passim) has written a classic book on private foundations. *See* foundation

private good. *See* good (sense 2)

private government: a *government of sorts that evolves when *nonprofit groups and businesses establish their own laws (rules) and subject people to them (cf. Lakoff 1973, passim; McConnell 1966, passim). These "private governments" have their own *leaders (some elected, some not) and their own forms of taxation (e.g., *association dues). They are considered "private," because they operate largely outside the jurisdiction of (public, elected) government. Streeck and Schmitter (1985, passim) have written in detail about what they call "private interest government."

private interest group. *See* special interest group

private-market failure: when the economy or business sector (*sector of society) fails to provide a certain *good or *service, because doing so will not generate enough profit. Said by some analysts to lead, at times, to a *nonprofit group arising or stepping in to fill the perceived "need" for the good or service, assuming a sufficient number of clients or customers is likely to be available (cf. Weisbrod 1988, passim).

private operating foundation. *See* operating foundation

private sector. *See* sector of society

private welfare: the philanthropic (*philanthropy) activity of the *nonprofit sector (cf. Critchlow and Parker 1998, passim; DeGrazia 1957, passim: Powell and Clemens 1998, passim). The term is synonymous with *charity (sense 2) and with *charitable sector, narrowly viewed. Little (1995, passim) compares private welfare and public welfare (*welfare, sense 2) in her history of the Ontario Mothers Allowance, in which she traces the complicated interplay of the two systems.

privatization: tendency in the past few decades for governments in *welfare states to cut back on direct service delivery to clients (*target of benefits) having particular unmet *needs. Governments then "privatize" these services, by contracting private for-profit, or more commonly, not-for-profit social service agencies (*nonprofit agency) to offer them, the agencies being supplied with governmental money to carry out such functions. Business firms may also receive governmental *contracts for delivery of the needed *services. Rekart (1993, passim) explores the pros and cons of this practice for nonprofit agencies and governments in Canada, as do Smith and Lipsky (1993, passim) for America and Kramer et al. (1993, passim) for four European nations. Savas (2000, passim) takes a broad analytical view of both for-profit and nonprofit privatization, while Minow (2002, passim) emphasizes that privatization involves a partnership for the *public good (sense 2). Ascoli and Ranci (2002, passim), using Italy as an example, discuss how privatization affects the structure of *welfare (sense 2) in a society.

pro bono professional work: *professionals (e.g., lawyers, physicians) volunteering their time to perform with little or no pay for poor or otherwise deserving clients (*targets of benefits) their usual professional work (cf. Tucker 1972, passim). The term derives from the Latin *pro bono publico,* or "for the public good." Weinstein (1993, passim) recounts his life as lawyer, soldier, teacher, and pro bono *activist.

problem: a doubtful or difficult matter, for which, however, an individual *volunteer or a *nonprofit group has the *resources needed to solve (McWhinney 1992:62–64). *See also* issue

process evaluation in program evaluation: investigation, by any of a variety of methods, designed to examine the process by which a *nonprofit group's *program unfolds. This type of evaluation looks at the steps taken to reach the intended outcomes of a program (Thomas 1994:362–364). Sometimes termed "formative evaluation." *See also* program evaluation

process of nonprofit groups: a routine or common operation of *nonprofit groups such as a *meeting, activity, workshop, or session of socialization (Smith 2000:127–148).

producer cooperative: a *for-profit organization, structured along *cooperative lines, made up of producers of a particular *good or *service (cf. Ben-Ner 1987, passim). In the United States agricultural producer cooperatives are most common. Contrasts with *consumer cooperatives, which may be *nonprofit groups. Shifley (2003, passim) conducted a case study of a worker-owned and-managed cooperative to explore how fundamental changes in the organization of work can affect the well-being of workers and their families. He found that expanding personal choice is one of several changes that can have a positive effect.

profession: 1. an occupation that controls its own work, as this control is organized by a special set of institutions (e.g., education, government) and sustained by an *ideology of expertise and service based on advanced skill, knowledge, or training (cf. Freidson 1994:10, n.1). 2. (loosely) a paid occupation.

professional: 1. someone engaged in a *profession (sense 1). 2. someone engaged for money in a specified occupation or activity. In the United States many *volunteer administrators in the *nonprofit sector are professional only in sense 2; that is, they are most accurately described as *paid staff rather than as workers in a profession (sense 1) (Smith 2000: 153–154).

professional association: an *association of and for professionals (sense 1) of some kind such as physicians, lawyers, and teachers. One kind of *occupational association. The U.S. Census Bureau prefers the term "professional organization" for professional associations (O'Neill 2002: 214). Krause (1996, passim) presents a comparative, cross-national, historical study of the decline of four traditional professions (medicine, law, university teaching, and engineering) and the power of their professional associations in the past few decades, as capitalism and state power have increasingly overcome the *influence of professional *values.

professional organization. *See* professional association

professional/volunteer tension: discord that sometimes emerges when *professionals and *volunteers in a *paid-staff nonprofit group perform the same tasks. Pearce (1993:142) observed that such tension arises, in part, because the professionals have more legitimacy (are formally trained), whereas the volunteers have more dedication (are fired by *altruism). Pearce notes (pp. 143–144) that tension can also occur between the two types over the level of expertise itself, as in formal training (professional) vis-à-vis long experience (volunteer). *See also* professionalization of volunteers and volunteerism

professionalism: the *ideology and special set of institutions that help *members of a *profession (sense 1) organize and sustain it (Freidson 1994:10, n.1).

professionalization of volunteers and volunteerism: process in which *volunteers and the *volunteering they do increasingly take on the qualities of professional work (*professional). These qualities include, for the professionalizing volunteers, increased formal training, skill and knowledge, seriousness, experience, certification, and the like. Nichols (2004:203), in writing about sports volunteering, holds that pressure toward professionalization emerges in the *nonprofit sector when it faces substantial competition from the business and governmental sectors (*sector of society).

professional-lay partnership: partnerships between networks of agency-based *professionals and members of *professional associations interested in *community-based initiatives and lay people who are part of *networks of individual *volunteers, *voluntary associations, and religious *congregations (Israel 1988). Requires sensitivity to varying cultures and customs of *organizations and *communities, the encouragement of lay *participation and control of programmatic and organizing efforts, and the promotion of interdependence with or independence from professionals rather than dependence on them.

profits of nonprofit groups: 1. excess of returns over outlays (*excess revenue) gained by a *nonprofit group through its commercial dealings. Starkweather (1993:107) observes that many hospitals in the United States engage in for-profit activities (*see* for-profit group), while seeking the advantages of classification as an *exempt organization. 2. *unfair competition by nonprofits, in which commercial activities of nonprofits, subsidized by governmental tax-exemption for *excess revenues, unfairly hamper the businesses that compete or would compete with nonprofits in certain industries (Bennett and DiLorenzo 1989, passim).

program: in the *nonprofit sphere, relatively permanent *organization, *project, or procedure created to meet particular *needs of a *target group (Barker 2003:342). Martin (2003) examines an assistance program for the homeless in Australia and its relationship to *volunteering and post-industrial society.

program evaluation: research that provides information on the effects of public and nonprofit activities and *programs (Thomas 1994:342). Wholey and Hatry (2004) have compiled recently a most comprehensive handbook of practical program evaluation. *See also* outcome evaluation for program evaluation; process evaluation in program evaluation

program evaluation review: examination by the staff (paid and volunteer) of a *nonprofit group under *program evaluation of the data collected during this process and their preliminary interpretation made by the evaluators (Thomas 1994:364).

program officer: *foundation staff member who screens and processes *grant proposals from *nonprofit groups, sending the most promising to the *board of directors or trustees for action. Not present in most smaller foundations (see the Foundation Center Glossary at http://www.fdn center.org/learn/ufg/glossary.html).

program volunteer: *volunteer who works in a *volunteer program (Smith

2000:224). Program *volunteers, because they work in such service programs, constitute one of the main types of volunteers who are motivated by the nonmember type of *service incentive (Smith 2000:98–99), as contrasted with most *associational volunteers, who tend to be motivated by the *co-member service incentive and other aspects of *member benefit *voluntary altruism. *See* volunteer

program volunteering: the *volunteer activities of *program volunteers (Smith 2000:224 and passim).

program volunteering, participation in: being an active *volunteer in a *volunteer program. Studies of predictors of *participation in volunteer programs include Chambré (1987, passim), Smith (1994, passim), and Kirsch et al. (1999).

project: a planned, short-term, individual or collective undertaking that, says Barker (2003:342), is more flexible than a *program. *Volunteers undertaking projects are engaged in *project-based leisure.

project-based leisure: a short-term, moderately complicated, either one-shot or occasional though infrequent, creative undertaking carried out in *free time. It requires considerable planning, effort, and sometimes skill or knowledge, but for all that is neither *serious leisure nor intended to develop into such (Stebbins 2005b, passim). Some *volunteering is project-based *leisure (e.g., volunteering at a major convention or major sports competition, volunteering to help restore human life or wildlife after a natural or human-made disaster). *See also* casual leisure

proposal. *See* grant proposal

proselytizing: actively seeking *converts to one's own *religion from among those with no religion or another religion (cf. Sheffer 1999, passim).

prosocial behavior: *helping behavior aimed at someone in need of help (Burlingame 2004:387); if reciprocity sought is low (Bar-Tal 1976), may be seen as altruistic action (*altruism) taken by an individual or group in any sector intended to benefit society and the *public interest. Staub (1978; 1979, passim) wrote a classic literature review on prosocial behavior and morality. Ciarrocchi (2003, passim) found that spiritual and personality variables mediate differently the prosocial behavior of men and women.

protected zone: arena of social life in which people feel free from the money economy and the dictates of the state and free to operate according to the dictates of *compassion. According to Wuthnow (1991:279), *volunteers often view their *volunteer work as activity in such a protected zone. Wuthnow saw this zone as falling within Habermas's broader conceptualization of the life world, an area of personal and interpersonal life that is increasingly intruded upon by the system (the state and market).

protest. *See* activity, protest

protest movement. *See* social movement

proud amateurishness of grassroots association leaders: sentiment many *leaders have toward running their *grassroots associations, which is expressed in such processes as trial and error and learning by experience. Smith (2000:154) says that these leaders are often proud of the amateurish quality of their *leadership, proud that it is *not* professional. *See* professional; profession

pseudo-nonprofit group. *See* nonprofit group

psychic benefit: a nonmaterial reward, or advantage, gained from *volunteering or *quasi-volunteering. Smith, Reddy, and Baldwin (1972:163) observed that *volunteers experience psychic benefits when *volunteering meets their cognitive *needs, particularly those of *self-fulfillment and self-actualization. *See also* satisfaction; development of volunteers

psychic income. *See* psychic benefit; satisfaction

psychological empowerment. *See* empowerment (sense 2)

psychological empowerment impact: positive change in a person's life created by self-perception of competence, understanding of the relevant sociopolitical environment, and personal control over relevant conditions, all combined in a proactive approach to the desired change (see Zimmerman 1995:581). *See also* impact of nonprofits

psychological factor in volunteering: a psychological reason why people volunteer in the many different kinds of *volunteering. There are two main sets of such reasons: (a) presence of certain personality traits (e.g., self-confidence, extraversion, sense of efficacy) and (b) presence of certain attitudes (e.g., perceived *effectiveness of *nonprofit groups, preferences for *service in *leisure time, sense of *civic obligation, sense of civic pride, *altruism). These traits are among those comprising the *democratic personality and the *active-effective character. The intensive study of psychological factors in volunteering has helped offset the inadequacy of research that has relied largely, if not entirely, on *motive talk. Smith (1994a:250–252) explores these factors in his review of the literature on determinants of *participation in voluntary *associations and *program volunteering.

psychological trait of leaders. *See* leadership, trait approach

public: 1. the people as a whole in a *community or a nation. 2. a set of people sharing a common social, cultural, or political *interest, but who, as individuals, often have no contact with one another. Both theory and practice in the *nonprofit sector revolve mostly around sense 1 and the idea of *public benefit (Smith 1993, passim). By contrast *amateurs and public-centered *professionals (those in art, science, sport, entertainment, Stebbins 1992:22) relate to particular publics, as does public opinion centered on a given *issue (sense 2).

public advocacy. *See* advocacy

public benefit. *See* benefit (sense 2)

public benefit in nonprofits: 1. of or pertaining to the *public interest in the broadest sense. 2. something valuable that *targets of benefits (recipients) or the general *public receive as the intended result of activities and *programs of a *nonprofit group. Smith (1993, passim) compares *member benefits with public benefits and argues that "public" is a misnomer, with "nonmember benefit" being preferred as the more accurate term (Smith 2000:115–116).

public benefit nonprofit group: *nonprofit group whose principal *goal is to benefit and serve in the *public interest nonmembers (i.e., the *public, sense 1) rather than *members. The *target of benefits is rarely a cross section of the society but rather selected *social categories of people such as the poor, aged, or homeless, hence the term *"nonmember benefit group" is preferred. Smith (2000:114–117) compares *member benefit and *nonmember benefit groups.

public charity: a specialized type of *nonprofit organization distinguished by parts of the Internal Revenue Code in America because these *organizations "either have wide public support or . . . actively function in a supporting relationship to such organizations" (Milani 1988:5.4). The latter source gives (ibid.) as examples (from Section 509 of the Internal Revenue Code) "a church or . . . *association of churches," "an educational organization (e.g., school, college)," "a hospital," "a publicly supported organization (e.g., museum, library, American Red Cross)." More technicalities about public charities are given in Wood (1988, sections 4.13–4.14). But Bowen et al. (1994:7) make it all clear with a diagram, which shows that public charities are roughly the same as Internal Revenue Service (IRS) 501(c)(3) groups (omitting about 10 percent that are private foundations), and which, in October 1991, constituted about 41 percent of all IRS *tax-exempt entities. All public charities are designated as 509(a) groups by the IRS, meeting the *public support test. In their table 2.1, Bowen et al. (1994:21) show that public charities run the gamut of purposive types of nonprofits, from mutual benefit to health and human services, from religion to science, from disaster relief to *civil rights. *See also* nonprofit organization; nonprofit agency

public foundation: a *nonprofit group that gets at least one-third of its total annual *revenue from the *public, including *government and other *foundations, and that engages mainly in *grant making, though it may also provide some direct charitable services. A form of *public charity (see the Cleveland Foundation Glossary of Terms at http://www .clevelandfoundation.org/page1691.cfm).

public good: 1. a commodity whose *benefits are indivisibly spread among the entire *community, whether or not particular individuals desire to consume the public good (Samuelson and Nordhaus 1995:761). A *good in sense 1. Clean air is one example. 2. as in the "public good" (*see* public interest [the]) (Smith 1977:1108).

public goods theory: a set of propositions centered on the observation that *nonprofit groups emerge to provide collective *goods to those social groups having preferences other than those of the median voter. By contrast government provides such goods to median voters (Weisbrod 1988). *See also* contract failure theory; voluntary failure theory

public interest (the): 1. the joint satisfaction of *public needs (cf. Fellmeth and Nader 1970, passim; Kohlmeier 1969, passim; Smith 1977:1108). 2. (as in the expression "in the public interest") the meeting of one or more public needs (Smith 2000:22–23). There is a journal devoted to discussions of this topic: *The Public Interest.*

public interest group: *nonprofit organization or *collectivity of like-minded individuals interested in changing or retaining a particular arrangement by influencing a certain governmental *social policy, candidate for office, governmental *agency, or the general *public (sense 1). Unlike *special interest groups, public interest groups purport to serve the *public interest and the general *welfare (sense 2) of the whole society. Jordan and Maloney (1996, passim) found, in a study conducted in England, that group activity is important in shaping the preferences of potential *members of interest groups and in stimulating their *participation there. Hrebenar (1997, chap. 12) discusses the rise of public interest groups (*nonprofit organizations) in America from the late 1960s as counterbalancing forces to more traditional lobbies that are *special interest groups. Two public interest groups that have stood the test of time are Common Cause (McFarland 1984, passim) and Public Citizen, Inc. founded by Ralph Nader (cf. Marcello 2004, passim). Other important books on public interest groups in the United States have been written by, among others, Berry (1977), McCann (1986), and Rothenberg (1992). *See also* interest group; lobbyist

public need: a collective good (*good, senses 1 and 3) widely accepted by society. In the United States these *needs seem to include physical and mental health, economic well-being, justice/freedom/security, education and communication, science/technology/ inquiry, *religion,/philosophy/ idealism, peace and social integration, esthetic experience/"culture"/entertainment, *leisure/recreation/relaxation, emotional expression and interpersonal relations, *participation/involvement/efficacy/power, ecological balance/decent environment, social *welfare and social *services, and social change/adaptation (Smith 1977, passim). To qualify as *nonprofit sector concerns, all must be addressed within the framework of *voluntary altruism (Smith 2000:22–23).

public participation. *See* community involvement

public philanthropy: both private support of the government through philanthropy and voluntarism as well as government support of nonprofits and voluntarism (Burlingame 2004:402). For instance, includes government financing of nonprofit activity through *grant making together with private volunteering for government agencies at different territorial levels (Brudney and Kellough 2000, passim). The relationship between the government sector and the nonprofit sector is a complex one (cf. Boris and Steuerle 1999, passim).

public policy. *See* social policy

public purpose. *See* public need

public relations in nonprofits. *See* marketing in nonprofits

public sector. *See* sector of society

public service: 1. an adjective used to modify such terms as "announcement," "commission," and the like, and signifying a *public need (cf. Bowen 1973, passim; Millet 1966, passim). 2. a specific service performed usually by an individual and recognized as being in the *public interest. Ganje and Kenny (2004, passim) describe the public service performed by the *Grand Forks Herald* (sense 2), when it covered extremely well the 1997 flood of the Red River, which runs through the city of Grand Forks, North Dakota. *See* social service (sense 2).

public support test: a test of whether a *nonprofit receives substantial support from the general public, as set out in two alternative versions in Section *509(a) of the U.S. Internal Revenue Code (cf. Burlingame 2004: 539). Both versions require one-third of the nonprofit's support to come from the general public (including donations, grants, sales, fees, etc.) in order to qualify as a *public charity rather than as a *private foundation.

public welfare. *See* welfare (sense 2); public interest

public worship: religious worship open to the *public (sense 1), as opposed to worship restricted to *members of a religious *congregation or *organization. Tax exemption for property owned by *ecclesiastical corporations was originally tied to its use for public worship, but this has gradually become justified on the broader grounds as use of a religious nature (Cummins 1986).

purchase of services: shorthand term for the contractual relationship between governmental *agencies and *nonprofit groups (almost always *nonprofit agencies, not *associations), in which government supplies the money nonprofits use to provide *services to specified *targets of benefits. Purchase of services is central to *privatization of *social services in *welfare states. S. Smith and Lipsky (1993, passim) have studied the purchase of services in the United States.

pure volunteer. *See* volunteer, pure

purpose of nonprofit group. *See* mission

purposive incentive: type of *nonprofit group *incentive rooted in the desire to gain certain normative or ideological rewards, hence sometimes called "normative incentive." In gaining these rewards *active members also find special *satisfaction through sharing the *ideology of their *nonprofit group, as it determines what the group's *goals should be and how they should be achieved (Knoke 1988, passim; 1990:115). Purposive incentives trace back to Clark and Wilson (1961, passim). *See also* incentive type

purposive type classification of nonprofit groups. *See* classification of non-profit groups

purposive type of flat-earth paradigm: *nonprofit sector model that *nonprofit groups can be described and explained by classifying them according to purpose (*goal), or *mission, and, by implication, that such classifications can help us understand these groups and how they work (Smith 2000:232–233). Neglects relevance of the more profound analytic classifications (*see* classification of nonprofit groups). *See also* paradigm

Q

qualified donee (for charitable contribution tax deduction): generally includes *governments (*government agency) and Internal Revenue Service 501(c)(3) charitable organizations mainly, plus veterans organizations, domestic fraternal lodges (for charitable purposes), and nonprofit cemetery organizations. The first four can also receive tax-deductible gifts for estate and gift tax purposes (Fishman and Schwarz 2000:868–869). Individuals are not qualified donees (Fishman and Schwarz 2000:874).

quality assurance (quality control): in the *nonprofit sector, maintenance of the desired quality of the *service or product offered by a *nonprofit group (cf. Juran and Gryna 1974, passim). Bradshaw and colleagues (1998, passim) examined complaint procedures as part of quality assurance in the *voluntary sector of Great Britain. They studied *nonprofit groups contracted to provide various services.

QUANGO. *See* quasi-nongovernmental organization

quasi-nongovernmental organization (QUANGO): a *nonprofit group that has significant governmental or *for-profit characteristics. For instance, a legal *nonprofit service *organization operating as a *business (e.g., the American Automobile Association in the United States) or a legal *nonprofit research *organization started by a national *government (e.g., the RAND Corporation in the United States). Taylor (1999, passim) applied the principles of critical discourse analysis to the materials produced by a QUANGO for landlords to reveal how this *organization manages communication with tenants.

quasi-volunteer: 1. person who works for a *public service *goal, is recognized socially as a type of *volunteer, and receives a stipend that is significantly less than market value of the labor provided (e.g., Peace Corps volunteers) (Smith 2000:25, 47). Sometimes referred to as a "stipended volunteer." A *volunteer who receives a stipend that is very low albeit commensurate with the value of that person's volunteer labor, because work skills are also very low is, at bottom, a "false quasi-volunteer" (cf. Smith, Reddy, and Baldwin 1972:172). 2. when paid employees in the *nonprofit sector receive less pay than employees in the business sector for doing the same or similar jobs, the former can be viewed as "career quasi-volunteers" or what Stebbins (2004a, passim) calls "occupational devotees." Inspired by *voluntary altruism and various special, highly attractive conditions of their work, they forego higher pay.

quasi-volunteer action: *voluntary action that is significantly underremunerated (Smith 2000:24). It issues, in large part, from *quasi-volunteer altruism. *See also* quasi-volunteer; volunteer action

quasi-volunteer altruism: *voluntary altruism that motivates *paid staff in a *nonprofit group to engage in *under*remunerated activity, as opposed to *un*remunerated or remunerated activity (Smith 2000:24).

quasi-volunteer group: a *nonprofit group 50 percent or more of whose cumulative group-related hours of action by *analytic members over a particular period of time qualify as *quasi-volunteer action (Smith 2000: 25–26). Roughly speaking, a *paid-staff nonprofit in which most paid staff are *under*remunerated and motivated by *quasi-volunteer altruism.

quasi-volunteering: the role activities of *quasi-volunteers (cf. Smith 2000: 24–25).

R

rabbi: a Jewish *religious functionary who has completed a recognized course of study with other existing rabbis (cf. Harris 1998b:216).

rainbow coalition: a formal or informal *nonprofit group composed of people from different minority groups or other disadvantaged parts of society working together to achieve particular social or political *goals held in common (cf. Janvier 1984; McKelvey 1994). Originally an American term, Klineberg's (1998, passim) data suggest that the diverse Black and Hispanic *communities in the United States are unlikely to unite in a new rainbow coalition until efforts to promote a healthier natural environment are combined with a firmer *commitment to economic and social justice.

randomization for program evaluation: the process of assigning by chance subjects in an experiment. Experiments are sometimes used in *outcome evaluation designs as part of *program evaluation (Thomas 1994:356).

rank and file: ordinary *members of a *nonprofit group or an entire society, as distinguished from its *leaders or *societal insiders. The adjectival form is hyphenated (e.g., rank-and-file members). Gapasin (1996, passim) studied change from 1970 to 1992 in a *private sector *union, during which a rank-and-file movement (see social movement) for greater *democracy resulted in unseating an incumbent president of twenty-five years. See also democracy in nonprofit groups

rationale for charitable tax exemption: legal doctrine that certain charitable *nonprofits deserve *501(c)(3) *tax-exempt status because they serve a *charitable purpose, have a *nondistribution constraint, do not try substantially to influence legislation, do not participate in political campaigns of any candidates for public office, and do not violate the law or public policy generally (Fishman and Schwarz 2000:229–230). There are various additional rationales as well (pp. 329–348).

rationalization of organizations: 1. the process during which *leaders of *nonprofit groups and, to varying degrees, their ordinary *members consider ways to reach group *goals, using in the most effective and efficient way possible given group *resources (Smith 2000:167). 2. the results of the rationalization process. Weber (1947) was one of the first to suggest that organizations engage in rationalization in these senses.

rebellion: 1.open or determined disobedience by a *group or *collectivity to an authority. 2. organized armed resistance to the established ruler or government usually undertaken by *volunteers (cf. Gurr 1969, passim). Rebellions in sense 2 have often been organized by *grassroots associations or *social movements and have involved force or threat of it against people and property. Thus, in 1837 in Lower Canada (Quebec), Louis-Joseph Papineau established a political party known as the Parti Patriote, which fomented the Patriote Rebellion in hope of achieving greater francophone representation in the largely anglophone legislative assembly then governing that part of Canada (Crystal 1994:924). And Katz and his colleagues (1988, passim) write of peasant rebellions in Mexico as one type of dramatic ramification of the various peasant social movements and *collectivities operating between the sixteenth and twentieth centuries.

recipient of helping services. *See* target of benefits

reciprocity: returning something for something received; a form of mutual action (cf. Becker 1986, passim; Burlingame 2004:409–411). Trivers (1971, passim) explains *altruism to unrelated others by noting that it roots in the probability of reciprocity. Given humankind's lengthy lifespan and high degree of interdependence, it is adaptive to be altruistic, assuming others will reciprocate at some point in the future.

recognition of paid staff: the practice in *paid-staff nonprofit organizations of providing formal or informal rewards to paid staff for work well done. Vineyard (2001, passim) discusses this function in *nonprofit groups.

recognition of volunteers/members: major administrative function in *nonprofit groups and *volunteer programs that involves providing formal awards as part of the *program, the larger *organization, or an external volunteer recognition process (e.g., National Volunteer Week). Such awards may be for outstanding service, length of service, or unusual service (see volunteer service). More informal rewards are treated, in this dictionary, in the entry on *motivating volunteers. Connors (1995:178–179, chap. 11, and passim), Fisher and Cole (1993, chap. 4), Vineyard

(2001, passim), and Wittich (2003b, passim) all give practical advice on volunteer recognition practices. Battle (1988, chap. 6) gives brief advice about recognition of *members with awards in *associations.

recreation/recreational activity: 1. synonym for *leisure activity. 2. activity done in *free time, which, after work, refreshes and restores the person to return to work again (Godbey 1999:12–13); included in *voluntary action if done in a *nonprofit group (Smith 2000:23).

recreational club. *See* recreational group

recreational group: 1. synonym for *leisure group. 2. *club or *group one *goal of which is to provide an activity that regenerates *members for work. Clubs and groups in sense 2 have long been out of fashion, though several were in operation in the days of the Puritans (Weber 1952:167). Many recreational groups (sense 1) exist today in America (Verba et al. 1995:63); national random adult survey data show 21 percent of respondents are affiliated with a *nonprofit group, usually an *association, classified as "Hobby, Sports, Leisure."

recruitment of nonprofit group paid staff: the process of finding and hiring people to fill remunerated posts in *paid-staff nonprofit groups. Sturgeon (1994:535–556) writes on the ins and outs of finding and keeping the best employees in these groups.

recruitment of volunteers/members: the process of persuading people to become *members or *volunteers, whether as unaffiliated individuals or as unpaid staff of a *nonprofit group. Nonprofit groups, in general, and *grassroots associations, in particular, tend to informally recruit *members or volunteers (Smith 2000:139). Smith (1985:235–248) discusses general volunteer recruitment modes (word of mouth, general public recruitment through mass media, mass canvassing door-to-door or by telemarketing, volunteer fairs, recruitment presentations at other groups' meetings, volunteer registers or skillsbanks) and key factors in recruitment tactics, using his *ISSTAL model. McCurley (1994, passim) looks at recruitment of volunteers for *volunteer programs. There are many practical guides to volunteer recruitment (e.g., Connors 1995, chap. 4; Ellis 2002; Fisher and Cole 1993, chap. 5; Little 1999; McBee 2002; McCurley and Vineyard 1988; Rusin 1999; Wilson 1983; Wittich 2003a). Battle (1988, chap. 6) treats member recruitment. *See also* staffing

regional association: a supralocal *association that draws its *members from and offers a *service to a region of a state, province, or nation. Skeldon (1977, passim) studied two conflicting interpretations of the role of regional associations for migrants using data from Peru. He concluded it is more fruitful to view these entities as products of urbanization than as urban enclaves.

regular volunteer. *See* habitual volunteer

relations, external. *See* environment, organizational

religion: 1. *denomination, *sect, *church, or *new religion (cult). 2. set of beliefs, sentiments, and activities dealing with the ultimate questions of human existence such as the supernatural (e.g., God, gods, Satan, angels) and life after death or the basic moral principles for human life on earth (e.g., compassion, kindness, love thy neighbor). Some religious systems are built on both components. Johnstone (1992, passim) examines religion from the sociological perspective, concluding that, because of the multiplicity of denominations there, America is a denominational society.

religiosity: religious feeling (including emotion) or belief (including *ideology) or both, which may be expressed, formally or informally, through religious *interest and *participation in religious *rituals and religious experiences (*religious activity; Johnstone 1992, chap. 4; Stark and Glock 1968, passim). One of many measures of religiosity is frequent (e.g., weekly) attendance at religious services. In the United States, weekly attendance at church or synagogue rose in the population from 40 percent in 1980 to 44 percent in 2000 (U.S. Bureau of the Census 2002:56, table 64).

religious: 1. (adj.) characterized by *religiosity. 2. (n.) member of a *religious order (cf. Turcotte 2001, passim).

religious activity/commitment: *group, collective, or individual activity mainly directed toward religious *goals. It can run from individual prayer to *participation in worship services to administration of a religious *organization to working for a *religious nonprofit group. Stark and Glock (1968:14–16) distinguish five dimensions of religious commitment or activity. Religious activity is part of the *nonprofit sector, though this fact has, until recently (Harris 1998, passim), often been overlooked by nonprofit scholars (Smith 1984, passim). *See also* religiosity; ritual

religious belief/knowledge: the dimension of *religious activity that focuses on what people believe about God, the Bible, the supernatural, or other religious topics pertaining to a given *religion, along with their commitment to such beliefs (cf. Stark and Glock 1968:14, chaps. 2, 3, 7). Religious knowledge refers to the subset of religious beliefs that are actual knowledge of religious facts about rites, scriptures, traditions, and so forth. Stark and Glock (1968:14–16) view belief and knowledge as separate but related dimensions.

religious consequences: that aspect of *religious practice that refers to how religion affects an individual's everyday life and activities (cf. Stark and Glock 1969:16).

religious conversion. *See* conversion, religious

religious convert. *See* convert, religious

religious cult. *See* new religion

religious denomination. *See* denomination

religious experience/feeling: the dimension of *religious activity that focuses on what people experience and feel about religion, God, the Bible, the supernatural, church, and related matters (Stark and Glock 1968:15, chap. 6). James (1902/1958, passim) wrote an early classic work on the varieties of religious experience.

religious functionary: general social science term for religious leader of any *religion or *denomination (cf. Ranson et al. 1977, passim).

religious group. *See* religious nonprofit group

religious mission: 1. a *nonprofit group with the religious *goal of converting or evangelizing people with no *religion or a different religion or *denomination. 2. a religious *nonprofit *mission or principal *goal. Flory (2002, passim) examined the impact of recently established, nontraditional, adult degree completion *programs on the educational mission of two evangelical colleges. Nevertheless the colleges have so far been able to maintain their religious identity.

religious movement: a *social movement oriented toward one or more central religious *goals. Toth (2003, passim) mounted a case study of Islamism in Southern Egypt, considered there a radical religious movement. Absence of legitimate channels for economic assistance, *political participation, and *social protest have radicalized the region.

religious nonprofit group: a *nonprofit group organized according to religious *goals and principles. Verba et al. (1995:63) found that 12 percent of randomly selected American adults reported affiliation with such religious groups, usually *grassroots associations and not *churches. Cnaan and Milofsky (1991:S7–S9) note that such groups are subdivisions of larger, formally organized religious entities (e.g., church, *denomination) whose *missions include provision of specific *social services, especially for the needy who owe their lot to, for example, war, famine, natural disaster, economic problems, or social and political persecution (cf. Cnaan et al. 1999, passim).

religious order: a religious *brotherhood or *sisterhood in which *members live, worship, and work communally, usually in a *monastery or *convent. Common in the Roman Catholic Church. Turcotte (2001, passim) writes that the religious order is a historical form of Christianity, especially Catholicism. It purports to have a vision of the world that is independent in some significant way of the dominant vision of the Church or surrounding society.

religious organization: an *organization with one or more central religious *goals. Usually a *religious nonprofit group. Christerson and Emerson (2003, passim) studied the costs of ethnic diversity in a sample of religious organizations. One problem is that minority groups in these organizations, compared with the majority group there, tend to disproportionately bear these costs.

religious philanthropy: the intersection of *religion and *philanthropy, including religion as a prime motivation for giving and volunteering, congregations as the prime recipients of philanthropic giving and sources of further giving, religious origins of many social agencies and the structure of national associations, and religion as a major historical factor in the development of the nonprofit sector (Burlingame 2004:411–415). The last point is especially supported by the readings in Hammack (1998, passim) and by Stackhouse (1990, passim).

religious pluralism. *See* pluralism, religious

religious practice: one of the major dimensions of *religious activity/commitment that refers to how religion affects *ritual behavior, *devotional activities, and *religious consequences in everyday activities as influenced by religious beliefs (cf. Battin 1990, passim; Hall 1997, passim; Stark and Glock 1968:15, chaps. 4, 5; Wilkinson 1999, passim).

religious right (in America): a religious movement of the last few decades of the twentieth century and early twenty-first century that combines earlier *fundamentalism (Gasper 1963, passim) with the idea that conservative Christians should try to influence the political process if they can, serving God in so doing (Johnstone 1992:148–153). Choosing issues to fight over like abortion, gay rights, evolution, and morality in general, the religious right in America has become a potent political force (Brown 2002; passim; Martin 1996, passim; Utter and Storey 1995, passim).

religious settlement: an *intentional community with central religious goals and ideology. Of the many utopian intentional communities studied by Kanter (1972:244–248) founded in America from 1780–1860, the most successful in terms of longevity were all religious settlements. *See also* commune

religious tolerance: 1. attitude of personal acceptance in society of the existence and operation of *religions and *denominations different from one's own (cf. Newman 1982, passim). Often, but not necessarily, accompanies the right of *freedom of religion. 2. societal condition in which the existence and operation of multiple religions and denominations are accepted; existence of freedom of religion (cf. Newman 1982, passim). Budziszewski (1992, pt. 5) raises the question of whether religious tolerance is even possible, when many religions claim that, according to their special deity, they are superior to all others. In this stance, *tolerance can easily become sin.

repertoire of collection action. *See* action norm, distinctive

request for proposal (RFP): general solicitation of *grant proposals by a *foundation or *governmental agency from *nonprofit groups or individuals for a particular, often new, foundation or agency *program area. RFPs typically list *project specifications and application procedures. Nevertheless most foundations still prefer to receive proposals initiated by nonprofits rather than requesting them for specified areas of interest (see the Foundation Center Glossary at http://www.fdncenter.org/learn/ufg/glossary.html).

research literature on nonprofit sector. *See* literature on the nonprofit sector

residential longevity: length of time a person has resided in the same residence or locality. Hodgkinson (1990) cited research by Hodgkinson and Weitzman (1988) to the effect that length of residence in a *community did not affect extent of *program volunteering, while *membership in a religious *congregation did. They concluded that congregations may dampen the otherwise presumably negative effect of lack of rootedness in the geographic community, by providing an avenue for linkage to the community through the congregation. As predicted by the *dominant status model, a subpart of the *ISSTAL model, residential longevity has been found to be positively associated with greater *associational volunteering and *program volunteering (Smith 1994:247, 250).

resistance movement: a *social movement formed to resist or oppose an incumbent *government, often a new *government forced on a territory from outside (cf. Chambard 1976, passim). Frequently operates underground (secretly). Goldberg (1991, passim) discusses twentieth-century American resistance movements. Some resistance fails to coalesce into a social movement, however, as seen, for instance, in resistance activities intended to undermine stereotyped images of females in sport and *leisure. Mishal (2003, passim) argues that, following the attack in 2001 on the World Trade Center in New York, the Hamas resistance movement in Palestine has shown itself to be a dynamic, flexible phenomenon characterized by far greater complexity than conventionally assumed. *See also* underground group

resistance to complexity: opposition in *nonprofit groups, especially the *grassroots association variety, to bureaucratic structure and procedure (*bureaucracy) (cf. Smith 2000:112). Harrison (1960, passim), after reviewing Weber's thoughts on the matter, concluded that nonprofit groups (especially smaller ones) strive for balance between *need for bureaucratic procedure and distrust of centralized authority (*centralization). *See also* complexity in nonprofits

resource: a means of supplying a deficiency; a stock or reserve to be drawn on when needed. The main resources of *nonprofit groups are financial (*revenue and, rarely, *assets) and personnel (*volunteers, *paid staff). The term "fund" is synonymous with financial resource. According to Smith (2000:119), *grassroots associations tend to operate with a low level of resources. Paid-staff nonprofits, by contrast, operate with substantial resources, especially the largest nonprofits (Salamon 1999, passim).

resource acquisition: the obtaining by one or more *leaders of a *nonprofit group of such *resources as *donations and *members and the *dues they pay as well as monies gained from *grants and *fund-raising events. Smith (2000:160) observes that some *grassroots association leaders also try to organize *membership drives, even though success here is elusive.

resource mobilization approach: theoretic perspective emphasizing both societal support and constraint of *social movement phenomena. It considers the many *resources that must be mobilized, links of movements to other movements, dependence of movements on external sources for success, and *tactics authorities use to control or incorporate movements (Zald and McCarthy 1987:16).

responsibilities of the board of directors: a *nonprofit *board of directors has legal responsibilities they must adhere to, including selection of the chief executive officer, strategic planning, securing needed resources, monitoring management performance, and so forth (cf. Fishman and Schwarz 2000:145–146). *See also* fiduciary obligations of board of directors

responsibility accounting. *See* management control system

responsive philanthropy: reformist approach to philanthropy championed initially by the Donee Group (1975) of the Filer Commission and by its successor, the National Committee for Responsive Philanthropy (NCRP) (whose newsletter since 1978 has been named *Responsive Philanthropy*). While initially focusing on pushing for more responsiveness of traditional philanthropy to the have-nots of our society (e.g., the poor, minorities, women, etc.), NCRP and the larger responsive philanthropy movement have gone on to other issues like accountability of foundations, *alternative federated funds, and social justice and advocacy philanthropy generally (Burlingame 2004:415–417; Rabinowitz 1990, passim).

restricted fund: 1. *fund consisting of money or other *gifts as well as the income they generate, use of which must conform with restrictions established by the *donor or *grantor. 2. an *operating fund may be restricted, in that it may be established for a particular purpose or for a particular period of time (Anthony and Young 1994:417). Restricted operating funds are, for example, used to administer *grants and *contracts. *See also* designated fund

retaining volunteers/members. *See* retention of volunteers/members

retention of volunteers/members: 1. the process of trying to hold on to *associational *members, *program volunteers, or other *nonprofit group members. McCurley (1994, passim) discusses retaining program volunteers. 2. the outcome of this process. Ross (1976:140–142) suggests that primary *groups existing within larger *nonprofit groups tend to encourage *members to remain in the fold (sense 1). Smith (1985:248–249) suggests that effective *volunteer (or *member) retention involves adequate *training of members/volunteers, their proper *placement, and a variety of other *personnel practices centered on retaining them. Other practical guides to retention practices for volunteers include Connors

(1995, chap. 4), Fisher and Cole (1993, chap. 4), Ilsley (1990), Little (1999), McBee (2002), McCurley and Lynch (1996), Rusin (1999), and Wittich (2002). Battle (1988, chap. 4) deals briefly with member retention.

retrenchment in nonprofit groups: synonymous with *cutback: the act of cutting back *funding, *services, or *resources. Smith (1985:231–233) discusses retrenchment and cutbacks in funding for *nonprofit groups in the United States, resulting from economic recession and *policies of the Reagan administration. Byron (2003) examines the problems of retrenchment and regeneration in the rural areas of the province of Newfoundland. Burlingame et al. (1996, passim) present essays on different facets of retrenchment and *devolution in the nonprofit world.

retrospective reciprocity: A form of *reciprocity in which a person who engages in *giving or *volunteering in the interests of an *organization or *cause does so in part because that person previously received some *benefit from the existence of that organization or cause. This concept was suggested by the findings of Chambré (1987) that 10 percent of older adult volunteers had previously received *services from the organization for which they volunteered. *See also* reciprocity; anticipatory reciprocity; concurrent reciprocity; lateral reciprocity

reunion: a temporary *leisure gathering of people belonging to a particular family or having attended a particular school. A short-term celebration of the existence of a particular family or school (including institutions of higher education). Vinitzky-Seroussi (1998, passim) examined the high school reunion as an autobiographical occasion.

revenue: a *nonprofit group's annual income from all sources. Data on the revenue of *grassroots associations are difficult to find, given that these associations are seldom audited on a national level or even on a lower territorial level (Smith 2000:57). Data on the revenue of larger nonprofits are reported annually in the United States to the Internal Revenue Service on Form 990 and are available for statistical summary (cf. Toepler 2003:239–240) and research.

revolt. *See* rebellion

revolution: a substantial number of people engaging as *volunteers in *political voluntary action, involving force or threat of it against people or property or both in an attempt to replace certain structural and operational principles of the existing *government. Revolutions, which can last for years, still may not succeed. They may also be the cumulative result of several shorter *rebellions. Kimmel (1990, passim) offers a comprehensive overview of revolutions.

reward system: scheme of payment or other return for contributions made to a *nonprofit group by its *paid staff and *volunteers. Writing on *ethics in *nonprofit management, Jeavons (1994:203) holds that *leaders and *managers of such groups must reward members for honesty whatever the sphere.

RFP. *See* request for proposal

riot: a substantial number of people acting mainly as *volunteers engaged in *voluntary action, who use force or threat of it against people or property or both to *protest a perceived injustice or terrorize others (cf. Miller 1985:238). Riots are usually short-lived, lasting a few hours or days. Lofland (1990:432–433), in a classic statement, categorizes the riot as a form of *collective behavior. His examples included race riots and riots generated by captives (e.g., prisoners). Kettle and Hodges (1982, passim) described and analyzed the race riots in British cities in the summer of 1981, which followed a long history of occasional riots in Britain since the fourteenth century (p. 12).

risk management and liability for volunteers/members: major administrative function in *nonprofit groups and *volunteer programs that involves careful selection of *volunteers who seem to have low-risk potential (a) for harming *clients, the larger *organization, and the *volunteer program, and (b) for harming themselves. Liability insurance is recommended for the volunteer program and its *participants. Connors (1995) reviews general *liability and immunities in chapter 14, *risk management strategies in chapter 16, and volunteers and employment law in chapter 17. Fisher and Cole (1993:48–51) discuss risk management in selection of volunteers. Tremper and Kortin (1993, passim) have written a book on controlling risks in volunteer programs. *Grassroots associations seldom concern themselves with risk management, for they have little to lose in a lawsuit, but nonetheless, some carry liability insurance. *Board members of *associations of any size or territorial level have certain legal responsibilities and liabilities (Connors 1995, chap.15), which can be covered by directors and *officers liability insurance. Battle (1988:142–143) discusses insurance and bonding in associations. *See also* charitable immunity and liability

risk management in nonprofits: a *project, or more properly, a regular *program in a *nonprofit group of assessing risk and finding effective ways of reducing it (M. Herman 2005, passim). The *goal is to avoid harm from risky events and avoid causing harm to both *members and *targets of benefits. Mainly found in *paid-staff nonprofit organizations, risk management aims at lowering accidents and work stoppage; reducing insurance rates; and increasing numbers of *clients, *members, and *volunteers by protecting and enhancing the nonprofit's reputation for safety. Risk management reduces likelihood of legal suit, while improving the group's position if sued (Tremper 1994:486). *See also* charitable immunity and liability; liability; risk management and liability for volunteers/members

ritual: 1. a prescribed order of performing a religious or other devotional service. Stark and Glock (1968, chap. 4) take a broader view and include in religious ritual such activities as church attendance (worship), mass media worship, communion, religious organization participation (church-connected), financial support, and saying grace. 2. a rite or ceremonial procedure. With respect to sense 1, Rappaport (1999) argued that survival of a religious *denomination requires a delicate balance of continuity of ritual and adaptation of ritual to changing social conditions. Writing on sense 2, Smith (1972c:44–49) argues that emotionally powerful rituals in sociability *grassroots associations (e.g., college fraternities and sororities) play a key role in developing and maintaining *member *commitment. Hobsbawm (1965, chap. 6) writes of ritual in social movements. *See also* religious activity; religiosity

rotating credit: a system of lending money, wherein individual *members of a *grassroots association established for this purpose contribute, often monthly, to a credit pool, either fixed or variable amounts. Loans are then made from the pool to contributors in amounts and according to a schedule of eligibility determined by the members (Fisher 1993:43). Rotating savings and credit associations (ROSCAs) are popular in many parts of the world, especially in developing nations (Van den Brink and Chavas 1997:746).

round physical earth controversy: long-standing, historical dispute over whether the earth is round or flat (cf. Zerubavel 1992, passim). Using this controversy as a model, Smith (2000:13–15) develops his flat- and round-earth metaphors and accompanying *paradigms. *See also* metaphor, flat-earth nonprofit sector; metaphor, round-earth nonprofit sector; Flat-Earth Research Society International

round-earth nonprofit sector paradigm. *See* paradigm, round-earth nonprofit sector

rule of reprimand in volunteer service: principle stating that, if *volunteers can be reprimanded in the same manner as *paid staff for such violations of group rules as being late or absent, then the *value of their *service can be acknowledged (Anthony and Young 1994:411). That is, services of volunteers, as those of paid staff, can be counted as *revenue or an expense when *management can control the former as it does the latter.

rural youth group: a youth development *association, such as 4-H or Future Farmers of America, developed primarily for rural farm youth. Found in the United States at both local and national levels. Goreham (2004, passim) studied four hundred rural *church *youth groups in the Northern Plains states. He found, among other things, that, on average and compared with Catholic and mainline Protestant groups, evangelical Protestant youth groups met more frequently, had higher *participation rates, and had greater turnover among youth workers.

S

sacrifice: 1. the act of surrendering something valued or desired (e.g., a life, *goal, *resource) to achieve something regarded as more worthy or important or to avoid having a greater loss (cf. Bakan 1968; Hubert and Mauss 1964). 2. the loss incurred by the act of sacrificing something. Often seen in a Christian context of current sacrifice for eternal salvation. *See also* altruism (various entries). Lomnitz (2003, passim) holds that the economic crisis of the 1980s in Mexico reshaped the meaning of secular sacrifice (senses 1 and 2). The long-standing Christian idea of sacrifice has, as a result, also undergone change.

sampling frame creation strategy for nonprofits: plan for developing a list of all types of *nonprofit groups, from which sampling units can then be drawn. Smith (2000:267–274) discusses such a *strategy for creating an all-inclusive sampling frame of nonprofits in the United States.

satisfaction: 1. action of meeting or fact of having met a *need, want, desire, or expectation, of becoming or being content, or satisfied, along these lines. 2. action of becoming or state of being satisfied by way of gratification or pleasure received from something. Stebbins (2004a:1) argues that *volunteering as *serious leisure engenders deep *fulfillment, which includes a feeling of satisfaction as defined in sense 1, whereas volunteering as *casual leisure engenders more superficial satisfaction, as in sense 2. Csikszentmihalyi (1990) argues for a special kind of satisfaction, the flow experience, that comes from competing optimally with oneself.

See also direct satisfaction; indirect satisfaction; psychic benefits; extrinsic satisfaction; intrinsic satisfaction

scientific philanthropy. *See* philanthropy, scientific

screening of volunteers/members: major administrative function in *nonprofit groups and *volunteer programs that involves assessing the fit of a potential *volunteer with a volunteer program and the potential risks of taking on that person. Screening often consists of administering a questionnaire, an interview, an assessment of background and references, and so on. The volunteer program hopes to find useful volunteer workers, who will be unlikely to damage in any way the organization's *morale, *clients, or reputation. Connors (1995:164–172) and Fisher and Cole (1993:48–51) give practical advice and a sample of volunteer screening instruments used as part of the application process. Compared with *paid-staff nonprofits, *grassroots associations are generally more accepting of potential new *members, and any screening is usually quite loose and informal.

seasonality in nonprofits: the condition of being dependent on the seasons, of something recurring during a particular season. Various *nonprofit groups operate seasonally, among them sports booster clubs, volunteer teams that serve at annual fairs and civic festivals, and parental groups that help out in the schools. Seasonality is one of several factors affecting the functioning of such groups (Smith 2000:129).

Second World nonprofit group: a *nonprofit group in a former Communist bloc country. Golinowska (1994, passim) discusses the growth of market-oriented nonprofits in Poland's *nonprofit sector. These groups are supported primarily by the intelligentsia (e.g., artists, teachers, physicians).

secondary group: *large organization of people who, for the most part, have only indirect, impersonal contact, but who nonetheless work together in specialized roles to reach particular *goals (Stebbins 1990:121–122). A largely outmoded term for *organization and *association (cf. Stark 1994:16). *See also* primary group

secondary satisfaction. *See* indirect satisfaction

secondary/tertiary association: a secondary association is a type of *nonprofit group, namely a *grassroots association characterized by face-to-face interaction, whereas a tertiary *association is a mass membership *organization without regular means of face-to-face *participation. Putnam (1995) argued that secondary associations enhance *social capital, whereas tertiary associations often restrict participation to check writing or other forms of indirect involvement. The family/household exemplifies a primary association, which has the characteristics of a *primary group.

secret society: *nonprofit group formed to promote, through covert methods, a particular *cause. *Members are sworn to secrecy about existence of the society, its cause, and its proceedings (Wolff 1950, pt. 4). Possibly the most notorious secret society in American history is the Ku Klux Klan (Sims 1996, passim). Picardie (1988, passim) reveals the workings of the Oddfellows, a British secret society of long standing. Barrett (1999, passim) presents a historical overview of secret societies worldwide.

sect: 1. a *religion. 2 a small, nonprofit, often deviant, religious group (*deviant group) born in a schism within a mainline faith or established sect (*sect, established). Although many cults (*new religion) fail, some do succeed, eventually going on to become sects. Johnstone (1992, chap. 5) discusses at length the church-sect continuum of religious organization. Wilson (1970, passim) reviews the nature of various analytic types of sects, and much earlier, Clark (1937, passim) examined the small sects in America. Zellner and Petrowsky (1998, passim) present chapters by various authors on sects and *new religions. Stark and Bainbridge (1985, pt. 2) describe sects in America, as does Bainbridge (1997, chaps. 6–9). Yinger (1970:266–273) discusses the church-sect continuum. Other important writings on sects include Aldridge (2000, passim), Bromley and Hadden (1992, passim), Cousineau (1998, passim), Halperin (1983, passim), Martin (1990, passim), Johnson (1963, passim), Mann (1955, passim), and Mather and Nichols (1993, passim). *See also* denomination

sect, established: a *sect that has stabilized midway in the transition from sect to *denomination, such as the Amish or Quakers (Society of Friends). Yinger (1970:266) notes that "established *sects" differ only in degree from "pure sects." The former are somewhat more inclusive, less alienated, and more structured than the pure variety, and therefore somewhat closer to mainline faiths.

sectarian relief organization. *See* religious nonprofit group

sectarian service: *service of a *religious nonprofit group, which is often available only to adherents of the *religion supporting that group (Barker 2003:385). Catholic Charities USA and Combined Jewish Appeal are two of many such services in the United States. Cnaan and Boddie (2002, passim) describe sectarian service by religious congregations. Jeavons (1994, passim) discusses Christian service organizations.

sector of society: a distinct part of the social organization of a society; in economics, an area of industry or economic activity. (a) Before the mid-1960s social scientists tended to subscribe to a two-sector model of modern society: government and private. The latter included both businesses and *nonprofit groups, with businesses receiving by far the most attention. This approach reflected the *nonprofit sector is unimportant flat-earth paradigm (Smith 2000:219–221). (b) Since approximately 1970 a three-sector model has been recognized: government, business (for-profit), and nonprofit, with the latter often being referred to as the *third sector. This reflected the *three-sector model of society flat-earth paradigm (Smith 2000:221–222). (c) Somewhat later family and household were added, thereby giving birth to the four-sector model (e.g., Ortmeyer and Fortune 1985, passim; Smith 1991:138–139). (d) Finally, Smith (2000:225) has proposed a fifth sector, namely dividing the nonprofit sector into the *volunteer nonprofit groups subsector and the *paid-staff nonprofit groups subsector.

secular humanism: a form of liberalism, of American origin, that stresses the conviction that *religion should not be taught or practiced in publicly funded educational systems. More broadly, a philosophy and nontheistic religion practiced through universalistic moral and ethical conduct, helping other people (*see* helping behavior) as well as saving and improving the environment (cf. Lamont 1957, passim). Roberts (1999, passim) examined the relationship between Marxism and secular humanism, noting that, although they share considerable common ground, there has been little dialogue between their exponents.

secularist focus flat-earth paradigm: nonprofit sector model that *nonprofit groups are largely profane rather than sacred, or linked in some way to religious considerations (Smith 2000:235–236). Although *church *congregations are now increasingly recognized as *associations, nonprofit scholars in the past have tended to overlook their existence and the existence of other *religious nonprofits (Smith 1984, passim).

secularization: process occurring in most modern societies in which (a) *religion, God, the supernatural, and the sacred decline in importance and relevance to everyday life and thought, while explanations and beliefs based on science and rationality increase in importance correspondingly (Johnstone 1992:316–320); and (b) there is increasing separation between the religious and the secular (nonreligious) aspects of life and society as well as increasing differentiation within the religious sphere (ibid.). Many different definitions of secularization have been used in empirical research (Shriner 1967), but the foregoing two aspects sum up the thrust of them.

seed money: *grant or *donation, usually modest in size, given to start up a new *nonprofit project or new *nonprofit organization (see the Foundation Center Glossary at http://www.fdncenter.org/learn/ufg/glossary .html).

self-fulfillment. *See* fulfillment/self-fulfillment; satisfaction (sense 1)

self-help group (SHG): a relatively informal *member benefit group, in which *members with an admitted personal *problem or defect seek to overcome it by drawing on the skills and experiences of others in the group. Self-help groups often form in reaction to critical inadequacies perceived to dilute the *effectiveness of their counterparts in the medical and helping *professions. Katz (1993, passim) examines, from a *social movement perspective, self-help in the United States (see also Smith and Pillemer 1983, passim). Kropotkin (passim) wrote an early book (first published in 1914) that reviewed mutual aid among animals and then among humans through our history. Katz and Bender (1976, passim) wrote a key early contemporary book that gave an overview of self-help groups in the United States and elsewhere. Now many books comprehensively treat American SHGs (e.g., Borkman 1999; Borman 1982; Gartner and Riessman 1977, 1984; Gitterman and Shulman 1994; Katz 1992; Katz and Bender 1990; Kurtz 1997; Madara and White 2002; Powell 1994; Riessman and Carroll 1995; Wuthnow 1994), collectively dealing with over a hundred types including those dealing with abuse, addiction, bereavement, disabilities, family and parenting, health, mental health, and miscellany. See Madara and White (2002) for SHG contact information. There are also numerous books on subtypes of SHGs (e.g., Humphreys 2004; Kaye 1997) and on SHGs for specific problems (e.g., Rudy 1986; Yale 1995). Lavoie et al. (1994) and Mäkelä (1996) take a more international perspective on SHGs. There are many studies of SHGs in different regions of the world (e.g., Kwok et al. 2002, passim) and in different nations (e.g., Thomas-Slayton 1985, passim).

self-interest: pursuit of one's own personal profit, benefit, or ascendancy and whatever advantage is required to accomplish this. When pursuit of self-interest excludes regard for others, when it is exploitative, it can be qualified as *selfishness (Stebbins 1993c:51).

selfishness: an imputation most commonly hurled at perceived self-seekers by their victims, where the self-seekers seem to demonstrate a concern for their own *welfare or advantage at the expense of or disregard for those victims. Objectively, selfishness is a breach of etiquette. Subjectively, it is seen by its victims as exploiting their *needs and *interests. Hence the true opposite of selfishness is self-sacrifice (*sacrifice) (Stebbins 1993c:50–51). *See also* self-interest; unselfishness; altruism

self-study in nonprofits: in the *nonprofit sector, a *nonprofit group's *evaluation of itself, designed to establish whether its *goals, *mission, procedures, *programs, and the like meet certain criteria. The criteria are often set by external *agencies on whom the nonprofit group is dependent for *funding or other *resources. Bocialetti and Kaplan (1986, passim) argue that self-studies are a way of avoiding the deficiencies of traditional evaluation. The former deal specifically with the funder-agency relationship (*see* exchange, philanthropic) in the evaluation process (*evaluation of nonprofit groups/programs), something the latter fails to do as effectively.

semiformal nonprofit group: *nonprofit group lacking clear boundaries and sometimes a clear *leadership structure, but having, nonetheless, a unique proper name. It is a nonprofit group that is more formal than an *informal group and less formal than a *formal group (Smith 1992b: 252). Semiformal nonprofits are often evolving, moving along the continuum from informal to formal group. They are inclined to treat as a *member anyone who turns up at meetings or other group events. *Associations tend to be semiformal nonprofits initially, whereas the opposite holds for *nonprofit agencies, which usually start life as formal entities.

semiprofession: an occupation that meets some, but not all, of the criteria used to distinguish *professions from other types of occupations. Hall (1986:50) points out that the semiprofessions (e.g., teaching, librarianship), because they are often practiced in *organizations, come to be significantly dominated by those organizations and hence lack the power of the more independent professions.

senior (citizens') center: both an *organization and a building offering *leisure or *social services or both to the elderly. May be run by a *nonprofit group or by a *governmental agency. Cusack (1994, passim) explored the motives seniors give for taking on *leadership roles in a seniors' center in Canada. The motives sprang from their interests in being active in retirement, relating to the *needs and abilities of seniors, holding power and *influence, and leading others.

sense of community: a personal belief that a particular *community exists (e.g., ethnic, neighborhood, municipality, interest-based) and the believer's feeling of being part of it (cf. Lowie 1948:3). Liu and Besser (2003, passim) found that sense of community among seniors was positively related to their tendency to participate in community improvement activities.

serious leisure: serious leisure is the systematic pursuit of an *amateur, *hobbyist, or *volunteer activity that participants find so substantial, interesting, and fulfilling (*fulfillment) that, in the typical case, they launch themselves on a (leisure) career centered on acquiring and expressing its special skills, knowledge, and experience (Stebbins 1992:3). The term was coined by Stebbins (1982, passim). *See also* volunteering as leisure; casual leisure; project-based leisure

service: activity by individuals, done often but not necessarily as *members of a *group, and intended to improve for one or more other people their objective situation or subjective *satisfaction or both (cf. Reimer 1982, passim; Sarri and Hasenfeld 1978, passim). Provision of such service is not the exclusive domain of *nonprofit groups nor of *nonmember benefit nonprofits, contrary to the *traditional nonmember service flat-earth paradigm (Smith 2000:227–228). Salamon (2002:9–10) observes that, so far as *nonprofit organizations are concerned, they are, in the first place, service providers. *See also* informal care; service volunteers; quality assurance; service, personal social

service club: an *association that combines the *goal of *sociability with that of helping the local *community. The Lions, Kiwanis, Soroptimists, and Rotary International number among the many service clubs in the United States. Charles (1993, passim) provides an extensive study of three of the aforementioned groups.

service incentive: type of *incentive rooted in the desire to serve other *members of the *nonprofit group to which the individual belongs (*co-member service incentive) or, while participating in that group, to serve a particular category of nonmember (*nonmember service incentive) (Smith 2000:98–99). *See also* incentive type

service learning: school or university-based *program in which students receive course credit for *volunteer work, usually doing *community service in a *nonprofit agency or *volunteer program in their *community (Burlingame 2004:433–435; Jacoby et al. 1996, passim; O'Grady 2000, passim; Roberts and Yang 2002, passim; Wade 1997, passim). The pioneers of the service learning movement (*social movement) initially targeted higher education, but later spread to primary and secondary schooling as well (Stanton et al. 1999, passim). Tends to result in many desirable outcomes, including academic learning, personal development, interpersonal development, decreased stereotyping, and increased social responsibility (Burlingame 2004:434–435).

service, personal social: 1. direct, face-to-face *benefit offered by a *volunteer or a *nonprofit group to a *target, or recipient, of that benefit (cf. Halmos 1970, passim; Mehr 2001, passim). 2. Smith (2000:228) observes that many scholars so narrowly define the concept of *service that they exclude from consideration *self-help and other *member benefit activities, which should be included as *co-member services.

service program volunteer. *See* program volunteer

service provision. *See* service

service recipient. *See* target of benefits

service volunteer: *volunteer whose activities are seen as providing *service to others outside the volunteer's household and family (cf. Kipps 1997, passim; Raynolds and Raynolds 1988, passim). *Service volunteering includes *informal volunteering, *board volunteering, and *associational volunteering as well as traditional *service volunteering. In the United States the service volunteer is sometimes confused with a much narrower conception: the *service program volunteer who works in a *volunteer service program (e.g., Brudney 1994:280).

service volunteer, traditional: a *service volunteer who works in a *nonmember benefit (*public benefit) nonprofit or a *volunteer program. Excludes *service volunteering in *member benefit nonprofits, where the *services are given to co-members (*co-member service) (Smith 2000: 227–228).

service volunteer program. *See* volunteer program

service volunteering: 1. serving a particular category of *nonmembers who are the *target of benefits of the *nonprofit group for which the individual is volunteering. Salamon (2002:9–10), writing in sense 1, points out that, through their service role, nonprofits make many crucial contributions to local and national life. 2. serving as a *program volunteer.

3. the broadest definition includes senses 1 and 2 but allows the target of benefits to include the members of the nonprofit group itself, as in *member benefit groups. The latter approach is ignored by many mainstream nonprofit scholars, because they adhere to the *traditional non-member service flat-earth paradigm of the *nonprofit sector (Smith 2000:227–228). Smith (2000:197–201, 204–205) reviews research showing the internal impact of member benefit groups on their members, including *social support, *helping, self-expression, stimulation, information, sociopolitical activation (politicization), *psychological empowerment, happiness, and health.

settlement house: a *nonprofit community center, usually in a poor urban area, offering educational and neighborhood assistance, social activities, and help to local people; begun in the late nineteenth century and flourishing in the early decades of the twentieth century, these centers were usually staffed by young, college-educated, unmarried men and women from higher status homes who wanted to help working-class people and were supported by donations from wealthy benefactors (Barbuto 1999, passim; Burlingame 2004:437–439). For the past sixty years or so, remaining settlement houses have been nonresidential and staffed by professional social workers (ibid.). Koerin (2003, passim), in a rare look at contemporary settlement houses, examines this tradition, with an eye to its trends and future concerns.

shadow wage in nonprofits: an indirect social wage enjoyed by employed taxpayers whose tax obligation is reduced by the extent to which their *volunteering reduces the necessity of tax-supported social services (Smith 1981: 26).

sheltered workshop: a *nonprofit workshop and training center in which things are made or repaired by people with disabilities who are sheltered from the demands of the typical *for-profit organization or other *businesses. Copp (1998, passim) explores how employees at a sheltered workshop for people with developmental disabilities try to manage their emotions under such difficult conditions as boredom and low pay.

SIC. *See* Standard Industrial Classification

sisterhood: 1. an *association of women formed to pursue a particular religious, social, or other *goal. In the narrowest sense, a female *religious order (cf. Donovan 1989, passim; Mumm 2001, passim). Traditional term no longer commonly used. 2. the general *collectivity of women in a nation, world region, or the entire world (cf. Melder 1977, passim; Morgan 1970, passim). In this second sense, Davis (2002, passim) writes that global feminism has been criticized as a form of cultural imperialism, whereby under the heading of universal sisterhood, a white, Western model of feminism is imposed on women in non-Western situations.

sit-down strike: form of *passive resistance by a *collectivity in which participants interfere with the normal functioning of an *organization by obstructing human movement and other activity in critical areas of its operations (cf. Sharp 1973, passim). Torigian (1999, passim) found that, in France and the United States, the radical and illegal sit-down strike was widely and effectively used in the modern labor movement (*see* social movement) to reach the *goal of factory unionization.

site visit: visit by *foundation or governmental grant-making *agency staff to the offices or operating site of a *nonprofit group to meet with its *directors, staff (*paid staff), *volunteers, and *clients. The aim of the visit is to assess the group's qualifications for a *grant or other type of funding.

sit-in: *direct action protest involving, in essence, protesters physically occupying space (e.g., chairs, seats, the floor) in a building or other place belonging to the person or group whose *policies are under protest (cf. Sharp 1973, passim). Wallenstein and Clyburn (2003, passim) stress the urban nature of the many civil rights (*see* civil liberty) sit-ins held in Virginia over a six-month period in 1960.

sliding scale dues: *membership cost paid to a *nonprofit group based on a *member's financial capacity to pay it. Laband and Beil (1998, passim) found a fairly extensive degree of noncompliance among members of the American Sociological Association (ASA) having the highest income and the ASA's requirement that they pay the highest *dues on its sliding dues scale.

small group: *group small enough for all *members to interact simultaneously, to talk with each other, or at least to be known to each other. Members of such groups also clearly recognize that they belong to them; they have a strong sense of "we" and "they" (nonmembers) (Back 1981: 320). Of course, by definition, all groups have some significant sense of collective identity, so with small groups, it is a matter of higher degree or intensity on this dimension. *See also* small group paradox; primary group; collectivity; informal group

small group paradox: when a *nonprofit group meets the structural criteria for being semiformal or formal but has a set of operating procedures and norms that encourage informal relationships and sharing (Wuthnow 1994:158). *See also* small group

sociability: quality of being sociable, of having a friendly disposition, of being inclined toward friendly interaction. Some *nonprofit groups, especially *associations, have as their principal *mission promoting sociability among *members, as Schmidt and Babchuk (1972:51) found in their study of the historical transformation of American fraternal orders. Clawson's (1989) similar historical study emphasizes male social solidarity in such associations. *See also* small group; primary group; informal group

sociability incentive: the desire to belong to a *nonprofit group for the *sociability and solidarity offered to its *members. Knoke (1988:315–

316), in his discussion of "social incentives," stresses the attractiveness of coordinated social and *leisure activities enjoyed exclusively by *members of the group. *See also* incentive type in nonprofits

sociability value. *See* value, humane core

social action: 1. individual behavior that takes one or more other persons or *groups into account (e.g., Parsons 1949, passim). 2. a vague term for *protest activities by a *collectivity or *social movement (cf. Chambers 1987, passim). Tarrow (1991, passim) discusses social action (sense 2) and cycles of protest. Barker (2003:401) notes that those involved in such social action may be *professionals (e.g., clergy, social workers, politicians) or *nonprofessionals (e.g., people whose problem the social action is centered on). *See also* community involvement; citizen participation; political participation; community action

social aesthetics value. *See* value, humane core

social agency. *See* nonprofit agency

social capital. *See* capital, social

social category: a set of two or more individuals who share one or more social or sociodemographic characteristics, and who may have a sense of collective identity but do not usually intercommunicate systematically. For instance, women and men in a society each constitute a social category. Blau (1977) discusses how social categories influence intergroup contact. *See also* collectivity

social change: change in the structure or processes of a society or smaller territory (Stark 1994, chap. 17). Weinstein (2005, passim) offers a comprehensive view of the many social forces generating social and cultural change.

social change fund: one of the many funds or foundations that have in recent decades been supporting advocacy and social change rather than traditional charities, seeking to empower the poor, minorities, women, and other disadvantaged populations (cf. Burlingame 2004:447–451; Perlmutter 1988a, passim; Rabinowitz 1990, passim). Sometimes involved in workplace fund-raising (*federated fund, alternative). Ostrander (1995, passim) has written a case study of one social change foundation/fund.

social change nonprofit group. *See* social influence nonprofit group; advocacy group

social change role of nonprofit groups/nonprofit sector. *See* pioneering role of nonprofits/nonprofit sector

social community theory of volunteering: a theory that argues that people engage in *volunteering because others in their *social network also do so (Henderson 1984). Thus, members of *religious congregations or in a university dormitory may decide together to be involved in *volunteer activity.

social economy. *See* economy, social

social group. *See* group

social influence nonprofit group: a *nonprofit group the *mission of which is to change in some substantial way the thoughts or actions of a certain set of people. Nonprofits, in their *advocacy role, contribute enormously to social life, by identifying and publicizing *community *problems and giving voice to a range of community *interests (Salamon 2002:10). Social *influence can also be exerted at supralocal levels of *government and society (Berry 1997, passim). *See also* advocacy group

social innovation activity. *See* informal social innovation activity

social isolation: a *problem for individuals, families, *social networks, *neighborhoods and entire *communities, characterized by weak social networks and insufficient *social support (cf. Gordon 1976, passim; Lynch 1977, passim; Weiss 1973, passim). Checkoway (1988b) viewed social isolation as a serious problem in both industrial and developing areas. Because of normative bias in much of social theory, there has been more attention to positively framed dependent variables such as social support, life *satisfaction, successful aging, productive aging, aging well, and so on, than there has been to negatively framed factors such as *barriers and limitations to *voluntary action, social isolation, and the like.

social movement: initially a *collectivity, who, working from a shared *ideology, try over time either to effect change or to maintain the status quo on a particular *issue using in a significant way unconventional *political voluntary action (*protest activities). In time the collectivity may coalesce into one or more *nonprofit groups (Lofland 1996, passim). In turn some of these social movement groups may eventually become formal *nonprofit organizations, as in the environmental movement in America (Dunlap and Mertig 1992, passim) and Western Europe (Dalton 1994, pt. 3). McAdam and Snow (1997, introduction) define social movements and review major conceptual issues covered in more depth by chapters in this book of readings with a very large bibliography of the field. Nonprofit researchers studying social movements often fail to relate adequately such movements to the rest of the *nonprofit sector, thus reflecting the *social movement/protest flat-earth paradigm (Smith 2000:226–227). On the other hand, mainstream nonprofit researchers who ignore social movement phenomena are reflecting the *status quo/ establishment flat-earth paradigm (Smith 2000:225–226). There are well over a hundred books, mostly recent, on different types of social movements (e.g., Adam 1995; Aptheker 1989; Basu and McGrory 1995; Blanchard 1994; Blumberg 1991; Chatfield 1992; Ferree and Hess 1995; Ferriss et al. 1997; Finsen and Finsen 1994; Goldberg 1991; Hawes 1991; Jenkins and Klandermans 1995; Josephy 1970; Katz 1993; Knobel 1996; Manes 1990; Mayer 1989; McAdam 1982; Morris 1984; Piven and Cloward 1979; Powell et al. 1996; Price 1990; Scholsberg 1999; Shapiro 1993;

Siebold 1992; Unger 1974; Zakin 1995) and at least two thousand articles and book chapters (McAdam and Snow 1997, references, as well as more recent references). A number of authors have also attempted to analyze more generally the structure and dynamics of social movements (e.g., Alvarez et al. 1998; Della Porta 1999; Gamson 1990; Jenkins and Klandermans 1995; Laraña, Johnston, and Gusfield 1994; Lofland 1996; McAdam and Snow 1997; McAdam, McCarthy, and Zald 1996; Morris and Mueller 1992; Smith 1996; Tarrow 1998; Tilly 2004; Zald and McCarthy 1979, 1987).

social movement bureaucratization: process whereby a *social movement organization becomes socially and economically established, and its original *charismatic leadership is gradually replaced with a bureaucratic structure (Zald and Ash 1966:327). *See also* bureaucratization

social movement group: a *nonprofit group and, usually, small unit in a larger *social movement that, based on a shared *ideology, tries to effect change or maintain the status quo on a particular *issue. The social movement group is actually a subtype of *political nonprofit. Sometimes incorrectly referred to as *social movement organizations, most social movement groups are, at most, informal or semiformal. Lofland and Jamison (1984) wrote a classic article on social movement groups or "locals," and Lofland (1996) later wrote a book-length treatment of these nonprofit groups that are often ignored by mainstream nonprofit scholars because of the *status quo/establishment flat-earth paradigm of the nonprofit sector they often use (Smith 2000:225–226). Basu and McGrory (1995) describe local feminist movement groups around the world. Wood and Jackson (1982, passim) provide a detailed overview of many aspects of the social movement. *See also* advocacy group; social movement organization; social influence nonprofit group

social movement leader. *See* leader, social movement

social movement nonprofit group. *See* social movement group

social movement organization: a *social movement group that is formally organized (*formal group), as described in Lofland (1996, passim). Zald and Denton (1987, passim) describe the transformation of the Young Men's Christian Association (YMCA) into a modern general-service organization from its origins as an organ of the evangelistic social movement. Ferree and Martin (1995) describe new feminist social movement organizations. *See also* social influence nonprofit group; social movement group

social movement/protest flat-earth paradigm: nonprofit sector model that centers on oppositional, or *protest, *social movements, ignoring thereby mainstream, non-protest-oriented *nonprofit groups, unless the latter also have oppositional *missions (Smith 2000:226–227).

social movement sector: all the *social movements of a society seen together as comprising a distinct sector with *social change *goals and

*unconventional political action as common characteristics. Loya (1998), in studying this sector, presents data on the history, organization, and structure of 178 *transnational (*see* transnational association), pro-democracy movement *organizations.

social network: a set of relationships, according to Israel (1988), centered on an individual and having characteristics that are structural (e.g., size, density, and presumably, composition, or degree of heterogeneity), interactional (e.g., degree of mutual support, frequencies of interaction), and functional (e.g., instrumental and expressive and informational functions, identity maintenance and facilitation of *social participation inside and outside the network). Low social network involvement could be one operationalization of the concept of social isolation. Bott (1957) wrote an early work on family and social network. Community-based social network interventions are one form of *community-based initiative (Checkoway 1988b). The journal *Social Networks* is devoted to this topic. *See also* network

social participation: broadly defined, a wide variety of forms of public and semipublic activity by individuals taking place in a broader social context. In the context of *volunteer roles, as discussed by Payne and Bull (1985:268), social participation is provided through opportunities for access to various types of involvement with peers who have mutual *interests and concerns. Other contexts include adult education; structured participation for isolated widows/widowers and newcomers; singles groups; and political participation in local, state, and national elections and *issues.

social policy: *policy of a society or nation that guides how it directs its citizens, groups, and institutions and their interrelationship. Barker (2004:405) observes that such policy emerges from the society's *values and customs, and determines the distribution of *resources and level of well-being of its people. Thus social policy centers on such concerns as health, education, deviance, and *social welfare. Not to be confused with public policy—a field of study devoted to identifying *policy *problems and governmental responses to them as well as suggesting how the problems can be solved. See Bochel (2005, passim) and Manning, Baldock, and Vickerstaff (2003, passim) for an overview of social policy.

social protest. *See* activity, protest

social religiosity value. *See* value, humane core

social service: 1. an adjective used to modify such terms as "social service *agencies," implying the delivery of some specific *service (cf. Chambers 1963, passim; Romanofsky and Chambers 1978, passim). 2. a specific *service delivered as part of the overall system of *social services (cf. Chambers 1963, passim). Roose and De Bie (2003, passim) explore the several ramifications that followed when youth in Belgium changed from conducting *participatory action research to providing the service of participative *care. This topic is treated regularly in the journal *Social Service Review*. *See also* social services

social services: the sphere of activities of *service-providing personnel who foster the health and well-being of a *community or society (cf. Huttman 1985, passim; Kamerman and Kahn 1976, passim). Such people provide individual *social service like helping people achieve a level of self-sufficiency, strengthen their family relationships, and restore themselves and their *groups and *communities to successful social functioning (Barker 2003:407). Van Til (1988:115–116) notes that governmentally supported social services have voluntary roots, and that many of these services are now being returned to the *nonprofit sector. *See also* service

social support: a very common term in the social scientific literature, it is used by Israel (1988) to refer to a mixture of four kinds of supportive behavior: emotional support, instrumental support, informational support, and what she called "appraisal support" (affirmation, feedback, etc.). Social support so defined is one of the important functions provided by a *social network. Social networks then vary in degree of social support as well as in degree of *social isolation. Social networks with high levels of social interaction and advantageous structural characteristics are more likely to have low levels of social isolation, while not necessarily providing high levels of social support because not all social ties are supportive. But low levels of social interaction and the disadvantageous aspects of network structure associated with social isolation may be more likely to be associated with low social support. As Israel (1988:37) pointed out, an individual's network may include social ties that do not provide social support, and concomitantly, an examination of only supportive ties could exclude relationships having other important dimensions. Israel concluded that social network interventions may include not only social supportive interventions but also other forms of intervention. Clary (1982) also highlights social support.

socialization: the complex learning process through which people develop their self-concepts as well as acquire the skills, knowledge, and motivation needed to participate in social life (Mackie 1987:77). Smith (2000: 140–141) observes that, whereas *paid-staff *nonprofit groups tend nowadays to seek educated, specially trained, formally socialized *leaders, *grassroots associations informally socialize their newcomers and rarely provide formal training for their leaders.

socialization by nonprofit groups. *See* socialization

socialization, religious: *socialization, both formal and informal, of *members of *religious nonprofit groups along lines of the *religion each group espouses. Religious socialization, such as through Sunday school, catechism, and Hebrew school, is a main activity for these groups (Johnstone 1992, chap. 4)

socially responsible investing: investment (e.g., of *endowments) in companies that reflect the socially responsible *mission and *values of a *foundation or other *nonprofit group. Entine (2003, passim) traces the evolution of socially responsible investing, starting with the screening practices used by the Quakers to the social *activism in the United States during the 1960s.

societal corporatism. *See* neocorporatism

societal insider. *See* insider, societal

societal outsider. *See* outsider, societal

sociodemographic homogeneity. *See* homogeneity, sociodemographic

sociodemographic participation predictors flat-earth paradigm: nonprofit sector model that uses exclusively or nearly exclusively sociodemographic variables to predict individual *volunteer *participation (Smith 2000: 236–237).

sociopolitical change orientation. *See* orientation of nonprofit groups

sociopolitical innovation: identifying and defining new social problems and unmet *public needs; providing responsible sociopolitical dissent re-garding these *needs; mobilizing individuals and *groups to seek change in the *public interest; and using new approaches to *political action and *social change that will benefit the larger *community (Smith 2000: 22). Rogers (1983, passim) has written a classic work on the diffusion of innovations of all types. Conger (1973, passim) describes and lists major social inventions in history *See also* social innovation activity

sociopolitical innovation values. *See* value, humane core

sodality: 1. term used by anthropologists to refer to a (common *interest) *association in a preliterate society (Lowie 1948:14). 2. an official (church-recognized), lay, Roman Catholic association for women having a philanthropic purpose. Originated in Europe in medieval times (Trex-ler 1991:14).

solidary incentive. *See* sociability incentive

sorority: female social *club, particularly for undergraduate college and uni-versity students. Scott (1965, passim) wrote a classic empirical study of college fraternities and sororities. Giddings (1988, passim) presents a history of Delta Sigma Theta, a national black sorority in America first chartered in 1913 (p. 52). Drout and Corsoro (2003, passim) studied the differences in perception of the hazing conducted in fraternities accord-ing to male and female students belonging to a sorority or a *fraternity or having no "Greek" (fraternity/sorority) affiliation. Robbins (2004, passim) exposes the dark side of sororities in a muckraking narrative.

spare time. *See* free time; leisure time

spatial diffusion of nonprofits: the spread over geographic space and through time of *nonprofit groups, in general, or of a type of nonprofit, in particular. Hedstrom (1994, passim) studied the spatial diffusion of Swedish trade *unions between 1890 and 1940 and how distances and relations between people influenced the growth and spread of this *social movement.

special events fund-raising: the process of using special *fund-raising events, among them fairs, sports matches, arts festivals, pancake breakfasts, and entertainment events, to raise money for a charitable *cause (Allen 2001:480).

special interest group: a formal or informal group, though not necessarily nonprofit, seeking to influence a governmental *social policy, political candidate, governmental *agency, proposal of law, or even the general public (sense 1) (cf. Truman 1955, passim). Unlike the *public interest group, actions of the special interest group revolve around a single *issue, which serves as a rallying point for its *members and tends to benefit mainly them and similar people. Street (1997, passim) examines elderly political actors as a special interest group and their view of Social Security and Medicare as citizen rights (*civil liberty). Clawson et al. (1992, passim) describe and analyze as special interest groups the nature and impact of corporate *political action committees (PACs). *Labor unions also have their PACs. *See also* political participation; political voluntary action; interest group

specificity of goals. *See* diffuseness vs. specificity of goals

splinter group: in the *nonprofit sector, a *nonprofit group, often informal, that splits off from a larger group or *organization—it may also be nonprofit—so as to function independently of the latter. Epstein and Sardiello (1999, passim) studied the Wharf Rats, an informal twelve-step drug and alcohol recovery group that split off from the traditional Alcoholics Anonymous and Narcotics Anonymous programs. This splinter group, though successful to some extent, was, however, less so than its predecessors.

sponsor: 1. a person or *organization that, by pledging meeting space, supports a *nonprofit group or *fund-raising activity. Having one or more sponsors is a form of horizontal *collaboration for nonprofits, and a reasonably common arrangement among *grassroots associations (Smith 2000:141). 2. a person in a *twelve-step (*self-help) group who acts as *mentor for another, usually newer, *member of the group (Rudy 1986, passim).

spontaneous volunteer: one who helps (*see* helping/helping behavior) out at a disaster site (natural or human-made), so-called because *motivation to do so emerges at the moment of learning about the disaster. Such a person, who may have come from afar, may not possess the skills needed at the disaster site, may not be wanted there, and is likely to abandon this role after having served there. Sharon (2004:15) found that one of the motives behind spontaneous volunteering is a powerful desire to help, fueled by the emotional impact of the disaster itself. Also known as "unaffiliated volunteer," in contrast to affiliated *volunteers who, for instance, work for the Red Cross and are trained in disaster relief. The Points of Light Foundation (2002, passim) has written a manual on how to effectively use this spontaneous help.

sporadic volunteer. *See* episodic volunteer; *see also* habitual volunteer

squatters' neighborhood nonprofit group: local *nonprofit group serving the *interests of a *group of people occupying illegally or in other unauthorized fashion otherwise unoccupied land or premises. Fisher (1984, passim) describes several neighborhood improvement associations (*neighborhood nonprofit group) in Latin America that were formed by squatters.

staff development: the ensemble of activities and *programs created by a *nonprofit group to enhance the ability of its personnel (*paid staff, *volunteer) to fulfill their functions. Staff development, which is usually organized by the nonprofit for meeting certain of its requirements, can also help personnel improve their broader career (*career in nonprofits) objectives and opportunities as well as their *human capital (Barker 2003:415). *See also* in-service training

staffing: to supply a *nonprofit group with staff (*see* nonprofit staff; resource), whether *paid or *volunteer. Staffing involves recruitment of new personnel, assignment of all personnel as well as their promotion, transferring, and firing. Starr (2001, passim) examined the role of staffing, among other organization-building activities, in creating the Pittsburgh Alliance for Progressive Action. *See also* staff development; in-service training; recruitment of volunteers/members; recruitment of nonprofit group paid staff

staff of nonprofits. *See* nonprofit staff; resource

staff-volunteer relations. *See* building paid staff-volunteer relations

stakeholder: person, *group, or *organization who can make a claim on a *nonprofit group's attention, *resources, or output, or who is affected by this output (Bryson 1994:160).

stakeholder analysis in strategic planning: that aspect of *strategic planning that consists of identifying the *stakeholders of a *nonprofit group and the criteria they use to judge its performance. Such analysis also includes examining the group's ability to meet these criteria as well as the stakeholders' *influence on the group. Finally, the *needs nonprofit stakeholders are expected to meet are also analyzed (Bryson 1994:160).

Standard Industrial Classification (SIC): scheme for categorizing the diverse industries in the United States, which is set out in a publication of the Office of Management and Budget (1987). Bradford Smith (1992, passim) has proposed a way to use SIC codes to classify the activities of nonprofit tax-exempt organizations (*tax-exempt status).

state association: *association that is, in essence, statewide (or province-wide) in *membership, scope, activity, or *mission. Operationally, such an association is sometimes defined as a *group active in or seeking *members from all major regions of the state (province) and from one-third or more of its cities and towns. Hammer and Wazeter (1993, passim) developed a model of *effectiveness of state-wide teachers' *unions.

state and local tax-exemption, charitable: Internal Revenue Service *501(c)(3) exempt charitable organizations generally receive state exemptions on income tax, state and local exemptions on real property taxes, and sometimes state and local exemptions on sales and use taxes (Fishman and Schwarz 2000:458–463).

status quo/establishment flat-earth paradigm: nonprofit sector model that focuses exclusively, or nearly exclusively, on mainstream *nonprofit groups and *volunteers serving *societal insiders. Thus this paradigm tends to ignore such entities as *protest, *advocacy, and *social movement nonprofits (Smith 2000:225–226).

status recognition in nonprofits: practice that links *commitment and subjective well-being and that helps reinforce *voluntary action (Mannell 1993). Status recognition functions to sustain commitment and subjective well-being, despite the possibility of short-term imbalances in the costs (*cost of volunteer participation) and *benefits of *participation. Status recognition is consistent with the observation of Fischer and Schaffer (1993) that the benefits of *volunteering are often indirect or deferred, until some time following the volunteer's contribution. Status recognition gives more immediate (if less tangible) rewards for volunteering and can involve both status maintenance and status acquisition. *See also* prestige incentive; incentive type

Statute of Charitable Uses: 1601 English law that was the beginning of modern charity law; established charity watchdog commissions in each county and specified acceptable charitable purposes (Fishman and Schwarz 2000:27)

stewardship: the use of time, skills, and money of individuals in a religious *congregation to serve the *community. Hodgkinson (1990) defined this Christian concept, describing it as an all-encompassing activity of life and purpose of life rather than an isolated duty.

stewardship and fund-raising: *stewardship includes the practice of ethical accounting, conducted using the *resources at hand, a process that Fogal (1994:377) says applies equally to *fund-raising by a *nonprofit group and to success in fulfilling its *mission. He notes, further, that fund-raising managers must help the group's *leaders meet their stewardship responsibilities.

stigmatized nonprofit group: *nonprofit group with an unsavory, if not deviant, image in the larger *community, such that *members are inclined to hide from all but close friends and relatives the fact of their *membership in it. Smith (2000:102) observes that the prestige-stigma dimension of nonprofits has been little studied (cf. Goffman 1963, passim). *See also* deviant nonprofit group; deviant group

stipended volunteer: a *quasi-volunteer who is acting significantly from *voluntary altruism and is underremunerated for the *services or work performed in a job or role (cf. Smith 2000:25, 47). A Peace Corps *volunteer is one example (cf. Peace Corps 1997, passim; Willsen 2003, passim). A poorly paid museum staff member (*paid staff) is another example. Korstad and Leloudis (1999, passim) report on a field experiment conducted in the 1960s using a set of college students as stipended volunteers to work in an antipoverty *program in North Carolina. The volunteers found *participation in the program to be most enriching, while its effect on recipients (*target of benefits) was unclear.

strong democracy. *See* democracy

strategic management in nonprofits: administration of a *nonprofit group's strategic plan (*strategic planning). Walker (1983, passim) argues that, when it comes to *leadership and *management, nonprofits differ substantially from businesses and, therefore, strategic management, a business practice, can harm these groups. Most authors in the area of *paid-staff nonprofit organizations would disagree strongly with Walker, seeing strategic management as an important part of making a nonprofit successful in today's competitive climate (e.g., Bryce 2000; Koteen 1997; Oster 1995). Walker's point is, however, well taken in the context of *grassroots associations, where the strategic management process is administrative overkill (Smith 2000, chaps. 5–7).

strategic planning in nonprofits: process of setting broad *policy and direction for a *nonprofit group and of allowing for internal and external assessments (*evaluation of nonprofits), attention to key *stakeholders, identification of key *issues, and development of strategies (*strategy in nonprofits) to deal with the issues. Such planning also includes *decision making and action as well as monitoring the results of these two (Bryson 1994:154). Allison and Kaye (1997), Bryson (2004), Burkhart and Reussi (1993), and Wilbur (2000, chap. 1) are all similarly favorable to the promise and proved value of strategic planning for *paid-staff nonprofit organizations. The value of the process is less clear in *grassroots associations, where organization tends to be informal and *management styles are loose (Smith 2000, chaps. 5–7). This is not to say, however, that *strategy in nonprofits is wholly valueless for the latter type of nonprofit. *See also* action planning

strategy in nonprofits: a long-range set of all or a combination of the following: purposes (*goal), *policies, *programs, actions, decisions, and *resource allocations. Strategy describes what an *organization is, what it does, and why it does it (Bryson 1994:169). *See also* tactics

strike: *direct action protest in which employees, as a *group, withhold their labor as a *tactic for influencing the *organization or business with which they are at loggerheads. Altman (1994, passim) describes the Pullman strike of 1894, interpreting it as a major turning point in American labor history.

structural form of nonprofit groups: the way a *nonprofit group is organized with reference to its *mission. Smith (2000:9–10) lists several of the many different forms nonprofits have taken in modern times, among them *associations, *foundations, *federations, universities, museums, hospitals, social *agencies, *underground groups, loose *networks, charismatic cults (*new religion), and *rotating credit associations.

structure of nonprofit group: ways in which *nonprofit groups are set up in lasting social patterns, usually in *formal nonprofit groups using such documents as *charters, *constitutions, articles of incorporation (*articles of organization), and *by-laws (Smith 2000:107). Smith (ibid., chap. 5) analyzes the internal structure of *grassroots associations in terms of nine patterns, including informal *tax-exempt status, tending toward informal *organization, more internal *democracy, substantial *sociodemographic homogeneity, and few financial *resources—all of which contrast markedly with the structure of *paid-staff nonprofits. *See also* structural form of nonprofit groups

subgovernment. *See* iron triangle, the

subsector, nonprofit: subdivision of the *nonprofit sector. In this regard, Smith (2000:115) writes that two principal subsectors are the *paid-staff nonprofits subsector (mostly made up of *nonmember [public] benefit *nonprofit groups) and the *volunteer nonprofits subsector (*mostly made up of member benefit *grassroots associations and other *associations). Smith (2000, pt. 2) demonstrates how markedly grassroots associations differ from paid-staff nonprofits on over fifty structural and processual dimensions.

succession of leaders. *See* leaders, succession of

summative evaluation: 1. an evaluation of the overall or general outcomes and impacts of a *nonprofit group or *volunteer program; *outcome evaluation (cf. Bloom et al. 1971, passim; Center for the Study of Evaluation,1974, passim). 2. an assessment that measures, qualitatively and quantitatively, the progress of either *volunteer or *paid-staff trainees in meeting the educational objectives of a particular training *program. This evaluation is designed to determine the levels of success and *effectiveness of such programs (Macduff 1994:610).

Sunday school: 1. the religious education department or subgroup of a local *church, usually operating classes on Sunday (e.g., mornings) that involve prayer, Bible study, and emotional support. 2. the sessions of Sunday school attended by students. Although Sunday school has been conventionally for children and youth, in recent decades in many churches, there have been classes for adults (Wuthnow 1994:66–68).

supervision of volunteers/members: major administrative function in *nonprofit groups and *volunteer programs that involves monitoring the performance of *volunteers in their assigned roles (*volunteer role), giving, when appropriate, both positive and corrective feedback. May be done by the *volunteer administrator or by a regular *paid-staff member of the larger *organization whom the volunteer works with. Connors

(1995:176–178), Fisher and Cole (1993, chap. 7), and Lee et al. (1999) give practical advice on supervising volunteers. Supervision of *members is very loose in *grassroots associations, in keeping with their *informal style of operation (Smith 2000, chap. 5).

support group: *nonprofit group, usually rather small and informal, that provides social and emotional advice and encouragement to *members, while group *goals may be as varied as discussion, support, prayer, religious education, *self-help, therapy, recovery, *sociability, and the like (Wuthnow 1999:65). Wuthnow (pp. 2–5) argues that support groups have recently been on the rise in America, with about 40 percent of adult Americans belonging to one (p. 47), while more traditional *associations have been in decline (Putnam 2000, sec. 2; Wuthnow 1998, passim).

supralocal nonprofit group: a *nonprofit group that serves a territory larger than a local *community, such as a state, province, region, or nation. Supralocal groups are thus not *grassroots associations but may nonetheless be similar to them as *associations and important in their own right (Smith 2000:8). *State associations, *national voluntary associations, and *transnational associations are three examples.

supralocal volunteer association. *See* supralocal nonprofit group

survival of the fittest group: a *social movement or other *nonprofit group that, in attempting to survive, must compete for *members with similar groups, as all try to adapt to changes in public sentiment and to the organizational environment (*environment, organizational) in which each is embedded (Zald and Ash 1966:332).

survivalist nonprofit group. *See* citizen militia; paramilitary group

symbolic protest: irritating, unconventional, *political voluntary action that is content with a nonviolent, public show of displeasure (cf. Carter 1974, passim; Sharp 1973, passim). Examples include burning draft cards, holding vigils, and organizing *marches in neutral territory. Being symbolic the *protest never reaches the location of the people in power who could do something about the contentious *policy or practice. Often compared with *direct action protest (Carter 1974, passim). Marullo and Edwards (1994, passim) recommend a set of survival *strategies for peace groups, observing nonetheless that symbolic protest tends to increase mortality among protesters.

synagogue: 1. the local religious *congregation of the orthodox and conservative branches of the *religion of Judaism (cf. De Breffney 1978, passim; Heilman 1976, passim; Wertheimer 1987, passim). 2. the building in which such local Jewish religious *congregations meet. Shokeid (2001, passim) studied the *problems of gaining access to organizational power faced by women trying to assume *leadership positions in a formerly male-dominated gay/lesbian synagogue.

T

tactics in nonprofits: short-range plans (*planning) and procedures used to carry out a scheme or achieve a *goal. In the *nonprofit sector, usage of this word is always in the plural, the singular form referring, by contrast, to a military ploy or maneuver. Cannold (2002, passim) discusses both the strategies and the tactics used by "women-centered" antichoice proponents opposing abortion in Australia and the United States. The tactics considered were, for the most part, legislative. *See also* strategy in nonprofits

tainted money in nonprofits: money acquired by corrupt means. Van Til (1994:58) raises the ethical question of *nonprofit groups receiving money as a *donation from a *donor who acquired it unscrupulously and quite possibly took a tax deduction on the donation.

target of benefits: the recipient, or "helpee," whom a *nonprofit group or other *donor or *volunteer is trying to aid in some way (Gamson 1990: 16; Smith 2000:17). The target is usually either another entity or a particular population of individuals or groups. In *member benefit groups, their own *members are, in the main, the target of benefits.

tax deduction and philanthropy: the nature, rationale, and role of federal income tax deductions for charitable contributions, which date back to 1917 (cf. Burlingame 2004:464–469; Fishman and Schwarz 2000, pt. 3).

tax-exempt organizations registered with the Internal Revenue Service (IRS): Small subset of all tax-exempt organizations (cf. O'Neill 2002:7;

Smith 2000:36–45) that are officially recognized by the IRS as tax exempt in IRS categories 501(c)(1)–(21), 501(d)–(f), 501(k), 501(n), 521, 527–529 (Fishman and Schwarz 2000:57; O'Neill 2002:4–5).

tax-exempt sector: in general a synonym for *nonprofit sector, but one stressing that *nonprofit groups in this sector serve social *values and the *public interest sufficiently well to receive from state and federal *governments a tax-exemption on *excess revenues as well as exemption from state and local property and sales taxes generally (Burlingame 2004: 356). Additionally, most *philanthropic foundations and *charities receive tax exemptions for their *donors (i.e., in the United States, Internal Revenue Service category *501[c][3]). Other nations vary in amount of tax exemption they grant nonprofits as well as the kinds of nonprofits so favored. Weisbrod (1992, passim) has surveyed the tax *policies for *nonprofit organizations in ten countries. *See also* sector of society

tax-exempt status of nonprofits: nearly all *nonprofit groups are *exempt organizations, even if, in the United States, only a minority are officially recognized as such by either the Internal Revenue Service (IRS) (e.g., category *501[c][3]) or the state taxation agencies. This informal exemption is possible because many *grassroots associations, being too poor or too small, being religious in nature, or being linked to a larger tax-exempt organization, are not obliged to register with the IRS or, if obliged, fail to do so (Smith 2000:109). Tax-exempt status means that federal and state taxes on *excess revenues need not be paid. Certain tax-exempt groups (e.g., IRS category 501[c][3]) can receive *donations that are tax deductible to the *donor.

teach-in: a form of *direct action protest in which *participants take over conventional classrooms, often in a college or university, and offer alternative teaching related to *social change and the *social movement the *protest *participants belong to (cf. Sharp 1973, passim). Fraser and Freeman (1997, passim) studied a teach-in New York in 1996 that was designed to ally progressive American intellectuals with the working classes and labor movement.

technical assistance: management or operating advice given to a *nonprofit group by an outside consultant (*consultant use by nonprofits), *foundation staff member (*paid staff), or corporate staff member, often as an addition to a *grant the nonprofit has received. Advice may be given on, among other technical areas, *fund-raising, marketing, legal matters, financial planning, and budgeting (*budget) (see the Foundation Center Glossary at http://www.fdncenter.org/learn/ufg/glossary.html).

temple: 1. in ancient times, a place where a god or gods dwelled and hence were worshipped, along with the *religious functionaries who worked there (Pearce 1984, passim; Wilkinson 2000, passim). 2. the local religious *congregation of the reformed branch of Judaism or the building in which such a *congregation meets (Sell 1986, passim). 3. the local *congregation or building in which it meets for some Asian *religions like Buddhism and Taoism (cf. Ellwood 1979, passim). Chen (2002, passim) compared a Taiwanese immigrant Buddhist temple with a Taiwanese evangelical immigrant Christian church to explore the paradox of why the first is more publicly engaged in American society than the second.

tenant association. *See* building association

tenant management: an arrangement in public housing that enables residents to participate in making and executing decisions (*decision making) affecting their homes and quality of residential life. O'Brien (1995, passim) interviewed twelve African-American women, all long-time residents of a public housing complex in Kansas and engaged in tenant management activities. She concluded that although such activity failed to bring about collective *empowerment, it nonetheless fostered personal development (*see* developmental incentive) of the women.

tenant organization. *See* building association

territorial scope: the geographic area in which the *target of benefits of a *nonprofit group is found. Smith (2000:81) observes that, depending on the nonprofit, territorial scope may be as small as a local apartment building or as large as a nation or even many nations.

terrorism: 1. principles and practices used to create terror in a population (Laqueur 1977, passim). 2. act or series of acts based on these principles and practices carried out by a *terrorist (sense 2) or *terrorist group, which are intended, by means of violence, to intimidate or coerce a *government or *community (ibid.). Often done to force acceptance of specified political demands. Giroux (2004, passim) discusses how terrorism directed against Americans can be conceived of as a war on *democracy in the United States, while Rubenstein (1987, passim) discusses various aspects of terrorism throughout the modern world. Laqueur (1977, passim) analyzes terrorism in depth, as do Bell (1975, passim), Holms with Burke (1994, passim), Rubenstein (1987, passim), and Schweitzer and Schweitzer (2002, passim).

terrorist: a person who practices *terrorism, usually as a *member of a *terrorist group (cf. Alexander et al. 2001, passim). Holms with Burke (1994, passim) have written a book about groups of terrorists, their tools of the trade, and counter-terrorism.

terrorist group: a *group in any *sector of society (including the *nonprofit sector), which may be part of a larger *social movement, who engage in *terrorism. Holmes with Burke (1994, frontispiece) offer the FBI definition: a *group that uses unlawful "force or violence against persons or property to intimidate or coerce a government, the civilian population or any segment thereof, in furtherance of political or social objectives." These two authors have written a book about terrorist groups, their tools of the trade, and counter-terrorism. Raczynski (2004, passim) develops a discrete-event simulation model of the dynamics of the structures of terrorist and antiterrorist *organizations and agents and their interactions. Rubenstein (1987, pt. 3) discusses three forms of modern terrorist groups—Anarcho-communists, Left-nationalists, and Far-right *terrorism—whereas Bell (1975, chap. 2) classifies them into four types. Weinberg and Pedahzun (2003, passim) examine the relationship of political parties and terrorist groups. Alexander et al. (2001, passim) and Carr (1975, passim) describe particular terrorist groups.

tertiary time. *See* free time; leisure time/leisure; leisure activity; noncoercion

third-party government: government by *nonprofit groups. Based on the observation that, in *welfare states, nonprofits have considerable power because of the diverse functions delegated to them by *government through *contracts and *grants for *social services. Salamon has written extensively on third-party government (e.g., Salamon 1987, passim).

third sector: in general, a synonym for *nonprofit sector, albeit one stressing that *nonprofit groups in this sector differ from groups comprising the *business and *government sectors (*see* sector of society). The term "third sector" does, however, omit consideration of the household/family sector, which came first historically. Thus *"fourth sector" is a historically more accurate ordinal label for the former. Salamon and Anheier (1992, passim) and Smith (1991, passim) discuss the various definitions of the several sectors of society.

Third World: the developing nations, many being in Africa, Asia, and Latin America, that are not aligned with either the former Communist bloc (*Second World) or the developed (mostly Western) non-Communist bloc (Horowitz 1966, passim). Although considerable published material exists on Third-World *nonprofit groups (e.g., Clark 1991; Esman and Uphoff 1984; Fisher 1993, 1998), mainstream scholars, because they adhere to the *developed world flat-earth paradigm, tend to be unaware of it or, if aware, fail to incorporate it in their work (Smith 2000:234). Harris (1986, passim) argues that the Third World is vanishing, as certain key former Third-World countries industrialize while others sink into the *Fourth World of underdevelopment.

Third-World development/aid nonprofit: 1. *transnational nonprofit group specializing in aid to or development of *Third- or *Fourth-World nations (e.g., Clark 1991; Lissner 1977; Smith and Elkin 1981; Sommer 1977; Van de Fliert 1994, pt. 2). 2. *indigenous nonprofit group, national or subnational in scope, that works on development or aid in a Third or Fourth World nation. Fisher (1993, passim; 1998, passim) examines the work of indigenous nonprofits in various developing nations, concluding that they have helped significantly in recent times. See also related books by Anheier and Salamon (1998), Carroll (1992), Clark (1991), and Esman and Uphoff (1984), which further support Fisher's conclusions. Jedlicka (1990) sees *volunteerism as a key pathway to world development.

three-sector model of society. *See* model of society

three-sector model of society flat-earth paradigm: nonprofit sector model stating (erroneously, *see* sectors of society) that industrial society can be analyzed according to three sectors: *government, *business, and non-profit, with the latter often being referred to as the *third sector* (Smith 2000:221–222). Omits the household/family sector, which came first historically. *See also* nonprofit sector

time-budget/time diary method: a procedure for estimating how people spend their time, asking them to record their current time use in small intervals (cf. Szalai 1972, chap. 4). Horne (2003:502–503) maintains that the most accurate way to estimate personal use of time is either to make random telephone calls to respondents or to ask them to wear a buzzer and, when it sounds (at random), to record what they are doing in a time diary. *See also* volunteer time

time-money scheme: an arrangement whereby an hour of *volunteering equals an hour of time credit. Such credits are "banked," to be used later in "purchasing" the *services of another *volunteer. Also known as "local exchange [for employment] trading system," or LETS, such schemes are now in operation in several countries, including the United States and the United Kingdom (Boyle 1997).

tokenism: principle or practice of granting minimal concessions, often to a minority or other underrepresented group, as a token gesture intended to appease extreme demands, comply with legal requirements, and the like (cf. Davis 1963). Pazy and Oron (2001, passim) found in an *evaluation of Israeli Defense Forces that female performance rates were lower than male rates when the women were token *members of their units.

tolerance: an attitude or orientation that individuals hold toward certain activities or thoughts of others that differ substantially from their own (Stebbins 1996b:3). It is a relatively passive disposition, falling roughly midway between scorn or disdain toward an activity or thought pattern on the one hand, and embracement or acceptance of it on the other. Both scorn and embracement, in contrast to tolerance, are active approaches to the behavior in question. When something is tolerated it is accorded legitimacy, though perhaps grudgingly. At the same time, because tolerated thought and behavior are nonetheless mildly threatening, people have little interest in actually adopting tolerated behaviors or thought patterns as their own, or even accepting them as alternatives they might conceivably adopt in the future.

total quality management (TQM): a managerial approach in *nonprofit groups that aims to achieve high-level client and consumer as well as employee and *volunteer *satisfaction (senses 1 and 2) (Carr and Littman 1990, passim; Feigenbaum 1983, passim; George and Weimerskirch 1994). Rothschild and Ollilainen (1999, passim) observe that TQM is frequently misunderstood. They show, through an examination of egalitarian *cooperative organizations, that profound differences separate TQM from other managerial approaches and that practitioners would do well to learn from these *grassroots associations. *See also* management; nonprofit group management

totalitarian state. *See* dictatorship

trade association: *association whose principal *goal is to foster improvement in a certain kind of business, serving thus *member businesses or their representatives and managers, if not all three. Knoke (1993, passim) considers the role of trade associations in the American political economy.

trade union. *See* union

trademark fund-raising event. *See* fund-raising

traditional nonmember service flat-earth paradigm: *nonprofit sector model that centers more or less exclusively on personal, direct, face-to-face *social services and *welfare activities for nonmembers, as if this were the whole of the nonprofit sector (Smith 2000:227–228). *See also* service, personal social; Lady Bountiful; noblesse oblige

traditional service volunteer. *See* service volunteer, traditional

traditional service volunteering: *service volunteering (senses 1 and 2) in which the *target of benefits is outside one's *nonmember nonprofit group or outside one's *volunteer program. The main kind of *volunteering focused on when one works from the *traditional nonmember service flat-earth paradigm (Smith 2000:227–228).

training in nonprofits. *See* in-service training in nonprofits

training of volunteers/members: major administrative function in *nonprofit groups and *volunteer programs that involves providing information and learning experiences for newly recruited *volunteers or *members regarding the *volunteer role they will be expected to play and how to perform its tasks successfully. This function is generally given more attention in volunteer programs and *nonprofit agencies than in *associations, except associations with *paid staff. Macduff (1994) writes about the principles of training for both volunteers and paid staff in nonprofit groups and volunteer programs. Other sources of practical guidance on training volunteers include Connors (1995, chaps. 5 and 6) and Fisher and Cole (1993, chap. 6). Battle (1988, chap. 4) covers the training of *association members.

trait approach to leadership. *See* leadership, trait approach to

transfer. *See* exchange

transnational activity in nonprofits: although some nonprofits are transnational by nature and basic *mission (*see* transnational association/transnational nonprofit), it has been argued recently that all nonprofits should consider the transnational or international dimension of their activities (Wilbur 2000, chap. 10). Anheier and Themudo (2005) argue that, today, the *nonprofit sector is steadily internationalizing.

transnational association/transnational nonprofit: *association whose *membership or activities or both are multinational, even though in practice, many are only bi-national. In the *nonprofit sector transnational associations may be composed of individuals or *nonprofit groups and are often formed to provide relief for or development of *Third-World countries, among many other types of *goals. See Bennett (1995, passim), Feld et al. (1994, passim), Iriye (2002, passim), Jordan and Feld (2001, passim), and Muldoon (2004, passim) for detailed consideration of transnational associations (cf. also Burlingame 2004:264–268). Osigweh (1993, passim) examines some local transnational associations. *See also* nongovernmental organization (NGO)

troop: a type of local *association. In the United States, local associations of the Boy Scouts and of Girl Scouts are called "troops." Mechling (1984, passim) studied language use among a troop of Boy Scouts at summer camp, as interpreted through Freudian theory.

trust: 1. state or condition of being trusted or relied upon; state of being entrusted with something (e.g., *board of trustees entrusted with ensuring democratic procedure). 2. faith or confidence that a *nonprofit group will accept and honor in practice the set of humane core social values (*value, humane core) (e.g., integrity, openness, accountability, *service, and *charity) that constitute a major part of the philosophical and religious foundation of the *nonprofit sector and that meet the public's current expectations for nonprofits (Jeavons 1994:186). 3. a *charitable trust.

trustee. *See* board member; board of trustees

turbulent field as environment: rapid social, political, and economic change (*social change), which for *nonprofit groups wanting to remain current and effective, requires continual *organizational transformation (Perlmutter and Gummer 1994:230–231).

twelve-step (anonymous) group: 1. a local *self-help, *member benefit, volunteer *nonprofit group modeled after Alcoholics Anonymous (AA) (AA was founded in 1935, Rudy 1986:7) and that adapts the Twelve Steps and Twelve Traditions of AA (Mäkelä 1996, passim) to deal with recovery from other problems and addictions such as narcotics addiction, compulsive gambling, workaholism (overworking), overeating, incest, sex addiction, mental illness, excessive debt, codependency, living with an alcoholic, and the like (Mäkelä 1996, chap. 16; Beattie 1990:229–240). Twelve-step groups also tend to use and adapt the structures and processes of AA such as first-name-only anonymity, weekly meetings, *sponsorship, rotating *leadership of meetings, no cross talk, use of approved helpful printed literature (pamphlets and books), welcoming back people who have relapsed, and so on (Rudy 1986, passim; Mäkelä 1996, passim). 2. a *national association made up of local *groups as in sense 1.

two-sector model of society. *See* model of society

U

unaffiliated volunteer. *See* spontaneous volunteer

unbeliever: a person who believes in no particular religion at all (cf. Turner 1985).

unconventional participation: individual *participation in a *deviant group or *deviant collective action. One of the most celebrated studies of unconventional participation is Humphreys' (1970, chap. 4) ethnography of homosexual "tearooms" (men's public toilets), which includes a section describing the interaction that typically takes place there.

unconventional voluntary political action: *political voluntary action that makes significant intentional use of *protest activities, while being motivated by unconventional (deviant) *goals or means of achieving them (Gamson 1990, passim).

underdeveloped country. *See* Third World; Fourth World

underground economy. *See* economic activity, informal

underground group: *deviant nonprofit group that attempts to keep secret the fact of its existence. Crowley (1989, passim) studied the age-old Wicca and its adaptation to modern times. Golden and McConnell (1986, passim) focus on a new underground railroad in America transporting illegal aliens from Latin America.

underground movement: a *social movement that operates underground (secretly) to avoid negative sanctions by governmental authorities, who are reacting to the movement's deviant goals or means it uses to achieve them. Some underground movements are secret *resistance movements, as with the anti-Nazi underground movements in occupied European nations during World War II (Files 1991, passim; Miller 1979, passim). Bromwich (2004, passim) laments the demise of the underground movement of the dissident left wing in the United States, which began in the late 1950s and lasted for approximately a decade. He predicts it will return, however, for there is, these days, much to protest.

underground railroad: informal network of abolitionists and former slaves in America prior to emancipation who helped slaves escape to safety in nonslave states, usually in the North, or in Canada (Burlingame 2004: 475–477; Gara 1996, passim).

understaffed volunteer setting: setting for *volunteer work in which there is insufficient *volunteer leadership, particularly *paid staff. According to Pearce (1993), there is in understaffed volunteer settings a high degree of dependence on *volunteers. Since volunteers are *nondependent workers this gives them leverage. If their leverage is acknowledged by providing sufficient time for them to exercise their role as perceived owners of the *organization and their roles related to delivery of *service, reduced role conflict and reduced volunteer subordination is likely to follow.

unfair competition by nonprofits: claim (Bennett and DiLorenzo 1989:xi) that "government is competing unfairly with small [business] firms . . . indirectly by granting tax exemptions and giving taxpayer subsidies to profit-making 'nonprofit' organizations. [As a result of unfair competition from government and tax-exempt nonprofits,] many private firms are driven from the marketplace; others struggle to survive. Competition from the commercial *nonprofit sector also discourages the formation of new firms, which would provide employment and stimulate economic growth." Bennett and DiLorenzo (1989, chap. 3) describe in detail the political economy of this unfair competition and then go on to analyze unfair competition by commercial *nonprofit groups in a variety of industries such as hospital and medical care, physical fitness, and audiovisual and computer software (chaps. 4–6). They also describe unfair governmental competition with the business sector (chap. 7) and what can be done generally about unfair competition (chap. 7). Weisbrod (2000, passim) more recently addresses himself to these same concerns, and the point in general seems well taken. Brody (1996, passim), in a related study, discusses the economic convergence of the *nonprofit and for-profit organization (*for-profit group) forms. The nonprofit researchers in this area tend to operate according to the *damned nonprofit flat-earth paradigm (Smith 2000:230–231).

unincorporated nonprofit: a *nonprofit, usually a *grassroots association, that is unincorporated in any state; often new, small, or religious; can still obtain Internal Revenue Service (IRS) tax-exemption under IRS category 501(c)(3) if it qualifies otherwise (*charitable federal tax exemption requirements) (Fishman and Schwarz 2000:61),

union: *association whose *mission is to establish and improve for its *members their rate of remuneration, conditions of work, fringe benefits, and certain other features of employment and worker *welfare (sense 1). Some unions represent workers at a particular factory or industry (industrial unions), whereas others represent those in a certain job or occupation (craft or trade unions). Members of a craft or trade union are relatively skilled at a (usually manual) form of work and may work alone, whereas those in an industrial union include all lower-level employees in a particular *for-profit organization. Zieger (1995, passim) and Galenson and Lipset (1990, passim), for example, offer a comprehensive view of unions in the United States in the late twentieth century. Rayback (1959, passim) and Galenson (1994, passim; 1996, passim) provide histories of American unions. Lipset et al. (1977, passim) studied the bases of union *democracy in a classic book, and Galenson (1976, passim) studied democracy in European unions. Union locals have been examined by Barbash (1974, passim), Stepan-Norris and Zeitlin (1996, passim), Tannenbaum and Kahn (1982, passim), and Wellman (1995, passim). Galenson (1983, passim) wrote a history of a national union, the United Brotherhood of Carpenters, and Ferriss et al. (1997, passim) wrote a history of the national United Farm Workers. Masters (1997, passim) and Erem (2001, passim) discuss recent issues and problems with unions in America. Galenson (1998) describes the world's strongest trade unions, which are in Scandinavia.

union local: the local chapter, branch, or unit of a larger regional, national, or international *union. Union locals have been studied by Stepan-Norris and Zeitlin (1996, passim) and Wellman (1995, passim).

United Fund. *See* United Way

United Way: a local organization established to conduct annual United Way or, more rarely, United Fund fund-raising campaigns and to manage subsequent distribution of the proceeds to *community *charities. The first federation of local United Ways (then Community Chests) was established in 1918, giving rise eventually to the present-day United Way of America, which now represents approximately 1,400 local units (http://www.national.unitedway.org). United Ways also exist in Canada and several other countries. Brilliant (1990, passim) has studied the history and *problems of United Ways and the United Way of America. Smith (1978, passim) has sharply criticized the United Way system on a number of grounds, but especially for its mainly successful attempts to maintain a monopoly over corporate payroll deduction as charitable *fund-raising in America. *See also* Community Chest; Black United Fund; fund-raising intermediary

unofficial nonprofit goal. *See* goal, unofficial

unprofessional: 1. of an act seen as being contrary to professional conduct and standards, often seen as violating a *profession's code of ethics (cf. Manley 1992, passim). 2. of a person who does not belong to a *profession; of an *amateur (senses 1 and 2) or a *nonprofessional (sense 1). Groves (2001, passim) studied the animal rights movement (*see* social movement) in the United States, focusing on the emotions of female *activists. He found that, to gain legitimacy without seeming to be unprofessional (many were *professionals serving in *grassroots associations), women intentionally used emotional behavior in interaction with the media and biomedical *community.

unrelated business income tax: federal income tax on the revenues of a *nonprofit that are unrelated to its tax-exempt mission or function (Hopkins 1998:632).

unselfishness: unselfishness, selflessness, and *altruism are often considered synonymous with being not selfish, with being mindful of the *interests and *needs of others. Stebbins (1993c:50–51) argues, however, that the true opposite of *selfishness is not unselfishness but rather self-sacrifice (*sacrifice). In the latter, not only are generous people mindful of other's needs, they also give up to those others something of their own that they *value.

uprising. *See* rebellion

utilitarian incentive: desire to gain economic returns from *membership in a *nonprofit group, be the returns monetary, occupational, professional, or some other material *benefit (cf. Clark and Wilson 1961, passim). Two studies of national associations (King and Walker 1992:407; Knoke 1990:119) revealed that occupational and professional benefits were more important to *members than other (minor) material benefits. *See also* incentive type

utility. *See* satisfaction

utopia: 1. a utopian (ideal) community or *commune; an idealistic *intentional community (cf. Richter 1971, passim). 2. an imaginary ideal community or society with a particular social structure and particular social processes. Thomas More (1989, passim), in 1516, wrote a classic statement on utopia (sense 2).

utopian community. *See* commune

V

value: a belief transcending specific actions and situations and serving as a standard guide for selection or evaluation of behavior, people, and events. Furthermore, values, which individuals rank according to their importance relative to one another, also refer to desired *goals and to modes of conduct promoting these goals (Smith and Schwartz 1997:80).

value-based concern. *See* voluntary altruism

value, humane core: a *value centered on humane caring, sharing, and social support (*see* voluntary altruism), which serves to motivate *volunteers to act or *nonprofit groups to establish *goals. Smith (2000:22–24) sets out seven humane core values: *civic engagement (civic pride, responsibility, etc.), *sociopolitical innovation (identify new social problems), social religiosity (faith-based concerns), *sociability (creating and sharing in friendly interaction), social aesthetics (creating, performing, preserving art), *economic system support (auxiliary support for economy and business), and *personal social service (satisfying beyond family the needs and wishes of others).

value judgment: evaluation asserting the merit or demerit of the object being evaluated, such as a person or group. Maslovaty and Dor-Shav (1990, passim) found in their study of Tel Aviv high school students that all respondents had a high level of value judgment, though when it came to content, there were some gender differences.

value orientation: direction of a person's attitudes and thinking toward some object, as based on certain beliefs, standards, moral principles, or social customs. Joireman and colleagues (2003, passim) studied, in an experiment, how a sample of people with different value orientations construed the rationality, morality, and power that could underlie their most pro-social or least aggressive choices.

venture philanthropy: using venture capital approaches with *nonprofit groups to help the latter not only with *grants but also with *technical assistance, *networking, and other support *services. Frumkin (2003, passim) discusses venture philanthropy as a way to improve the *effectiveness of *philanthropic foundations. He argues that such *philanthropy becomes social investing, because it uses the discipline of the investment world in a field that has traditionally relied on *trust and good faith.

vertical collaboration of nonprofits. *See* collaboration

vigilante: a person who, without governmental (*government) authorization, takes law and order into (usually) *his* own hands, punishing one or more others considered to have committed a crime. Tucker (1985, passim) discusses vigilantes in the backlash against crime in America.

vigilante group: a *nonprofit group, usually an *association, that without governmental (*government) authorization, takes law and order into its own hands, punishing a person or persons considerrd to have committed a crime. Tucker (1985) observes that, today, most vigilantism is not of the group variety, however, but conducted instead by individual *vigilantes. In earlier times, the Ku Klux Klan has been a vigilante group harassing African-Americans (Sims 1997, passim). *See also* posse

violent protest: irritating, unconventional *political voluntary action intending to use violence, defined as harm to people or property or both. *Symbolic or *direct action protest that unintentionally escalates into violence is not, in fact, violent protest (cf. Carter 1974, passim). Such escalation may be caused by an overreaction of police or other authorities. Stone (1971, passim) examined the infamous Kent State University shootings in 1970, in which four students were killed during a direct action protest that went wrong.

virtual foundation: a *grant-making foundation operating only or mainly through the Internet, using e-mail and electronic transfers of *funds. Examples of such foundations include the Virtual Foundation, which supports grassroots projects around the world (http://www.virtual foundation.org), and the Cystic Fibrosis Foundation (http://www.global .mci.com/casestudies/emea/fibrosisen.pdf).

virtual volunteering: use of information and communications technology to enable and facilitate *volunteering at a distance from its group or organizational base (Murray and Harrison 2005:31–33). Also known as online volunteering and e-volunteering. *See also* Internet activism; e-philanthropy

vision of success: an *organization's ideal picture of itself in the future, as it carries out its *mission and achieves success. Such vision is important for developing effective *strategies for running the organization (Bryson 1994:169).

VOLAG: acronym for voluntary agency (*nonprofit agency), usually in a developing country (cf. Keeny 1973, passim; Lissner 1977, passim). Kothari (1995, passim) studied approximately ten thousand VOLAGs in India established to serve the poor and disadvantaged. Based on successes observed in the Young India Project and other programs, he proposes a blueprint for *government to encourage these *organizations to increase their efforts to raise people above the poverty line.

voluntariness, freely chosen quality of: proposition stating that people freely choose to volunteer in a certain activity (for a discussion of this proposition, see Cnaan, Handy, and Wadsworth 1996:369–372). Stebbins (2005a, passim) argues, however, that the free choice of any *leisure activity, *volunteering included, is hedged about by so many qualifying conditions as to render the idea useless in definitions of leisure. The nature and degree of choice cannot be assumed, Stebbins holds, rather, it must be analyzed for every activity and category of participant.

voluntarism: all people and groups involved in *informal voluntary action, *associational activity, *volunteering, or paid employment in a *nonprofit group. Roughly synonymous with *nonprofit sector. Manser and Cass (1976, passim) described voluntarism and several external forces and internal *issues affecting it. Van Til (1988:9) holds that voluntarism, as a concept, has a normative side, namely, that *voluntary groups are both good and good for society. Handy (1966, passim) discusses the importance of the voluntary principle in American *religion in the nineteenth and twentieth centuries as a key facet of *freedom of religion and, more generally, *freedom of association. (Indeed, the roots of voluntarism based on these two freedoms go back, in one sense, to the beginnings of the Protestant Reformation in Europe and even earlier to the *"heresies" and *sects of the eleventh and twelfth centuries there [Moore 1995, passim].) Von Hoffman (1994:122) suggests that the voluntarism, central to "nineteenth century Protestant religious life as it was, had enormous impact on American society, particularly in the North." Crucial here (ibid.) "is the fact that the local-chapter structure [*polymorphic nonprofit group] elaborated first by Protestant *church members was adopted by a wide range of religious and secular neighborhood organizations." Many other authors have written on voluntarism from a variety of perspectives (e.g., Brackney 1997; Brown 1998; Freedman 1993; Hall 1992; Layton 1987; Macleod and Hogarth 1999, chap. 1; Ogilvie 2004; Schwartz 1984; Smith with Dixon 1973; Verba et al. 1995).

voluntary action: action by individuals or *nonprofit groups stemming from *voluntary altruism. In voluntary action individuals, alone or in groups, reach beyond their own personal, often selfish (*selfishness), *interests to act in harmony with a combination of the following: *service, *citizenship, socio-religious *values and other values (*value, humane core). In their broadest sense such beliefs motivate people to act as if others in their society mattered, an outgrowth of certain cultural and subcultural values of a nation. National societies vary, albeit with some overlap, as to the nature of these values and how they are expressed within their legal systems. People in business and government (*see* sectors of society) act using mainly an economic calculus, while in the *nonprofit sector, they act mainly from a social value calculus. Voluntary action includes *quasi-volunteering, but to the extent it is based strictly on *self-interest, not certain kinds of *informal leisure. Smith (2000, chap. 1), who popularized the term, examines some complexities of voluntary action. An early use of the term is found in Smith, Reddy, and Baldwin (1972:168 and passim). He borrowed the term from the book by Lord Beveridge (1948) entitled *Voluntary Action*, incorporating the term into the interdisciplinary, interprofessional association he founded in 1971 now called *ARNOVA and that focuses on nonprofit and voluntary action research. Broader than the concepts of *volunteering and *volunteer work, in that voluntary action can also refers to certain informal activity motivated by voluntary altruism (*see* individual voluntary action). Indeed, it is the most general, all-embracing concept of all at the behavioral and interactional levels of the *nonprofit sector. Various authors have used the term "voluntary action" in writing about nonprofit sector phenomena, but usually without necessarily having in mind the foregoing, more detailed definition (e.g., Acheson and Williamson 1995; Galdston 1961; Gladstone 1979; Korten 1990; Lewis 1999; Lohmann 1992; Smith 1972c, 2001; Smith with Dixon 1973; Smith and Van Til 1983).

voluntary action center. *See* volunteer center

voluntary activity: 1. activity done of one's own free will. 2. synonym for *"voluntary action" (Smith 2000, chap. 1).

voluntary agency. *See* nonprofit agency; VOLAG

voluntary altruism: a special set of values (*value, humane core) and attitudes that underlie *participation in all *nonprofit groups and the entire *nonprofit sector. According to Smith (2000:19–20) *altruism is voluntary when there is (a) a mix of humane caring and sharing of oneself and one's resources; (b) at least a moderate freedom to chose the activity; (c) a lack of coercion from biophysical, biosocial, or socially compelling forces; (d) a sensitivity to certain *needs and wants of a *target of benefits; (e) an expectation of little or no remuneration or payment in kind; and (f) an expectation of receiving some sort of *satisfaction for action undertaken on behalf of the target. Monroe (1996, chap. 10) writes about the altruistic perspective in a way that is consonant with voluntary altruism, stressing perception of a shared humanity (*value, humane core).

See also altruism, volunteer; self-serving; voluntariness, freely chosen quality of; voluntary action

voluntary altruistic action. *See* voluntary action

voluntary association. *See* association

voluntary century. *See* century, voluntary

voluntary community. *See* commune; intentional community

voluntary failure theory: a set of propositions centered on the observation that *nonprofit groups are the first response to the desire for *public goods. According to this theory government supplies only those goods beyond what the nonprofits provide (Salamon 1995, passim). *See also* contract failure; public goods theory

voluntary group. *See* nonprofit group

voluntary group incidence. *See* nonprofit group incidence

voluntary group prevalence. *See* nonprofit group prevalence

voluntary organization: one of two types of *nonprofit organizations (Smith 1981), the first of which uses largely *paid staff, albeit staff who may be engaged in a form of quasi-volunteerism, or work for below the market value of similar services and skills applied elsewhere. The second is an organization made up largely of *volunteers. The measure for distinction is number of paid vs. volunteer hours. *See also* nonprofit organization

voluntary participation. *See* voluntary action

voluntary sector: preferred term in some nations for the *nonprofit sector, such as in the United Kingdom, because it emphasizes the noncompulsory, nonstatutory (nongovernmental) aspect of that sector (Billis 1989, passim). Also the term preferred by those scholars who espouse a positive, humane core value-based (*value, humane core) definition of the sector (e.g., Smith 2000, chap. 1). Kendall et al. (1996), in their overview of the British nonprofit sector, show their preference for the term "voluntary sector" in their book title, while most other books surveying the national nonprofit scene use the term "nonprofit sector" in their titles. *See also* nonprofit sector, national studies of

voluntary service. *See* volunteer service

voluntary society. *See* civil society

voluntary spirit: the attitude of *charity, *altruism, and *philanthropy expressed through voluntary *giving, *service, and association with others (O'Connell 1983, passim). Broadly put the voluntary spirit inspires *participation in the *nonprofit sector in either the sphere of social concern or that of *political action, sometimes both. *Voluntary altruism is a broader, less ideologically (*ideology) charged term for this attitude, in that the first avoids such offensive connotations as *Lady Bountiful and *noblesse oblige while including areas the second excludes like *sociability and *religious activity.

volunteer: 1. an individual who performs, even for a short period of time, *volunteer work in an informal setting (*see* informal volunteer) or a formal one (*see* formal volunteer) as *board member of a *nonprofit group, active association *member or *leader (*associational volunteer), or participant in a *volunteer program of a nonprofit, governmental *agency, or unusually, certain type of business firm (cf. Lauffer and Gorodezky 1977, passim; Smith 2000, chap. 1). The volunteer provides a *service or benefit (*member benefit, *public benefit) to one or more individuals outside that person's family, usually receiving no pay, though some volunteers in *volunteer programs are compensated for out-of-pocket expenses (e.g., transportation costs for low-income participants, *see* *expense reimbursement), as are some nonprofit group board members who come from out of town. Ellis and Noyes (1990, passim) sketch the history of the volunteer in the United States. Other books examine particular aspects of being a volunteer (Allahyari 2000; Pearce 1993; Sills 1957), certain types of volunteers (Chambré 1987; Cionca 1999; Gora and Nemerowicz 1985), and the positive *value of volunteers and *volunteering (Hybels 2004; Kilpatrick and Danziger 1996; O'Connell and Taylor 1999; Perry 2000; Pidgeon 1998; Yount 1998). Still other volumes give practical advice on working with (*volunteer administration) or as a volunteer (Battle 1988; Calmes 1997; Pidgeon 1998; Thomas and Thomas 1998; Vineyard and McCurley 2001) or list volunteer opportunities (Powell 2000). 2. one who voluntarily joins the armed services of a country rather than be conscripted involuntarily by a governmental "draft" (selective service system). Emilio (1849/1969, passim) presents the history of a black volunteer army infantry unit in the Civil War. Cross (2004, passim) presents a history of a Tennessee volunteer infantry regiment in the same war. *See also* volunteering; quasi-volunteer; philanthropy; altruism; board volunteer; association; service volunteer; associational volunteer; program volunteer; voluntary altruism

volunteer action: significantly unremunerated *voluntary action by an individual or a group that results substantially from *voluntary altruism (Smith 2000:24). Volunteer action usually refers to individual *volunteering or *participation, rather than *group voluntary action (e.g., Ross and Wheeler 1971; Smith 1985). As such, it includes the activity of all kinds of *volunteers, especially *associational volunteers, *program volunteers, *board volunteers, *service volunteers, and *informal service volunteers. *See also* quasi-volunteer action

volunteer activity. *See* volunteering

volunteer administration: 1. process of managing (*management) *volunteers in *volunteer programs. Brudney (1990:56–57) considers the matter of *effectiveness of volunteers working in volunteer *programs in for-profit hospitals and government agencies (*for-profit group). McCurley and Lynch (1989, passim) and Fischer and Schaffer (1993, passim) consider many of the *problems of volunteer administration, as do other authors (e.g., Battle 1988; Bradner 1999; Campbell and Ellis 1995; Connors 1995; Fisher and Cole 1993; Goodlad and McIvor 1998;

Lee et al. 1999; Macleod and Hogarth 1999; McCurley and Lynch 1989; McSweeney and Alexander 1996; Vineyard and McCurley 1998, 2001; Wilson 1976, 1983; Wittich 2003a). 2. occupational role, paid or unpaid, of managing volunteers in volunteer programs. Volunteer administrators, especially those who are part-time or full-time *paid staff, are striving to professionalize (*see* professionalization of volunteers and volunteerism) but lack appropriate and widespread linkages to institutions of higher education for professional credentialing and degrees, unlike the emerging *nonprofit management profession. For the past four decades or so, the Association for Volunteer Administration has spearheaded the professionalization that has taken place. Fisher and Cole (1993, chap. 9) give a fine overview of professionalization in volunteer administration. Connors (1995:157–159, 184) and Ellis et al. (1996, passim) discuss the executive role in volunteer programs. Some key facets of volunteer administration not mentioned elsewhere in this dictionary include communications, program *policies (Connors 1995, chap. 7; Graff 1997, passim), use of volunteers in *fund-raising (Connors 1995, chap. 12), *advocacy for volunteer programs, public relations, volunteer promotion and career ladders (*see* career volunteering), volunteer access to equipment and supplies, *resources (Vineyard and McCurley 1989, passim), accounting, and record keeping. *See also* job creation for volunteers/members; recruitment of volunteers/members; screening of volunteers/members; orientation of volunteers/members; training of volunteers/members; development of volunteers/members; placement of volunteers/members; motivating of volunteers/members; supervision of volunteers/members; personnel practices for volunteers/members; recognition of volunteers/members; retention of volunteers/members; accountability of volunteers/members; risk management and liability with volunteers/members; building paid staff-volunteer relations; recruitment of nonprofit group paid staff; evaluation of volunteer programs/associations; expense reimbursement of volunteers; formation of a volunteer program/association

volunteer administrator: supervisor of a *volunteer program and the *volunteers serving within it. Concerning remuneration may be paid full-time, part-time, or, as volunteer, not paid at all. Brudney (1990:109–114) discusses the training of volunteer administrators. *See also* volunteer administration

volunteer as intern. *See* intern as volunteer

volunteer association: membership group composed of *volunteers, although it may also have *paid support staff (Ellis and Noyes 1990). Some host settings for volunteers welcome volunteer associations, for example Friends of the Library. The organization of associations of volunteers has been cited as an important element of volunteer *empowerment (Dover 1997).

volunteer avoidance of direct participation in decision making: the tendency of *volunteers to want to influence organizational *policy, but by and large to avoid actually participating in *management roles or *decision-making roles (Pearce 1993:156). There may be a certain aversion to playing such roles. The implication is that ways need to be devised for volunteer input and *influence or playing indirectly *decision-making roles, but advocates of volunteer *empowerment should not assume volunteers wish to be involved in the nuts and bolts of decision making.

volunteer bureau. *See* volunteer center

volunteer career. *See* career volunteering

volunteer center (voluntary action center, volunteer bureau): 1. local *nonprofit organization whose *goals include promoting *volunteerism as well as coordinating, recruiting, placing, and recognizing *volunteers (cf. Community Chests and Councils of America 1952, passim; United Way of Wake County 1988, passim). Many centers operate on a *community-wide basis, while attempting to meet the volunteer *needs of particular *nonprofit agencies and *projects. Garbarino and Jacobson (1978, passim) studied the operations of the specialized Youth Helping Youth Volunteer Bureau, which supplied young volunteers to a variety of local agencies dealing with youth.

volunteer coordinator. *See* volunteer administrator

volunteer department: sub-*group of an *organization that operates a *volunteer program or *group (e.g., the *volunteer program of a hospital, whether the hospital is *governmental, *for-profit, or *nonprofit; a *volunteer advisory board of a governmental *agency or *program). Maneker (1973, passim) views such departments as an extention of Webers's theory of *bureaucracy. He argues that, though the work is demeaning for the *volunteers he observed in a voluntary hospital in New York, prestige comes with serving there and in doing the "noble" work the hospital needs.

volunteer evaluation: the process or result of evaluating *volunteers in their roles (*volunteer role). Vineyard (1988, passim) discusses evaluating volunteers.

volunteer exploitation: use of *volunteers in ways that disregard their *needs and desires or that involves too many hours of *service or substandard conditions for *volunteering. Given the *workplace metaphor often applied to *volunteer work, Pearce (1993:178) has asked whether it is possible to exploit volunteers in the same manner as other workers are sometimes exploited.

volunteer functions inventory: an inventory of thirty motivations for *volunteering based on up to five possible responses (each measured on a seven-point scale) for each of six theorized functions of volunteering (social, value, career, understanding, protective, and esteem functions). Clary, Snyder, and Ridge (1992), whose research was guided by functional analysis, developed this inventory. The instrument can be used in surveys of volunteers and nonvolunteers as well, and it can be administered in group or individual settings.

volunteer group. *See* volunteer nonprofit group

volunteer, habitual: literally, one who makes a habit of *volunteering, of serving a *nonprofit group or acting as an *informal service volunteer for a half-year or more. Viewed from the *leisure perspective, one for whom volunteering is a main *leisure activity pursued either *regularly* (e.g., more or less every week, fortnight, or month in, say, friendly visiting at a hospital or attending monthly *board meetings) or *frequently,* albeit irregularly (e.g., working different *volunteer roles such as helping with Scouts one night, collecting trash in a local park the next Saturday, and serving coffee after *church the following day). Regular and frequent habitual volunteers contrast with *episodic volunteers and *sporadic* volunteers, or people who volunteer only occasionally, and irregularly at that. Stebbins (1998, passim) studied regular habitual volunteers, who were serving as *key volunteers in the francophone communities located in Calgary and Edmonton. *See also* continuous-service volunteer

volunteer, key: a *volunteer in a *nonprofit group who numbers among its most skilled, knowledgeable, and hard-working *members in helping the group reach its *goals. Such a person is usually an *officer but could also be, for example, chair of a major *committee or organizer of a major event (Stebbins 1998:4).

volunteer leadership: a concept encompassing three types of roles centered, partly or wholly, on coordinating *volunteer work: elected *leaders of a *volunteer nonprofit group, especially a *grassroots association; salaried staff (*paid staff) who, as part of their job, supervise *volunteers in a *volunteer program; and full-time *volunteer administrators (Ellis and Noyes 1990).

volunteer management. *See* volunteer leadership; volunteer administration

volunteer nonprofit group: *nonprofit group led and operated primarily by *volunteers striving to accomplish group *goals (cf. Pearce 1993, passim); usually *associations in structural form (*associational form of organization). Stands in contrast to *paid-staff nonprofit groups and *paid-staff nonprofit organizations, The concept of volunteer nonprofit group includes the many and varied *self-help groups, such as the one studied by Karp (1992, passim), which was established for people coping with affective disorders. Nonprofit researchers who study volunteer nonprofits but neglect other types of nonprofit groups are operating according to the *volunteer and membership flat-earth paradigm (Smith 2000:224–225).

volunteer nonprofit group management: *management of a *volunteer nonprofit group, usually a *grassroots association or other *association; volunteer-level alternative to *nonprofit management, which deals with *paid-staff nonprofits. Books on this kind of management are rare, but see Battle (1988), Calmes (1997), Flanagan (1984), Milligan and Milligan (1965), Scheier (1992), Tropman (1997), and Wolfe (1991).

volunteer nonprofit group sector. *See* sector of society

volunteer participation. *See* volunteer action

volunteer/professional tension. *See* professional/volunteer tension

volunteer program: a *program designed for *service volunteers to work within a larger *nonprofit group, *for-profit organization, or governmental *agency, which runs the program (cf. Brudney 1994, passim; Lauffer and Gorodezky 1977, passim). Some volunteer programs serve governmental agencies, while others serve business firms (primarily volunteer services in *for-profit hospitals and other for-profit health institutions [*for-profit group]). Brudney (1990:56–57) considers the question of *effectiveness of volunteers working in volunteer programs in for-profit hospitals and governmental agencies (*see* for-profit organization). Various authors examine school volunteer programs (Brown 1998; Burke and Picus 2001; Carter 1974), church *congregation *volunteer service programs (Cnaan et al. 1999), volunteers in courts and corrections (Cook and Scioli 1975; Morris 1970), museum volunteer programs (Goodlad and McIver 1998), older volunteers in volunteer programs (Fischer and Schaffer 1993), child volunteers in volunteer programs (Ellis et al. 2003), workplace employee volunteer programs (Vineyard 1996), and the future of volunteer programs (Allen 1981; Vineyard 1993).

volunteer program activity: execution of the various tasks that, together, implement a *volunteer program. Allahyari (2000, chaps. 1–2) describes the different involvements of the *volunteers who serve in two California *charities set up to serve the poor.

volunteer, pure: a *volunteer who receives no remuneration at all (unstipended) and no reimbursement for out-of-pocket expenses (*expense reimbursement) (Smith 2000:24). This person, who therefore gains only *psychic benefits for *volunteer work, is the most prevalent type of volunteer in *volunteer nonprofit groups and *volunteer programs.

volunteer recognition. *See* recognition of volunteers/members

volunteer, regular. *See* volunteer, habitual

volunteer reliability. *See* volunteer unreliability

volunteer role: a concept that generalizes any one of the various roles set out in several typologies of volunteer roles, such as those outlined in the *hierarchy of volunteer role engagement or the typology of Fischer et al. (1991). The latter identifies volunteer roles that are formal or informal, regular (see *habitual volunteer) or occasional (*occasional volunteer), and that involve person-to-community *services, person-to-object services, or person-to-person services.

volunteer satisfaction: analogous to job satisfaction, a construct measured by an index of such factors as sense of belonging, feeling needed, meeting others, sense of self-worth, and recognition and appreciation (Stevens 1991). Volunteer satisfaction is typically measured in *volunteer programs, although grassroots associations rarely measure it. *See also* satisfaction; self-fulfillment

volunteer service: 1. *pure volunteering. 2. *pure volunteering and *quasi-volunteer action or *stipended volunteering. Wilson, Adams, and Carlson (1993, passim) examined a volunteer service consisting of youth (volunteers in sense 1) matched with an adult social worker for the purpose of establishing youth-adult friendships. *See also* service

volunteer spirit. *See* voluntary altruism

volunteer-staff relations. *See* building paid staff-volunteer relations

volunteer support organization: professional *association, such as the Association for Volunteer Administration and the American Society of Directors of Volunteers, which is composed of *professionals (sense 2) who help administer and advise *volunteers and *volunteer programs (Barker 2003:458).

volunteer time: time spent *volunteering, typically as recorded for a specified week in a time diary. Formal volunteer time is volunteer time spent acting in and for a *formal nonprofit group or *volunteer program. Informal volunteer time is volunteer time spent as an *informal service volunteer. Smith (2000:53–54) discusses some of the methodological difficulties that emerge when measuring volunteer time. *See also* volunteer; volunteering; time-budget/time diary method

volunteer tourism: the *leisure activity of tourists who, in organized fashion, spend their vacation time *volunteering outside their home community. A volunteer tourist might help with alleviating poverty, restoring the environment, or doing research on an aspect of a foreign society (Wearing 2001:1). McMillion et al. (2003, passim) give an alternative overview of volunteer vacations. A kind of *cross-national volunteering.

volunteer unreliability: a *problem identified by Pearce (1993:111–112) that springs from using *volunteers. It is manifested in, for instance, failure to be punctual, to honor *commitments, or to execute roles (*volunteer role) properly, as well as in absenteeism. *See also* nondependent volunteer; antivolunteerism

volunteer vacation. *See* volunteer tourism

volunteer work: The valuable activity of *volunteers, as they help provide a *public or *member benefit to another person or group outside the volunteer's family or help reach a broader philanthropic or altruistic *goal. It includes *associational volunteering, *board volunteering, *program volunteering, *service volunteering, *informal service volunteering, and possibly other types of *volunteering. Smith (2000:108) observes that the vast majority of *grassroots associations function entirely with help from volunteers. *See also* imputed value of volunteer work

volunteer worker. *See* volunteer

volunteering: act of doing *volunteer work, whether in a formal or an informal context, whether in a *public benefit or a *member benefit group, which is nevertheless done outside one's family. Uncoerced *helping activity not done primarily for financial gain (Van Til 1988:6). Raynolds and Stone (1998, passim) argue that volunteering not only enriches your life but also boosts your work career. *See also* volunteer; development of volunteers; psychic benefit

volunteering as leisure: a volitional conception of *volunteering, which revolves in significant part around a central subjective motivational question: it must be determined whether *volunteers feel they are engaging in enjoyable (*casual leisure) or fulfilling (*serious leisure) activity that they have had the option to accept or reject on their own terms. A key element in the leisure conception of volunteering is the felt absence of moral coercion to do the volunteer activity, an element that, in *marginal volunteering, may be experienced in degrees, as more or less coercive (Stebbins 2001:1). *See also* noncoercion; motivation

volunteering as unpaid work: an economic conception of *volunteering—which dominates in *nonprofit sector research—that defines it as absence of payment as livelihood, whether in money or in kind. This definition largely avoids the messy question of *motivation so crucial to the leisure conception (*volunteering as leisure) (Stebbins 2001:1).

volunteering history: a personal record of *volunteering or other forms of unpaid productive activity done over the life course (Morgan 1986; Caro and Bass 1985). *See also* career volunteering

volunteerism: that part of the *nonprofit sector (also known as *voluntarism) centered specifically on *volunteering. Major components include *informal volunteering, *board volunteering, *traditional service volunteering, and *associational volunteering. Van Til (1988:9) observes that this concept has a normative side, in that it often presumes the goodness of volunteering and *volunteers in society. Cull and Hardy (1974, passim) present an overview of *volunteer programs and *volunteer administration as well as research and communication needs in *voluntary action. Other books exploring volunteerism include Ellis and Noyes (1990), Ford and Ford (1996), Forward (1994), Harman (1982), Jedlicka (1990), Kouri (1990), Ladd (1999), Marcovitz and Crest (2004), Poplau (2004), Self and Wyman (1992), Steele (2000), and Vineyard (1993).

Volunteerism Commission (World Leisure): World Leisure (formerly World Leisure and Recreation Association) founded in 1997 and formally approved in 2000 its Volunteerism Commission (VOLCOMM). It is animated by two main objectives: (a) to organize and encourage research in all countries on all aspects of *volunteering related to *leisure, and (b) to the extent deemed useful there, to disseminate worldwide to the *nonprofit sector's many applied fields relevant theory and research in this area. The applied fields are made up of individual *volunteers, their "employers" (those who engage them), and various *nonprofit groups (Stebbins 2004a:2–4).

W

watchdog: in the *nonprofit sector, a person or group (*formal or *informal, *nonprofit or *for-profit) appointed or organized to safeguard the rights, activities, *programs, and the like of a *target group (*see* target of benefits). Watchdogs serve as monitors of possible abuse of the target by governmental, business, or other powerful *interests. Cable and Degutis (1997, passim) traced the history of a local *social movement against a proposed landfill that, though it failed to win its *cause, became a watchdog *organization committed to monitoring governmental landfill policies. *See also* ombudsperson

welfare: 1. the personal condition of physical health, emotional comfort, economic security, and meeting of other *public needs. 2. the *programs in a society designed to help its members achieve this condition (Barker 2003:462), usually referred to as "public welfare" (*public interest). 3. in popular usage "welfare" sometimes refers to public assistance given to the poor, as in Gabe and Falk's (1995) discussion of incentives and disincentives in the welfare system.

welfare state: a nation or the different wings of its national government that assume responsibility for the *welfare of citizens, including their health and educational *needs. Van Til (1988:160–166) compares development of the welfare state in Britain with that of the United States, where it is less extensive.

work: 1. performance of useful activity, broadly conceived of (Applebaum

1992, passim). 2. performance of useful activity that some people in the society are paid to do (narrow economic version of term). Schor (1993, passim) argues that there has been, in recent decades, an increase in the paid-work time of Americans. In neither usage is work confined solely to *occupational activity but rather includes *volunteer work, housework, childcare, *informal care, and other *obligations. Rifkin (1995, passim) argues, contrary to Schor (1993), that technology is resulting in a net global decline of work, jobs, and the labor force that will either lead to "the demise of our civilization" or a "great social transformation and a rebirth of the human spirit" (back cover of book). The rebirth referred to involves, among other things, expanding the role of the *nonprofit sector and empowering *nonprofit groups and *volunteers in new ways to take up the slack left by the decline of paid work (Rifkin 1995, chap. 17).

work activity. *See* work

work group: *group in which most or all of the work is done by paid employees (Smith 2000:168). If the group is a *formal group, it is considered a *work organization. Informal work groups (*informal group) also exist, as exemplified in the traditional family farm and the family-run convenience store.

work organization: a *formal group in which most or all of the work is done by paid employees (Smith 2000:168). Work *organizations include businesses, governmental *agencies, and *paid-staff *nonprofit groups.

workplace metaphor: a metaphor in which *volunteering is seen as a form of *work: *volunteers are unpaid employees in *associations, *nonprofit agencies, *volunteer programs, and other *nonprofit groups (Ilsley 1990: 112).

world religion: 1. one of the roughly ten major world religions extant today (cf. Parrinder 1983, passim). 2. one of the many religions ever extant in human society (cf. Bowker 1997, passim; Losch 2001, passim).

Y

youth gang. *See* gang

youth group: a *group, usually an *association, comprised mainly of youth, often with the *goal of youth development. Goreham (2004, passim) conducted research on four hundred rural church youth groups (*see* rural youth group) from eight denominations in the Northern Plains states. He found, among other things, that, on average and compared with Catholic and mainline Protestant groups, evangelical Protestant youth groups met more frequently, had higher *participation rates, and had greater turnover among youth workers.

Z

---

zero-based budgeting in nonprofits: financial procedure whereby, every fiscal year, an *organization is forced to examine and justify each item in its *budget. The object, says Connell (2001:89–90), is to continue only those *programs that meet the group's *planning goals and are financially feasible.

Bibliography

Abbott, Andrew. 1988. *The System of Professions: An Essay in the Division of Expert Labor.* Chicago: University of Chicago Press.

Abraham, Henry J., and Barbara A. Perry. 1998. *Freedom and the Court: Civil Rights and Liberties in the United States.* New York: Oxford University Press.

Abramson, Alan J., and Rachel McCarthy. 2002. "Infrastructure Organization." Pp. 331–354 in *The State of Nonprofit America,* ed. Lester M. Salamon. Washington, D.C.: Brookings Institution Press.

Acheson, Nicholas, and Arthur Williamson, eds. 1995. *Voluntary Action and Social Policy in Northern Ireland.* Aldershot, UK: Avebury.

Adam, Barry D. 1995. *The Rise of a Gay and Lesbian Movement.* Rev. ed. New York: Twayne.

Adler, Margot. 1986. *Drawing Down the Moon.* Rev. ed. Boston: Beacon.

Adler, Peter. 1981. *Momentum, a Theory of Social Action.* Beverly Hills, Calif.: Sage.

Ahlbrandt, Roger S. 1994. *Neighborhoods, People, and Community.* New York: Plenum Press.

Aldrich, John H. 1995. *Why Parties? The Origin and Transformation of Political Parties in America.* Chicago: University of Chicago Press.

Aldridge, Alan. 2000. *Religion in the Contemporary World.* Cambridge, UK: Blackwell.

Alexander, Yonah, Michael S. Swetnam, and Herbert M. Levine. 2001. *ETA: Profile of a Terrorist Group.* Ardsley, N.Y.: Transnational Publishers.

Aliabadi, Youssef S. 2000. "The Idea of Civil Liberties and the Problem of Institutional Government in Iran." *Social Research* 67(2):345–376.

Alinsky, Saul D. 1969. *Reveille for Radicals.* New York: Random House.

Allahyari, Rebecca A. 2000. *Visions of Charity: Volunteer Workers and Moral Community.* Berkeley, Calif.: University of California Press.

Allen, Katherine, and Victoria Chin-Sang. 1990. "A Lifetime of Work: The Context and Meanings of Leisure for Aging Black Women." *Gerontologist* 30(6):734–740.

Allen, Kerry K. 1981. *Will Volunteering Survive?* Washington, D.C.: Volunteer.

Bibliography

Allen, Sylvia. 2001. "Benefit Event Fundamentals." Pp. 480–499 in *The Nonprofit Handbook: Fund Raising*, 3rd ed., ed. James M. Greenfield. New York: Wiley.

Allison, Michael, and Jude Kaye. 1997. *Strategic Planning for Nonprofit Organizations: A Practical Guide and Workbook*. New York: Wiley.

Altman, Linda J. 1994. *The Pullman Strike of 1894: Turning Point for American Labor*. Brookfield, Conn.: Millbrook Press.

Alvarez, Sonia E., Evelina Dagnino, and Arturo Escobar, eds. 1998. *Cultures of Politics, Politics of Culture: Re-Visioning Latin American Social Movements*. Boulder, Colo.: Westview Press.

American Society of Association Executives. 1988. *Principles of Association Management*. Washington, D.C.: American Society of Association Executives.

———. 1994. *Fund Raising for Associations and Association Foundations*. Washington, D.C.: American Society of Association Executives.

———. 2001. *Policies and Procedures in Association Management*. Washington, D.C.: American Society of Association Executives.

———. 2002. *Generating & Managing Nondues Revenues in Associations*. Washington, D.C.: American Society of Association Executives.

Anderson, Robert T. 1973. "Voluntary Associations in History: From Paleolithic to Present Times." Pp. 9–28 in *Voluntary Action Research 1973*, ed. David H. Smith. Lexington, Mass.: Lexington Books.

Anderson, Ronald, and Jack Engledow. 1977. "A Factor Analytic Comparison of U.S. and German Information Seekers." *Journal of Consumer Research* 3:185–196.

Andreason, Alan R. 1995. *Marketing Social Change*. San Francisco: Jossey-Bass.

Andrews, Gregg. 1991. *Shoulder to Shoulder? The American Federation of Labor, the United States, and the Mexican Revolution 1910–1924*. Berkeley, Calif.: University of California Press.

Angell, Robert Cooley. 1941. *The Integration of American Society: A Study of Groups and Institutions*. New York: Russell and Russell.

Anheier, Helmut K. 1987. "Indigenous Voluntary Associations, Nonprofits, and Development in Africa." Pp. 416–433 in *The Nonprofit Sector*, ed. Walter W. Powell. New Haven, Conn.: Yale University Press.

Anheier, Helmut K., and Kusuma Cunningham. 1994. "Internationalization of the Nonprofit Sector." Pp. 100–116 in *The Jossey-Bass Handbook of Nonprofit Leadership and Management*, ed. Robert D. Herman and Associates. San Francisco: Jossey-Bass.

Anheier, Helmut, and Lester M. Salamon. 1998. *The Nonprofit Sector in the Developing World: A Comparative Analysis*. New York: Manchester University Press.

Anheier, Helmut, and Wolfgang Seibel. 2001. *The Nonprofit Sector in Germany*. New York: Palgrave.

Anheier, Helmut, and Stefan Toepler. 1999. *Private Funds, Public Purpose: Philanthropic Foundations in International Perspective*. New York: Kluwer Academic/Plenum Publishers.

Anonymous. 2000. *Communities Directory: A Guide to Intentional Communities and Cooperative Living*. Rutledge, Mo.: Fellowship for Intentional Community.

Anthony, Robert N., and David W. Young. 1984. *Management Control in Nonprofit Organizations*. Homewood, Ill.: R. D. Irwin.

———. 1994. "Accounting and Financial Management." Pp. 403–443 in *The Jossey-Bass Handbook of Nonprofit Leadership and Management*, ed. Robert D. Herman and Associates. San Francisco: Jossey-Bass.

———. 2004. "Financial Accounting and Financial Management." Pp. 466–512 in *The Jossey-Bass Handbook of Nonprofit Leadership and Management*, 2nd ed, ed. Robert D. Herman and Associates. San Francisco: Jossey-Bass.

Appel, Willa. 1983. *Cults in America.* New York: Holt.

Applebaum, Herbert. 1992. *The Concept of Work: Ancient, Medieval, and Modern.* Albany: State University of New York Press.

Aptheker, Herbert. 1989. *Abolitionism: A Revolutionary Movement.* Boston: Twayne.

Archambault, Edith. 1997. *The Nonprofit Sector in France.* New York: Manchester University Press.

Armstrong, Charles K., ed. 2002. *Korean Society: Civil Society, Democracy and the State.* London: Routledge.

Armstrong, James S. 2001. *Planning Special Events.* San Francisco: Jossey-Bass.

Armstrong, Karen. 2002. *Islam: A Short History.* New York: Modern Library.

Arsenault, Jane. 1998. *Forging Nonprofit Alliances.* San Francisco: Jossey-Bass.

Aryee, Samuel, and Yaw A. Debrah. 1997. "Members' Participation in the Union: An Investigation of Some Determinants in Singapore." *Human Relations* 50: 129–147.

Asbury, H. 1927. *The Gangs of New York.* Garden City, N.J.: Garden City Publishing Co.

Ascoli, Ugo, and Costanzo Ranci. 2002. *Dilemmas of the Welfare Mix: The New Structure of Welfare in an Era of Privatization.* New York: Kluwer Academic.

Aspen Institute. 2002. *Government: The Nonprofit Sector and Government; Clarifying the Relationship.* Washington, D.C.: Nonprofit Sector Strategy Group.

Atingdui, Lawrence. 1995. *Defining the Nonprofit Sector: Ghana.* Baltimore: Johns Hopkins Institute for Policy Studies.

Austin, D. Mark. 1991. "Community Context and Complexity of Organizational Structure in Neighborhood Associations." *Administration and Society* 22:516–531.

Avner, Marcia. 2002. *The Lobbying and Advocacy Handbook for Nonprofit Organizations.* St. Paul, Minn.: Amherst H. Wilder Foundation.

Axelrod, Nancy R. 1994. "Board Leadership and Board Development." Pp. 119–136 in *The Jossey-Bass Handbook of Nonprofit Leadership and Management,* ed. Robert D. Herman and Associates. San Francisco: Jossey-Bass.

Ayman, Roya. 2000. "Leadership." Pp. 1563–1574 in *Encyclopedia of Sociology,* 2nd ed., vol. 3, ed. Edgar F. Borgatta and Rhonda J. V. Montgomery. New York: Macmillan Reference USA.

Back, Kurt W. 1981. "Small Groups." Pp. 320–343 in *Social Psychology,* ed. Morris Rosenberg and Ralph H. Turner. New York: Basic Books.

———. 1988. "Encounter Groups Revisited." *Society* 26 (Nov./Dec.):50–53.

Baghramian, Maria, and Attracta Ingram. 2000. *Pluralism: The Philosophy and Politics of Diversity.* London: Routledge.

Bailey, Darlyne, and Kelly M. Koney. 2000. *Strategic Alliances among Health and Human Service Organizations.* Thousand Oaks, Calif.: Sage.

Bainbridge, William S. 1997. *The Sociology of Religious Movements.* London: Routledge.

Bakan, David. 1968. *Disease, Pain & Sacrifice: Toward a Psychology of Suffering.* Chicago: University of Chicago Press.

Baker, Colin, Alan Johnson, and Michael Lavalette. 2001. "Introduction." Pp. 1–18 in *Leadership and Social Movements,* ed. Colin Baker, Alan Johnson, and Michael Lavalette. Manchester, UK: Manchester University Press.

Balmer, Randall H., and Lauren F. Winner. 2002. *Protestantism in America.* New York: Columbia University Press.

Balsamo, William, and George Carpozi, Jr. 1999. *Crime Incorporated or Under the Clock: The Inside Story of the Mafia's First Hundred Years.* Far Hills, N.J.: New Horizon Press.

Banaszak-Holl, Jane, Susan Allen, Vincent Mor, and Thomas Schott. 1998. "Organizational Characteristics Associated with Agency Position in Community Care Networks." *Journal of Health and Social Behavior* 39:368–385.

Banks, James A., and Cherry A. McGee. 1995. *Handbook of Research on Multicultural Education.* New York: Prentice Hall International.

Banks, Robert J. 1980. *Paul's Idea of Community: The Early House Churches in Their Historical Setting.* Grand Rapids, Mich.: Eerdmans.

Banting, Keith G., ed. 1999. *The Nonprofit Sector in Canada: Roles and Relationships.* Montreal: McGill-Queens University Press.

Banting, Keith G., and Kathy Brock, ed. 2002. *The Nonprofit Sector and Government in a New Century.* Montreal: McGill-Queens University Press.

Barabási, Albert-Laszlo. 2002. *Linked: The New Science of Networks.* Cambridge, Mass.: Perseus.

Barbash, Jack. 1974. *Labor's Grass Roots: A Study of the Local Union.* Westport, Conn.: Greenwood Press.

Barber, Benjamin R. 1984. *Strong Democracy: Participatory Politics for a New Age.* Berkeley: University of California Press.

Barbetta, Gian P., ed. 1997. *The Nonprofit Sector in Italy.* New York: Manchester University Press.

Barbuto, Domenica M. 1999. *American Settlement Houses and Progressive Social Reform: An Encyclopedia of the American Settlement Movement.* Phoenix: Oryx Press.

Barker, Robert L. 2003. *The Social Work Dictionary,* 5th ed. Washington, D.C.: National Association of Social Workers Press.

Barnes, Andrew. 1991. "Poor Relief and Brotherhood." *Journal of Social History* 24(3):603–611.

Barrett, David V. 1999. *Secret Societies: From the Ancient and Arcane to the Modern and Clandestine.* London: Blandford.

Bar-Tal, Daniel. 1976. *Prosocial Behavior.* New York: Wiley.

Barth, Alan, and James E. Clayton. 1983. *The Rights of Free Men: An Essential Guide to Civil Liberties.* New York: Knopf.

Bartholdi, John L., III, Loren K. Platzman, R. Lee Collins, and William H. Warden III. 1983. "A Minimal Technology Routing System for Meals on Wheels." *Interfaces* 13(3):1–8.

Basu, Amrita, and C. E. McGrory. 1995. *The Challenge of Local Feminisms: Women's Movements in Global Perspective.* Boulder, Colo.: Westview Press.

Batson, C. D. 1991. *The Altruism Question.* Hillsdale, N.J.: Erlbaum.

Battin, M. Pabst. 1990. *Ethics in the Sanctuary: Examining the Practices of Organized Religion.* New Haven, Conn.: Yale University Press.

Battle, Richard V. 1988. *The Volunteer Handbook: How to Organize and Manage a Successful Organization.* Austin, Tex.: Armstrong Printing.

Beaford, Robert D., Timothy B. Gongaware, and Danny L. Valadez. 2000. "Social Movements." Pp. 2717–2727 in *Encyclopedia of Sociology,* 2nd ed., vol. 4, ed. Edgar F. Borgatta and Rhonda J. V. Montgomery. New York: Macmillan Reference USA.

Beattie, Melody. 1990. *Codependents' Guide to the Twelve Steps.* New York: Simon & Schuster.

Beck, Ulrich. 2000. *The Brave New World of Work,* trans. Patrick Camiller. New York: Polity Press.

Becker, Howard S. 1963. *Outsiders: Studies of Sociology of Deviance.* Glencoe, Ill.: Free Press.

Becker, Lawrence C. 1986. *Reciprocity.* London: Routledge and Kegan Paul.

Becker, Lawrence C., and Charlotte B. Becker., eds. 1992. *The Encyclopedia of Ethics.* New York: Garland.

Bee, Malcolm. 2003. "Within the Shelter of the Old Elm Tree: Oddfellowship and Community in North Oxfordshire." *Family and Community History* 6(2):85–96.

Beierle, Thomas C., and Jerry Cayford. 2002. *Democracy in Practice: Public Participation in Environmental Decisions.* Washington, D.C.: Resources for the Future.

Beito, David T. 2000. *In Mutual Aid to Welfare State: Fraternal Societies and Social Services, 1890–1967.* Chappel Hill: University of North Carolina Press.

Bell, J. Bowyer. 1975. *Transnational Terror.* Washington, D.C.: American Enterprise Institute for Public Policy Research.

Bellah, Robert N. 1975. *The Broken Covenant: American Civil Religion in a Time of Trial.* New York: Seabury Press.

Bellah, Robert N., Richard Madsen, William M. Sullivan, Ann Swidler, and Steven M. Tipton. 1985. *Habits of the Heart: Individualism and Commitment in American Life.* New York: Perennial Library.

Bellamy, J. 1973. *Crime and Public Order in England in the Later Middle Ages.* London: Routledge and Kegan Paul.

Ben-Ner, Avner. 1987. "Producer Co-operatives: Why Do They Exist in Capitalist Economies?" Pp. 434–449 in *The Nonprofit Sector,* ed. Walter W. Powell. New Haven, Conn.: Yale University Press.

Ben-Ner, Avner, and Benedetto Gui. 1993. *The Nonprofit Sector in a Mixed Economy.* Ann Arbor: University of Michigan Press.

Bennett, James T., and Thomas J. DiLorenzo. 1989. *Unfair Competition: The Profits of Nonprofits.* New York: Hamilton.

———. 1994. *Unhealthy Charities: Hazardous to Your Health and Wealth.* New York: Basic Books.

Berger, Peter L., and Richard J. Neuhaus. 1977. *To Empower People: The Role of Mediating Structures in Public Policy.* Washington, D.C.: American Enterprise Institute for Public Policy Research.

Bergsträsser, Arnold. 1950. *Goethe and the Modern Age: The International Convocation at Aspen, Colorado 1949.* Chicago: Regnery.

Bernikow, Louise. 1986. *Alone in America: The Search for Companionship.* New York: Harper & Row.

Bernstein, Susan R. 1991. *Managing Contracted Services in the Nonprofit Agency.* Philadelphia: Temple University Press.

Berry, Jeffrey M. 1977. *Lobbying for the People: The Political Behavior of Public Interest Groups.* Princeton, N.J.: Princeton University Press.

———. 1997. *The Interest Group Society.* 3rd ed. New York: Addison-Wesley Longman.

Berry, Jeffrey M., and David F. Arons. 2003. *A Voice for Nonprofits.* Washington, D.C.: Brookings Institution Press.

Berry, Jeffrey M., Kent E. Portney, and Ken Thomson. 1993. *The Rebirth of Urban Democracy.* Washington, D.C.: Brookings Institution Press.

Besnard, Pierre. 1980. *Animateur Socioculturel: Une Profession Différente?* Paris: Éditions ESF.

Best, Joel, and David F. Luckenbill. 1982. *Organizing Deviance.* Englewood Cliffs, N.J.: Prentice Hall.

Bestor, Theodore C. 1985. "Tradition and Japanese Social Organization: Institutional Development in a Tokyo Neighborhood." *Ethnology* 24:121–135.

Bethel, Sheila M. 1993. *Beyond Management to Leadership: Designing the 21st Century Association.* Washington, D.C.: American Society of Association Executives Foundation.

Bianchi, Robert. 1989. *Unruly Corporatism: Associational Life in Twentieth-Century Egypt.* New York: Oxford University Press.

Bibby, John F., and Thomas M. Holbrook. 1996. "Parties and Elections." Pp. 78–
121 in *Politics in the American States,* 6th ed., ed. Virginia Gray and Herbert
Jacob. Washington, D.C.: CQ Press.

Biggart, Nicole W. 1998. "The Creative-Destructive Process of Organizational
Change: The Case of the Post Office." Pp. 240–260 in *Qualitative Studies of
Organizations,* ed. John Van Maanen. Thousand Oaks, Calif.: Sage.

Billis, David. 1993. *Organising Public and Voluntary Agencies.* London: Routledge
and Kegan Paul.

Blair, Karen J. 1994. *The Torchbearers: Women and Their Amateur Arts Associations
in America, 1890–1930.* Bloomington: Indiana University Press.

Blanchard, Dallas A. 1994. *The Anti-Abortion Movement and the Rise of the Religious Right.* New York: Twayne.

Blank, Carla. 2003. *Rediscovering America: The Making of Multicultural America,
1900–2000.* New York: Three Rivers Press.

Blanken, Rhea L., and Allen Liff. 1999. *Facing the Future: A Report on the Major
Trends and Issues Affecting Associations.* Washington, D.C.: American Society
of Association Executives.

Blasi, Joseph. 1986. *The Communal Experience of the Kibbutz.* New Brunswick, N.J.:
Transaction Publishers.

Blau, Judith. 2000. "Relational Wealth in the Commons: Local Spaces of Work and
Residence in a Global Economy." Chapter 12 in *Relational Wealth: The Ad-
vantages of Stability in a Changing Economy,* ed. Carrie R. Leana and Denise
M. Rousseau. New York: Oxford University Press.

Blau, Judith R., Kenneth C. Land, and Kent Redding. 1992. "The Extension of Religious Affiliation: An Explanation of the Growth of Church Participation in
the United States." *Social Science Research* 21(4):329–352.

Blau, Peter M. 1977. *Inequality and Heterogeneity.* New York: Free Press.

Blau, Peter M., and Marshall W. Meyer. 1987. *Bureaucracy in Modern Society.* 3rd
ed. New York: Random House.

Blau, Peter M., and W. Richard Scott. 1962. *Formal Organizations.* San Francisco:
Chandler Publishing Co.

Blazek, Jody. 1996. *Financial Planning for Nonprofit Organizations.* New York: Wiley.

Block, Stephen R. 2001. "A History of the Discipline." Pp. 97–111 in *The Nature of
the Nonprofit Sector,* ed. J. Steven Ott. Boulder, Colo.: Westview Press.

———. 2004. *Why Nonprofits Fail.* San Francisco: Jossey-Bass.

Blokland, Talja. 2001. "Bricks, Mortar, Memories: Neighbourhood and Networks in
Collective Acts of Remembering." *International Journal of Urban and Regional Development* 25:268–283.

Blondel, Jean. 1982. *The Organization of Government: A Comparative Analysis of
Governmental Structures.* Beverly Hills, Calif.: Sage.

Bloom, Benjamin S., Thomas J. Hastings, and George F. Madaus. 1971. *Handbook
of Formative and Summative Evaluation of Student Learning.* New York: Mc-
Graw-Hill.

Blumberg, Rhoda L. 1991. *Civil Rights: The 1960s Freedom Struggle.* Rev. ed. New
York: Twayne.

Bode, Carl. 1956. *The American Lyceum: Town Meeting of the Mind.* New York: Oxford University Press.

Bochel, Hugh M. 2005. *Social Policy: Issues and Developments.* New York: Pearson/
Prentice Hall.

Bocialetti, Gene, and Robert E. Kaplan. 1986. "Self-Study for Human Services
Agencies: Managing a Three-Sided Relationship." *Evaluation and Program
Planning* 9(1):1–11.

Bonk, Kathy, Henry Griggs, and Emily Tynes. 1999. *The Jossey-Bass Guide to Strategic Communications for Nonprofits.* San Francisco: Jossey-Bass.

Bordt, Rebecca L. 1997. *The Structure of Women's Nonprofit Organizations.* Bloomington: Indiana University Press.

Boris, Elizabeth T., and Jeff Krehely. 2002. "Civic Participation and Advocacy." Pp. 299–330 in *The State of Nonprofit America,* ed. Lester M. Salamon. Washington, D.C.: Brookings Institution Press.

Boris, Elizabeth T., and C. Eugene Steuerle., eds. 1999. *Nonprofits and Government: Collaboration and Conflict.* Washington, D.C.: Urban Institute Press.

Bork, Robert H., and Waldemar Nielsen. 1993. *Donor Intent.* Indianapolis: Philanthropy Roundtable.

Borkman, Thomasina J. 1976. "Experiential Knowledge: A New Concept for the Analysis of Self-Help Groups." *Social Services Review* 50:445–456.

———. 1999. *Understanding Self-Help/Mutual Aid.* New Brunswick, N.J.: Rutgers University Press.

Borman, Leonard D. 1982. *Helping People to Help Themselves: Self-Help and Prevention.* New York: Haworth Press.

Bott, Elizabeth. 1957. *Family and Social Network.* New York: Free Press.

Boulding, Kenneth. 1953. *The Organizational Revolution.* New York: Harper.

———. 1973. *Economy of Love and Fear: A Preface to Grants Economics.* Belmont, Calif.: Wadsworth.

Bourdieu, Pierre. 1977. *Outline of a Theory of Practice.* Cambridge, UK: Cambridge University Press.

Bouvard, Marguerite. 1975. *The Intentional Community Movement.* New York: National University Publications Kennikat Press.

Bowen, Don L. 1973. *Public Service Professional Associations and the Public Interest.* Philadelphia: American Academy of Political and Social Science.

Bowen, William G., Thomas I. Nygren, Sarah E. Turner, and Elizabeth A. Duffy. 1994. *The Charitable Nonprofits.* San Francisco: Jossey-Bass.

Bowker, John W. 1997. *The Oxford Dictionary of World Religions.* New York: Oxford University Press.

Boyle, David. 1997. "Time as Currency: A New Approach to Building Communities." *Voluntary Action* 1:25–38.

Boyte, Harry C. 1980. *The Backyard Revolution: Understanding the New Citizen Movement.* Philadelphia: Temple University Press.

Brackney, William H. 1997. *Christian Voluntarism.* Grand Rapids, Mich.: Eerdmans.

Bradner, Jeanne H. 1993. *Passionate Volunteerism.* Winnetka, Ill.: Conversation Press.

———. 1999. *Leading Volunteers for Results.* Winnetka, Ill.: Conversation Press.

Bradshaw, Yvonne, Ian Kendall, Martin Blackmore, Norman Johnson, and Sandra Jenkinson. 1998. "Complaining Our Way to Quality: Complaints, Contracts, and the Voluntary Sector." *Social Policy and Administration* 32:209–225.

Brainard, Lori A., and Jennifer M. Brinkerhoff. 2004. "Lost in Cyberspace: Shedding Light on the Dark Matter of Grassroots Organizations." *Nonprofit and Voluntary Sector Quarterly* 33(3):32S–53S.

Brakeley, George A., Jr. 2001. "Major Gifts from Individuals." Pp. 733–754 in *The Nonprofit Handbook: Fund Raising,* 3rd ed., ed. James M. Greenfield. New York: Wiley.

Brasnett, Margaret. 1969. *Voluntary Social Action.* London: National Council of Social Service.

Braunstein, Peter, and Michael W. Doyle. 2002. *Imagine Nation: The American Counterculture of the 1960s and 70s.* New York: Routledge.

Breault, Marc, and M. King. 1993. *Inside the Cult.* New York: Penguin.

Bremner, Robert H. 1960. *American Philanthropy.* Chicago: University of Chicago Press.

———. 1988. *American Philanthropy.* 2nd ed. Chicago: University of Chicago Press.

———. 1996. *Giving: Charity and Philanthropy in History.* New Brunswick, N.J.: Transaction Publishers.

Bresler, Robert J. 2004. *Freedom of Association: Rights and Liberties under the Law.* Santa Barbara, Calif.: ABC-CLIO.

Bright, Jennifer. 2001. "Commitment of Board Members to Nonprofit Organizations." *Dissertation Abstracts International, A: The Humanities and Social Sciences* 62(5):1957A.

Brightbill, Charles. 1960. *The Challenge of Leisure.* Englewood Cliffs, N.J.: Prentice Hall.

Brilliant, Eleanor. 1990. *The United Way.* New York: Columbia University Press.

Britton, N. 1991. "Permanent Disaster Volunteers: Where Do They Fit?" *Nonprofit and Voluntary Sector Quarterly* 20:395–414.

Brock, Kathy, ed. 2003. *Delicate Dances: Public Policy and the Nonprofit Sector.* Montreal: McGill-Queen's University Press.

Brody, Evelyn. 1996. "Agents without Principals: The Economic Convergence of the Nonprofit and For-Profit Organizational Forms." *New York Law School Law Review* 40:457–536.

Bromley, David G. 1988. *Falling from Faith: Causes and Consequences of Religious Apostasy.* Newbury Park, Calif.: Sage.

Bromley, David G., and Jeffrey K. Hadden, eds. 1992. *Handbook of Cults and Sects in America.* Greenwich, Conn.: JAI Press.

Bromwich, David. 2004. "The Disappearing Underground." *Dissent* 51 (winter):40–42.

Brown, Daniel J. 1998. *Schools with Heart: Voluntarism and Public Education.* Boulder, Colo.: Westview Press.

Brown, Eleanor, and Janice H. Zahrly. 1990. *Commitment and Tenure of Highly Skilled Volunteers: Management Issues in a Nonprofit Agency.* San Francisco: Institute for Nonprofit Organizations, University of San Francisco.

Brown, Harold O. J. 1998. *Heresies: Heresy and Orthodoxy in the History of the Church.* Peabody, Mass.: Hendrickson.

Brown, Michele C., and H. Peter Karoff, eds. 2004. *Just Money: A Critique of Contemporary American Philanthropy.* Boston: TPI Editions.

Brown, R. Khari, and Ronald E. Brown. 2003. "Faith and Works: Church-Based Social Capital." *Social Forces* 82:617–641.

Brown, Ruth M. 2002. *For a "Christian America": A History of the Religious Right.* Amherst, N.Y.: Prometheus Books.

Brown, William H. 1944. *The Rochdale Pioneers: A Century of Cooperation.* Manchester, UK: Co-operative Union Ltd.

Brudney, Jeffrey L. 1990. *Fostering Volunteer Programs in the Public Sector.* San Francisco: Jossey-Bass.

———. 1994. "Designing and Managing Volunteer Programs." Pp. 279–302 in *The Jossey-Bass Handbook of Nonprofit Leadership and Management,* ed. Robert D. Herman and Associates. San Francisco: Jossey-Bass.

Brudney, Jeffrey L., and J. Edward Kellough. 2000. "Volunteers in State Government: Involvement, Management, and Benefits." *Nonprofit and Voluntary Sector Quarterly* 29(1):111–130.

Brunton, Bruce C. 1988. "Institutional Origins of the Military-Industrial Complex." *Journal of Economic Issues* 22:599–607.

Bruyn, Severyn T. 1977. *The Social Economy: People Transforming American Business.* New York: Wiley.

Bryan, Hobson. 1977. "Leisure Values Systems and Recreational Specialization: The Case of Trout Fishermen." *Journal of Leisure Research* 9:174–187.

Bryce, Herrington J. 2000. *Financial & Strategic Management for Nonprofit Organizations.* San Francisco: Jossey-Bass.

Bryman, Alan. 1986. *Leadership and Organizations.* Boston: Routledge.

Bryson, John M. 1994. "Strategic Planning and Action Planning for Nonprofit Organizations." Pp. 154–183 in *The Jossey-Bass Handbook of Nonprofit Leadership and Management,* ed. Robert D. Herman and Associates. San Francisco: Jossey-Bass.

———. 1995. *Strategic Planning for Public and Nonprofit Organizations.* Rev. ed. San Francisco: Jossey-Bass.

Bryson, John M., and Barbara C. Crosby. 1992. *Leadership for the Common Good.* San Francisco: Jossey-Bass.

Buchanan, David, and Richard Bedham. 1999. "Politics and Organizational Change: The Lived Experience." *Human Relations* 52:609–629.

Buchbinder, H., Gerry Hunnius, and E. Stevens. 1974. *Citizen Participation: A Research Framework and Annotated Bibliography.* Ottawa: Ministry of State, Urban Affairs Canada.

Budziszewksi, J. 1992. *True Tolerance: Liberalism and the Necessity of Judgment.* New Brunswick, N.J.: Transaction Publishers.

Bullard, Sara. 1993. *Free at Last: A History of the Civil Rights Movement and Those Who Died in the Struggle.* New York: Oxford University Press.

Burke, Mary A., and Lawrence O. Picus. 2001. *Developing Community-Empowered Schools.* Thousand Oaks, Calif.: Corwin Press.

Burkhart, Patrick J., and Suzanne Reussi. 1993. *Successful Strategic Planning: A Guide for Nonprofit Agencies and Organizations.* Newbury Park, Calif.: Sage.

Burlingame, Dwight F., ed. 2004. *Philanthropy in America: A Comprehensive Historical Encyclopedia.* Santa Barbara, Calif.: ABC-CLIO.

Burlingame, Dwight F., William F. Diaz, Warren F. Ilchman, and Associates. 1996. *Capacity for Change: The Nonprofit World in the Age of Devolution.* Indianapolis: Indiana University Center on Philanthropy.

Burlingame, Dwight F., and Lamont J. Hulse, eds. 1991. *Taking Fund Raising Seriously: Advancing the Profession and Practice of Raising Money.* San Francisco: Jossey-Bass.

Burns, James M. 1978. *Leadership.* New York: Harper & Row.

Burwell, Yolanda. 1995. "Lawrence Oxley and Locality Development: Black Self-Help in North Carolina 1925–1928." *Journal of Community Practice* 2:49–69.

Butler, John R. 2003. "Transgender DeKalb: Observations of an Advocacy Campaign." *Journal of Homosexuality* 45:277–296.

Bútora, Martin, and Zuzana Fialová. 1995. *Nonprofit Sector and Volunteering in Slovakia.* Bratislava, Slovakia: Slovak Academic Information Agency.

Byron, Reginald, ed. 2003. *Retrenchment and Regeneration in Rural Newfoundland.* Toronto: University of Toronto Press.

Cable, Sherry, and Beth Degutis. 1997. "Movement Outcomes and Dimensions of Social Change: The Multiple Effects of Local Mobilizations." *Current Sociology/Sociologie Contemporaine* 45:121–135.

Cage, John. 2001. *Anarchy.* Middletown, Conn.: Wesleyan University Press.

Cahn, Moise. 1960. Preface (p. vii) in *The Citizen Volunteer: His Responsibility, Role, and Opportunity in Modern Society,* ed. Nathan E. Cohen. New York: Harper & Brothers.

Caille, Alain. 2001. "The Double Inconceivability of the Pure Gift." *Angelaki* 6(2):23–39.

Calmes, Anne M. 1997. *Community Association Leadership: A Guide for Volunteers.* Alexandria, Va.: Community Associations Institute.

Campbell, Katherine N., and Susan J. Ellis. 1995. *The (Help!) I-Don't-Have-Enough-Time Guide to Volunteer Management.* Philadelphia: Energize.

Cannold, Leslie. 2002. "Understanding and Responding to Anti-Choice Women-Centered Strategies." *Productive Health Matters* 10 (19 May):171–179.

Capozzola, Christopher. 1999. "Thorstein Veblen and the Politics of War 1914–1920." *International Journal of Politics, Culture, and Society* 13(2):255–271.

Carlson, Mim. 2003. *The Executive Director's Survival Guide: Thriving as a Nonprofit Leader.* San Francisco: Jossey-Bass.

Caro, Francis G., Scott A. Bass, and Yung-Ping Chen. 1993. "Introduction: Achieving a Productive Aging Society." Pp. 3–25 in *Achieving a Productive Aging Society,* ed. Scott A. Bass, Francis G. Caro, and Yung-Ping Chen. Westport, Conn.: Auburn House.

Carr, David K., and Ian D. Littman. 1990. *Excellence in Government: Total Quality Management in the 1990s.* Arlington, Va.: Coopers & Lybrand.

Carr, Gordon. 1975. *The Angry Brigade: The Cause and the Case.* London: Gollancz.

Carroll, Thomas F. 1992. *Intermediary NGOs: The Supporting Link in Grassroots Development.* Bloomfield, Conn.: Kumarian Press.

Carson, Carol. S. 1984. "The Underground Economy: An Introduction." *Survey of Current Business* 64 (May):21–37; (July):106–117.

Carter, April. 1973. *Direct Action and Liberal Democracy.* New York: Harper Torchbooks.

Carter, Barbara. 1974. *Organizing School Volunteer Programs.* New York: Citation Press.

Carter, Richard. 1961. *The Gentle Legions.* Garden City, N.Y.: Doubleday.

Carver, John. 1990. *Boards that Make a Difference.* San Francisco: Jossey-Bass.

Carver, John, and Miriam M. Carver. 1997. *Reinventing Your Board: A Step-by-Step Guide to Implementing Policy Governance.* San Francisco: Jossey-Bass.

Cavallo, Sandra. 1995. *Charity and Power in Early Modern Italy.* Cambridge, UK: Cambridge University Press.

Center for the Study of Evaluation. 1974. *Step by Step Guide for Conducting A Summative Evaluation.* Los Angeles: Center for the Study of Evaluation, University of California, Los Angeles.

Chadwick, Henry. 1993. *The Early Church.* Rev. ed. London: Penguin.

Chait, Richard P., William P. Ryan, and Barbara E. Taylor. 2005. *Governance as Leadership: Reframing the Work of Nonprofit Boards.* Hoboken, N.J.: Wiley.

Chambard, Claude. 1976. *The Maquis: A History of the French Resistance Movement.* Indianapolis: Bobbs-Merrill.

Chambers, Clark A. 1963. *Seedtime of Reform: American Social Service and Social Action 1918–1933.* Minneapolis: University of Minnesota Press.

Chambré, Susan M. 1987. *Good Deeds in Old Age: Volunteering by the New Leisure Class.* Lexington, Mass.: Lexington Books.

Charles, Jeffrey A. 1993. *Service Clubs in American Society: Rotary, Kiwanis, and Lions.* Urbana: University of Illinois Press.

Chase, Mary E. 1939. *A Goodly Fellowship.* New York: Macmillan.

Chatfield, Charles. 1992. *The American Peace Movement.* New York: Twayne.

Chaves, Mark. 2004. *Congregations in America.* Cambridge, Mass.: Harvard University Press.

Checkoway, Barry. 1988a. "Aging, Isolation and Community Health: Propositions from an International Meeting." *Danish Medical Bulletin: Journal of the Health Sciences* Gerontology Special Supplement Series (6):90–91.

———. 1988b. "Community-Based Initiatives to Improve Health of the Elderly." *Danish Medical Bulletin: Journal of the Health Sciences* Gerontology Special Supplement Series (6):30–36.

———. 1995. "Six Strategies of Community Change." *Community Development Journal* 30(1):2–20.

Chen, Carolyn. 2002. "The Religious Varieties of Ethnic Presence: A Comparison between a Taiwanese Immigrant Buddhist Temple and an Evangelical Christian Church." *Sociology of Religion* 63:215–238.

Chetkovich, Carol, and Peter Frumkin. 2003. "Balancing Margin and Mission: Nonprofit Competition in Charitable versus Fee-Based Programs." *Administration and Society* 35:564–596.

Cho, Paul Y. 1981. *Successful Home Cell Groups.* Los Angeles: Logos International.

Chrislip, David D., and Carl E. Larson. 1994. *Collaborative Leadership: How Citizens and Civic Leaders Can Make a Difference.* San Francisco: Jossey-Bass.

Christerson, Brad, and Michael Emerson. 2003. "The Costs of Diversity in Religious Organizations: An In-Depth Case Study." *Sociology of Religion* 64:163–181.

Christy, Carol A. 1987. *Sex Differences in Political Participation: Processes of Change in Fourteen Nations.* New York: Praeger.

Ciarrocchi, Joseph W., Ralph L. Piedmont, and Joseph E. G. Williams. 2003. "Love Thy Neighbor: Spirituality and Personality as Predictors of Prosocial Behavior in Men and Women." *Research in the Social Scientific Study of Religion* 14:61–75.

Cigler, Allan J., and Burdett A. Loomis. 2002. *Interest Group Politics.* 6th ed. Washington, D.C.: CQ Press.

Cionca, John. 1999. *Inviting Volunteers to Minister.* Cincinnati, Ohio: Standard Publishing.

Cizakca, Murat. 2000. *A History of Philanthropic Foundations: The Islamic World from the Seventh Century to the Present.* Istanbul, Turkey: Bogazici University Press.

Clark, B., and J. Q. Wilson. 1961. "Incentive Systems: A Theory of Organization." *Administrative Science Quarterly* 6:129–166.

Clark, Elmer T. 1937. *The Small Sects in America.* Rev. ed. New York: Abingdon Press.

Clark, John. 1991. *Democratizing Development: The Role of Voluntary Organizations.* West Hartford, Conn.: Kumarian Press.

Clarke, Brian P. 1993. *Piety and Nationalism: Lay Voluntary Associations and the Creation of an Irish-Catholic Community in Toronto, 1850–1895.* Montreal: McGill-Queen's University Press.

Clary, E. G. 1982. "Social Support as a Unifying Concept in Voluntary Action." *Journal of Voluntary Action Research* 16:58–68.

Clary, E. G., Mark Snyder, and Robert Ridge. 1992. "Volunteers' Motivations: A Functional Strategy for the Recruitment, Placement, and Retention of Volunteers." *Nonprofit Management and Leadership* 2(4):333–350.

Clawson, Dan, Alan Neustadtl, and Denise Scott. 1992. *Money Talks: Corporate PACs and Political Influence.* New York: Basic Books.

Clemens, Elisabeth S. 1997. *The People's Lobby: Organizational Innovation and the Rise of Interest Group Politics in the United States, 1890–1925.* Chicago: University of Chicago Press.

Clifton, Robert L., and Alan M. Dahms. 1993. *Grassroots Organizations: A Resource Book for Directors, Staff, and Volunteers of Small, Community-Based, Nonprofit Agencies.* 2nd ed. Prospect Heights, Ill.: Waveland Press.

Clotfelter, Charles T., ed. 1992. *Who Benefits from the Nonprofit Sector?* Chicago: University of Chicago Press.

Clotfelter, Charles T., and Thomas Ehrlich, eds. 1999. *Philanthropy and the Nonprofit Sector in a Changing America.* Bloomington: Indiana University Press.

Cnaan, Ram A., and Stephanie C. Boddie. 2002. *The Invisible Caring Hand: American Congregations and the Provision of Welfare.* New York: New York University Press.

Cnaan, Ram A., Femida Handy, and Margaret Wadsworth. 1996. "Defining Who Is a Volunteer: Conceptual and Empirical Considerations." *Nonprofit and Voluntary Sector Quarterly* 25(3):364–386.

Cnaan, Ram, and Carl Milofsky. 1997. "Editorial." *Nonprofit and Voluntary Sector Quarterly* 26 (Supplemental):S3–S13.

Cnaan, Ram A., Robert Wineberg, and Stephanie C. Boddie. 1999. *The Newer Deal: Social Work and Religion in Partnership.* New York: Columbia University Press.

Cobban, Alfred. 1971. *Dictatorship: Its History and Theory.* New York: Haskell House.

Cohen, Anthony P. 1985. *The Symbolic Construction of Community.* London: Tavistock.

Cohen, Lilly, and Dennis R. Young. 1989. *Careers for Dreamers & Doers: A Guide to Management Careers in the Nonprofit Sector.* New York: Foundation Center.

Cohen, Nathan E. 1960. *The Citizen Volunteer: His Responsibility, Role, and Opportunity in Modern Society.* New York: Harper & Bros.

Cole, Richard L. 1974. *Citizen Participation and the Urban Policy Process.* Lexington, Mass.: Lexington Books.

Colwell, Mary A. C. 1993. *Private Foundations and Public Policy: The Political Role of Philanthropy.* New York: Garland Publishing.

Commager, Henry S. 1954. *Freedom, Loyalty, Dissent.* New York: Oxford University Press.

Commission on Private Philanthropy and Public Needs. 1975. *Giving in America: Toward a Stronger Voluntary Sector.* Washington, D.C.: Commission on Private Philanthropy and Public Needs.

Community Chests and Councils of America. 1952. *A Volunteer Bureau Handbook.* New York: Community Chests and Councils of America.

Conger, D. Stuart. 1973. *Social Inventions.* Prince Albert, Canada: Saskatchewan New Start.

Connell, James E. 2001. "Budgeting for Fund-Raising." Pp. 52–95 in *The Nonprofit Handbook: Fund Raising,* 3rd ed., ed. James M. Greenfield. New York: Wiley.

Connors, Tracy D. 1988a. "Committees of the Nonprofit Organization." Pp. 12.1–12.9 in *The Nonprofit Organization Handbook,* 2nd ed., ed. Tracy D. Connors. New York: McGraw-Hill.

———. 1988b. *The Nonprofit Organization Handbook.* 2nd ed. New York: McGraw-Hill.

———. 1995. *The Volunteer Management Handbook.* New York: Wiley.

———. 2001. *The Nonprofit Handbook: Management.* 3rd ed. New York: Wiley.

Connors, Tracy D., and Stephan R. Wise. 1988. "Seeking Revenue or Support from Corporations." Pp. 35.1–35.17 in *The Nonprofit Organization Handbook,* 2nd ed., ed. Tracy D. Connors. New York: McGraw-Hill.

Conrad, W. R., Jr., and W. E. Glenn. 1983. *The Effective Voluntary Board of Directors.* Rev. ed. Athens, Ohio: Swallow Press.

Constantelos, Demetrios J. 1991. *Byzantine Philanthropy and Social Welfare.* New Rochelle, N.Y.: Caratzas.

Constantine, Larry L., and Joan M. Constantine. 1973. *Group Marriage: A Study of Contemporary Multilateral Marriage.* New York: Collier Books.

Conway, M. M. 1991. *Political Participation in the United States.* 2nd ed. Washington, D.C.: Congressional Quarterly Press.

Cook, Thomas J., and Frank P. Scioli. 1975. *The Effectiveness of Volunteer Programs in Courts and Corrections.* Chicago: University of Illinois at Chicago Circle.

Cooley, Charles H. 1909. *Social Organization.* New York: Charles Scribner's Sons.

———. 1965. *Social Process.* Carbondale: Southern Illinois University Press.

Copp, Martha. 1998. "When Emotion Work Is Doomed to Fail: Ideological and Structural Constraints on Emotion Management." *Symbolic Interaction* 21: 299–328.

Corcoran, James. 1995. *The Birth of Paramilitary Terrorism in the Heartland.* New York: Penguin.

Cornes, Richard, and Todd Sandler. 1996. *The Theory of Externalities, Public Goods, and Club Goods.* Cambridge, UK: Cambridge University Press.

Cornforth, Chris, ed. 2003. *The Governance of Public and Non-Profit Organizations.* London: Routledge.

Council on Foundations. 1986. *Principles and Practices for Effective Grantmaking.* Rev. ed. Washington, D.C.: Council on Foundations.

Cousineau, Madeleine. 1998. *Religion in a Changing World.* Westport, Conn.: Praeger.

Couto, Richard A. 1999. *Making Democracy Work Better: Mediating Structures, Social Capital, and the Democratic Prospect.* Chapel Hill: University of North Carolina Press.

Covey, Herbert C., Scott Menard, and Robert J. Franzese. 1992. *Juvenile Gangs.* Springfield, Ill.: C. C. Thomas.

Cowlishaw, Gillian. 2003. "Disappointing Indigenous People: Violence and the Refusal of Help." *Public Culture* 15(1):103–125.

Cox, John B. 1997. *Professional Practices in Association Management.* Washington, D.C.: American Society of Association Executives.

Creighton, W. B. 1977. "The Bullock Report—The Coming of the Age of Democracy." *British Journal of Law and Society* 4(Summer):1–17.

Crimmins, James C., and Mary Keil. 1983. *Enterprise in the Nonprofit Sector.* New York: Rockefeller Brothers Fund.

Critchlow, Donald T., and Charles H. Parker. 1998. *With Us Always: A History of Private Charity and Public Welfare.* Lanham, Md.: Rowman & Littlefield.

Cross, C. Wallace. 2004. *Cry Havoc: A History of the 49th Tennessee Volunteer Infantry Regiment, 1861–1865.* Franklin, Tenn.: Hillsboro Press.

Crouch, David, and Colin Ward. 1994. *The Allotment: Its Landscape and Culture.* Nottingham, UK: Mushroom Bookshop.

Crowley, Vivianne. 1989. *Wicca: The Old Religion in the New Age.* San Francisco: Aquarium/Thorsons.

Crystal, David, ed. 1994. "Rebellions of 1837." *The Cambridge Encyclopedia.* 2nd ed. New York: Cambridge University Press.

Csikszentmihalyi, Mihalyi. 1990. *Flow: The Psychology of Optimal Experience.* New York: Harper-Perennial.

Cuadrado, Mary A. F. 1999. "A Comparison of Hispanic and Anglo Calls to a Gambling Help Hotline." *Journal of Gambling Studies* 15:71–81.

Cull, John G., and Richard E. Hardy, eds. 1974. *Volunteerism: An Emerging Profession.* Springfield, Ill.: C. C. Thomas.

Cummins, John R. 1986. "Real Property Tax Exemptions for Religious Institutions in Ohio: Bishop Ordains a Faulty Progeny." *Ohio State Law Journal* 47(2): 535–64.

Curti, Merle. 1963. *American Philanthropy Abroad: A History.* New Brunswick, N.J.: Rutgers University Press.

Curtis, James E., Edward Grabb, and Douglas Baer. 1992. "Voluntary Association Membership in Fifteen Countries: A Comparative Analysis." *American Sociological Review* 57:139–152.

Cusack, Sandra A. 1994. "Developing Leadership in the Third Age: An Ethnographic Study of Leadership in a Seniors' Center." *Journal of Applied Gerontology* 13:127–142.

Bibliography

Cutlip, Scott. 1965. *Fund Raising in the United States: Its Role in American Philanthropy.* New Brunswick, N.J.: Rutgers University Press.

Dahl, Robert A. 1967. *Pluralist Democracy in the United States.* Chicago: Rand McNally.

Dale, Harvey P. 1997. *The Work of Operating Foundations.* Gütersloh, Germany: Bertelsmann Foundation.

Dalton, Russell J. 1994. *The Green Rainbow: Environmental Groups in Western Europe.* New Haven, Conn.: Yale University Press.

Danes, Sharon M., and Yoon G. Lee. 2004. "Tensions Generated by Business Issues in Farm Business-Owning Couples." *Family Relations* 53:357–366.

Daniels, Arlene K. 1988. *Invisible Careers: Women Civic Leaders from the Volunteer World.* Chicago: University of Chicago Press.

Daniels, Roger. 1993. *Concentration Camps: North America-Japanese in the United States and Canada during World War II.* Malabar, Fla.: Krieger Publishing Co.

Danis, Heather, and Julie A. Burke. 1996. *Grant Proposal: Wake County Department of Health.* Chapel Hill: School of Public Health, University of North Carolina.

Darsey, James. 1995. "Joe McCarthy's Fantastic Moment." *Communication Monographs* 62 (March):65–86.

Davis, Benjamin J. 1963. *Must Negro-Americans Wait Another Hundred Years for Freedom? Against Tokenism and Gradualism.* New York: New Century Publishers.

Davis, John H. 1993. *Mafia Dynasty.* New York: Harper Paperbacks.

Davis, Kathy. 2002. "Feminist Body/Politics as World Traveller: Translating Our Bodies, Ourselves." *European Journal of Women's Studies* 9:223–247.

Davis, Keith. 1953. "Management Communication and the Grapevine." *Harvard Business Review* 31(5):43–49.

Dawley, David. 1992. *A Nation of Lords: The Autobiography of the Vice Lords.* Prospect Heights, Ill.: Waveland Press.

Day, Nancy E. 1994. "Designing and Managing Compensation and Benefits Programs." Pp. 557–590 in *The Jossey-Bass Handbook of Nonprofit Leadership and Management,* ed. Robert D. Herman and Associates. San Francisco: Jossey-Bass.

De Breffny, Brian. 1978. *The Synagogue.* New York: Macmillan.

De Grazia, Alfred. 1957. *Grass Roots Private Welfare.* New York: New York University Press.

Dekieffer, Donald E. 1997. *The Citizen's Guide to Lobbying Congress.* Chicago: Chicago Review Press.

Delgado, Gary. 1986. *Organizing the Movement: The Roots and Growth of ACORN.* Philadelphia: Temple University Press.

Della Porta, Donatella. 1999. *Social Movements: An Introduction.* Oxford, UK: Blackwell.

Demerath, N. J., III, and Rhys H. Williams. 1985. "Civil Religion in an Uncivil Society." *The Annals of the American Academy of Political and Social Science* 480 (July):154–166.

Department of Commerce. 1982. *Measuring Nonmarket Economic Activity: BEA Working Papers.* Washington, D.C.: Department of Commerce.

DeSario, Jack, and Stuart Langton. 1987. *Citizen Participation in Public Decision Making.* New York: Greenwood Press.

Devinatz, Victor G. 2001. "The Antipolitics and Politics of a New Left Union Caucus: The Workers' Voice Committee of the UAW Local 6 1970–1975." *Nature, Society, and Thought* 14:285–321.

Diaz, William. 2002. "For Whom and For What? The Contributions of the Nonprofit Sector." Pp. 517–535 in *The State of Nonprofit America,* ed. Lester M. Salamon. Washington, D.C.: Brookings Institution Press.

Dilger, Robert J. 1992. *Neighborhood Politics: Residential Community Associations in American Governance.* New York: New York University Press.

Dionne, E. J., Jr., Kayla Drogosz, and Robert Lotan, eds. 2003. *United We Serve: National Service and the Future of Citizenship.* Washington, D.C.: Brookings Institution Press.

Disch, Lisa J. 2002. *The Tyranny of the Two-Party System.* New York: Columbia University Press.

DiMaggio, Paul J., and Helmut K. Anheier. 1990. "The Sociology of Nonprofit Organizations and Sectors." *Annual Review of Sociology* 16:137–159.

DiMaggio, Paul J., and Walter W. Powell. 1983. "The Iron Cage Revisited: Institutional Isomorphism and Collective Rationality in Organization Fields." *American Sociological Review* 48 (April):147–160.

Dobratz, Betty A., and Tim Buzzell. 2002. *Sociological Views on Political Participation in the 21st Century.* New York: JAI Press.

Dominguez, Jorge I., ed. 1994a. *Parties, Elections, and Political Participation in Latin America.* New York: Garland.

Dominguez, Jorge I., ed. 1994b. *The Roman Catholic Church in Latin America.* New York: Garland.

Donelan, Brenda. 2002. "Extremist Groups of the Midwest: A Content Analysis of Internet Websites." *Great Plains Sociologist* 16:1–27.

Donovan, Mary A. 1989. *Sisterhood as Power: The Past and Passion of Ecclesial Women.* New York: Crossroad.

Douglas, James. 1987. "Political Theories of Nonprofit Organizations." Pp. 43–54 in *The Nonprofit Sector,* ed. Walter W. Powell. New Haven, Conn.: Yale University Press.

Dove, Kent E. 2000. *Conducting a Successful Capital Campaign.* San Francisco: Jossey-Bass.

———. 2001. *Conducting a Successful Fundraising Program.* San Francisco: Jossey-Bass.

Dover, Michael A. 1992. "Pairing and Intentional Activist Groups: Building Diverse Movement Organizations." Conference Panel Presentation, Workshop on Grassroots Empowerment, Perspectives for Democracy and Socialism in the Nineties, July, San Francisco.

———. 1997. "Enhancing Older Volunteer Empowerment, Activism and Effectiveness: Theoretical and Research Support for Developing a Senior Citizen Volunteer Association." Paper presented at the 16th Annual Conference, Association for Research on Nonprofit Organizations and Voluntary Action, December, Indianapolis.

———. 2003. The Social System of Real Property Ownership: Public and Nonprofit Property Tax Exemptions and Corporate Tax Abatements in City and Suburb 1955–2000. Ph.D. Dissertation. University of Michigan, Ann Arbor.

Dowie, Mark. 1988. *We Have a Donor: The Bold New World of Organ Transplanting.* New York: St. Martin's Press.

Downton, J. V. 1973. *Rebel Leadership.* New York: Free Press.

Driedger, S. Michelle, and John Eyles. 2001. "Organochlofines and Breast Cancer: The Use of Scientific Evidence in Claimsmaking." *Social Science and Medicine* 52:1589–1605.

Dropkin, Murray, and Allyson Hayden. 2001. *The Cash Flow Management Book for Nonprofits.* San Francisco: Jossey-Bass.

Drout, Cheryl E., and Corsoro, Christie L. 2003. "Attitudes toward Fraternity Hazing among Fraternity Members, Sorority Members, and Non-Greek Students." *Social Behavior and Personality* 31:535–543.

Drucker, Peter F. 1974. *Management: Tasks, Responsibilities, Practices.* New York: Harper & Row.

———. 1992. *Managing the Non-Profit Organization.* New York: HarperBusiness.

———. 1995. *Managing in a Time of Great Change.* New York: Dutton.

Duca, Diane J. 1996. *Nonprofit Boards.* New York: Wiley.

Duck, Steve. 1992. *Human Relationships.* 2nd ed. Newbury Park, Calif.: Sage.

Dumazedier, Joffre. 1967. *Toward a Society of Leisure.* New York: Free Press.

———. 1988. *Révolution Culturelle du Temps Libre 1968–1988.* Paris: Méridiens Klincksieck.

Duncan, Harriet H., Shirley S. Travis, and William J. McAuley. 1995. "Emergent Theoretical Model for Interventions Encouraging Physical Activity (Mall Walking) among Older Adults." *Journal of Applied Gerontology* 14(1):64–77.

Dunlap, Riley E., and Angela G. Mertig, eds. 1992. *American Environmentalism: The U.S. Environmental Movement, 1970–1990.* Philadelphia: Taylor & Francis.

Dunlop, James J. 1989. *Leading the Association: Striking the Right Balance between Staff and Volunteers.* Washington, D.C.: American Society of Association Executives.

Eadie, Douglas C. 1997. *Changing by Design: A Practical Approach to Leading Innovation in Nonprofit Organizations.* San Francisco: Jossey-Bass.

Eadie, Douglas C., and Linda Daily. 1994. *Boards That Work: A Practical Guide to Building Effective Association Boards.* Washington, D.C.: American Society of Association Executives.

Eastland, Terry. 2000. *Freedom of Expression in the Supreme Court: The Defining Cases.* Lanham, Md.: Rowman & Littlefield.

Ebata, Michi, and Beverly Neufeld. 2000. *Confronting the Political in International Relations.* New York: St. Martin's Press.

Ebaugh, Helen R., Paula F. Piper, Janet S. Chafetz, and Martha Daniels. 2003. "Where's the Religion? Distinguishing Faith-Based from Secular Social Service Agencies." *Journal for the Scientific Study of Religion* 42:411–426.

Eberly, Don E., ed. 2000. *The Essential Civil Society Reader.* Lanham, Md.: Rowman & Littlefield.

Eberly, Don E., and Ryan Streeter. 2002. *The Soul of Civil Society: Voluntary Associations and the Public Value of Moral Habits.* Lanham, Md.: Lexington Books.

Eckenstein, Lina. 1963. *Women under Monasticism: Chapters on Saint-Lore and Convent Life between A.D. 500 and A.D. 1500.* New York: Russell & Russell.

Ecklein, Joan. 1984. *Community Organizers.* 2nd ed. New York: Wiley.

Edwards, Michael. 2004. *Civil Society.* Cambridge, UK: Polity Press.

Edwards, Richard L., and John A. Yankey. 1998. *Skills for Effective Management of Nonprofit Organizations.* Washington, D.C.: National Association of Social Workers Press.

Eisemon, Thomas O., and Charles H. Davis. 1997. "Kenya: Crisis in the Scientific Community." Pp. 105–128 in *Scientific Communities in the Developing World,* ed. Jacques Gaillard, V. V. Krishna, and Roland Waast. New Delhi: Sage.

Ellis, Susan J. 2002. *The Volunteer Recruitment (and Membership Development) Book.* Philadelphia: Energize.

Ellis, Susan J., Jeffrey D. Kahn, and Alan S. Glazer. 1996. *From the Top Down: The Executive Role in Volunteer Program Success.* Rev. ed. Philadelphia: Energize.

Ellis, Susan J., and Katherine H. Noyes. 1990. *By the People: A History of Americans as Volunteers.* Rev. ed. San Francisco: Jossey-Bass.

Ellis, Susan J., Anne Weisbrod, and Katherine H. Noyes et al. 2003. *Children as Volunteers: Preparing for Community Service.* Philadelphia: Energize.

Ellsworth, Frank L., and Joe Lumarda, eds. 2003. *Foundation Management*. Hoboken, N.J.: Wiley.

Ellwood, Robert S. 1979. *Alternative Altars: Unconventional and Eastern Spirituality in America*. Chicago: University of Chicago Press.

Ember, Carol R., and Melvin Ember. 2004. *Cultural Anthropology*. 11th ed. Upper Saddle River, N.J.: Pearson Prentice Hall.

Emilio, Luis F. 1894/1969. *A Brave Black Regiment: The History of the Fifty-Fourth Regiment of Massachusetts Volunteer Infantry, 1863–1865*. New York: Arno Press.

Emmons, Robert A. 1997. "Motives and Life Goals." Pp. 485–512 in *Handbook of Personality Psychology*, ed. Robert Hogan, John Johnson, and Stephen Briggs. San Diego: Academic Press.

Endres, Kirsten W. 2001. "Local Dynamics of Renegotiating Ritual Space in Northern Vietnam: The Case of the *Dinh*." *SOJOURN: Journal of Social Issues in Southeast Asia* 16:70–101.

Eng, Eugenia. 1988. "Extending the Unit of Practice from Individual to Community to Reduce Social Isolation among the Elderly." *Danish Medical Bulletin: Journal of the Health Sciences* Gerontology Special Supplement Series (6):45–51.

English, T. J. 1990. *The Westies: Inside the Hell's Kitchen Irish Mob*. New York: G. P. Putnam's Sons.

Engstrom, John, and Paul A. Copley. 2004. *Essentials of Accounting for Governmental and Not-for-Profit Organizations*. Boston: McGraw-Hill/Irwin.

Entine, Jon. 2003. "The Myth of Social Investing: A Critique of Its Practice and Consequences for Corporate Social Performance Research." *Organization and Environment* 16:352–368.

Epstein, Barbara. 1991. *Political Protest and Cultural Revolution: Nonviolent Direct Action in the 1970s and 1980s*. Berkeley: University of California Press.

Epstein, Jonathon S., and Robert Sardiello. 1990. "The Wharf Rats: A Preliminary Examination of Alcoholics Anonymous and the Grateful Dead Head Phenomena." *Deviant Behavior* 11:245–257.

Epstein, Steven. 1991. *Wage Labor and Guilds in Medieval Europe*. Chapel Hill: University of North Carolina Press.

Erem, Suzan. 2001. *Labor Pains: Inside America's New Union Movement*. New York: Monthly Review Press.

Ermann, M. David, and Richard J. Lundman, eds. 2002. *Corporate and Governmental Deviance*. 6th ed. New York: Oxford University Press.

Ernstthal, Henry L., and Bob Jones. 2001. *Principles of Association Management*. 3rd ed. Washington, D.C.: American Society of Association Executives.

Esman, Milton J., and Norman T. Uphoff. 1984. *Local Organizations: Intermediaries in Local Development*. Ithaca, N.Y.: Cornell University Press.

Estes, Richard J. 2000. "Social Development Trends in the Middle East 1970–1997: The Search for Modernity." *Social Indicators Research* 50:51–81.

Etzioni, Amitai. 1961. *A Comparative Analysis of Complex Organizations*. New York: Free Press.

———. 1968. *The Active Society*. New York: Free Press of Glencoe.

———. 1970. *Demonstration Democracy*. New York: Gordon and Breach.

———. 1975. *A Comparative Analysis of Complex Organizations*. Rev. and enlarged ed. New York: Free Press.

———. 1993. *The Spirit of Community*. New York: Simon & Schuster.

———. 2004. "The Emerging Global Normative Synthesis." *Journal of Political Philosophy* 12:214–244.

Evans, Bette N. 1997. *Interpreting the Free Exercise of Religion: The Constitution and American Pluralism*. Chapel Hill: University of North Carolina Press.

Bibliography

Evers, Adalbert, and Jean-Louis Laville. 2004. *The Third Sector in Europe.* Northampton, Mass.: Edward Elgas.

Eyre, Richard. 2003. *National Service: Diary of a Decade.* London: Bloomsbury.

Falomir-Pichastor, Juan M., Daniel Munoz-Rojas, Federica Invernizzi, and Gabriel Mugny. 2004. "Perceived In-Group Threat as a Factor Moderating the Influence of In-Group Norms on Discrimination against Foreigners." *European Journal of Social Psychology* 34:135–153.

Farcau, Bruce W. 1994. *The Coup: Tactics in the Seizure of Power.* Westport, Conn.: Praeger.

Feigenbaum, A. V. 1983. *Total Quality Control.* New York: McGraw-Hill.

Feld, Werner J., Robert S. Jordan, and Leon Hurwitz 1994. *International Organizations.* 3rd ed. Westport, Conn.: Praeger.

Fellmeth, Robert C., and Ralph Nader. 1970. *The Interstate Commerce Omission, the Public Interest, and the ICC.* New York: Grossman.

Ferguson, Charles W. 1937. *Fifty Million Brothers.* New York: Farrar and Rinehart.

Ferree, Myra M., and Beth B. Hess. 1995. *Controversy and Coalition: The New Feminist Movement.* Rev. ed. New York: Twayne.

Ferree, Myra M., and Patricia Y. Martin, eds. 1995. *Feminist Organizations: Harvest of the New Women's Movement.* Philadelphia: Temple University Press.

Ferriss, Susan, Ricardo Sandoval, and Diana Hembree. 1997. *The Fight in the Fields: Cesar Chavez and the Farmworkers Movement.* Orlando, Fla.: Harcourt Brace.

Fiedler, F. E. 1964. "A Contingency Model of Leadership Effectiveness." Pp. 149–190 in *Advances in Experimental Social Psychology. Volume I,* ed. Leonard Berkowitz. New York: Academic Press.

Files, Yvonne de Ridder. 1991. *The Quest for Freedom: Belgian Resistance in World War II.* Santa Barbara, Calif.: Fithian Press.

Filinson, Rachel. 2001. "Evaluation of the Impact of a Volunteer Ombudsman Program: The Rhode Island Experience." *Journal of Elder Abuse and Neglect* 13(4):1–19.

Fine, Gary A. 1998. *Morel Tales: The Culture of Mushrooming.* Cambridge, Mass.: Harvard University Press.

Fine, Seymour H. 1992. *Marketing the Public Sector: Promoting the Causes of Public and Nonprofit Agencies.* New Brunswick, N.J.: Transaction Publishers.

Finke, Roger, and Rodney Stark. 2005. *The Churching of America, 1776–2005: Winners and Losers in Our Religious Economy.* New Brunswick, N.J.: Rutgers University Press.

Finley, M. I. 1974. "Aristotle and Economic Analysis." In *Studies in Ancient Society,* ed. M. I. Finley. New York: Routledge & Kegan Paul.

Finsen, Lawrence, and Susan Finsen. 1994. *The Animal Rights Movement in America.* New York: Twayne.

Fischer, Lucy R., Daniel P. Mueller, and Philip W. Cooper. 1991. "Older Volunteers: A Discussion of the Minnesota Senior Study." *Gerontologist* 31(2):183–194.

Fischer, Lucy R., and Kay B. Schaffer. 1993. *Older Volunteers: A Guide to Research and Practice.* Newbury Park, Calif.: Sage.

Fisher, James C., and Kathleen M. Cole. 1993. *Leadership and Management of Volunteer Programs.* San Francisco: Jossey-Bass.

Fisher, Julie. 1984. "Development from Below: Neighborhood Improvement Associations in the Latin American Squatter Settlements." *Studies in Comparative International Development* 19:61–85.

———. 1993. *The Road from Rio: Sustainable Development and the Nongovernmental Movement in the Third World.* Westport, Conn.: Praeger.

———. 1998. *Nongovernments: NGOs and the Political Development of the Third World.* West Hartford, Conn.: Kumarian Press.

Fisher, Robert. 1994. *Let the People Decide: Neighborhood Organizing in America.* Rev. ed. New York: Twayne.

Fisher, Robert, and Joe Kling, eds. 1993. *Mobilizing the Community: Local Politics in the Era of the Global City.* Newbury Park, Calif.: Sage.

Fishman, James J., and Stephen Schwarz. 2000. *Nonprofit Organizations.* 2nd ed. New York: Foundation Press.

Flanagan, Joan. 1984. *The Successful Volunteer Organization.* Chicago: Contemporary Books.

———. 2002. *Successful Fund-Raising: A Complete Handbook for Volunteers and Professionals.* 2nd ed. New York: McGraw-Hill.

Floro, Maria S. 1995. "Economic Restructuring, Gender, and the Allocation of Time." *World Development* 23:1913–1929.

Flory, Richard W. 2002. "Intentional Change and the Maintenance of Mission: The Impact of Adult Education Programs on School Mission at Two Evangelical Colleges." *Review of Religious Research* 43:349–368.

Flynn, Patricia, and Virginia A. Hodgkinson. 2002. *Measuring the Impact of the Nonprofit Sector.* New York: Kluwer Academic.

Fogal, Robert E. 1994. "Designing and Managing the Fundraising Program." Pp. 369–381 in *The Jossey-Bass Handbook of Nonprofit Leadership and Management,* ed. Robert D. Herman and Associates. San Francisco: Jossey-Bass.

Ford, Henry E., and Jean L. Ford. 1996. *The Power of Association: Success through Volunteerism and Positive Associations.* Dubuque, Iowa: Kendall/Hunt.

Forward, David C. 1994. *Heroes After Hours: Extraordinary Acts of Employee Volunteerism.* San Francisco: Jossey-Bass.

Francis, Leslie J., and Laurence B. Brown. 1991. "The Influence of Home, Church, and School on Prayer among Sixteen-Year-Old Adolescents in England." *Review of Religious Research* 33:112–122.

Fraser, Steve, and Josh Freeman. 1997. "Rebuilding the Alliance." *Dissent* 44(1):29–30.

Frazier, Edward F., and C. Eric Lincoln. 1974. *The Negro Church in America.* New York: Schocken Books.

Freedman, Harry A., and Karen Feldman. 1998. *The Business of Special Events: Fundraising Strategies for Changing Times.* Sarasota, Fla.: Pineapple Press.

Freedman, Marc. 1993. *The Kindness of Strangers: Adult Mentors, Urban Youth, and the New Voluntarism.* San Francisco: Jossey-Bass.

Freeman, David F. 1981. *The Handbook on Private Foundations.* Cabin John, Md.: Seven Locks Press.

———. 1991. *The Handbook on Private Foundations.* Rev. ed. New York: Foundation Center.

Freidson, Eliot. 1994. *Professionalism Reborn: Theory, Prophecy, and Policy.* Chicago: University of Chicago Press.

Frey, R. Scott, Thomas Dietz, and Linda Kalof. 1992. "Characteristics of Successful American Protest Groups: Another Look at Gamson's Strategy of Social Protest." *American Journal of Sociology* 98:368–387.

Friedman, Lawrence J., and Mark D. McGarvie. 2003. *Charity, Philanthropy, and Civility in American History.* New York: Cambridge University Press.

Frishman, Martin, and Hasan-Uddin Khan. 1994. *The Mosque: History, Architectural Development and Regional Diversity.* New York: Thames and Hudson.

Fromkin, Howard L., and John J. Sherwood. 1976. *Intergroup and Minority Relations.* La Jolla, Calif.: University Associates.

Frumkin, Peter. 2003. "Inside Venture Philanthropy." *Society* 40(4):7–15.

Frumkin, Peter, and Jonathan B. Imber, eds. 2004. *In Search of the Nonprofit Sector.* New Brunswick, N.J.: Transaction Publishers.

Fry, Robert P. 1998. *Nonprofit Investment Policies.* New York: Wiley.

Fuller, Lon L. 1969. "Two Principles of Human Associations." Pp. 45–57 in *Voluntary Associations,* ed. J. R. Pennock and J. W. Chapman. New York: Atherton.

Fullinwider, Robert K., ed. 1999. *Civil Society, Democracy, and Civic Renewal.* Lanham, Md.: Rowman & Littlefield.

Gabe, Thomas, and Eugene H. Falk. 1995. *Welfare: (Dis)incentives in the Welfare System.* Washington, D.C.: Congressional Research Service, Library of Congress.

Galaskiewicz, Joseph. 1985. *Social Organization of an Urban Grants Economy.* Orlando, Fla.: Academic Press.

Galaskiewicz, Joseph, and Wolfgang Bielefeld. 1998. *Nonprofit Organizations in an Age of Uncertainty.* New York: Aldine de Gruyter.

Galdston, Iago. 1961. *Voluntary Action and the State.* New York: International Universities Press.

Galenson, Walter. 1976. *Trade Union Democracy in Europe.* Westport, Conn.: Greenwood Press.

———. 1983. *The United Brotherhood of Carpenters: The First Hundred Years.* Cambridge, Mass.: Harvard University Press.

———. 1994. *Trade Union Growth and Decline.* Westport, Conn.: Praeger.

———. 1996. *The American Labor Movement 1955–1995.* Westport, Conn.: Greenwood Press.

———. 1998. *The World's Strongest Trade Unions: The Scandinavian Labor Movement.* Westport, Conn.: Quorum.

Galenson, Walter, and Seymour M. Lipset, eds. 1990. *Labor and Trade Unions.* New York: Wiley.

Gallagher, Sally K. 1994. "Gender and Giving Help through Formal Volunteerism." Pp. 71–86 in *Older People Giving Care: Helping Family and Community.* Westport, Conn.: Auburn House.

Gamba, Michelle, and Brian H. Kleiner. 2001. "The Old-Boys' Network Today." *International Journal of Sociology and Social Policy* 21:101–107.

Gamson, William A. 1990. *The Strategy of Social Protest.* 2nd ed. Belmont, Calif.: Wadsworth Pub.

Gamwell, Franklin I. 1984. *Beyond Preference: Liberal Theories of Independent Association.* Chicago: University of Chicago Press.

Ganje, Lucy, and Lynda Kenny. 2004. "Come Hell and High Water: Newspaper Photographs, Minority Communities, and the Greater Grand Forks Flood." *Race, Gender, and Class* 11:78–89.

Gans, Herbert J. 1974. *Popular Culture and High Culture.* New York: Basic Books.

Gapasin, Fernando E. 1996. "Race, Gender and Other 'Problems' of Unity for the American Working Class." *Race, Gender and Class* 4(1):41–62.

Gara, Larry. 1996. *The Liberty Line: The Legend of the Underground Railroad.* Lexington: University Press of Kentucky.

Garbarino, J., and N. Jacobson. 1978. "Youth Helping Youth in Cases of Maltreatment of Adolescents." *Child Welfare* 57:505–510.

Garner, C. William. 1991. *Accounting and Budgeting in Public and Nonprofit Organizations.* San Francisco: Jossey-Bass.

Garner, Roberta A., and Mayer N. Zald. 1987. "The Political Economy of Social Movement Sectors." Pp. 293–317 in *Social Movements in an Organizational Society,* ed. Mayer N. Zald and John D. McCarthy. New Brunswick, N.J.: Transaction Publishers.

Garris, Sheron, and Julia Lettner. 1996. *Grant Proposal: Wellness Resource Center.* Chapel Hill: School of Public Health, University of North Carolina.

Garrow, David J. 1989. *The Walking City: The Montgomery Bus Boycott 1955–1956.* Brooklyn, N.Y.: Carlson Pub.

Gartner, Alan, and Frank Riessman. 1977. *Self-Help in the Human Services.* San Francisco: Jossey-Bass.

———. 1984. *The Self-Help Revolution.* New York: Human Sciences Press.

Gasper, Louis. 1963. *The Fundamentalist Movement.* The Hague: Mouton.

Gaudiani, Claire. 2003. *The Greater Good: How Philanthropy Drives the American Economy and Can Save Capitalism.* New York: Henry Holt.

Gaustad, Edwin S., and Leigh E. Schmidt. 2002. *The Religious History of America.* San Francisco: HarperSanFrancisco.

Gavron, Daniel. 2000. *The Kibbutz: Awakening from Utopia.* Lanham, Md.: Rowman & Littlefield.

Gelber, Steven M. 1999. *Hobbies: Leisure and the Culture of Work in America.* New York: Columbia University Press.

Gellner, Ernest. 1994. *Conditions of Liberty: Civil Society and Its Rivals.* London: Penguin Books.

George, John, and Laird Wilcox. 1996. *American Extremists: Militias, Supremacists, Klansmen, Communists, & Others.* Amherst, N.Y.: Prometheus Books.

George, Stephen, and Arnold Weimerskirch. 1994. *Total Quality Management.* New York: Wiley.

Gerth, Hans, and C. Wright Mills, eds. 1958. *From Max Weber: Essays in Sociology.* New York: Oxford University Press.

Ghanea-Hercock, Nazila. 2003. *The Challenge of Religious Discrimination at the Dawn of the New Millennium.* Boston: Martinus Nijhoff.

Gibelman, Margaret, and Steven Kraft, 1996. "Advocacy as a Core Agency Program: Planning Considerations for Voluntary Human Services Agencies." *Administration in Social Work* 20(4):43–59.

Giddings, Paula. 1988. *In Search of Sisterhood: Delta Sigma Theta and the Challenge of the Black Sorority Movement.* New York: William Morrow.

Gidron, Benjamin, Michael Bar, and Hagai Kats. 2004. *The Israeli Third Sector.* New York: Kluwer Academic.

Gidron, Benjamin, Ralph Kramer, and Lester M. Salamon, eds. 1992. *Government and the Third Sector.* San Francisco: Jossey-Bass.

Gilbert, Charles E. 1983. *Implementing Governmental Change.* Beverly Hills, Calif.: Sage.

Gillis, Chester. 1999. *Roman Catholicism in America.* New York: Columbia University Press.

Gilpatrick, Eleanor. 1989. *Grants for Nonprofit Organizations.* New York: Praeger.

Ginsberg, Paul. 2003. *Italy and Its Discontents: Family, Civil Society, State.* New York: Palgrave Macmillan.

Gintis, Herbert, Samuel Bowles, Robert Boyd, and Ernest Fehr. 2003. "Explaining Altruistic Behavior in Humans." *Evolution and Human Behavior* 24(3):153–172.

Giroux, Henry. 2004. "War Talk, the Death of the Social, and Disappearing Children: Remembering the Other War." *Cultural Studies—Critical Methodologies* 4(2):206–211.

Gittell, Marilyn. 1980. *The Limits to Citizen Participation: The Decline of Community Organizations.* Beverly Hills, Calif.: Sage.

Gittell, Ross, and Avis Vidal. 1998. *Community Organizing: Building Social Capital as a Development Strategy.* Thousand Oaks, Calif.: Sage.

Gitterman, Alex, and Lawrence Shulman. 1994. *Mutual Aid Groups, Vulnerable Populations, and the Life Cycle.* New York: Columbia University Press.

Bibliography

Gladstone, F. J. 1979. *Voluntary Action in a Changing World*. London: Bedford Square Press.

Glazer, Nathan. 1972. *American Judaism*. Chicago: University of Chicago Press.

Gleason, Philip. 1987. *Keeping the Faith: American Catholicism Past and Present*. Notre Dame, Ind.: Notre Dame University Press.

Glenn, Charles L. 2000. *The Ambiguous Embrace: Government and Faith-Based Schools and Social Agencies*. Princeton, N.J.: Princeton University Press.

Godbey, Geoffrey. 1999. *Leisure in Your Life: An Exploration*. 5th ed. State College, Pa.: Venture.

Goffman, Erving. 1963. *Stigma*. Englewood Cliffs, N.J.: Prentice Hall.

Goldberg, Robert A. 1991. *Grassroots Resistance: Social Movements in Twentieth Century America*. Belmont, Calif.: Wadsworth Publishing Co.

Golden, Renny, and Michael McConnell. 1986. *Sanctuary: The New Underground Railroad*. Maryknoll, N.Y.: Orbis Books.

Golden, Susan L. 1997. *Secrets of Successful Grantsmanship*. San Francisco: Jossey-Bass.

Goldstein, Joseph. 2002. *One Dharma: The Emerging Western Buddhism*. New York: HarperCollins.

Goldstein, Kenneth M. 1999. *Interest Groups, Lobbying, and Participation in America*. Cambridge, UK: Cambridge University Press.

Golomb, Sylvia L., and Andrea Kocsis. 1988. *The Halfway House: On the Road to Independence*. New York: Brunner/Mazel.

Goodin, Robert E., and Hans-Dieter Klingemann. 1996. "Political Science: The Discipline." Pp. 3–49 in *A New Handbook of Political Science*, ed. Robert E. Goodin and Hans-Dieter Klingemann. New York: Oxford University Press.

Goodlad, Sinclair, and Stephanie McIvor. 1998. *Museum Volunteers: Good Practice in the Management of Volunteers*. London: Routledge.

Goodman, Mervyn. 1996. "The Jewish Community of Liverpool." *The Jewish Journal of Sociology* 38:89–104.

Golinowska, Stanislawa. 1994. "Development of the Third Sector in Social Sphere during Transition." *Polish Sociological Review* 4(108):359–372.

Gora, Jo Ann G., and Gloria M. Nemerowicz. 1985. *Emergency Squad Volunteers: Professionalism in Unpaid Work*. New York: Praeger.

Gora, Joel M., and Sally Master. 1991. *The Right to Protest: The Basic ACLU Guide to Free Expression*. Carbondale: Southern Illinois University.

Gordon, Avery, and Christopher Newfield. 1996. *Mapping Multiculturalism*. Minneapolis: University of Minnesota Press.

Gordon, C. W., and Nicholas Babchuk. 1959. "Typology of Voluntary Associations." *American Sociological Review* 24:22–29.

Gordon, Suzanne. 1976. *Lonely in America*. New York: Simon and Schuster.

Goreham, Gary A. 2004. "Denominational Comparison of Rural Youth Ministry Programs." *Review of Religious Research* 45:336–348.

Gosden, P. H. J. H. 1961. *The Friendly Societies in England, 1815–1875*. Manchester, UK: Manchester University Press.

Gougler, Richard C. 1972. "Amish Barn-Raising." *Pennsylvania Folklife* 21 (Folk Festival Supplement):14–18.

Gould, Lewis L. 2003. *Grand Old Party: A History of the Republicans*. New York: Random House.

Gould, Roger V. 1996. "Patron-Client Ties, State Centralization, and the Whiskey Rebellion." *American Journal of Sociology* 102:400–429.

Graff, Linda L. 1997. *By Definition: Policies for Volunteer Programs*. 2nd ed. Dundas, Canada: Graff & Associates.

Graubard, Allen. 1972. *Free the Children: Radical Reform and the Free School Movement.* New York: Pantheon Books.

Gray, B. Kirkman. 1905/1967. *A History of English Philanthropy.* New York: Augustus Kelley.

Greeley, Andrew. 1972. *The Denominational Society.* Glenview, Ill.: Scott, Foresman.

Green, Gary P., and Anna Haines. 2002. *Asset Building and Community Development.* Thousand Oaks, Calif.: Sage.

Greene, Jack P. 1984. *Encyclopedia of American Political History: Studies of Principal Movements and Ideas.* New York: Scribner.

Greenfield, James M., and Tracy D. Connors. 2001. *The Nonprofit Handbook: Fund-Raising,* 3rd ed. New York: Wiley.

Greenwald, Carol S. 1977. *Group Power.* New York: Praeger.

Griffiths, Curt T., and Simon N. Verdun-Jones. 1994. *Canadian Criminal Justice.* 2nd ed. Toronto: Harcourt Brace Canada.

Grobman, Gary M. 2004. *An Introduction to the Nonprofit Sector.* Harrisburg, Pa.: White Hat Communications.

———. 2005. *The Nonprofit Handbook.* Harrisburg, Pa.: White Hat Communications.

Grønbjerg, Kirsten A. 1993. *Understanding Nonprofit Funding: Managing Resources in Social Services and Community Development Organizing.* San Francisco: Jossey-Bass.

Gross, Charles. 1890. *The Guild Merchant.* 2 vol. Oxford: Claredon Press.

Gross, Edward, and Amitai Etzioni. 1985. *Organizations in Society.* Englewood Cliffs, N.J.: Prentice Hall.

Gross, Malvern J., Richard F. Larkin, and John H. McCarthy. 2000. *Financial and Accounting Guide for Not-for-Profit Organizations.* 6th ed. New York: Wiley.

Groves, Julian M. 2001. "Animal Rights and the Politics of Emotion: Folk Construction of Emotion in the Animal Rights Movement." Pp. 212–229 in *Passionate Politics: Emotions and Social Movements,* ed. James M. Jasper and Francesca Polleta. Chicago: University of Chicago Press.

Gummer, Burton. 1988. "The Hospice in Transition: Organizational and Administrative Perspectives." *Administration in Social Work* 12:31–43.

Gurr, Ted R. 1969. *Why Men Rebel.* Princeton, N.J.: Princeton University Press.

Gutman, Amy, ed. 1998. *Freedom of Association.* Princeton, N.J.: Princeton University Press.

Guttmann, Allen. 2000. "The Development of Modern Sports." Pp. 248–259 in *Handbook of Sport Studies,* ed. Jay Coakley and Eric Dunning. Thousand Oaks, Calif.: Sage.

Hackenberg, Kirk A. 2002. *A Peace Corps Profile.* Victoria, B.C.: Trafford.

Hadaway, C. Kirk, Stuart A. Wright, and Francis M. Dubose. 1987. *Home Cell Groups and House Churches.* Nashville, Tenn.: Broadman.

Hadden, Jeffrey K. 2000. "Religious Movements." Pp. 2364–2376 in *Encyclopedia of Sociology,* 2nd ed., vol. 4, ed. Edgar F. Borgatta and Rhonda J. V. Montgomery. New York: Macmillan Reference USA.

Haggard, Thomas R. 1977. *Compulsory Unionism, the NLRB, and the Courts.* Philadelphia: Industrial Research Unit, University of Pennsylvania.

Hall, David D. 1997. *Lived Religion in America: Toward a History of Practice.* Princeton, N.J.: Princeton University Press.

Hall, Peter D. 1992. *Inventing the Nonprofit Sector and Other Essays on Philanthropy, Volunteerism, and Nonprofit Organizations.* Baltimore: Johns Hopkins University Press.

———. 1994. "Historical Perspectives on Nonprofit Organizations." Pp. 3–43 in

The Jossey-Bass Handbook of Nonprofit Leadership and Management, ed. Robert D. Herman and Associates. San Francisco: Jossey-Bass.

———. 1997. *A History of Nonprofit Boards in the United States.* National Center for Nonprofit Boards Occasional Paper. Washington, D.C.: National Center for Nonprofit Boards.

Hall, Richard H. 1986. *Dimensions of Work.* Beverly Hills, Calif.: Sage.

———. 1996. *Organizations.* 6th ed. Englewood Cliffs, N.J.: Prentice Hall.

Hall, Richard H., and Pamela S. Tolbert. 2005. *Organizations: Structures, Processes, and Outcomes.* 9th ed. New York: Pearson Prentice Hall.

Halmos, Paul. 1970. *The Personal Service Society.* New York: Schocken Books.

Halperin, David A. 1983. *Psychodynamic Perspectives on Religion, Sect, and Cult.* Boston: J. Wright, PSG.

Halpern, Thomas, and Brian Levin. 1996. *The Limits of Dissent: The Constitutional Status of Armed Citizen Militias.* Amherst, Mass.: Alethia Press.

Hamilton, Neil A. 1997. *The ABC-CLIO Companion to the 1960s Counterculture in America.* Santa Barbara, Calif.: ABC-CLIO.

Hamm, Keith. 1986. "The Role of 'Subgovernments' in U.S. State Policy Making: An Exploratory Analysis." *Legislative Studies Quarterly* 11:321–351.

Hamm, Mark S. 1994. *American Skinheads.* Westport, Conn.: Praeger.

Hammack, David C., ed. 1998. *Making the Nonprofit Sector in the United States: A Reader.* Bloomington: Indiana University Press.

Hammack, David C., and Dennis R. Young. 1993a. "Introduction: Perspectives on Nonprofits in the Marketplace." Pp. 1–22 in *Nonprofit Organizations in a Market Economy: Understanding New Roles, Issues, and Trends,* ed. David C. Hammack and Dennis R. Young. San Francisco: Jossey-Bass.

———, eds. 1993b. *Nonprofit Organizations in a Market Economy: Understanding New Roles, Issues, and Trends.* San Francisco: Jossey-Bass.

Hammer, Tove H., and David L. Wazeter. 1993. "The Dimensions of Local Union Effectiveness." *Industrial and Labor Relations Review* 46:302–319.

Hammond, Philip E. 1998. *With Liberty for All: Freedom of Religion in the United States.* Louisville, Ky.: Westminster John Knox Press.

Handy, Robert T. 1966. "The Voluntary Principle in Religion and Religious Freedom." Pp. 129–139 in *Voluntary Associations: A Study of Groups in Free Society,* ed. D. B. Robertson. Richmond, Va.: John Knox Press.

Hankin, Jo Ann, Alan G. Seidner, and John T. Zietlow. 1998. *Financial Management for Nonprofit Organizations.* New York: Wiley.

Hann, Chris. 1996. *Civil Society: Challenging Western Models.* London: Routledge.

Hannan, Michael T., and John Freeman. 1977. "The Population Ecology of Organizations." *American Journal of Sociology* 82(5):929–964.

Hansmann, Henry. 1980. "The Role of Nonprofit Enterprise." *Yale Law Journal* 89: 835–901.

Hanson, Charles G. 1982. *The Closed Shop.* New York: St. Martin's Press.

Hanson, Chris. 1996. *The Cohousing Handbook: Building a Place for Community.* Point Roberts, Wash.: Hartley & Marks Publishers.

Harcourt, Alexander, and Frans B. Waal. 1992. *Coalitions and Alliances in Human and Other Animals.* Oxford, UK: Oxford University Press.

Hardin, Garrett. 1968. "The Tragedy of the Commons." *Science* 162:1243–1248.

Harman, John D., ed. 1982. *Volunteerism in the Eighties.* Washington, D.C.: University Press of America.

Harootyan, Robert A., and Robert E. Vorek. 1994. "Volunteering, Helping and Gift Giving in Families and Communities." *Intergenerational Linkages: Hidden Connections in American Society,* ed. Vern L. Bengston and Robert A. Harootyan. New York: Springer.

Harris, Margaret. 1998a. "Doing It Their Way: Organizational Challenges for Voluntary Associations." *Nonprofit and Voluntary Sector Quarterly* 27:144–158.

———. 1998b. *Organizing God's Work.* New York: St. Martin's Press.

Harris, Nigel. 1986. *The End of the Third World.* New York: Meredith Press.

Harrison, Paul M. 1960. "Weber's Categories of Authority and Voluntary Associations." *American Sociological Review* 25(2):231–237.

Harrison, Reginald J. 1980. *Pluralism and Corporatism: The Political Evolution of Modern Democracies.* Boston: Allen & Unwin.

Hartnagel, Timothy F. 2004. "Correlates of Criminal Behavior." Pp. 120–163 in *Criminology: A Canadian Perspective,* 5th ed., ed. Rick Linden. Toronto: Thompson/Nelson.

Hartson, Louis D. 1911. "A Study of Voluntary Associations, Educational and Social, in Europe during the Period from 1100 to 1700." *Journal of Genetic Psychology* 18:10–30.

Harvard Business Review. 1999. *Harvard Business Review on Nonprofits.* Boston: Harvard Business Review Publishing.

Hassard, John. 1994. "Postmodern Organizational Analysis: Toward a Conceptual Framework." *Journal of Management Studies* 31:303–325.

Hausknecht, Murray. 1962. *The Joiners: A Sociological Description of Voluntary Association Membership in the United States.* New York: Bedminster Press.

Hawdon, James. 1996. *Emerging Organizational Forms: The Proliferation of Regional Intergovernmental Organizations in the Modern World-System.* Westport, Conn.: Greenwood Press.

Hawes, Joseph M. 1991. *The Children's Rights Movement.* New York: Twayne.

Haworth, John T. 1984. "Leisure, Work, and Profession." *Leisure Studies* 3:319–334.

———, ed. 1997. *Work, Leisure, and Well-Being.* London: Routledge.

Haynes, Jeff. 1997. *Democracy and Civil Society in the Third World: Politics and New Social Movements.* Cambridge, UK: Polity Press.

Heckenberg, Kirk A. 2002. *A Peace Corps Profile.* Victoria, Canada: Trafford.

Hedstrom, Peter. 1994. "Contagious Collectivities: On the Spatial Diffusion of Swedish Trade Unions, 1890–1940." *American Journal of Sociology* 99:1157–1179.

Heilman, Samuel C. 1976. *Synagogue Life.* Chicago: University of Chicago Press.

Heinze, Rolf G., and Helmut Voelzkow. 1993. "Organizational Problems for the German Farmers' Association and Alternative Policy Options." *Sociologia Ruralis* 33:25–41.

Henderson, Charles R. 1895. "The Place and Functions of Voluntary Associations." *American Journal of Sociology* 1 (June):327–334.

Henderson, John. 1997. *Piety and Charity in Late Medieval Florence.* New York: Oxford University Press.

Henderson, Karla. 1984. "Volunteerism as Leisure." *Journal of Voluntary Action Research* 13(1):55–63.

Herbst, Jurgen. 1976. "The American Revolution and the American University." *Perspectives in American History* 10:279–354.

Herman, Melanie L. 2005. "Risk Management." Pp. 560–584 in *The Jossey-Bass Handbook of Nonprofit Leadership and Management,* 2nd ed., ed. Robert D. Herman and Associates. San Francisco: Jossey-Bass.

Herman, Robert D. 2005. "The Future of Nonprofit Management." Pp. 731–735 in *The Jossey-Bass Handbook of Nonprofit Leadership & Management,* 2nd ed., ed. Robert D. Herman and Associates. San Francisco: Jossey-Bass.

Herman, Robert D., and Associates, eds. 1994. *The Jossey-Bass Handbook of Nonprofit Leadership & Management.* San Francisco: Jossey-Bass.

———. 2005. *The Jossey-Bass Handbook of Nonprofit Leadership & Management.* 2nd ed. San Francisco: Jossey-Bass.

Herman, Robert D., and Richard Heimovics. 1991. *Executive Leadership in Nonprofit Organizations.* San Francisco: Jossey-Bass.

———. 1994. "Executive Leadership." Pp. 137–153 in *The Jossey-Bass Handbook of Nonprofit Leadership and Management,* ed. Robert D. Herman and Associates. San Francisco: Jossey-Bass.

Herring, Cedric, Michael Bennett, Doug Gills, and Noah T. Jenkins, eds. 1998. *Empowerment in Chicago: Grassroots Participation in Economic Development and Poverty Alleviation.* Chicago: University of Illinois at Chicago.

Herron, Douglas B. 1997. *Marketing Nonprofit Programs and Services.* San Francisco: Jossey-Bass.

Hersey, P., and K. H. Blanchard. 1969. "Life-Cycle Theory of Leadership." *Training and Development Journal* 23:26–34.

Heunks, Felix J. 1991. "Varieties of Activism in Three Western Democracies." *Nonprofit and Voluntary Sector Quarterly* 20:151–172.

Hewitt, W. E. 1986. "Strategies for Social Change Employed by *Communidades Eclesiais de Base* (CEBs) in the Archdiocese of Sao Paulo." *Journal for the Scientific Study of Religion* 25:16–32.

Heywood, Andrew. 2002. *Politics.* 2nd ed. New York: Palgrave.

Himmelstein, Jerome L. 1997. *Looking Good and Doing Good: Corporate Philanthropy and Corporate Power.* Bloomington: Indiana University Press.

Hing, Bill O. 1997. *To Be an American: Cultural Pluralism and the Rhetoric of Assimilation.* New York: New York University Press.

Hirschfelder, Arlene B., and Paulette F. Molin. 2000. *The Encyclopedia of Native American Religions.* New York: Facts on File.

Hirschman, Albert O. 1970. *Exit, Voice, and Loyalty: Responses to Decline in Firms, Organizations, and States.* Cambridge, Mass.: Harvard University Press.

Hobsbawm, E. J. 1965. *Primitive Rebels.* New York: Norton.

Hobson, Burton, and Robert Obojski. 1980. *Coin Collecting as a Hobby.* New York: Sterling.

Hodgkinson, Virginia A. 1990. "The Future of Individual Giving and Volunteering: The Inseparable Link between Religious and Individual Generosity." Chapter 14 in *Faith and Philanthropy in American: Exploring the Role of Religion in American's Voluntary Sector,* ed. Robert Wuthnow and Virginia A. Hodgkinson. San Francisco: Jossey-Bass.

Hodgkinson, Virginia A., and Richard W. Lyman, eds. 1989. *The Future of the Nonprofit Sector.* San Francisco: Jossey-Bass.

Hodgkinson, Virginia A., and Christopher Toppe 1991. "A New Research and Planning Tool for Managers: The National Taxonomy of Exempt Entities." *Nonprofit Management & Leadership* 1:403–414.

Hodgkinson, Virginia A., and Murray S. Weitzman. 1988. *Giving and Volunteering in the United States.* Washington, D.C.: INDEPENDENT SECTOR.

———. 1996. *Nonprofit Almanac, 1996–1997.* San Francisco: Jossey-Bass.

Hodgkinson, Virginia A., Murray S. Weitzman, Christopher Toppe, and Stephen M. Noga. 1992. *Nonprofit Almanac, 1992–1993.* San Francisco: Jossey-Bass.

Hohl, Karen L. 1996. "The Effects of Flexible Work Arrangements." *Nonprofit Management and Leadership* 7(1):69–86.

Hollenbach, Margaret. 2004. *Lost and Found: My Life in a Group Marriage Commune.* Albuquerque: University of New Mexico Press.

Holmes, Mary. 2004. "Feeling Beyond Rules: Politicizing the Sociology of Emotion and Danger in Feminist Politics." *European Journal of Social Theory* 7:209–227.

Holms, John P., with Tom Burke. 1994. *Terrorism*. New York: Pinnacle Books.

Hopkins, Bruce R. 1998. *The Law of Tax-Exempt Organizations*. 7th ed. New York: Wiley.

———. 2001. *Starting and Managing a Nonprofit Organization: A Legal Guide*. 3rd ed. New York: Wiley.

Horne, William R. 2003. "Time-Budget Methods." Pp. 502–503 in *Encyclopedia of Leisure and Outdoor Recreation*, ed. John M. Jenkins and John J. Pigram. London: Routledge.

Horowitz, Irving L. 1966. *Three Worlds of Development*. New York: Oxford University Press.

Horvath, Terri. 1995. *Spread the Word: How to Promote Nonprofit Groups with a Network of Speakers*. Indianapolis: Publishing Resources.

Houle, Cyril O. 1989. *Governing Boards*. San Francisco: Jossey-Bass.

Howard, Marc M. 2003. *The Weakness of Civil Society in Post-Communist Europe*. Cambridge, UK: Cambridge University Press.

Howe, Fisher. 1995. *Welcome to the Board*. San Francisco: Jossey-Bass.

Howell, Jude. 2002. "In Their Own Image: Donor Assistance Civil Society." *Lusotopie* 9(1):117–130.

Hrebenar, Ronald J. 1997. *Interest Group Politics in America*. 3rd ed. Armonk, N.Y.: M. E. Sharpe.

Hubert, Henri, and Marcel Mauss. 1964. *Sacrifice*. Chicago: University of Chicago Press.

Hudock, Ann C. 1999. *NGOs and Civil Society: Democracy by Proxy?* Cambridge, UK: Polity Press.

Huizenga, Johan. 1955. *Homo Ludens*. Boston: Beacon Press.

Hula, Kevin W. 1999. *Lobbying Together: Interest Group Coalitions in Legislative Politics*. Washington, D.C.: Georgetown University Press.

Hula, Richard C., and Cynthia Jackson-Elmore, eds. 2000. *Nonprofits in Urban America*. Westport, Conn.: Quorum Books.

Hummel, Joan M. 1996. *Starting and Running a Nonprofit Organization*. Minneapolis: University of Minnesota Press.

Humphreys, Keith. 1998. "Can Addiction-Related Self-Help/Mutual Aid Groups Lower Demand for Professional Substance Abuse Treatment?" *Social Policy* 29 (Winter):13–17.

Humphreys, Keith, ed. 2004. *Circles of Recovery: Self Help Organizations for Addictions*. New York: Cambridge University Press.

Humphreys, Laud. 1970. *Tearoom Trade: Impersonal Sex in Public Places*. Chicago: Aldine.

Hunt, Geoff P., and S. Satterlee. 1986. "The Pub, the Village and the People." *Human Organization* 45:62–74.

Hunter, Floyd. 1953. *Community Power Structure: A Study of Decision Makers*. New York: Doubleday.

Hunter, James D. 1997. "Partisanship and the Abortion Controversy." *Society* 34(5): 30–31.

Hunter, K. I., and Margaret W. Linn. 1980–1981. "Psychosocial Differences between Elderly Volunteers and Non-Volunteers." *International Journal of Aging and Human Development* 12(3):205–213.

Hutcheson, John D., Jr., and Frank X. Steggart. 1979. *Organized Citizen Participation in Urban Areas*. Atlanta: Center for Research on Social Change, Emory University.

Hutchison, William R. 2003. *Religious Pluralism in America: The Contentious History of a Founding Ideal*. New Haven, Conn.: Yale University Press.

Huttman, Elizabeth D. 1985. *Social Services for the Elderly*. New York: Free Press.

Bibliography

Hybels, Bill. 2004. *The Volunteer Revolution: Unleashing the Power of Everybody.* Grand Rapids, Mich.: Zondervan.

Hyde, Cheryl A. 2000. "The Hybrid Nonprofit: An Examination of Feminist Social Movement Organizations." *Journal of Community Practice* 8(4):45–67.

Iannello, Kathleen P. 1992. *Decisions without Hierarchy: Feminist Interventions in Organization Theory and Practice.* New York: Routledge.

Ilsley, Paul J. 1990. *Enhancing the Volunteer Experience: New Insights on Strengthening Volunteer Participation, Learning, and Commitment.* San Francisco: Jossey-Bass.

INDEPENDENT SECTOR. 1991. *Ethics and the Nation's Voluntary and Philanthropic Community.* Washington, D.C.: INDEPENDENT SECTOR.

———. 1996. *Giving and Volunteering in the United States: Findings from a National Survey 1996 Edition.* Washington, D.C.: INDEPENDENT SECTOR.

INDEPENDENT SECTOR and Urban Institute. 2002. *The New Nonprofit Almanac and Desk Reference.* San Francisco: Jossey-Bass.

Ingersoll-Dayton, Berit, Margaret B. Neal, Jung-hwa Ha, and Leslie B. Hammer. 2003. "Collaboration among Siblings Providing Care for Older Parents." *Journal of Gerontological Social Work* 40:51–66.

Iriye, Akira. 2002. *Global Community: The Role of International Organizations in the Making of the Contemporary World.* Berkeley: University of California Press.

Irons, Peter H. 2005. *Cases and Controversies: Civil Rights and Liberties in Context.* Upper Saddle River, N.J.: Pearson Prentice Hall.

Isaacs, Stephen L., and James R. Knickman, eds. 1997. *To Improve Health and Health Care: The Robert Wood Johnson Foundation.* San Francisco: Jossey-Bass.

Israel, Barbara A. 1988. "Community-Based Social Network Interventions: Meeting the Needs of the Elderly." *Danish Medical Bulletin: Journal of the Health Sciences* Gerontology Special Supplement Series (6):36–44.

Jackson, Edgar L., and Thomas L. Burton, eds. 1999. *Leisure Studies: Prospects for the Twenty-First Century.* State College, Pa.: Venture.

Jackson, M. J. 1974. *The Sociology of Religion.* London: Batsford.

Jacobs, Janet. 1987. "Deconversion from Religious Movements." *Journal for the Scientific Study of Religion* 26(3):294–308.

Jacobs, Jerald A. 2002. *Associations and the Law.* Washington, D.C.: American Society of Association Executives.

Jacoby, Barbara. 2003. *Building Partnerships for Service Learning.* San Francisco: Jossey-Bass.

Jacoby, Barbara, and Associates. 1996. *Service-Learning in Higher Education.* San Francisco: Jossey-Bass.

James, Estelle. 2003. "Commercialism and the Mission of Nonprofits." *Society* 40(4): 29–35.

James, William. 1902/1958. *The Varieties of Religious Experience.* New York: Mentor.

Janoski, Thomas, March Musick, and John Wilson. 1998. "Being Volunteered? The Impact of Social Participation and Pro-Social Attitudes on Volunteering." *Sociological Forum* 13:495–519.

Janvier, Louis G. 1984. *Jesse Jackson for President Leading America's Rainbow Coalition.* Brooklyn, N.Y.: L. G. Janvier.

Jas, Pauline. 2000. *A Gift Relationship? Charitable Giving in Theory and Practice.* London: National Council of Voluntary Organizations.

Jeannotte, M. Sharon. 2003. "Singing Alone? The Contribution of Cultural Capital to Social Cohesion and Sustainable Communities." *International Journal of Cultural Policy* 9(1):35–49.

Jeavons, Thomas H. 1994a. "Ethics in Nonprofit Management: Creating a Culture of Integrity." Pp. 184–207 in *The Jossey-Bass Handbook of Nonprofit Leadership and Management,* ed. Robert D. Herman and Associates. San Francisco: Jossey-Bass.

———. 1994b. *When the Bottom Line Is Faithfulness: Management of Christian Service Organizations.* Bloomington: Indiana University Press.

———. 2005. "Ethical Nonprofit Management." Pp. 204–229 in *The Jossey-Bass Handbook of Nonprofit Leadership and Management,* ed. Robert D. Herman and Associates. San Francisco: Jossey-Bass.

Jeavons, Thomas H., and Ram A. Cnaan. 1997. "The Formation, Transitions, and Evolution of Small Religious Organizations." *Nonprofit and Voluntary Sector Quarterly* 26 (Supplemental):S62–S84.

Jedlicka, Allen D. 1990. *Volunteerism and World Development.* New York: Praeger.

Jenkins, J. Craig, and Bert Klandermans, eds. 1995. *The Politics of Social Protest.* Minneapolis: University of Minnesota Press.

Jensen, Dawn E. 2001. "Social Environment of Community Treatment Facilities: An Examination of Perception." *Dissertation Abstracts International, A: The Humanities and Social Sciences* 62(6):2244A.

Jinkins, Michael, and Deborah B. Jinkins. 1998. *The Character of Leadership: Political Realism and Public Virtue in Nonprofit Organizations.* San Francisco: Jossey-Bass.

Johnson, Benton. 1963. "On Church and Sect." *American Sociological Review* 28:539–549.

Johnston, Barbara Rose. 2003. "The Political Ecology of Water: An Introduction." *Capitalism, Nature, Socialism* 14(3):73–90.

Johnston, Hank, Enrique Laraña, and Joseph R. Gusfield. 1994. "Identities, Grievances, and New Social Movements." Pp. 3–35 in *New Social Movements: From Ideology to Identity,* ed. Enrique Laraña, Hank Johnston, and Joseph R. Gusfield. Philadelphia: Temple University Press.

Johnston, Michael. 1999. *The Fund Raiser's Guide to the Internet.* New York: Wiley.

Johnstone, Ronald L. 1992. *Religion in Society: A Sociology of Religion.* 4th ed. Englewood Cliffs, N.J.: Prentice Hall.

Joireman, Jeffrey A., D. Michael Kuhlman, Paul A. M. Van Lange, Toshiaki Doi, and Gregory P. Shelly. 2003. "Perceived Rationality, Morality, and Power of Social Choice as a Function of Interdependence Structure and Social Value Orientation." *European Journal of Social Psychology* 33:413–437.

Jones, Jerry. 1982. "Community Development in Senegal: Contradictions within Prevailing Social Structure." *Community Development Journal* 17:13–26.

Jones, Nicholas F. 1999. *The Associations of Classical Athens.* New York: Oxford University Press.

Jones-Johnson, Gloria, and W. Roy Johnson. 1992. "Subjective Underemployment and Psychosocial Stress: The Role of Perceived Social and Supervisor Support." *Journal of Social Psychology* 132:11–21.

Jordan, Grant. 1990. "The Pluralism of Pluralism: An Anti-Theory?" *Political Studies* 38:286–301.

———. 1993. "Pluralism." Pp. 49–68 in *Pressure Groups,* ed. Jeremy J. Richardson. New York: Oxford University Press.

Jordan, Grant, and William A. Maloney. 1996. "How Bumble-Bees Fly: Accounting for Public-Interest Participation." *Political Studies* 44(4):668–685.

Jordan, Robert S., and Warner J. Feld. 2001. *International Organizations.* 4th ed. Westport, Conn.: Praeger.

Jordan, W. K. 1959. *Philanthropy in England, 1480–1660.* London: Allen & Unwin.

Josephy, Alvin M., Jr. 1970. *Red Power: The American Indians' Fight for Freedom.* New York: McGraw-Hill.

Bibliography

Juran, J. M., and Frank M. Gryna. 1974. *Quality Control Handbook.* New York: Mc-Graw-Hill.

Kahera, Akel Ismail. 2002. "Urban Enclaves: Muslim Identity and the Urban Mosque in America." *Journal of Muslim Minority Affairs* 22(2):369–380.

Kahn, Richard, and Douglas Kellner. 2004. "New Media and Internet Activism: From the 'Battle of Seattle' to Blogging." *New Media and Society* 6(1):87–95.

Kahn, Si. 1982. *Organizing: A Guide for Grassroots Leaders.* New York: McGraw-Hill.

Kaldor, Mary. 2003. *Global Civil Society.* Cambridge, UK: Polity Press.

Kamen, Henry. 1998. *The Spanish Inquisition.* New Haven, Conn.: Yale University Press.

Kamerman, Sheila B., and Alfred J. Kahn. 1976. *Social Services in the United States.* Philadelphia: Temple University Press.

Kanter, Rosabeth M. 1972. *Commitment and Community: Communes and Utopias in Sociological Perspective.* Cambridge, Mass.: Harvard University Press.

Kanter, Rosabeth M., and Louis A. Zurcher, Jr. 1973. "Editorial Introduction." *Journal of Applied Behavioral Science* 9:137–143.

Kaplan, David E., and Andrew Marshall. 1996. *The Cult at the End of the World.* New York: Crown Publishers.

Kaplan, Matt. 1993. "Recruiting Senior Adult Volunteers for Intergenerational Programs: Working to Create a 'Jump on the Bandwagon' Effect." *Journal of Applied Gerontology* 12(1):71–82.

Kaplan, Matthew. 1986. "Cooperation and Coalition Development among Neighborhood Organizations: A Case Study." *Journal of Voluntary Action Research* 15:23–34.

Kaplan, Max. 1960. *Leisure in America.* New York: Wiley.

Kariel, Henry. 1981. *The Decline of American Pluralism.* Stanford, Calif.: Stanford University Press.

Karl, Jonathan. 1995. *The Right to Bear Arms: The Rise of America's New Militias.* New York: HarperCollins.

Karp, David A. 1992. "Illness Ambiguity and the Search for Meaning: A Case Study of a Self-Help Group for Affective Disorders." *Journal of Contemporary Ethnography* 21:139–170.

Kaseman, Dianne F. 1995. "Nonsystematic Happenings in Urban Health." Paper presented at the Annual Meeting of the Society for the Study of Social Problems, August.

Kasperson, Roger E., and Myna Breitbart. 1974. "Participating in Public Affairs: Theories and Issues." Pp. 1–16 in *Participation, Decentralization and Advocacy Planning.* Washington, D.C.: Association of American Geographers.

Kastner, Michael E. 1998. *Creating and Managing an Association Government Relations Program.* Washington, D.C.: American Society of Association Executives.

Katz, Alfred H. et al., eds. 1992. *Self-Help: Concepts and Applications.* Philadelphia: Charles Press.

———. 1993. *Self-Help in America: A Social Movement Perspective.* New York: Twayne.

Katz, Alfred H., and Eugene I. Bender. 1976. *The Strength in Us: Self-Help Groups in the Modern World.* New York: New Viewpoints/Franklin Watts.

———. 1990. *Helping One Another: Self-Help Groups in a Changing World.* Oakland, Calif.: Third Party Publishing Co.

Katz, Friedrich, ed. 1988. *Riot, Rebellion, and Revolution: Rural Social Conflict in Mexico.* Princeton, N.J.: Princeton University Press.

Kaufman, Jason. 1999. "Three Views of Associationalism in 19th Century America: An Empirical Examination." *The American Journal of Sociology* 104 (5 March):1296–1345.

Kaufman, Jason A. 2002. *For the Common Good? American Civic Life in the Golden Age of Fraternity.* New York: Oxford University Press.

Kaye, Lenard W. 1997. *Self-Help Support Groups for Older Women.* Washington, D.C.: Taylor & Francis.

Keane, John. 2003. *Global Civil Society?* New York: Cambridge University Press.

Keating, Barry P., and Maryanne O. Keating. 1980. *Not-for-Profit.* Glen Ridge, N.J.: Horton Publishing.

Keeler, John T. S. 1987. *The Politics of Neocorporatism in France.* New York: Oxford University Press.

Keeny, Sam M. 1973. "Voluntary Agencies in Transition." *Journal of Voluntary Action Research* 2(1):16–23.

Kelly, John R. 1983. *Leisure Identities and Interactions.* London: Allen & Unwin.

———. 1987. *Freedom to Be: A New Sociology of Leisure.* New York: Macmillan.

———. 1996. *Leisure.* 3rd ed. Boston: Allyn and Bacon.

Kelso, William A. 1978. *American Democratic Theory: Pluralism and Its Critics.* Westport, Conn.: Greenwood Press.

Kendall, Jeremy, Martin Kendall, and Martin Knapp. 1996. *The Voluntary Sector in the United Kingdom.* New York: Manchester University Press.

Kenedy, Robert A. 2004. *Fathers for Justice: The Rise of a New Social Movement in Canada as a Case Study of Collective Identity Formation.* Ann Arbor, Mich.: Caravan Books.

Kenney, Sally J. 2003. "Where Is Gender in Agenda Setting?" *Women & Politics* 25(1–2):179–207.

Keniston, Kenneth. 1971. *Youth and Dissent.* New York: Harcourt Brace Jovanovich.

Kephart, William M., and William W. Zellner. 1994. *Extraordinary Groups.* 5th ed. New York: St. Martin's Press.

Kerber, Linda K. 1997. "The Meanings of Citizenship." *Dissent* 44(4):33–37.

Kerr, Clark. 1967. *The University in America.* Santa Barbara, Calif.: Center for the Study of Democratic Institutions.

Kettle, Martin, and Lucy Hodges. 1982. *Uprising! The Police, the People and the Riots in Britain's Cities.* London: Pan Books.

Kiefer, Charles H. 1984. "Citizen Empowerment: A Developmental Perspective." *Prevention in Human Services* 3:9–36.

Kiger, Joseph C. 2000. *Philanthropic Foundations in the Twentieth Century.* Westport, Conn.: Greenwood Press.

Kilbane, Sally C. and John H. Beck. 1990. "Professional Associations and the Free Rider Problem: the Case of Optometry." *Public Choices* 25 (May):181–187.

Kilpatrick, Joseph, and Sanford Danziger. 1996. *Better than Money Can Buy: The New Volunteers.* Winston-Salem, N.C.: Innersearch Publications.

Kim, Hugh K. 1990. "Blacks Against Korean Merchants: An Interpretation of Contributory Factors." *Migration World Magazine* 18(5):11–15.

Kimmel, Michael S. 1990. *Revolution: A Sociological Interpretation.* Philadelphia: Temple University Press.

King, David C. 1997. *Freedom of Assembly.* Brookfield, Conn.: Millbrook Press.

King, David C., and Jack L. Walker. 1992. "The Provision of Benefits by Interest Groups in the United States." *Journal of Politics* 54:394–426.

King, Faye L. 2001. "Social Dynamics of Quilting." *World Leisure Journal* 43:26–29.

King, Richard M. 2000. *From Making a Profit to Making a Difference: How to*

Launch Your New Career in Nonprofits. River Forest, Ill.: Planning/Communications.

King, Samantha. 2001. "An All-Consuming Cause: Breast Cancer, Corporate Philanthropy, and the Market for Generosity." *Social Text* 19(4):115–143.

Kipps, Harriet C. 1997. *Volunteer America: A Comprehensive National Guide to Opportunities for Service, Training, & Work Experience*. Chicago: Ferguson Publishing Co.

Kirsch, Arthur D., Keith M. Hume, and Nadine T. Jalandoni. 1999. *Giving and Volunteering in the United States. 1999 Edition*. Washington, D.C.: INDEPENDENT SECTOR.

Kitagawa, Joseph M., ed. 1989. *The Religious Traditions of Asia*. New York: Macmillan.

Kleiber, Douglas A. 2000. "The Neglect of Relaxation." *Journal of Leisure Research* 32:82–86.

Klein, Kim. 1988. *Fundraising for Social Change*. 2nd ed. Inverness, Calif.: Chardon Press.

Klineberg, Stephen L. 1998. "Environmental Attitudes among Anglos, Blacks, and Hispanics in Texas: Has the Concern Gap Disappeared?" *Race, Gender & Class* 6:70–82.

Klonglan, Gerald E., and Benjamin Yep. 1972. *Theory and Practice of Interorganizational Relations*. Ames: Iowa State University Press.

Klonglan, Gerald E., Benjamin Yep, Charles L. Mulford, and Donald Dillman. 1973. "The Nature and Impact of Interorganizational Relations." Pp. 331–367 in *Voluntary Action Research 1973*, ed. David H. Smith. Lexington, Mass.: Lexington Books.

Kloppenborg, John S., and Stephen G. Wilson, eds. 1996. *Voluntary Associations in the Graeco-Roman World*. London: Routledge.

Kluger, Miriam P., William A. Baker, and Howard S. Garval. 1998. *Strategic Business Planning: Securing a Future for the Nonprofit Organization*. Washington, D.C.: CWLA Press.

Knauft, E. B., Renee A. Berger, and Sandra T. Gray. 1991. *Profiles of Excellence: Achieving Success in the Nonprofit Sector*. San Francisco: Jossey-Bass.

Knobel, Dale T. 1996. *America for the Americans: The Nativist Movement in the United States*. New York: Twayne.

Knoke, David. 1988. "Incentive in Collective Action Organizations." *American Sociological Review* 53:311–329.

———. 1993. "Trade Associations in the American Political Economy." Pp. 138–174 in *Nonprofit Organizations in a Market Economy*, ed. David C. Hammack and Dennis R. Young. San Francisco: Jossey-Bass.

Koerin, Beverly. 2003. "The Settlement House Tradition: Current Trends and Future Concerns." *Journal of Sociology and Social Welfare* 30:53–68.

Kohlmeier, Louis M. 1969. *The Regulators: Watchdog Agencies and the Public Interest*. New York: Harper & Row.

Kohn, Alfie. 1990. *The Brighter Side of Human Nature: Altruism and Empathy in Everyday Life*. New York: Basic Books.

Kolaric, Zinka, Andreja Meglic-Crnak, and Ivan Svetlik. 1995. "Slovenia." *Druzboslovne Razprave* 11(19–20):77–94.

Kornhauser, William. 1959. *The Politics of Mass Society*. Glencoe, Ill.: Free Press.

Korstad, Robert A., and James L. Leloudis. 1999. "Citizen Soldiers: The North Carolina Volunteers and the War on Poverty." *Law and Contemporary Problems* 62 (Autumn):177–187.

Korten, David C. 1990. *Getting to the 21st Century: Voluntary Action and the Global Agenda*. West Hartford, Conn.: Kumarian Press.

Koteen, Jack. 1997. *Strategic Management in Public and Nonprofit Organizations.* 2nd ed. Westport, Conn.: Praeger.

Kothari, Sanjay. 1995. "Role of Voluntary Agencies in India's Development." *Man and Development* 17:36–86.

Kottler, Jeffrey A. 2000. *Doing Good: Passion and Commitment for Helping Others.* Philadelphia: Brunner-Routledge.

Kouri, Mary K. 1990. *Voluntarism and Older Adults.* Santa Barbara, Calif.: ABC-CLIO.

Kramer, Ralph M., Hakon Lorentzen, Willem Melief, and Sergio Pasquinelli. 1993. *Privatization in Four European Countries.* Armonk, N.Y.: M. E. Sharpe.

Krause, Elliott A. 1996. *Death of the Guilds: Professions, States, and the Advance of Capitalism, 1930 to the Present.* New Haven, Conn.: Yale University Press.

Kraybill, Donald B., and Carl F. Bowman. 2001. *On the Back Road to Heaven: Old Order Hutterites, Mennonites, Amish, and Brethren.* Baltimore: Johns Hopkins University.

Kriesi, Hanspeter, and Ruud Koopmans. 1995. *New Social Movements in Western Europe.* Minneapolis: University of Minnesota Press.

Kropotkin, Petr. 1914. *Mutual Aid: A Factor in Evolution.* Boston: Porter Sargent.

Kubey, Robert W. and Mihalyi Csikszentmihalyi. 1990. *Television and Quality of Life.* Hillsdale, N.J.: Lawrence Erlbaum.

Kuhn, Thomas S. 1962. *The Structure of Scientific Revolutions.* Chicago: University of Chicago Press.

Kukathas, Chandran. 2003. *The Liberal Archipelago: A Theory of Diversity and Freedom.* New York: Oxford University Press.

Küng, Hans. 1969. *The Future of Ecumenism.* New York: Paulist Press.

Kurtz, Ernest. 2002. "Alcoholics Anonymous and the Disease Concept of Alcoholism." *Alcoholism Treatment Quarterly* 20:5–40.

Kurtz, Linda F. 1997. *Self-Help and Support Groups.* Thousand Oaks, Calif.: Sage.

Kuti, Eva. 1996. *The Nonprofit Sector in Hungary.* New York: Manchester University Press.

Kutner, Luis. 1970. "Due Process of Human Transplants: A Proposal." *University of Miami Law Review* 24(4):782–807.

Kwok, Joseph K. F., Raymond K. H. Chan, and W. T. Chan. 2002. *Self-Help Organizations of People with Disabilities in Asia.* Westport, Conn.: Auburn House.

Kymlicka, Will. 1995. *The Rights of Minority Cultures.* New York: Oxford University Press.

Laband, David N., and Richard O. Beil. 1998. "The American Sociological Association Dues Structure." *American Sociologist* 29 (Spring):102–106.

Ladd, Everett C. 1999. *The Ladd Report.* New York: Free Press.

Lagemann, Ellen C. 1999. *Philanthropic Foundations.* Bloomington: Indiana University Press.

Lakoff, Sanford A. 1973. *Private Government.* Glenview, Ill.: Scott, Foresman.

Lambert, Bernard. 1967. *Ecumenism: Theology and History.* New York: Herder & Herder.

Lambert, Malcolm. 1992. *Medieval Heresy: Popular Movements from the Gregorian Reform to the Reformation.* 2nd ed. Oxford, UK: Blackwell.

Lamont, Corliss. 1957. *The Philosophy of Humanism.* New York: Wisdom Library.

Lancourt, Joan E. 1979. *Confront or Concede: The Alinsky Citizen Action Organizations.* Lexington, Mass.: D. C. Heath.

Landim, Leilah. 1993. *Defining the Nonprofit Sector: Brazil.* Baltimore: Johns Hopkins Institute for Policy Studies.

Lane, John H., Jr. 1976. *Voluntary Associations among Mexican Americans in San Antonio, Texas.* New York: Arno Press.

Bibliography

Lappé, Francis M., and Paul M. DuBois. 1994. *The Quickening of America: Rebuilding Our Nation, Remaking Our Lives.* San Francisco: Jossey-Bass.

Laqueur, Walter. 1977. *Terrorism.* Boston: Little, Brown.

Laraña, Enrique, Hank Johnston, and Joseph R. Gusfield, eds. 1994. *New Social Movements: From Ideology to Identity.* Philadelphia: Temple University Press.

Lasswell, Harold D. 1936. *Politics: Who Gets What, When, How.* New York: McGraw-Hill.

———. 1951. *Democratic Character.* Glencoe, Ill.: Free Press.

Lauffer, Armand. 1997. *Grants, Etc.* Thousand Oaks, Calif.: Sage.

Lauffer, Armand, and Sarah Gorodezky. 1977. *Volunteers.* Newbury Park, Calif.: Sage.

Laumann, Edward O., and David Knoke. 1987. *The Organizational State: Social Choice in National Policy Domains.* Madison: University of Wisconsin Press.

Lavigne, Yves. 1993. *Hell's Angels.* New York: Carol.

Laville, Helen. 2003. "The Memorial Day Statement: Women's Organizations in the 'Peace Offensive.'" *Intelligence and National Security* 18(2):192–210.

Lavoie, Francine, Thomasina Borkman, and Benjamin Gidron. 1994. *Self-Help and Mutual Aid Groups.* New York: Haworth.

Lawler, Edward E. 1973. *Motivation in Work Organizations.* San Francisco: Jossey-Bass.

Lawrence, Paul, and Jay Lorsch. 1967. *Organization and Environment.* Cambridge, Mass.: Harvard University, Graduate School of Business Administration.

Lawson, R. 1983. "Origins and Evolution of a Social Movement Strategy: The Rent Strike in New York City, 1904–1980." *Urban Affairs Quarterly* 18:371–395.

Layton, Daphne N. 1987. *Philanthropy and Voluntarism: An Annotated Bibliography.* New York: Foundation Center.

Le Bon, Gustave. 1895/1960. *The Crowd.* New York: Viking Press.

Lee, Jarene F., Julia M Catagnus, and Susan J. Ellis. 1999. *What We Learned (the Hard Way) about Supervising Volunteers.* Philadelphia: Energize.

Lee, Raymond L. 2002. "Globalization and Mass Society Theory." *International Review of Sociology* 12(1):45–60.

Lehman, Edward W., ed. 2000. *Autonomy and Order: A Communitarian Anthology.* Lanham, Md.: Rowman & Littlefield.

Lemon, B. W., V. L. Bengston, and J. A. Peterson. 1972. "An Exploration of the Activity Theory of Aging: Activity Types and Life Satisfaction among Inmovers to a Retirement Community." *Journal of Gerontology* 275:11–23.

Lenkowsky, Leslie. 2002. "Foundations and Corporate Philanthropy." Pp. 355–386 in *The State of Nonprofit America,* ed. Lester M. Salamon. Washington, D.C.: Brookings Institution Press.

Leone, Richard C. 2003. *The War on Our Freedoms: Civil Liberties in an Age of Terrorism.* New York: BBS PublicAffairs.

Lester, Lori, and Robert Schneider. 2001. *Social Work Advocacy: A New Framework for Action.* Belmont Calif.: Brooks-Cole.

Leung, Patrick. 1996. "Is the Court-Appointed Special Advocate Program Effective? A Longitudinal Analysis of Time Involvement and Case Outcomes." *Child Welfare* 75:269–284.

Levitt, Theodore. 1973. *The Third Sector.* New York: AMACOM.

Levy, Barbara R., and R.L. Cherry. 1996. *The NSFRE* [National Society of Fund Raising Executives] *Fund-Raising Dictionary.* New York: Wiley.

Lewis, David. 1999. *International Perspectives on Voluntary Action: Reshaping the Third Sector.* London: Earthscan.

Lichterman, Paul. 1996. *The Search for Political Community: American Activists Reinventing Commitment.* New York: Cambridge University Press.

Liebman, Charles S., and Eliezer Don-Yehiya. 1983. *Civil Religion in Israel: Traditional Judaism and Political Culture in the Jewish State.* Berkeley: University of California Press.

Light, Paul C. 1998. *Sustaining Innovation: Creating Nonprofit and Government Organizations That Innovate Naturally.* San Francisco: Jossey-Bass.

———. 2000. *Making Nonprofits Work.* Washington, D.C.: Brookings Institution Press.

Lincoln, C. Eric, and Lawrence H. Mamiya. 1990. *The Black Church in the African American Experience.* Durham, N.C.: Duke University Press.

Linden, Russell M. 2002. *Working across Boundaries: Making Collaboration Work in Government and Nonprofit Organizations.* San Francisco: Jossey-Bass.

Linsk, Nathan L., Sharon Keigher, Lori Simon-Rusinowitz, and Suzanne England. 1992. *Wages for Caring: Compensating Family Care of the Elderly.* New York: Praeger.

Lippy, Charles H. 2000. *Pluralism Comes of Age: American Religious Cultures in the Twentieth Century.* Chapel Hill: University of North Carolina Press.

Lipset, Seymour M., Martin Trow, and James Coleman. 1977. *Union Democracy.* New York: Free Press.

Lissner, Jørgen. 1977. *The Politics of Altruism: A Study of the Political Behaviour of Voluntary Development Agencies.* Geneva, Switzerland: Lutheran World Federation.

Lister, Gwyneth. 2001. *Building Your Direct Mail Program.* San Francisco: Jossey-Bass.

Littell, Franklin H. 1962. *From State Church to Pluralism.* Garden City, N.J.: Anchor Books.

Little, Helen. 1999. *Volunteers: How to Get Them, How to Keep Them.* Naperville, Ill.: Panacea Press.

Little, Kenneth L. 1965. *West African Urbanization: A Study of Voluntary Associations.* Cambridge, UK: Cambridge University Press.

Little, Margaret. 1995. "The Blurring of Boundaries: Private and Public Welfare for Single Mothers in Ontario." *Studies in Political Economy* 47 (Summer):89–109.

Liu, Amy Q., and Terry Besser. 2003. "Social Capital and Participation in Community Involvement Activities by Elderly Residents in Small Towns and Rural Communities." *Rural Sociology* 68:343–365.

Livingstone, Elizabeth A., and F. L. Cross. 1997. *The Oxford Dictionary of the Christian Church.* 3rd ed. New York: Oxford University Press.

Livojevic, Michele, and Cornelius, Debra. 1998. "'Out of the Loop': The Dynamics of Citizen Activism in the Policy Process." *Humanity and Society* 22(2):207–215.

Lofland, John F. 1990. "Collective Behavior: The Elementary Forms." Pp. 411–446 in *Social Psychology: Sociological Perspectives,* ed. Morris Rosenberg and Ralph H. Turner. New Brunswick, N.J.: Transaction Publishers.

———. 1996. *Social Movement Organizations.* New York: Aldine de Gruyter.

Lofland, John, and Michael Jamison. 1984. "Social Movement Locals: Model Member Structures." *Social Analysis* 45:115–129.

Lohmann, Roger A. 1992. *The Commons: New Perspectives on Nonprofit Organizations and Voluntary Action.* San Francisco: Jossey-Bass.

———. 2001. "A New Approach: The Theory of the Commons." Chapter 14 in *The Nature of the Nonprofit Sector,* ed. J. S. Ott. Boulder, Colo.: Westview Press.

Lomnitz, Claudio. 2003. "Times of Crisis: Historicity, Sacrifice, and the Spectacle of Debacle in Mexico City." *Public Culture* 15(1):127–147.

Bibliography

London, Nancy R. 1991. *Japanese Corporate Philanthropy.* New York: Oxford University Press.

Loomis, Frank. D. 1962. *The Chicago Community Trust: A History of Its Development, 1915–1962.* Chicago: Chicago Community Trust.

Lopez, Donald S., Jr. 2001. *The Story of Buddhism: A Concise Guide to Its History and Teachings.* New York: HarperCollins.

Losch, Richard R. 2001. *The Many Faces of Faith: A Guide to World Religions and Christian Traditions.* Grand Rapids, Mich.: Eerdmans.

Lowe, James W. 1990. "Examination of Governmental Decentralization in New York City and a New Model for Implementation." *Harvard Journal on Legislation* 27:175–227.

Lowell, Stephanie. 2000. *The Harvard Business School Guide to Careers in the Nonprofit Sector.* Boston: Harvard Business School.

Lowery, David, and Holly Brasher. 2004. *Organizational Interests and American Government.* New York: McGraw-Hill.

Lowie, Robert H. 1948. *Social Organization.* New York: Rinehart.

Loya, Thomas A. 1998. "Global Democracy Movements: The Structure and Organization of the International Prodemocracy Social Movement Sector." Paper presented at the Annual Meeting of the American Sociological Association, August, Chicago.

Luke, Jeffrey S. 1998. *Catalytic Leadership.* San Francisco: Jossey-Bass.

Lummis, Adair T. 2004. "A Research Note: Real Men and Church Participation." *Review of Religious Research* 45:404–414.

Lundström, Tommy, and Filip Wijkström, eds. 1997. *The Nonprofit Sector in Sweden.* New York: Manchester University Press.

Luxton, Peter. 2001. *The Law of Charities.* New York: Oxford University Press.

Lynch, James J. 1977. *The Broken Heart: The Medical Consequences of Loneliness.* New York: Basic Books.

Lynch, Richard. 1993. *Lead! How Public and Nonprofit Managers Can Bring Out the Best in Themselves and Their Organizations.* San Francisco: Jossey-Bass.

Lynd, Robert S., and Helen M. Lynd. 1929. *Middletown.* New York: Harcourt Brace.

Lynn, Barry W., Marc D. Stern, and Oliver S. Thomas. 1995. *The Right to Religious Liberty.* Carbondale: Southern Illinois University Press.

Lyons, Mark. 2001. *Third Sector: The Contribution of Nonprofit and Cooperative Enterprises in Australia.* St. Leonards, Australia: Allen & Unwin.

Macaulay, David. 2003. *Mosque.* Boston: Houghton Mifflin.

Macduff, Nancy L. 1991. *Episodic Volunteering: Building the Short-Term Volunteer Program.* Walla Walla, Wash.: MBA Publications.

———. 1994. "Principles of Training for Volunteers and Employees." Pp. 591–615 in *The Jossey-Bass Handbook of Nonprofit Leadership and Management,* ed. Robert D. Herman and Associates. San Francisco: Jossey-Bass.

———. 1995. "Episodic Volunteering." Pp. 206–221 in *The Volunteer Management Handbook,* ed. Tracy D. Connors. New York: Wiley.

———. 2005. "Principles of Training for Volunteers and Employees." Pp. 703–730 in *The Jossey-Bass Handbook of Nonprofit Leadership and Management,* 2nd ed., ed. Robert D. Herman and Associates. San Francisco: Jossey-Bass.

Mackie, Marlene M. 1987. *Constructing Women and Men: Gender Socialization.* Toronto: Holt, Rinehart & Winston of Canada.

Macleod, David I. 1983. *Building Character in the American Boy: The Boy Scouts, YMCA, and Their Forerunners, 1870–1920.* Madison: University of Wisconsin Press.

Macleod, Flora, and Sarah Hogarth. 1999. *Leading Today's Volunteers.* 2nd ed. Bellingham, Wash.: Self-Counsel Press.

Madara, Edward, and Barbara J. White, eds. 2002. *The Self-Help Group Sourcebook: Your Guide to Community and Online Support Groups.* Cedar Knoll, N.J.: American Self-Help Clearinghouse.

Magat, Richard. 1989a. *An Agile Servant: Community Leadership by Community Foundations.* New York: Foundation Center.

———. 1989b. *Philanthropic Giving.* New York: Oxford University Press.

Mair, Peter, ed. 1990. *The West European Party System.* New York: Oxford University Press.

Majka, Theo J., and Linda C. Majka. 1992. "Decline of the Farm Labor Movement in California: Organizational Crisis and Political Changes." *Critical Sociology* 19:3–36.

Major, Wayne F. 2001. "The Benefits and Costs of Serious Running." *World Leisure Journal* 43:12–25.

Mäkelä, Klaus, et al., eds. 1996. *Alcoholics Anonymous as a Mutual-Help Movement: A Study in Eight Societies.* Madison: University of Wisconsin Press.

Malaparte, Curzio. 1932. *Coup d'Etat—The Technique of Revolution.* New York: Dutton.

Maltoni, Cesare, and Irving J. Selikoff. 1990. *Scientific Issues of the Next Century: Convocation of World Academies.* New York: New York Academy of Sciences.

Mancuso, Anthony. 2004. *How to Form a Nonprofit Corporation.* 6th ed. Berkeley, Calif.: Nolo Press.

Maneker, Jerry S. 1973. "An Extension of Max Weber's Theory of Bureaucracy." *Revista Internacional de Sociologia* 30:55–61.

Manes, Christopher. 1990. *Green Rage: Radical Environmentalism and the Unmaking of Civilization.* Boston: Little, Brown.

Manley, Will. 1992. *Unprofessional Behavior: Confessions of a Public Librarian.* Jefferson, N.C.: McFarland.

Mann, W. E. 1955. *Sect, Cult, and Church in Alberta.* Toronto: University of Toronto Press.

Mannell, Roger C. 1993. "High-Investment Activity and Life Satisfaction among Older Adults: Committed, Serious Leisure and Flow Activities." Pp. 125–145 in *Activity and Aging,* ed. John A. Kelly. Newbury Park, Calif.: Sage.

Mannell, Roger C., and Douglas A. Kleiber. 1997. *A Social Psychology of Leisure.* State College, Pa.: Venture.

Manning, Nick, John Baldock, and Sarah Vickerstaff. 2003. *Social Policy.* Oxford, UK: Oxford University Press.

Manser, Gordon, and Rosemary H. Cass. 1976. *Voluntarism at the Crossroads.* New York: Family Service Association of America.

Marcello, Patricia C. 2004. *Ralph Nader: A Biography.* Westport, Conn.: Greenwood Press.

Marcovitz, Hal, and Mason Crest. 2004. *Teens and Voluntarism.* Philadelphia: Mason Crest Publishers.

Maren, Michael. 1997. *The Road to Hell: The Ravaging Effects of Foreign Aid and International Charity.* New York: Free Press.

Margolis, Howard. 1982. *Selfishness, Altruism, and Rationality.* New York: Cambridge University Press.

Marshall, Alfred. 1930. *Principles of Economics.* 8th ed. London: Macmillan.

Martin, David. 1990. *Tongues of Fire: The Explosion of Protestantism in Latin America.* Oxford, UK: Blackwell.

Martin, Fiona. 2003. "The Changing Configurations of Inequality in Post-Industrial Society: Volunteering as a Case Study." *Alternate Routes* 19:79–108.

Martin, John L. 1998. "Authoritative Knowledge and Heteronomy in Classical Sociological Theory." *Sociological Theory* 16 (July):99–130.

Martin, William C. 1996. *With God on Our Side: The Rise of the Religious Right in America.* New York: Broadway Books.

Marty, Martin E. 1980. *Where the Spirit Leads: American Denominations Today.* Atlanta: John Knox Press.

Marullo, Sam, and Edwards, Bob. 1994. "Survival Strategies for Peace Groups." *Peace Review* 6(4):435–443.

Marwell, Nicole P. 2002. "Privatizing the Welfare State: Nonprofit Community-Based Organizations as Political Actors." *American Sociological Review* 69:265–291.

Marwell, Nicole and Paul-Brian McInerney. 2005. "The Nonprofit/For-Profit Continuum: Theorizing the Dynamics of Mixed-Form Markets." *Nonprofit and Voluntary Sector Quarterly* 34:7–28.

Mason, David E. 1984. *Voluntary Nonprofit Enterprise Management.* New York: Plenum.

Maslovaty, Nava, and Zecharia Dor-Shav. 1990. "Gender and the Structure and Salience of Values: An Example from Israeli Youth." *Sex Roles* 22:261–281.

Massarsky, Cynthia W. 1994. "Enterprise Strategies for Generating Revenue." Pp. 382–402 in *The Jossey-Bass Handbook of Nonprofit Leadership and Management,* ed. Robert D. Herman and Associates. San Francisco: Jossey-Bass.

Masters, Marick F. 1997. *Unions at the Crossroads.* Westport, Conn.: Quorum Books.

Mather, George A., and Larry A. Nichols. 1993. *Dictionary of Cults, Sects, Religions and the Occult.* Grand Rapids, Mich.: Zondervan.

Matson, Floyd W. 1990. *Walking Alone and Marching Together: A History of the Organized Blind Movement in the United States, 1940–1990.* Baltimore: National Federation of the Blind.

Mattesisch, Paul, Barbara Monsey, and C. Roy. 1997. *Community Building: What Makes It Work.* St. Paul, Minn.: Amherst H. Wilder Foundation.

Mauss, Marcel. 1925/1990. *The Gift.* New York: Norton.

Mayer, Robert N. 1989. *The Consumer Movement: Guardians of the Marketplace.* New York: Twayne.

Mayers, Raymond S. 2004. *Financial Management for Nonprofit Human Service Organizations.* Springfield, Ill.: C. C. Thomas.

McAdam, Doug. 1982. *Political Process and the Development of Black Insurgency, 1930–1970.* Chicago: University of Chicago Press.

McAdam, Doug, John D. McCarthy, and Mayer Zald, eds. 1996. *Comparative Perspectives on Social Movements.* Cambridge, UK: Cambridge University Press.

McAdam, Doug, and David A. Snow, eds. 1997. *Social Movements.* Los Angeles: Roxbury Publishing.

McAdam, Terry W. 1991. *Doing Well by Doing Good: The Complete Guide to Careers in the Nonprofit Sector.* Rockville, Md.: Fund Raising Institute.

McBee, Shar. 2002. *To Lead Is to Serve: How to Attract Volunteers and Keep Them.* Honolulu, Hawaii: To Lead Is to Serve.

McBride, Amanda M., and Michael Sherraden. 2004. "Toward a Global Research Agenda on Civic Service: Editors' Introduction to This Special Issue." *Nonprofit and Voluntary Sector Quarterly* (Supplement to volume 33, no. 4) 33:3S–7S.

McCaghy, Charles C., Timothy A Capron, and J. D. Jamieson. 2002. *Deviant Behavior: Crime, Conflict, and Interest Groups.* 6th ed. Boston: Allyn and Bacon.

McCamant, Kathryn, Charles Durrett, and Ellen Hartzman. 1994. *Cohousing: A Contemporary Approach to Housing Ourselves.* Berkeley, Calif.: Ten Speed Press.

McCann, Michael W. 1986. *Taking Reform Seriously: Perspectives on Public Interest Liberalism.* Ithaca, N.Y.: Cornell University Press.

McCarthy, John, and Mayer N. Zald. 1977. "Resource Mobilization and Social Movements: A Partial Theory." *American Journal of Sociology* 82(6):1212–1241.

McCarthy, Kathleen D. 1990. *Lady Bountiful Revisited: Women, Philanthropy, and Power.* New Brunswick, N.J.: Rutgers University Press.

———. 1991. *Women's Culture: American Philanthropy and Art, 1830–1930.* Chicago: University of Chicago Press.

McCarthy, Kathleen D., Virginia A. Hodgkinson, Russy D. Sumariwalla, and Associates. 1992. *The Nonprofit Sector in the Global Community: Voices from Many Nations.* San Francisco: Jossey-Bass.

McCarthy, Ronald M., Gene Sharp, and Brad Bennett. 1997. *Nonviolent Action: A Research Guide.* New York: Garland.

McConnell, Grant. 1966. *Private Power & American Democracy.* New York: Knopf.

McCool, Daniel. 1990. "Subgovernments as Determinants of Political Viability." *Political Science Quarterly* 105:269–293.

McCurley, Stephen. 1994. "Recruiting and Retaining Volunteers." Pp. 511–534 in *The Jossey-Bass Handbook of Nonprofit Leadership and Management,* ed. Robert D. Herman and Associates. San Francisco: Jossey-Bass.

McCurley, Steve, and Rick Lynch. 1996. *Volunteer Management.* Downers Grove, Ill.: Heritage Arts.

McCurley, Steve, and Sue Vineyard. 1988. *101 Tips for Volunteer Recruitment.* Downers Grove, Ill.: Heritage Arts.

———. 1997. *Measuring Up: Assessment Tools for Volunteer Programs.* Downers Grove, Ill.: Heritage Arts.

McDaniel, Terra. 2002. "Community and Transcendence: the Emergence of a House Church." Pp. 127–151 in *Postmodern Existential Sociology,* ed. Joseph A. Kotarba and John M. Johnson. Walnut Creek, Calif.: AltaMira.

McFall, Sally. 2002. *Government.* Danbury, Conn.: Grolier Educational.

McFarland, Andrew S. 1984. *Common Cause: Lobbying in the Public Interest.* Chatham, N.J.: Chatham House.

McGerr, Michael E. 1986/2000. *The Decline of Popular Politics: The American North, 1865–1892.* Bridgewater, N.J.: Republica Books.

McKelvey, Charles. 1994. *The African-American Movement: From Pan-Africanism to the Rainbow Coalition.* New York: General Hall.

McKenzie, Evan. 1994. *Privatopia: Homeowner Associations and the Rise of Residential Private Government.* New Haven, Conn.: Yale University Press.

McKinney, Jerome B. 2004. *Effective Financial Management in Public and Nonprofit Agencies.* Westport, Conn.: Praeger.

McLaughlin, Thomas A. 1995. *Streetsmart Financial Basics for Nonprofit Managers.* New York: Wiley.

———. 1998. *Nonprofit Mergers and Alliances.* New York: Wiley.

McLeish, Barry J. 1995. *Successful Marketing Strategies for Nonprofit Organizations.* New York: Wiley.

McLellan, Jeffrey A., and James Youniss. 2003. "Two Systems of Youth Service: Determinants of Voluntary and Required Youth Community Service." *Journal of Youth and Adolescence* 32:47–58.

McMillon, Bill, Doug Cutchins, and Anne Geissinger. 2003. *Volunteer Vacations: Short-Term Adventures that Will Benefit You and Others.* Chicago: Chicago Review Press.

McPherson, J. M. 1983. "The Size of Voluntary Organizations." *Social Forces* 61: 1044–1064.

McPherson, J. M., and Thomas Rotolo. 1996. "Testing a Dynamic Model of Social Composition: Diversity and Change in Voluntary Groups." *American Sociological Review* 61 (2 April):179–202.

McPherson, J. M., and Lynn Smith-Lovin. 1982. "Women and Weak Ties: Differences by Sex in the Size of Voluntary Organizations." *American Journal of Sociology* 87: 883–904.

McSweeney, Phil, and Don Alexander. 1996. *Managing Volunteers Effectively.* Broomfield, Vt.: Arena.

McWhinney, Will. 1992. *Paths of Change: Strategic Choices for Organizations and Society.* Newbury Park, Calif.: Sage.

McWhirter, Darien A. 1994. *Freedom of Speech, Press, and Assembly.* Phoenix: Oryx.

Mead, Frank S., and Samuel S. Hill. 1995. *Handbook of Denominations in the United States.* Nashville, Tenn.: Abingdon Press.

Mechling, Jay. 1984. "High Kybo Floater: Food and Feces in the Speech Play at a Boy Scout Camp." *The Journal of Psychoanalytic Anthropology* 7:256–268.

Megargee, Edwin I. 1997. "Internal Inhibitions and Controls." Pp. 581–614 in *Handbook of Personality Psychology,* ed. Robert Hogan, John Johnson, and Stephen Briggs. San Diego: Academic Press.

Mehr, Joseph. 2001. *Human Service: Concepts and Intervention Strategies.* Boston: Allyn and Bacon.

Meier, Andrea. 1997. "Inventing New Models of Social Support Groups: A Feasibility Study of an Online Stress Management Support Group for Social Workers." *Social Work with Groups* 20:35–53.

Meister, Albert. 1984. *Participation, Associations, Development, and Change,* ed. and trans. Jack C. Ross. New Brunswick, N.J.: Transaction Books.

Melder, Keith E. 1977. *Beginnings of Sisterhood: The American Woman's Rights Movement, 1800–1850.* New York: Schocken Books.

Mele, Alfred R. 2003. *Free Will and Determinism in Reflections on Philosophy: Introductory Essays.* 2nd ed., ed. Leemon McHenry and Takashi Yagisawa. New York: Longman Publications.

Melton, J. Gordon. 1986. *Encyclopedic Handbook of Cults in America.* New York: Garland.

———. 1993. *Encyclopedia of American Religions.* Detroit: Gale Research.

Melucci, Alberto. 1989. *Nomads of the Present: Social Movements and Individual Needs in Contemporary Society.* Philadelphia: Temple University Press.

Menchik, Paul, and Burton Weisbrod. 1987. "Volunteer Labor Supply." *Journal of Public Economics* 32:159–183.

Metzendorf, D., and Ram A. Cnaan. 1992. "Volunteers in Feminist Organizations." *Nonprofit Management and Leadership* 2:255–269.

Meyer, N. Dean. 1998. *Decentralization.* Ridgefield, Conn.: N. Dean Meyer and Associates.

Michels, Robert. 1915/1959. *Political Parties: A Sociological Study of the Oligarchical Tendencies of Modern Democracy.* New York: Dover Publications.

Mihlar, Fazil. 1999. *Unions and Right-to-Work Laws: The Global Evidence of Their Impact on Employment.* Vancouver, Canada: Frazer Institute.

Milani, Ken. 1988. "Nonprofit Organizations in a Technical Perspective." Pp. 5.1–5.8 in *The Nonprofit Organization Handbook,* 2nd ed., ed. Tracy D. Connors. New York: McGraw-Hill.

Milbrath, Lester, and M. Lal Goel. 1977. *Political Participation.* 2nd ed. Chicago: Rand McNally.

Milkas, Sidney M. 1999. *Political Parties and Constitutional Democracy.* Baltimore: Johns Hopkins University Press.

Miller, David L. 1985. *Introduction to Collective Behavior.* Belmont, Calif.: Wadsworth.

Miller, Donald E. 1997. *Reinventing American Protestantism: Christianity in the New Millennium.* Berkeley: University of California Press.

Miller, Henry, and Connie Phillip. 1983. "The Alternative Service Agency." Pp. 779–791 in *Handbook of Clinical Social Work,* ed. A. Rosenblatt and D. Waldfogel. San Francisco: Jossey-Bass.

Miller, Russell. 1979. *The Resistance.* Alexandria, Va.: Time-Life Books.

Millet, John D. 1966. *Organization for the Public Service.* Princeton, N.J.: Van Nostrand.

Milligan, Lucy R., and Harold V. Milligan. 1965. *The Club Member's Handbook.* Rev. ed. New York: Dolphin Books.

Milligan, Sharon, Patricia Maryland, Henry Ziegler, and Anna Ward. 1987. "Natural Helpers as Street Health Workers among the Black Urban Elderly." *Gerontologist* 27:712–715.

Mills, Jeannie. 1979. *Six Years with God: Life Inside Reverend Jim Jones's People's Temple.* New York: A & W.

Millspaugh, Arthur C. 1949. *Toward Efficient Government: The Question of Governmental Organization.* Washington, D.C.: Brookings Institution Press.

Milofsky, Carl. 1988. *Community Organizations: Studies in Resource Mobilization and Exchange.* New York: Oxford University Press.

Milofsky, Carl, and Stephen D. Blades. 1991. "Issues of Accountability in Health Charities: A Case Study of Accountability Problems among Nonprofit Organizations." *Nonprofit and Voluntary Sector Quarterly* 20:371–393.

Milofsky, Carl, and Carl Hunter. 1994. "Where Nonprofits Come from: A Theory of Organizational Emergence." Paper presented at the annual conference of the Association of Researchers on Nonprofit Organizations and Voluntary Action. Berkeley, Calif.

Minkler, Meredith. 1988. "Community-Based Initiatives to Reduce Social Isolation and Enhance Empowerment of the Elderly: Case Studies from the U.S." *Danish Medical Bulletin: Journal of the Health Sciences* Gerontology Special Supplement Series (6):52–57.

Minow, Martha. 2002. *Partners, Not Rivals: Privatization and the Public Good.* Boston: Beacon Press.

Mishal, Shaul. 2003. "The Pragmatic Dimension of the Palestinian Hamas: A Network Perspective." *Armed Forces and Society* 29(4):569–589.

Missingham, Bruce. 2002. "The Village of the Poor Confronts the State: A Geography of Protest in the Assembly of the Poor." *Urban Studies* 39(9):1647–1663.

Mixer, Joseph R. 1993. *Principles of Professional Fundraising.* San Francisco: Jossey-Bass.

Moctezuma, Pedro. 2001. "Community-Based Organization and Participatory Planning in South-East Mexico City." *Environment and Urbanization* 13:117–133.

Moland, John, Jr. 2002. "The Value-Oriented Civil Rights Movements and Passive Resistance: An Expressed Civility in the Pursuit of Social Justice." *Sociological Inquiry* 72:442–455.

Mondros, Jacqueline B., and Scott M. Wilson. 1994. *Organizing for Power and Empowerment.* New York: Columbia University Press.

Monroe, Kristen R. 1996. *The Heart of Altruism.* Princeton, N.J.: Princeton University Press.

Monsma, Stephen V., and J. Christopher Soper. 1998. *Equal Treatment of Religion in a Pluralistic Society.* Grand Rapids, Mich.: Eerdmans.

Monson, Craig. 1995. *Disembodied Voices: Music and Culture in an Early Modern Italian Convent.* Berkeley: University of California Press.

Moody, Harry R. 1988. "Mediating Policies." Chapter 8 in *Abundance of Life: Hu-*

man Development Policies for an Aging Society. New York: Columbia University Press.

Moore, Larry F. 1985. *Motivating Volunteers.* Vancouver, Canada: Vancouver Volunteer Centre.

Moore, R. I. 1977/1994. *The Origins of European Dissent.* Toronto: University of Toronto Press.

Moran, Mary H., and M. Anne Pitcher. 2004. "The 'Basket Case' and the 'Poster Child': Explaining the End of Civil Conflicts in Liberia and Mozambique." *Third World Quarterly* 25:501–519.

More, Thomas. 1989. *Utopia.* Cambridge, UK: Cambridge University Press.

Morgan, Gareth. 1986. *Images of Organization.* Beverly Hills, Calif.: Sage.

Morgan, James N. 1986. "Unpaid Productive Activity Over the Life Course." Pp. 73–109 in *Productive Roles in an Older Society,* ed. Committe on an Aging Society. Washington, D.C.: National Academy Press.

Morgan, Robin, ed. 1970. *Sisterhood Is Powerful: An Anthology of Writings from the Women's Liberation Movement.* New York: Random House.

Morris, Aldon D. 1984. *The Origins of the Civil Rights Movement.* New York: Free Press.

Morris, Aldon D., and Carol M. Mueller, eds. 1992. *Frontiers in Social Movement Theory.* New Haven, Conn.: Yale University Press.

Morris, Charles. 1997. *American Catholic: The Saints and Sinners Who Built America's Most Powerful Church.* New York: Vintage Books.

Morris, Joe A. 1970. *First Offender: A Volunteer Program for Youth in Trouble with the Law.* New York: Funk & Wagnalls.

Moser, Annalise. 2003. "Acts of Resistance: The Performance of Women's Grass Roots Protest in Peru." *Social Movement Studies* 2(2):177–190.

Moskos, Charles C. 1988. *A Call to Civic Service: National Service for Country and Community.* New York: Free Press.

Moyer, Mel. 1984. *Managing Voluntary Organizations.* Toronto: York University Press.

Moynihan, Daniel P. 1970. *Maximum Feasible Misunderstanding: Community Action in the War on Poverty.* New York: Free Press.

Muldoon, James P., Jr. 2004. *The Architecture of Global Governance: An Introduction to the Study of International Organizations.* Boulder, Colo.: Westview Press.

Mumm, Susan. 2001. *All Saints Sisters of the Poor: An Anglican Sisterhood in the Nineteenth Century.* Rochester, N.Y.: Boydell Press.

Murray, Vic, and Yvonne Harrison. 2005. "Virtual Volunteering." Pp. 31–47 in *Emerging Areas of Volunteering* (ARNOVA Occasional Paper Series, volume 1, no. 2), ed. Jeffrey L. Brudney. Indianapolis: Association for Research on Nonprofit Organizations and Voluntary Action.

Murray, Vic, and Bill Tassie. 1994. "Evaluating the Effectiveness of Nonprofit Organizations." Pp. 303–324 in *The Jossey-Bass Handbook of Nonprofit Leadership and Management,* ed. Robert D. Herman and Associates. San Francisco: Jossey-Bass.

Nagel, Jack H. 1987. *Participation.* Englewood Cliffs, N.J.: Prentice Hall.

Naidoo, Kumi, and Rajesh Tandon. 1999. "The Promise of Civil Society." Pp. 1–16 in *Civil Society at the Millennium,* ed. CIVICUS. West Hartford, Conn.: Kumarian Press.

Naisbitt, John. 1984. *MEGATRENDS.* New York: Warner.

Naisbitt, John, and Patricia Aburdene. 1990. *MEGATRENDS 2000.* New York: William Morrow.

Naples, Nancy A. 1998. *Community Activism and Feminist Politics: Organizing across Race, Class, and Gender.* New York: Routledge.

Nash, Roderick F. 1989. *The Rights of Nature: A History of Environmental Ethics.* Madison: University of Wisconsin Press.

National Committee for Responsive Philanthropy. 1987. *The Workplace Giving Revolution.* Washington, D.C.: National Committee for Responsive Philanthropy.

Ndegwa, Stephen N. 1996. *The Two Faces of Civil Society: NGOs and Politics in Africa.* Bloomfield, Conn.: Kumarian Press.

Nelson, Lisa S., Mark D. Robbins, and Bill Simonsen. 1998. "Introduction to the Special Issue on Governance." *Social Sciences Journal* 35:477–491.

Neptune, Robert. 1977. *California's Uncommon Markets: The Story of the Consumers Cooperatives, 1935–1977.* Richmond, Calif.: Associated Cooperatives.

Netanyahu, Benjamin. 1995. *Fighting Terrorism: How Democracies Can Defeat Domestic and International Terrorists.* New York: Noonday Press.

Neulinger, John. 1974. *The Psychology of Leisure.* Springfield, Ill.: C. C. Thomas.

———. 1989. *A Leisure Society: Idle Dream or Viable Alternative, Encroaching Menace or Golden Opportunity.* Reston, Va.: American Association for Leisure and Recreation.

Newman, Jay. 1982. *Foundations of Religious Tolerance.* Toronto: University of Toronto Press.

Nichols, Geoff. 2004. "Pressures on Volunteers in the UK." Pp. 197–208 in *Volunteering as Leisure/Leisure as Volunteering: An International Assessment,* ed. Margaret Graham and Robert A. Stebbins. Wallingford, Oxon, UK: CABI Publishing.

Nichols, Judith E. 1999. *Transforming Fundraising.* San Francisco: Jossey-Bass.

———. 2001. "Demographics: Our Changing World and How It Affects Raising Money." Pp. 332–346 in *The Nonprofit Handbook: Fund Raising,* 3rd ed., ed. James M. Greenfield. New York: Wiley.

Nicholls, Walter J. 2003. "Forging a 'New' Organizational Infrastructure for Los Angeles' Progressive Community." *International Journal of Urban and Regional Research* 27:881–896.

Niebuhr, H. Richard. 1929/1957. *The Social Sources of Denominationalism.* Cleveland, Ohio: Meridian Books.

Nielsen, Waldemar. 1972. *The Big Foundations.* New York: Columbia University Press.

———. 1979. *The Endangered Sector.* New York: Columbia University Press.

———. 1996. *Inside American Philanthropy: The Dramas of Donorship.* Norman: University of Oklahoma Press.

Norris, Pippa. 2001. *Civic Engagement, Information Poverty, and the Internet Worldwide.* New York: Cambridge University Press.

———. 2002. *Democratic Phoenix: Reinventing Political Activism.* Cambridge, UK: Cambridge University Press.

Northouse, Peter G. 1997. *Leadership: Theory and Practice.* Thousand Oaks, Calif.: Sage.

Nyang'oro, Julius E., and Timothy M. Shaw. 1989. *Corporatism in Africa.* Boulder, Colo.: Westview Press.

Nye, Mallory. 2001. *Multiculturalism and Minority Religions in Britain.* Richmond, UK: Curzon.

O'Brien, Geraldine, JoEllen Shannon, Deborah G. Booth, and Dianne Itterly. 1995. "East Coast Migrant Head Start Project: Continuity-Catalyst to Quality Service Delivery for Infants and Toddlers." *Infants and Young Children* 7(3):83–88.

O'Brien, Maeve. 2003. "Girls and Transition to Second-Level Schooling in Ireland: 'Moving On' and 'Moving Out.'" *Gender and Education* 15:249–267.

O'Brien, Patricia. 1995. "From Surviving to Thriving: The Complex Experience of Living in Public Housing." *Affilia* 10(2):155–178.

O'Connell, Brian. 1983. *America's Voluntary Spirit.* New York: Foundation Center.

———. 1997. *Powered by Coalition: The Story of Independent Sector.* San Francisco: Jossey-Bass.

———. 1999. *Civil Society: The Underpinnings of American Democracy.* Hanover, N.H.: University Press of New England.

O'Connell, Brian, and Rebecca B. Taylor. 1999. *Voices from the Heart: In Celebration of America's Volunteers.* San Francisco: Jossey-Bass.

Office of Management and Budget. 1987. *Standard Industrial Classification Manual 1987.* Rev. ed. Washington, D.C.: Government of the United States.

Ogilvie, Robert S. 2004. *Voluntarism, Community Life, and the American Ethic.* Bloomington: Indiana University Press.

O'Grady, Carolyn R. 2000. *Integrating Service Learning and Multicultural Education in Colleges and Universities.* Mahwah, N.J.: L. Erlbaum Associates.

O'Leary, Rosemary, Robert F. Durant, Daniel J. Fiorino, and Paul S. Welland. 1999. *Managing for the Environment.* San Francisco: Jossey-Bass.

Oldenbourg, Zoé. 1966. *The Crusades.* New York: Pantheon Books.

Oliner, Pearl M., and Samuel P. Oliner. 1995. *Toward a Caring Society: Ideas into Action.* Westport, Conn.: Praeger.

Oliner, Pearl M., Samuel P. Oliner, and Lawrence Baron. 1992. *Embracing the Other: Philosophical, Psychological, and Historical Perspectives on Altruism.* New York: New York University Press.

Olson, Mancur. 1965. *The Logic of Collective Action.* Cambridge, Mass.: Harvard University Press.

O'Neill, Michael. 1989. *The Third Sector.* San Francisco: Jossey-Bass.

———. 2002. *Nonprofit Nation: A New Look at the Third America.* 2nd ed. San Francisco: Jossey-Bass.

O'Neill, Michael, and Kathleen Fletcher, eds. 1998. *Nonprofit Management Education.* Westport, Conn.: Praeger.

O'Neill, Michael, and Dennis R. Young, eds. 1988. *Educating Managers of Nonprofit Organizations.* New York: Praeger.

Oppenheimer, Martin. 2004. "The Minorities 'Question': Does the Left Have Answers?" *New Politics* 9(4):121–135.

Orloff, Ann S. 1993. "Gender and the Social Rights of Citizenship: The Comparative Analysis of Gender Relations and Welfare States." *American Sociological Review* 58 (June):303–328.

Ornstein, Martha. 1913/1963. *The Role of Scientific Societies in the Seventeenth Century.* Hamden, Conn.: Archon Books.

Orosz, Joel J. 2000. *The Insider's Guide to Grantmaking.* San Francisco: Jossey-Bass.

Ortmeyer, D. L., and D. Fortune. 1985. "A Portfolio Model of Korean Household Sector Saving Behavior." *Economic Development and Cultural Change* 33:575–599.

Osigweh, Chimezie A. B. 1983. *Improving Problem-Solving Participation: The Case of Local Transnational Voluntary Organizations.* Lanham, Md.: University Press of America.

Oster, Sharon M. 1995. *Strategic Management for Nonprofit Organizations.* New York: Oxford University Press.

Ostrander, Susan A. 1995. *Money for Change: Social Movement Philanthropy at Haymarket People's Fund.* Philadelphia: Temple University Press.

Ostrom, Elinor, Joanna Burger, Christopher B. Field, Richard B. Norgard, and David Policansky. 1999. "Revisiting the Commons: Local Lessons, Global Challenges." *Science* 284 (9 April):278–282.

Ostrower, Francie. 1995. *Why the Wealthy Give.* Princeton, N.J.: Princeton University Press.

Ott, J. Steven. 2001. *Understanding Nonprofit Organizations: Governance, Leadership, and Management.* Boulder, Colo.: Westview Press.

Owusu, Thomas Y. 2000. "The Role of Ghanaian Immigrant Associations in Toronto." *International Migration Review* 34:1155–1181.

Oxhorn, Philip, Joseph S. Tulchin, and Andrew D. Seles, eds. 2004. *Decentralization, Democratic Governance, and Civil Society in Comparative Perspective: Asia, Africa, and Latin America.* Baltimore: Johns Hopkins University Press.

Ozinga, James R. 1999. *Altruism.* Westport, Conn.: Praeger.

Palisi, Bartolomeo J., and Bonni Korn. 1989. "National Trends in Voluntary Association Membership: 1974–1984." *Nonprofit and Voluntary Sector Quarterly* 18: 179–190.

Pammer, Michael. 2000. "Death and the Transfer of Wealth: Bequest Patterns and Culture Change in the Eighteenth Century." *Journal of Social History* 33:913–934.

Pappano, Laura. 2001. *The Connection Gap: Why Americans Feel So Alone.* New Brunswick, N.J.: Rutgers University Press.

Parker, Stanley R. 1976. *The Sociology of Leisure.* London: Allen & Unwin.

Parsons, Talcott. 1949. *The Structure of Social Action.* Glencoe, Ill.: Free Press.

Parrinder, Edward G. 1983. *World Religions.* New York: Facts on File.

Partridge, Christopher. 2004. *New Religions: A Guide.* New York: Oxford University Press.

Pateman, Carole. 1970. *Participation and Democratic Theory.* New York: Cambridge University Press.

Patton, M. Q. 1986. *Utilization-Focused Evaluation.* 2nd ed. Newbury Park, Calif.: Sage.

Payne, Barbara, and C. Neil Bull. 1985. "The Older Volunteer: The Case for Interdependence." Pp. 251–272 in *Social Bonds in Later Life: Aging and Interdependence,* ed. Warren E. Petersen and Jill Quadagno. Beverly Hills, Calif.: Sage.

Payne, Robert. 1974. *The Great Man; A Portrait of Winston Churchill.* New York: Coward, McCann and Geoghegan.

Pazy, Asya, and Israela Oron. 2001. "Sex Proportion and Performance Evaluation among High-Ranking Military Officers." *Journal of Organizational Behavior* 22:689–702.

Peace Corps. 1997. *Peace Corps: The Great Adventure.* Washington, D.C.: Peace Corps.

Pearce, Jone L. 1993. *Volunteers: The Organizational Behavior of Unpaid Workers,* London: Routledge.

Pearce, Kenneth. 1984. *The View from the Top of the Temple: Ancient Maya Civilization and Modern Maya Culture.* Albuquerque: University of New Mexico Press.

Pelling, Henry. 1963. *A History of British Trade Unionism.* London: Macmillan.

Pennington, M. Basil. 1983. *Monastery.* San Francisco: Harper & Row.

Pennock, J. Roland, and John W. Chapman. 1969. *Voluntary Associations.* New York: Atherton.

Pereira, Anthony W. 1997. *The End of the Peasantry.* Pittsburgh: University of Pittsburgh Press.

Perlmutter, Felice D. 1988a. "Alternative Federated Funds: Resourcing for Change." Pp. 95–108 in *Alternative Social Agencies,* ed. Felice D. Perlmutter. New York: Haworth.

Perlmutter, Felice D., ed. 1988b. *Alternative Social Agencies.* New York: Haworth.

Perlmutter, Felice D., and Ram A. Cnaan. 1993. "Challenging Human Service Organizations to Redefine Volunteer Roles." *Administration in Social Work* 17(4):77–95.

Perlmutter, Felice D., and Burton Gummer. 1994. "Managing Organizational Transformations." Pp. 227–246 in *The Jossey-Bass Handbook of Nonprofit Leadership and Management,* ed. Robert D. Herman and Associates. San Francisco: Jossey-Bass.

Perlmutter, Philip. 1992. *Divided We Fall: A History of Ethnic, Religious, and Racial Prejudice in America.* Ames: Iowa State University Press.

Perlstadt, Harry. 1975. "Voluntary Associations and the Community: The Case of Volunteer Ambulance Corps." *Journal of Voluntary Action Research* 4:85–89.

Perrow, Charles P. 1961. "The Analysis of Goals in Complex Organizations." *American Sociological Review* 26(6):854–866.

Perry, Susan K. 2000. *Catch the Spirit: Teen Volunteers Tell How They Made a Difference.* New York: Franklin Watts.

Pestoff, V. A. 1991. *Between Markets and Politics: Cooperatives in Sweden.* Boulder, Colo.: Westview Press.

Peters, F. E. 2004. *The Children of Abraham: Judaism, Christianity, Islam.* Princeton, N.J.: Princeton University Press.

Peters, Karl. 1988. "What Is *Zygon: Journal of Religion and Science*? Purpose, History, and Financial Goals." *Zygon* 23(4):489–496.

Peterson, Lorna. 1988. *Nonprofit Corporations and Competition between the For-Profit Sector: An Annotated Bibliography.* Monticello, Ill.: Vance Bibliographies.

Phelan, Marilyn E. 2000. *Nonprofit Enterprises: Corporations, Trusts, and Associations.* St. Paul, Minn.: West Group.

Philipose, Liz. 1996. "The Laws of War and Women's Human Rights." *Hypatia* 11(4):46–62.

Picardie, Justine. 1988. "Secrets of the Oddfellows." *New Society* 83 (Feb.):13–15.

Picker, Lester A. 2001. "The Corporate Support Marketplace." Pp. 615–637 in *The Nonprofit Handbook: Fund Raising,* 3rd ed., ed. James M. Greenfield. New York: Wiley.

Pidgeon, Walter P. 1998. *The Universal Benefits of Volunteering.* New York: Wiley.

Pipes, Daniel. 1999. *Conspiracy: How the Paranoid Style Flourishes and Where It Comes From.* New York: Free Press.

Pitcavage, Mark. 2001. "Camouflage and Conspiracy: The Militia Movement from Ruby Ridge to Y2K." *American Behavioral Scientist* 44(6):957–981.

Pitzer, Donald E., ed. 1997. *America's Communal Utopias.* Chapel Hill: University of North Carolina Press.

Piven, Frances F., and Richard A. Cloward. 1979. *Poor People's Movements: Why They Succeed, How They Fail.* New York: Vintage Books.

Pointer, Dennis D., and James E. Orlikoff. 2002. *The High-Performance Board.* San Francisco: Jossey-Bass.

Points of Light Foundation. 2002. *Preventing a Disaster within the Disaster: The Effective Use and Management of Unaffiliated Volunteers.* Washington, D.C.: Points of Light Foundation.

Poister, Theodore H. 2003. *Measuring Performance in Public and Nonprofit Organizations.* San Francisco: Jossey-Bass.

Pongsapich, Amara, and Nitaya Kataleeradaphan. 1997. *Thailand Nonprofit Sector and Social Development.* Bangkok, Thailand: Unknown.

Popenoe, David. 1996. "Family Caps." *Society* 33 (July–August):25–27.

Poplau, Ronald W. 2004. *The Doer of Good Becomes Good: A Primer on Volunteerism.* Lanham, Md.: Scarecrow Education.

Portes, Alejandro. 1998. "Social Capital: Its Origins and Applications in Modern Sociology." *Annual Review of Sociology* 24:1–24.

Post, Stephen G. 2003. *Research on Altruism and Love.* Philadelphia: Templeton Foundation Press.

Post, Stephen G., Lynn G. Underwood, Jeffrey Schloss, and William B. Hurlbut. 2002. *Altruism and Altruistic Love.* New York: Oxford University Press.

Poujol, Geneviève. 1989. *Profession, Animateur.* Toulouse, France: Privat.

Powell, Joan. 2000. *Alternatives to the Peace Corps: A Directory of Third World and U.S. Volunteer Opportunities.* 9th ed. Chicago: Food First Books.

Powell, Lawrence A., Kenneth J. Branco, and John B. Williamson. 1996. *The Senior Rights Movement.* New York: Twayne.

Powell, Thomas J. 1994. *Understanding the Self-Help Organization.* Thousand Oaks, Calif.: Sage.

Powell, Walter W., ed. 1987. *The Nonprofit Sector.* New Haven, Conn.: Yale University Press.

Powell, Walter W., and Elisabeth S. Clemens. 1998. *Private Action and the Public Good.* New Haven, Conn.: Yale University Press.

Power, R. J. 1993. *Cooperation among Organizations: The Potential of Computer Supported Cooperative Work.* (Research Reports ESPRIT). New York: Springer-Verlag.

Powers, Roger S., William B. Vogele, Christopher Kruegler, and Ronald M. McCarthy. 1997. *Protest, Power, and Change: An Encyclopedia of Nonviolent Action from ACT-UP to Women's Suffrage.* New York: Garland.

Pratt, Lloyd P. 2001. "The Undigested History of the Nantucket Atheneum: A Renovation Yields Treasure." *Common-Place* 2(1): http://www.common-place.org /vol-02/no-01.

Prelinger, Catherine M. 1992. *Episcopal Women: Gender Spirituality, and Commitment in an American Mainline Denomination.* New York: Oxford University Press.

Prestby, John E., Abraham Wandersman, Paul Florin, Richard Rich, and David Chavis. 1990. "Benefits, Costs, Incentive Management and Participation in Voluntary Organizations: A Means to Understanding and Promoting Empowerment." *American Journal of Community Psychology* 18(1):117–149.

Presthus, Robert V. 1978. *The Organizational Society.* New York: St. Martin's Press.

Prestoff, V. A. 1979. "Member Participation in Swedish Consumer Cooperatives." Stockholm, Sweden: Department of Political Science, University of Stockholm for the Cooperative Institute.

Price, Christine A. 2002. "Retirement for Women: The Impact of Employment." *Journal of Women and Aging* 14(3–4):41–57.

Price, Jerome. 1990. *The Antinuclear Movement.* Updated ed. Boston: Twayne.

Price, Richard H. 1990. "Whither Participation and Empowerment?" *American Journal of Community Psychology* 18(1):163–167.

Princenthal, Nancy, and Jennifer Dowley. 2001. *A Creative Legacy: A History of the National Endowment for the Arts Visual Artists' Fellowship Program 1966–1995.* New York: H. N. Abrams.

Pronovost, Gilles. 1998. "The Sociology of Leisure." *Current Sociology* 46:1–156.

Prusak, Bernard P. 2004. *The Church Unfinished: Ecclesiology through the Centuries.* New York: Paulist Press.

Pugliese, Donato J. 1986. *Voluntary Associations: An Annotated Bibliography.* New York: Garland.

Puka, Bill, ed. 1994. *Reaching Out: Caring, Altruism, and Prosocial Behavior.* New York: Garland.

Putnam, Robert D. 1993. *Making Democracy Work: Civic Traditions in Modern Italy.* Princeton, N.J.: Princeton University Press.

———. 1995. "Bowling Alone: Revisited." *Responsive Community* 5 (Spring):18–33.

———. 2000. *Bowling Alone: The Collapse and Revival of American Community.* New York: Simon & Schuster.

Pynes, Joan E. 1997. *Human Resources Management for Public and Nonprofit Organizations.* San Francisco: Jossey-Bass.

Quarrick, Gene. 1989. *Our Sweetest Hours: Recreation and the Mental State of Absorption.* Jefferson, N.C.: McFarland.

Queen, Edward L. 2000. *Serving Those in Need: A Handbook for Managing Faith-Based Human Services Organizations.* San Francisco: Jossey-Bass.

Rabinowitz, Alan. 1990. *Social Change Philanthropy in America.* New York: Quorum Press.

Raboteau, Albert J. 1995. *A Fire in the Bones: Reflections on African-American Religious History.* Boston: Beacon Press.

Raczynski, Stanislaw. 2004. "Simulation of the Dynamic Interactions between Terror and Anti-terror Organizational Structures." *Journal of Artificial Societies and Social Simulation* 7 (March):paragraphs 1.1–5.2.

Radtke, Janel M. 1998. *Strategic Communications for Nonprofit Organizations.* New York: Wiley.

Randall, Adrian, and Paul Palmer. 2002. *Financial Management in the Voluntary Sector.* London: Routledge.

Ranson, Stewart, Alan Bryman, and Bob Hinings. 1977. *Clergy, Ministers and Priests.* London: Routledge & Kegan Paul.

Rappaport, Roy A. 1999. *Ritual and Religion in the Making of Humanity.* New York: Cambridge.

Rauch, Jonathan. 1995. *Demosclerosis: The Silent Killer of American Government.* New York: Times Books.

Raush, Harold L., and Charlotte L. Raush. 1968. *The Halfway House Movement.* New York: Appleton-Century-Crofts.

Ray, Angela G. 2002. "Frederick Douglass on the Lyceum Circuit: Social Assimilation, Social Transformation?" *Rhetoric and Public Affairs* 5(4):625–647.

Rayback, Joseph G. 1959. *History of American Labor.* New York: Macmillan.

Raynolds, John, and Eleanor Raynolds. 1988. *Beyond Success: How Volunteer Service Can Help You Begin Making a Life Instead of Just a Living.* New York: Master Media.

Raynolds, John, and Gene Stone. 1998. *Volunteering.* New York: St. Martin's Press.

Reat, Noble R. 1994. *Buddhism: A History.* Berkeley, Calif.: Asian Humanities Press.

Reavis, Dick J. 1995. *The Ashes of Waco.* New York: Simon & Schuster.

Reger, Jo. 2004. "Organizational 'Emotional Work' through Consciousness-Raising: An Analysis of a Feminist Organization." *Qualitative Sociology* 27:205–222.

Reilly, Thom, and Nancy Peterson. 1997. "Nevada's University-State Partnership: A Comprehensive Alliance for Improved Services to Children and Families." *Public Welfare* 55:21–28.

Reimer, Frederic G. 1982. *Ethical Dilemmas in Social Service.* New York: Columbia University Press.

Reisig, Michael D., and Roger B. Parks. 2004. "Can Community Policing Help with the Truly Disadvantaged?" *Crime and Delinquency* 50:139–167.

Reitzes, Donald C., and Dietrich C. Reitzes. 1984. "Alinsky's Legacy: Current Applications and Extensions of His Principles and Strategies." *Research in Social Movements, Conflicts and Change* 6:31–55.

Rekart, Josephine. 1993. *Public Funds, Private Provision: The Role of the Volunteer Sector.* Vancouver, Canada: University of British Columbia Press.

Rheingold, Howard. 1994. *The Virtual Community.* New York: HarperCollins.

Rhoads, Robert A., and Lilliana Mina. 2001. "The Student Strike at the National

Autonomous University of Mexico: A Political Analysis." *Comparative Education Review* 45:334–353.

Richardson, James T., ed. 1978. *Conversion Careers: In and Out of the New Religions.* Beverly Hills, Calif.: Sage.

Richardson, Jeremy J., ed. 1993. *Pressure Groups.* New York: Oxford University Press.

Richey, Russell E. 1977. *Denominationalism.* Nashville, Tenn.: Abingdon.

Richter, Peyton E., ed. 1971. *Utopias.* Boston: Holbrook Press.

Riessman, Frank, and David Carroll. 1995. *Redefining Self-Help.* San Francisco: Jossey-Bass.

Rifkin, Jeremy. 1995. *The End of Work.* New York: Putnam.

Rigsby, Bruce. 1987. "Indigenous Language Shift and Maintenance in Fourth World Settings." *Multilingua* 6:359–378.

Riley-Smith, Jonathan S. C. 1995. *The Oxford Illustrated History of the Crusades.* New York: Oxford University Press.

Rimmerman, Craig A. 2001. *The New Citizenship: Unconventional Politics, Activism, and Service.* Boulder, Colo.: Westview Press.

Ripley, Randall B., and Grace A. Franklin. 1980. *Congress, the Bureaucracy, and Public Policy.* Homewood, Ill.: Dorsey Press.

Ritzer, George, and David Walczak. 1986. *Working: Conflict and Change.* 3rd ed. Englewood Cliffs, N.J.: Prentice Hall.

Robbins, Alexandra. 2004. *Pledged: The Secret Life of Sororities.* New York: Hyperion.

Robbins, Thomas, and Dick Anthony. 1981. *In Gods We Trust: New Patterns of Religious Pluralism in America.* New Brunswick, N.J.: Transaction Books.

Roberts, Edwin A. 1999. "Marxism and Secular Humanism: An Excavation and Reappraisal." *Nature, Society, and Thought* 12:177–201.

Roberts, Ken. 1999. *Leisure in Contemporary Society.* Wallingford, Oxon, UK: CABI Publishing.

Roberts, Pamela, and Alice Yang. 2002. *Kids Taking Action: Community Service Learning Projects, K–8.* Greenfield, Mass.: Northeast Foundation for Children.

Roberts, Ron E. 1971. *The New Communes.* Englewood Cliffs, N.J.: Prentice Hall.

Robertson, D. B., ed. 1966. *Voluntary Associations: A Study of Groups in Free Societies.* Richmond, Va.: John Knox Press.

Robinson, Andy. 2002. *Selling Social Change (without Selling Out): Earned Income Strategies for Nonprofits.* San Francisco: Jossey-Bass.

Robinson, B., and M.G. Hanna. 1994. "Lessons for Academics from Grassroots Community Organizing: A Case Study—The Industrial Areas Foundation." *Journal of Community Practice* 1:63–94.

Rock, Paul. 1988. "On the Birth of Organizations." *L.S.E. Quarterly* 2:123–153.

Rogers, Everett M. 1983. *Diffusion of Innovations.* 3rd ed. New York: Free Press.

Rohracher, Harald. 2003. "The Role of Users in the Social Shaping of Environmental Technologies." *Innovation: The European Journal of Social Science Research* 16(2):177–192.

Rojek, Chris. 2000. *Leisure and Culture.* New York: Palgrave.

———. 2002. "Civil Labour, Leisure, and Post Work Society." *Loisir et Société/Society and Leisure* 25(1):21–36.

Romanofsky, Peter, and Clarke A. Chambers. 1978. *Social Service Organizations.* Westport, Conn.: Greenwood Press.

Roose, Rudi, and De Bie, Maria. 2003. "From Participative Research to Participative Practice—A Study in Youth Care." *Journal of Community and Applied Social Psychology* 13:475–485.

Rose, Arnold M. 1965. *Minority Problems: A Textbook of Readings in Intergroup Relations.* New York: Harper & Row.

———. 1967. *The Power Structure: Political Process in American Society.* New York: Oxford University Press.

Rose-Ackerman, S. 1982. "Charitable Giving and Excessive Fundraising." *Quarterly Journal of Economics* 97:193–212.

———. 1990. "Competition between Non-Profits and For-Profits: Entry and Growth." *Voluntas* 1(1):13–25.

Rosenblum, Nancy L. 1998. *Membership and Morals.* Princeton, N.J.: Princeton University Press.

Rosenstone, Steven J., and John M. Hansen. 1993. *Mobilization, Participation, and Democracy in America.* New York: Macmillan.

Ross, Jack C. 1976. *An Assembly of Good Fellows: Voluntary Associations in History.* Westport, Conn.: Greenwood.

Ross, Jack C., and Raymond H. Wheeler. 1971. *Black Belonging.* Westport, Conn.: Greenwood.

Ross, Robert J. 1977. "Primary Groups in Social Movements: A Memoir and Interpretation." *Journal of Voluntary Action Research* 6:139–152.

Rosso, Henry A., ed. 1991. *Achieving Excellence in Fund Raising.* San Francisco: Jossey-Bass.

Roszak, Theodore. 1969. *The Making of a Counterculture.* Garden City, N.Y.: Doubleday.

Rothbart, Myron, and Oliver P. John. 1985. "Social Categorization and Behavior Episodes: A Cognitive Analysis of the Effects of Intergroup Contact." *Journal of Social Issues* 41:81–104.

Rothenberg, Lawrence S. 1992. *Linking Citizens to Government: Interest Group Politics at Common Cause.* New York: Cambridge University Press.

Rothschild, Joyce, and Marjukka Ollilainen. 1999. "Obscuring but Not Reducing Managerial Control: Does TQM Measure up to Democracy Standards?" *Economic and Industrial Democracy* 20:583–623.

Rothschild-Whitt, Joyce. 1979. "The Collectivist Organization." *American Sociological Review* 44:509–527.

Roue, Marie. 2003. "US Environmental NGOs and the Cree: An Unnatural Alliance for the Preservation of Nature?" *International Social Science Journal* 55(4): 619–627.

Rubinstein, Richard E. 1987. *Alchemists of Revolution: Terrorism in the Modern World.* New York: Basic Books.

Ruckle, James E. 1993. *Distinctive Qualities of Third Sector Organizations.* New York: Garland.

Rudy, David R. 1986. *Becoming an Alcoholic: Alcoholics Anonymous and the Reality of Alcoholism.* Carbondale: Southern Illinois University Press.

Rummel, R. J. 1994. *Death by Government.* New Brunswick, N.J.: Transaction Publishers.

Ruppel, Warren. 2002. *Not-for-Profit Accounting Made Easy.* New York: Wiley.

Rusch, William G. 1985. *Ecumenism—a Movement toward Church Unity.* Philadelphia: Fortress Press.

Rusin, Jo B. 1999. *Volunteers Wanted.* Mobile, Ala.: Magnolia Mansions Press.

Sagarin, Edward. 1969. *Odd Man In: Societies of Deviants in America.* Chicago: Quadrangle Books.

Sajoo, Amyn B. 2002. *Civil Society in the Muslim World.* New York: I. B. Tauris Publishers.

Salamon, Lester M. 1987. "Of Market Failure, Voluntary Failure, and Third-Party Government: Toward a Theory of Government-Nonprofit Relations in the Modern Welfare State." *Journal of Voluntary Action Research* 16: 29–49.

———. 1992. *America's Nonprofit Sector: A Primer.* New York: Foundation Center.

———. 1994. "The Nonprofit Sector and the Evolution of the American Welfare State." Pp. 83–99 in *The Jossey-Bass Handbook of Nonprofit Leadership and Management,* ed. Robert D. Herman and Associates. San Francisco: Jossey-Bass.

———. 1995. *Partners in Public Service: Government-Nonprofit Relations in the Modern Welfare State.* Baltimore: Johns Hopkins University Press.

———. 1999. *America's Nonprofit Sector: A Primer.* 2nd ed. New York: Foundation Center.

———. 2002. "The Resilient Sector: The State of Nonprofit America." Pp. 3–64 in *The State of Nonprofit America,* ed. Lester M. Salamon. Washington, D.C.: Brookings Institution Press.

———. 2003. *The Resilient Sector: The State of Nonprofit America.* Washington, D.C.: Brookings Institution Press.

Salamon, Lester M., and Helmut Anheier. 1992a. "In Search of the Non-Profit Sector I: The Question of Definitions." *Voluntas* 3(2):125–151.

———. 1992b. "In Search of the Non-Profit Sector II: The Problem of Classification." *Voluntas* 3(3):267–309.

———. 1994. *The Emerging Sector.* Baltimore: Johns Hopkins University Institute for Policy Studies.

Salamon, Lester M., Helmut K. Anheier, Regina List, Stefan Toepler, S. Wojciech Sokolowsi, and Associates. 1999. *Global Civil Society: Dimensions of the Nonprofit Sector.* Baltimore: Johns Hopkins Center for Civil Society Studies.

Salzman, Jason. 1998. *Making the News: A Guide for Nonprofits and Activists.* Boulder, Colo.: Westview Press.

Samuelson, Paul A., and William D. Nordhaus. 1995. *Economics.* 15th ed. New York: McGraw-Hill.

Sanders, Clinton R. 1995. "Killing with Kindness: Veterinary Euthanasia and the Social Construction of Personhood." *Sociological Forum* 10:195–214.

Sanoff, Henry. 2000. *Community Participation Methods in Design and Planning.* New York: Wiley.

Sanyal, Rajat. 1980. *Voluntary Associations and the Urban Public Life in Bengal (1815–1876).* Calcutta, India: Riddhi-India.

Sarri, Rosemary C., and Yeheskel Hasenfeld. 1978. *The Management of Human Services.* New York: Columbia University Press.

Sarna, Jonathan D. 2004. *American Judaism: A History.* New Haven, Conn.: Yale University Press.

Savas, Emanuel S. 2000. *Privatization and Public-Private Partnerships.* New York: Chatham House.

Savedoff, William D. 1998. *Organization Matters.* Washington, D.C.: Inter-American Development Bank.

Scarboro, Allen, Nancy Campbell, and Shirley Stone. 1994. *Living Witchcraft: A Contemporary American Coven.* Westport, Conn.: Praeger.

Schaff, Terry, and Doug Schaff. 1999. *The Fundraising Planner.* San Francisco: Jossey-Bass.

Schattschneider, E. E. 1960. *The Semisovereign People.* New York: Holt, Rinehart and Winston.

Schaw, Walter A. 2002. *International Handbook on Association Management.* Washington, D.C.: American Society of Association Executives.

Schehr, Robert C. 1997. *Dynamic Utopia: Establishing Intentional Communities as a New Social Movement.* Westport, Conn.: Bergin & Garvey.

Scherr, Avron. 1989. *Freedom of Protest, Public Order, and the Law.* New York: Blackwell.

Scheier, Ivan H. 1992. *When Everyone's a Volunteer: The Effective Functioning of All-Volunteer Groups.* Philadelphia: Energize.

———. 1993. *Building Staff/Volunteer Relations.* Philadelphia: Energize.

Schevitz, Jeffrey M. 1967. "The Do-Gooder as Status Striver." *Phylon* 28 (Winter): 386–398.

Schlesinger, Arthur M., Jr. 1993. *The Disuniting of America: Reflections on a Multicultural Society.* New York: Norton.

Schmaedick, Gerald L., ed. 1993. *Cost-Effectiveness in the Nonprofit Sector.* Westport, Conn.: Quorum Books.

Schmid, Hillel. 2001. *Neighborhood Self-Management: Experiments in Civil Society.* New York: Kluwer Academic.

Schmidt, Alvin J., and Nicholas Babchuk. 1972. "Formal Voluntary Groups and Change Over Time: A Study of Fraternal Associations." *Journal of Voluntary Action Research* 1(1):46–55.

Schmitter, Philippe, and G. Lehmbruch, eds. 1979. *Trends toward Corporatist Intermediation.* London: Sage.

Scholsberg, David. 1999. *Environmental Justice and the New Pluralism.* New York: Oxford University Press.

Schor, Juliet B. 1993. *The Overworked American.* New York: Basic Books.

Schuler, Douglas, and Peter Day, eds. 2004. *Shaping the Network Society: The New Role of Civil Society in Cyberspace.* Cambridge: MIT Press.

Schumacher, Edward C. 2003. *Building Your Endowment.* San Francisco: Jossey-Bass.

Schwartz, Florence. 1984. *Voluntarism and Social Work Practice: A Growing Collaboration.* Lanham, Md.: University Press of America.

Schwartz, Frank J., and Susan Pharr, eds. 2003. *The State of Civil Society in Japan.* Cambridge, UK: Cambridge University Press.

Schweder, Richard A., Martha Minow, and Hazel Markus. 2002. *Engaging Cultural Differences: The Multicultural Challenge in Liberal Democracies.* New York: Russell Sage Foundation.

Schweitzer, Glenn E., and Carole D. Schweitzer. 2002. *A Faceless Enemy: The Origins of Modern Terrorism.* Cambridge, Mass.: Perseus Publishing.

Scott, Anne F. 1992. *Natural Allies: Women's Associations in American History.* Urbana: University of Illinois Press.

Scott, Katherine T. 2000. *Creating Caring & Capable Boards.* San Francisco: Jossey-Bass.

Scott, William A. 1965. *Values and Organizations: A Study of Fraternities and Sororities.* Chicago: Rand McNally.

Seabrook, Jeremy. 1988. *The Leisure Society.* Oxford, UK: Blackwell.

Sealander, Judith. 1997. *Private Wealth and Public Life: Foundation Philanthropy and the Reshaping of American Social Policy from the Progressive Era to the New Deal.* Baltimore: Johns Hopkins University Press.

Seaton, Craig E. 1996. *Altruism and Activism.* Lanham, Md.: University Press of America.

Seiler, Timothy L. 2001. *Developing Your Case for Support.* San Francisco: Jossey-Bass.

Self, Donald R., and Walter W. Wymer. 1999. *Volunteerism Marketing: New Vistas for Nonprofit and Public Sector Marketing.* New York: Haworth Press.

Seligman, Adam. 1992. *The Idea of Civil Society.* New York: Free Press.

Sell, Alan P. F. 1986. *Reformed Theology and the Jewish People.* Geneva, Switzerland: World Alliance of Reformed Churches.

Sen, Rinku, and Kim Klein. 2003. *Stir It Up: Lessons in Community Organizing and Advocacy*. San Francisco: Jossey-Bass.

Sen, Siddhartha. 1993. *Defining the Nonprofit Sector: India*. Baltimore: Johns Hopkins Institute for Policy Studies.

Shaiko, Ronald G. 1997. "Female Participation in Association Governance and Political Representation: Women as Executive Directors, Board Members, Lobbyists, and Political Action Committee Directors." *Nonprofit Management and Leadership* 8(2):121–139.

Shapiro, Joseph P. 1993. *No Pity: People with Disabilities Forging a New Civil Rights Movement*. New York: Times Books.

Shapiro, Samuel B. 1987. *A Coming of Age: A History of the Profession of Association Management*. Washington, D.C.: American Society of Association Executives.

Sharma, Mahesh. 1999. "Artisans and Monastic Credit in Early Twentieth Century Himachal." *Indian Economic and Social History Review* 36(2):239–257.

Sharon, Liath. 2004. "Averting a Disaster within a Disaster: The Management of Spontaneous Volunteers following the 11 September 2001 Attacks on the World Trade Center in New York." *Voluntary Action* 6(2):11–20.

Sharp, Gene. 1973. *Methods of Nonviolent Action*. Boston: Porter Sargent.

Shaw, Randy. 2001. *The Activist's Handbook*. Updated ed. Berkeley: University of California Press.

Shaw, Sondra C., and Martha A. Taylor. 1995. *Reinventing Fundraising: Realizing the Potential of Women's Philanthropy*. San Francisco: Jossey-Bass.

Sheffer, Martin S. 1999. *God versus Caesar: Belief, Worship, and Proselytizing under the First Amendment*. Albany: State University of New York Press.

Sherr, Avrom. 1998. *Freedom of Protest, Public Order, and the Law*. New York: Blackwell.

Shifley, Rick L. 2003. "The Organization of Work as a Factor in Social Well-Being." *Contemporary Justice Review* 6:105–125.

Shim, Jae K., and Joel Siegel. 1997. *Financial Management for Nonprofits*. Chicago: Irwin Professional Publications.

Shokeid, Moshe. 2001. " 'The Women are Coming': The Transformation of Gender Relationships in a Gay Synagogue." *Ethnos* 66:5–26.

Shostak, Arthur. 1998. "Cocreating a Futures Studies Course with Unionists." *American Behavioral Scientist* 42:539–542.

Shriner, Larry. 1967. "The Concept of Secularization in Empirical Research." *Journal for the Scientific Study of Religion* 6(2):207–220.

Shy, John W. 1976. *A People Numerous and Armed: Reflections on the Military Struggle for American Independence*. New York: Oxford University Press.

Siciliano, Julie I. 1997. "The Relationship between Formal Planning and Performance in Nonprofit Organizations." *Nonprofit Management and Leadership* 7(4):387–403.

Sidjanski, Dusan. 1974. "Interest Groups in Switzerland." *Annals of the American Academy of Political and Social Science* 413:101–123.

Siebold, Cathy. 1992. *The Hospice Movement*. New York: Twayne.

Sifrey, Micah L. 2003. *Spoiling for a Fight: Third Party Politics in America*. New York: Routledge.

Silber, Norman I. 2001. *A Corporate Form of Freedom: The Emergence of the Nonprofit Sector*. Boulder, Colo.: Westview Press.

Silk, Thomas. 2004. "The Legal Framework of the Nonprofit Sector in the United States." Pp. 63–80 in *The Jossey-Bass Handbook of Nonprofit Leadership and Management*, 2nd ed., ed. Robert D. Herman and Associates. San Francisco: Jossey-Bass.

Sills, David L. 1957. *The Volunteers: Means and Ends in a National Organization.* Glencoe, Ill.: Free Press.

Simmel, Georg. 1955. *Conflict and the Web of Group-Affiliations,* trans. Kurt H. Wolff and Reinhard Bendix. New York: Free Press.

Simon, David R., ed. 2002. *Elite Deviance.* 7th ed. Boston: Allyn and Bacon.

Simon, Judith S., and J. Terence Donovan. 2001. *The Five Life Stages of Nonprofit Organizations.* St. Paul, Minn.: Amherst H. Wilder Foundation.

Simonsen, William, and Mark D. Robbins. 2000. *Citizen Participation in Resource Allocation.* Boulder, Colo.: Westview Press.

Simpson, Richard L., and William H. Gulley. 1962. "Goals, Environmental Pressures, and Organizational Characteristics." *American Sociological Review* 27: 344–351.

Sims, Patsy. 1996. *The Klan.* 2nd ed. Lexington: University Press of Kentucky.

Singer, Margaret T., with Janja Lalich. 1995. *Cults in Our Midst.* San Francisco: Jossey-Bass.

Sink, David W. 1992. "Response to Federal Cutbacks by Nonprofit Agencies and Local Funding Sources." *New England Journal of Human Services* 11(3):29–35.

Siriani, Carmen, and Lewis Friedland. 2001. *Civic Innovation in America: Community Empowerment, Public Policy, and the Movement for Civic Renewal.* Berkeley: University of California Press.

Skeldon, Ronald. 1977. "Regional Associations: A Note on Opposed Interpretations." *Comparative Studies in Society and History* 19:506–510.

Skrtic, Thomas M. 1991. "The Special Education Paradox: Equity and the Way of Excellence." *Harvard Educational Review* 61:148–206.

Slaton, Christa D. 1992. *Televote: Expanding Participation in the Quantum Age.* New York: Praeger.

Slesinger, Larry. 2004. *Search: Winning Strategies to Get Your Next Job in the Nonprofit World.* Glen Echo, Md.: Piemonte Press.

Slyke, David M., and Christine H. Roch. 2004. "What Do They Know, and Whom Do They Hold Accountable? Citizens in the Government-Nonprofit Contracting Relationship." *Journal of Public Administration Research and Theory* 14:191–210.

Smelser, Neil. 1962. *Theory of Collective Behavior.* New York: Free Press.

Smith, Bradford. 1992. *The Use of Standard Industrial Classification (SIC) Codes to Classify the Activities of Nonprofit, Tax-Exempt Organizations.* Working Paper No. 19. San Francisco: Institute for Nonprofit Organization Management, University of San Francisco.

Smith, Bradford, Sylvia Shue, Jennifer L. Vest, and Joseph Villarreal, eds. 1999. *Philanthropy in Communities of Color: Sharing and Helping in Eight Communities of Color.* Bloomington: Indiana University Press.

Smith, Bradford, Sylvia Shue, and Joseph Villarreal. 1992. *Asian and Hispanic Philanthropy.* San Francisco: University of San Francisco Press.

Smith, Bruce L. R. 1966. *The Rand Corporation: Case Study of a Nonprofit Advisory Corporation.* Cambridge, Mass.: Harvard University Press.

Smith, Christian. 1996. *Disruptive Religion: The Force of Faith in Social-Movement Activism.* New York: Routledge.

Smith, Constance, and Anne Freedman. 1972. *Voluntary Associations: Perspectives on the Literature.* Cambridge, Mass.: Harvard University Press.

Smith, David Horton. 1967. "A Parsimonious Definition of 'Group': Toward Conceptual Clarity and Scientific Utility." *Sociological Inquiry* 37(2): 141–167.

———. 1969. "Evidence for a General Activity Syndrome: A Survey of Townspeople in Eight Massachusetts Town and Cities." Pp. 453–454 in *Proceedings of the 77th Annual Convention of the American Psychological Association, 1969*, vol. 4. Washington, D.C.: American Psychological Association.

———. 1972a. Organizational Boundaries and Organizational Affiliates. *Sociology and Social Research* 56:494–512.

———. 1972b. "The Journal of Voluntary Action Research: An Introduction." *Journal of Voluntary Action Research* 1(1):2–5.

———. 1972c. "Ritual in Voluntary Associations." *Journal of Voluntary Action Research* 1(4):39–53.

———. 1973. "The Impact of the Voluntary Sector on Society." Pp. 387–399 in *Voluntary Action Research: 1973*, ed. David Horton Smith. Lexington, Mass.: Lexington Books.

———. 1973/2001. "The Impact of the Voluntary Sector on Society." Pp. 79–87 in *The Nature of the Nonprofit Sector*, ed. J. Steven Ott. Boulder, Colo.: Westview Press.

———, ed. 1974. *Voluntary Action Research: 1974*. Lexington, Mass.: Lexington Books.

———. 1975. "Voluntary Action and Voluntary Groups." Pp. 247–270 in *Annual Review of Sociology*, vol. 1, ed. Alex Inkeles, James Coleman, and Neil Smelser. Palo Alto, Calif.: Annual Reviews Inc.

———. 1977. "Values, Voluntary Action, and Philanthropy: The Appropriate Relationship of Private Philanthropy to Public Needs." Pp. 1093–1108 in *Research Papers, Volume II. Philanthropic Fields of Interest. Part II—Additional Perspectives*, ed. Commission on Private Philanthropy and Public Needs. Washington, D.C.: Department of the Treasury.

———. 1978. "The Philanthropy Business." *Society* 15:8–15.

———. 1980a. "Methods of Inquiry and Theoretical Perspectives." Pp. 8–33 in *Participation in Social and Political Activities*, ed. David Horton Smith, Jacqueline Macaulay, and Associates. San Francisco: Jossey-Bass.

———. 1980b. "Theoretical Models of Informal Social Activity." Pp. 400–530 in *Participation in Social and Political Activities*, ed. David Horton Smith, Jacqueline Macaulay, and Associates. San Francisco: Jossey-Bass.

———. 1981. "Altruism, Volunteers, and Volunteerism." *Journal of Voluntary Action Research* 10(1):21–36.

———. 1983. "Synanthrometrics: On Progress in the Development of a General Theory of Voluntary Action and Citizen Participation." Pp. 80–94 in *International Perspectives on Voluntary Action Research*, ed. David Horton Smith and Jon Van Til. Lanham, Md.: University Press of America.

———. 1984. "Churches Are Generally Ignored in Contemporary Voluntary Action Research: Causes and Consequences." *Journal of Voluntary Action Research* 13(4):11–18.

———. 1985. "Volunteerism: Attracting Volunteers and Staffing Shrinking Programs." Pp. 225–251 in *Social Planning and Human Service Delivery in the Voluntary Sector*, ed. Gary A. Tobin. Westport, Conn.: Greenwood Press.

———. 1991. "Four Sectors or Five? Retaining the Member-Benefit Sector." *Nonprofit and Voluntary Sector Quarterly* 20:137–150.

———. 1992a. "National Nonprofit, Voluntary Associations: Some Parameters." *Nonprofit and Voluntary Sector Quarterly* 21(1):81–94.

———. 1992b. "A Neglected Type of Voluntary Nonprofit Organization: Exploration of the Semiformal, Fluid-Membership Organization." *Nonprofit and Voluntary Sector Quarterly* 21(3):251–269.

———. 1993. "Public Benefit and Member Benefit Nonprofit, Voluntary Groups." *Nonprofit and Voluntary Sector Quarterly* 22(1):53–68.

———. 1994a. "Determinants of Voluntary Association Participation and Volunteering: A Literature Review." *Nonprofit and Voluntary Sector Quarterly* 23(3): 243–263.

———. 1994b. "Some Understudied Research Topics: The 1994 ISTR Conference and Beyond." *Voluntas* 5(3):349–358.

———. 1995a. "Democratic Personality." Pp. 941–943 in *The Encyclopedia of Democracy. Volume 3,* ed. Seymour Martin Lipset. Washington, D.C.: Congressional Quarterly Books.

———. 1995b. "Some Challenges in Nonprofit and Voluntary Action Research." *Nonprofit and Voluntary Sector Quarterly* 24(2):99–101.

———. 1996a. "Defining Nonprofit/Voluntary Sector Terms: A Search for Practical and Theoretical Consensus." Unpublished paper. Department of Sociology, Boston College, Chestnut Hill, Mass.

———. 1996b. "Teaching a Course in Deviant Groups: A Neglected Side of Deviance." *Teaching Sociology* 24:177–188.

———. 1997a. "Grassroots Associations Are Important: Some Theory and a Review of the Impact Literature." *Nonprofit and Voluntary Sector Quarterly* 26 (3, September):269–306.

———. 1997b. "The International History of Grassroots Associations." *International Journal of Comparative Sociology* 38(3–4):189–216.

———. 1997c. "The Rest of the Nonprofit Sector: Grassroots Associations as the Dark Matter Ignored in Prevailing 'Flat-Earth' Maps of the Sector." *Nonprofit and Voluntary Sector Quarterly* 26:114–131.

———. 1999. "Researching Volunteer Associations and Other Nonprofits: An Emergent Interdisciplinary Field and Possible New Discipline." *American Sociologist* 30 (4, Winter):5–35.

———. 2000. *Grassroots Associations.* Thousand Oaks, Calif.: Sage.

———. 2003. "A History of ARNOVA." *Nonprofit and Voluntary Sector Quarterly* 32(3):458–72.

Smith, David Horton, Dan Bernfeld, Ernst Abma, and David Zeldin. 1992. "International Terminology on Nonprofit Organizations and Voluntary Action in Some European Languages and American English." Paper presented at the Third International Conference of Research on Voluntary and Nonprofit Organizations, Center on Philanthropy, Indiana University at Indianapolis, March.

Smith, David Horton, with John Dixon. 1973. "The Voluntary Society." Pp. 202–227 in *Challenge to Leadership,* ed. Edward C. Bursk. New York: Free Press.

Smith, David Horton, and Frederick Elkin, eds. 1981. *Volunteers, Voluntary Organizations, and Development.* Leiden, Netherlands: E. J. Brill.

Smith, David Horton, Jacqueline Macaulay, and Associates. 1980. *Participation in Social and Political Activities.* San Francisco: Jossey-Bass.

Smith, David Horton, and Karl Pillemer. 1983. "Self-Help Groups as Social Movement Organizations: Social Structure and Social Change." Pp. 203–233 in *Research in Social Movements, Conflicts and Change, Volume 5,* ed. Louis Kriesberg. Greenwich, Conn.: JAI Press.

Smith, David Horton, R. D. Reddy, and B. R. Baldwin. 1972. "Types of Voluntary Action: A Definitional Essay." In *Voluntary Action Research: 1972,* ed. D. H. Smith, R. D. Reddy, and B. R. Baldwin. Lexington, Mass.: Lexington Books.

Smith, David Horton, and Ce Shen. 2002. "The Roots of Civil Society: A Model of Voluntary Association Prevalence Applied to Data on Larger Contemporary Nations." *International Journal of Comparative Sociology* 42(2):93–133.

Smith, David Horton, and Nancy Theberge. 1987. *Why People Recreate: An Overview of Research.* Champaign, Ill.: Life Enhancement Publications.

Smith, David Horton, and Jon Van Til, eds. 1983. *International Perspectives on Voluntary Action Research.* Lanham, Md.: University Press of America.

Smith, Garry. 1994. "The Status of Gambling in Canadian Society." Pp. 19–26 in *Gambling in Canada: The Bottom Line,* ed. Colin S. Campbell. Burnaby, BC: Criminology Research Centre, School of Criminology, Simon Fraser University.

Smith, Justin D., Angela Ellis, and Georgina Brewis. 2005. "Cross-National Volunteering: A Developing Movement?" Pp. 63–76 in *Emerging Areas of Volunteering* (ARNOVA Occasional Paper Series, volume 1, no. 2), ed. Jeffrey L. Brudney. Indianapolis: Association for Research on Nonprofit Organizations and Voluntary Action.

Smith, Justin D., Colin Rochester, and Rodney Hedley. 1995. *An Introduction to the Voluntary Sector.* London: Routledge.

Smith, M. J. 1990. "Pluralism, Reformed Pluralism, and Neopluralism: The Role of Pressure Groups in Policy-Making." *Political Studies* 37:302–322.

Smith, Maria P. 1989. "Taking Volunteerism into the Twenty-first Century: Some Conclusions from the American Red Cross Volunteer 2000 Study." *Journal of Volunteer Administration* 8 (Fall):3–10.

Smith, Peter B., and Shalom Schwartz. 1997. "Values." Pp. 77–118 in *Handbook of Cross-Cultural Psychology, Volume 3: Behavior and Applications,* 2nd ed., ed. John W. Berry, Marshall H. Segall, and Cigdem Kagitcibasi. Boston: Pearson Allyn and Bacon.

Smith, Steven R. 2005. "Managing the Challenges of Government Contracts." Pp. 371–390 in *The Jossey-Bass Handbook of Nonprofit Leadership and Management,* 2nd ed. Robert D. Herman and Associates. San Francisco: Jossey-Bass.

Smith, Steven R., and Michael Lipsky. 1993. *Nonprofits for Hire.* Cambridge, Mass.: Harvard University Press.

Smock, Kristina. 2004. *Democracy in Action: Community Organizing and Urban Change.* New York: Columbia University Press.

Smucker, Bob. 1991. *The Nonprofit Lobbying Guide: Advocating Your Cause and Getting Results.* San Francisco: Jossey-Bass.

———. 2004. "Nonprofit Lobbying." Pp. 230–253 in *The Jossey-Bass Handbook of Nonprofit Leadership and Management,* 2nd ed., ed. Robert D. Herman and Associates. San Francisco: Jossey-Bass.

Snow, David A. 2003. "Social Movements." Pp. 811–834 in *Handbook of Symbolic Interactionism,* ed. Larry T. Reynolds and Nancy J. Herman-Kinney. Walnut Creek, Calif.: AltaMira Press.

Snow, Robert L. 1999. *Terrorists among Us: The Militia Threat.* Cambridge, Mass.: Perseus Publishing.

Solomon, Barbara. 1976. *Black Empowerment: Social Work in Oppressed Communities.* New York: Columbia University Press.

Solomon, Lewis D. 2003. *In God We Trust? Faith-Based Organizations and the Quest to Solve America's Social Ills.* Lanham, Md.: Lexington Books.

Somers, Margaret R. 1993. "Citizenship and the Place of the Public Sphere: Law, Community and Political Culture in the Transition to Democracy." *American Sociological Review* 58(5):587–621.

Sommer, John G. 1977. *Beyond Charity: U.S. Voluntary Aid for a Changing Third World.* Washington, D.C.: Overseas Development Council.

Sommer, Robert, Katharine Hess, and Sandra Nelson. 1985. "Funeral Co-Op Members' Characteristics and Motives." *Sociological Perspectives* 28:487–500.

Sosis, Richard, and Bressler, Eric R. 2003. "Cooperation and Commune Longevity:

A Test of the Costly Signaling Theory of Religion." *Cross-Cultural Research* 37(2):211–239.

Soysal, Yasemin N. 1994. *Limits of Citizenship: Migrants and Postnational Membership in Europe.* Chicago: University of Chicago Press.

Spergel, Irving A. 1995. *The Youth Gang Problem.* New York: Oxford University Press.

Spiegel, Hans B. C., ed. 1968. *Citizen Participation in Urban Development. Volume I: Concepts and Issues.* Washington, D.C.: NTL Institute for Applied Behavioral Science.

———, ed. 1974. *Decentralization: Citizen Participation in Urban Development— Volume 3.* Fairfax, Va.: Learning Resources Corporation/NTL.

Stackhouse, Max L. 1990. "Religion and the Social Space for Voluntary Institutions." Pp. 22–37 in *Faith and Philanthropy in America,* ed. Robert Wuthnow and Virginia Hodgkinson. Washington, D.C.: INDEPENDENT SECTOR.

Stammen, Theo. 1981. *Political Parties in Europe.* Westport, Conn.: Meckler Publishing.

Stanton, Esther. 1970. *Clients Come Last: Volunteers and Welfare Organizations.* Beverly Hills, Calif.: Sage.

Stanton, Timothy K., Dwight E. Giles, and Nadinne I. Cruz. 1999. *Service-Learning.* San Francisco: Jossey-Bass.

Staples, Lee. 1984. *Roots to Power: A Manual for Grassroots Organizing.* New York: Praeger.

Stark, Rodney. 1994. *Sociology.* 5th ed. Belmont, Calif.: Wadsworth.

Stark, Rodney, and Charles Y. Glock. 1968. *American Piety: The Nature of Religious Commitment.* Berkeley: University of California Press.

Stark, Rodney, and William S. Bainbridge. 1985. *The Future of Religion: Secularization, Revival and Cult Formation.* Berkeley: University of California Press.

Starkweather, D. B. 1993. "Profit Making by Nonprofit Hospitals." Pp. 105–137 in *Nonprofit Organizations in a Market Economy,* ed. David C. Hammack and Dennis R. Young. San Francisco: Jossey-Bass.

Starr, Jerold M. 2001. "The Challenges and Rewards of Coalition Building: Pittsburgh's Alliance for Progressive Action." Pp. 107–119 in *Forging Radical Alliances across Difference: Coalition Politics for the New Millennium,* ed. Jill M. Bystydzienski and Steven P. Schacht. Lanham, Md.: Rowman & Littlefield.

Staub, Ervin. 1978. *Positive Social Behavior and Morality. Volume 1, Social and Personal Influences.* New York: Academic.

———. 1979. *Positive Social Behavior and Morality. Volume 2, Socialization and Development.* New York: Academic.

Stebbins, Robert A. 1979. *Amateurs: On the Margin between Work and Leisure.* Beverly Hills, Calif.: Sage.

———. 1982. "Serious Leisure: A Conceptual Statement." *Pacific Sociological Review* 25 (April):251–272.

———. 1990. *Sociology: The Study of Society.* 2nd ed. New York: Harper & Row.

———. 1992. *Amateurs, Professionals, and Serious Leisure.* Montreal; McGill-Queen's University Press.

———. 1993a. *Canadian Football: The View from the Helmet.* Toronto: Canadian Scholars Press.

———. 1993b. *Career, Culture, and Social Psychology in a Variety Art: The Magician.* Malabar, Fla.: Krieger.

———. 1993c. *Predicaments: Moral Difficulty in Everyday Life.* Lanham, Md.: University Press of America.

———. 1994. *The Franco-Calgarians: French Language, Leisure and Linguistic Life-Style in an Anglophone City.* Toronto: University of Toronto Press.

———. 1996a. *The Barbershop Singer: Inside the Social World of a Musical Hobby.* Toronto: University of Toronto Press.

———. 1996b. *Tolerable Differences: Living with Deviance.* 2nd ed. Toronto: Mc-Graw-Hill Ryerson.

———. 1996c. "Volunteering: A Serious Leisure Perspective." *Nonprofit and Voluntary Sector Quarterly* 25:211–224.

———. 1998. *The Urban Francophone Volunteer: Searching for Personal Meaning and Community Growth in a Linguistic Minority,* Volume 3, No. 2 (New Scholars-New Visions in Canadian Studies quarterly monographs series). Seattle: University of Washington, Canadian Studies Centre.

———. 2000. "Obligation as an Aspect of Leisure Experience." *Journal of Leisure Research* 32:152–155.

———. 2001. "Volunteering—Marginal or Mainstream: Preserving the Leisure Experience." Pp. 1–10 in *Leisure Volunteering: Marginal or Inclusive?* ed. Margaret Graham and Malcolm Foley. Eastbourne, UK: Leisure Studies Association, University of Brighton.

———. 2002. *The Organizational Basis of Leisure Participation: A Motivation Exploration.* State College, Pa.: Venture.

———. 2003a. "Boredom in Free Time." *Leisure Studies Association Newsletter* 64 (March 2003):29–31.

———. 2003b. "Casual Leisure." Pp. 44–46 in *Encyclopedia of Leisure and Outdoor Recreation,* ed. John Jenkins and John Pigram. London: Routledge.

———. 2003c. "Hobby." Pp. 238–239 in *Encyclopedia of Leisure and Outdoor Recreation,* ed. John Jenkins and John Pigram. London: Routledge.

———. 2003d. "Volunteering." Pp. 541–542 in *Encyclopedia of Leisure and Outdoor Recreation,* ed. John Jenkins and John Pigram. London: Routledge.

———. 2004a. *Between Work and Leisure: The Common Ground of Two Separate Worlds.* New Brunswick, N.J.: Transaction Publishers.

———. 2004b. "Introduction." Pp. 1–12 in *Volunteering as Leisure/Leisure as Volunteering: An International Assessment,* ed. Robert A. Stebbins and Margaret Graham. Wallingford, Oxon, UK: CABI Publishing.

———. 2005a. "Choice and Experiential Definitions of Leisure." *Leisure Sciences* 27: 349–352.

———. 2005b. "Project-Based Leisure: Theoretical Neglect of a Common Use of Free Time." *Leisure Studies* 24:1–11.

Stebbins, Robert A., and Margaret Graham. 2004. *Volunteering as Leisure/Leisure as Volunteering: An International Assessment.* Wallingford, Oxon, UK: CABI Publishing.

Steele, Betty. 2000. *My Heart, My Hands: A Celebration of Volunteerism in Canada.* Toronto: Stoddart.

Steinberg, Richard. 1990. "Labor Economics and the Nonprofit Sector: A Literature Review." *Nonprofit and Voluntary Sector Quarterly* 19:151–169.

Stepan-Norris, Judith, and Maurice Zeitlin. 1996. *Talking Union.* Urbana: University of Illinois Press.

Sterk, Claire E. 1999. "Building Bridges: Community Involvement in Drug and HIV Research among Minority Populations." *Drugs and Society* 14:107–121.

Sterne, Evelyn S. 2000. "Bringing Religion into Working-Class History." *Social Science History* 24:149–182.

Stevens, Ellen S. 1991. "Toward Satisfaction and Retention of Senior Volunteers." *Journal of Gerontological Social Work* 16(3–4):33–41.

Stewart, David W., and Henry A. Spille. 1988. *Diploma Mills: Degrees of Fraud.* New York: Macmillan.

Stewart, Frank H. 1977. *Fundamentals of Age-Group Systems.* New York: Academic Press.

Stewman, Shelby. 1988. "Organizational Demography." *Annual Review of Sociology* 14:173–202.

Stiglitz, Joseph. 1986. *Economics of the Public Sector.* New York: W. W. Norton and Company.

Stogdill, R. M. 1948. "Personal Factors Associated with Leadership: A Survey of the Literature." *Journal of Psychology* 25:35–71.

Stone, I. F. 1971. *The Killings at Kent State.* New York: Vintage.

Stonebraker, Robert J. 2003. "Allocating Local Church Funds to Benevolence: The Impact of Congregational Size." *Review of Religious Research* 45:48–58.

Strain, Laurel A., and Audrey A. Blandford. 2003. "Caregiving Networks in Later Life: Does Cognitive Status Make a Difference?" *Canadian Journal on Aging* 22:261–273.

Streeck, Wolfgang, and Phillipe Schmitter. 1985. *Private Interest Government: Beyond Market and State.* London: Sage.

Street, Debra. 1997. "Special Interest or Citizens' Rights? 'Senior Power,' Social Security, and Medicare." *International Journal of Health Services* 27(4):727–751.

Streitmatter, Rodger. 2001. *Voices of Revolution: The Dissident Press in America.* New York: Columbia University Press.

Stroecker, Randy. 1999. "Are Academics Irrelevant? Roles for Scholars in Participatory Research." *American Behavioral Scientist* 42(5):840–854.

Stromberg, Ann H. 1968. *Philanthropic Foundations in Latin America.* New York: Russell Sage Foundation.

Sturgeon, M. Sue. 1994. "Finding and Keeping the Right Employees." Pp. 535–556 in *The Jossey-Bass Handbook of Nonprofit Leadership and Management,* ed. Robert D. Herman and Associates. San Francisco: Jossey-Bass.

Sturtevant, William T. 1997. *The Artful Journey: Cultivating and Soliciting the Major Gift.* Chicago: Bonus Books.

Sullivan, Mercer L. 2004. "Youth Perspectives on the Experience of Reentry." *Youth Violence and Juvenile Justice* 2(1):56–71.

Summers, Martin. 2003. "Diasporic Brotherhood: Freemasonry and the Transnational Production of Black-Middle Class Masculinity." *Gender and History* 15:550–574.

Sylves, Richard T. 1998. "How the Exxon Valdez Disaster Changed America's Oil Spill Emergency Management." *International Journal of Mass Emergencies and Disasters* 16(1):13–43.

Szalai, Alexander. 1972. *The Use of Time.* The Hague: Mouton.

Tannenbaum, Arnold S., and Robert L. Kahn. 1982. *Participation in Union Locals.* Evanston, Ill.: Row Peterson.

Tarrow, Sidney G. 1991. *Struggle, Politics, and Reform: Collective Action, Social Movements, and Cycles of Protest.* Ithaca, N.Y.: Center for International Studies, Cornell University.

Tarrow, Sidney G., et al. 1998. *Power in Movement: Social Movements and Contentious Politics.* Cambridge, UK: Cambridge University Press.

Taylor, Mark C. 1998. *Critical Terms for Religious Studies.* Chicago: University of Chicago Press.

Taylor, Mary. 1999. "Unwrapping Stock Transfers: Applying Discourse Analysis to Landlord Communication Strategies." *Urban Studies* 36:121–135.

Taylor, Samuel H., and Robert W. Roberts. 1985. *Theory and Practice of Community Social Work.* New York: Columbia University Press.

Tecker, Glenn, and Marybeth Fidler. 1993. *Successful Association Leadership.* Washington, D.C.: American Society of Association Executives Foundation.

Tester, Keith. 1992. *Civil Society.* London: Routledge.

Thomas, Clive S., ed. 2004. *Research Guide to U.S. and International Interest Groups.* Westport, Conn.: Praeger.

Thomas, Clive S., and Ronald Hrebenar. 1996. "Interest Groups in the States." Pp. 122–158 in *Politics in the American States,* 6th ed., ed. Virginia Gray and Herbert Jacob. Washington, D.C.: CQ Press.

Thomas, John C. 1994. "Program Evaluation and Program Development." Pp. 342–366 in *The Jossey-Bass Handbook of Nonprofit Leadership and Management,* ed. Robert D. Herman and Associates. San Francisco: Jossey-Bass.

Thomas, Ret, and Dorine M. Thomas. 1998. *The Service Volunteer's Handbook.* San Jose, Calif.: Resource Publications.

Thomas-Slayter, Barbara P. 1985. *Politics, Participation, and Poverty: Development through Self-Help in Kenya.* Boulder, Colo.: Westview Press.

Thompson, Mark S. 1980. *Benefit-Cost Analysis for Program Evaluation.* Beverly Hills, Calif.: Sage.

Thompson, Mary C. 1997. "Employment-Based Volunteering: Leisure or Not?" *World Leisure & Recreation* 39(3):30–33.

Thoreau, Henry David. 1849/1960. *Walden and Civil Disobedience,* ed. Paul Sherman. Boston: Houghton Mifflin.

Tilgher, Adriano. 1977. *Work, What It Has Meant to Men through the Ages.* New York: Arno Press.

Tilly, Charles. 1978. *From Mobilization to Revolution.* Reading, Mass.: Addison-Wesley.

———. 2004. *Social Movements, 1768–2004.* Boulder, Colo.: Paradigm Publishers.

Timbs, John. 1865. *Club Life of London.* 2 vols. London: Chatto and Windus.

Titmuss, Richard M. 1971. *The Gift Relationship.* New York: Pantheon Books.

Toepler, Stefan. 2003. "Grassroots Associations versus Larger Nonprofits: New Evidence from a Community Case Study in Arts and Culture." *Nonprofit and Voluntary Sector Quarterly* 32(2):236–251.

Tomeh, Aida K. 1981. "The Value of Voluntarism among Minority Groups." *Phylon* 42(1):86–96.

Todd, Malcolm J., and Gary Taylor. 2004. *Democracy and Participation: Popular Protest and New Social Movements.* London: Merlin.

Tonry, Michael, and Albert J. Reiss, Jr., eds. 1993. *Beyond the Law: Crime in Complex Organizations.* Chicago: University of Chicago Press.

Torigian, Michael. 1999. "The Occupation of Factories: Paris 1936, Flint 1937." *Comparative Studies in Society and History* 41:324–347.

Toth, James. 2003. "Islamism in Southern Egypt: A Case Study of a Radical Religious Movement." *International Journal of Middle East Studies* 35(4):547–572.

Tremper, Charles. 1994. "Risk Management." Pp. 485–508 in *The Jossey-Bass Handbook of Nonprofit Leadership and Management,* ed. Robert D. Herman and Associates. San Francisco: Jossey-Bass.

Tremper, Charles, and Gwynne Kortin. 1993. *No Surprises: Controlling Risks in Volunteer Programs.* Washington, D.C.: Nonprofit Risk Management Center.

Trexler, Richard C. 1991. *Public Life in Renaissance Florence.* Ithaca, N.Y.: Cornell University Press.

Trivers, R. 1971. "The Evolution of Reciprocal Altruism." *Quarterly Review of Biology* 46:35–57.

Tropman, John E. 1997. *Successful Community Leadership: A Skills Guide for Volunteers and Professionals.* Washington, D.C.: National Association of Social Workers.

————. 2003. *Making Meetings Work.* Thousand Oaks, Calif.: Sage.

Trueblood, Elton. 1967. *The Incendiary Fellowship.* New York: Harper.

Truman, David B. 1955. *The Governmental Process.* New York: Knopf.

Tsouderos, John E. 1955. "Organizational Change in Terms of a Series of Selected Variables." *American Sociological Review* 20(2):206–210.

Tucker, Marna S. 1972. *The Lawyer as Volunteer: Pro Bono Publico Programs for Bar Associations and Professional Organizations.* Chicago: American Bar Association.

Tucker, Richard K. 1991. *The Dragon and the Cross: The Rise and Fall of the Ku Klux Klan in Middle America.* Hamden, Conn.: Archon Books.

Tucker, William. 1985. *Vigilante: The Backlash against Crime in America.* New York: Stein and Day.

Tuckman, Howard P. 1996. *Competition among Nonprofits and between Nonprofits and For-Profits.* Indianapolis: Indiana University Center on Philanthropy.

Turcott, Paul-André. 2001. "The Religious Order as a Cognitive Minority in the Church and in Society." *Social Compass* 48:169–191.

Ture, Kwame, and Charles V. Hamilton. 1967. *Black Power.* New York: Random House.

Turner, Howard B. 1992. "Older Volunteers: An Assessment of Two Theories." *Educational Gerontology* 18(1):41–55.

Turner, James. 1985. *Without God, Without Creed: The Origins of Unbelief in America.* Baltimore: Johns Hopkins University Press.

Unger, Donald G., and Abraham Wandersman. 1983. "Neighboring and Its Role in Block Organizations: An Exploratory Report." *American Journal of Community Psychology* 11(3):291–300.

Unger, Irwin. 1974. *The Movement: A History of the American New Left, 1959–1972.* New York: Dodd, Mead.

Union of International Associations. 1994a. *International Congress Calendar.* Brussels: Union of International Associations.

Union of International Associations. 1994b. *Yearbook of International Organizations.* Brussels: Union of International Associations.

United Way of Wake County, Voluntary Action Center. 1988. *Cornucopia 88: A Guide to Getting Involved.* Raleigh, N.C.: United Way of Wake County, Voluntary Action Center.

Uphoff, Norman. 2000. "Understanding Social Capital: Learning from the Analysis and Experience of Participation." Pp. 215–249 in *Social Capital: A Multifaceted Perspective,* ed. Partha Dasgupta and Ismail Serageldin. Washington, D.C.: World Bank.

U.S. Bureau of the Census. 2002. *Statistical Abstract of the United States: 2002,* 112th ed. Washington, D.C.: U.S. Dept. of Commerce, U.S. Census Bureau.

Utter, Glenn H., and John W. Storey. 1995. *The Religious Right: A Reference Handbook.* Santa Barbara, Calif.: ABC-CLIO.

Van Aelst, Peter, and Stefaan Walgrave. 2002. "New Media, New Movements? The Role of the Internet in Shaping the 'Anti-Globalization' Movement." *Information, Communication, and Society* 5:465–493.

Van de Fliert, Lydia, ed. 1994. *Indigenous Peoples and International Organisations.* Nottingham, UK: Spokesman.

Van den Brink, Rogier, and Jean-Paul Chavas. 1997. "The Microeconomics of an Indigenous African Institution: The Rotating Savings and Credit Association." *Economic Development and Cultural Change* 45:745–772.

Van Deth, Jan W., ed. 1997. *Private Groups and Public Life: Social Participation, Voluntary Associations, and Political Involvement in Representative Democracies.* London: Routledge.

Van Loo, M. F. 1990. "Gift Exchange: A Brief Survey with Applications for Non-profit Practitioners." 1990 Spring Research Forum Working Papers. Washington, D.C.: INDEPENDENT SECTOR.

Van Maanen, John, ed. 1998. *Qualitative Studies of Organizations.* Thousand Oaks, Calif.: Sage.

Van Til, Jon. 1988. *Mapping the Third Sector: Voluntarism in a Changing Social Economy.* New York: Foundation Center.

———. 1990. *Critical Issues in American Philanthropy.* San Francisco: Jossey-Bass.

———. 1994. "Nonprofit Organizations and Social Institutions." Pp. 44–64 in *The Jossey-Bass Handbook of Nonprofit Leadership and Management,* ed. Robert D. Herman and Associates. San Francisco: Jossey-Bass.

———. 2000. *Growing Civil Society.* Bloomington: Indiana University Press.

Veblen, Thorstein. 1899. *The Theory of the Leisure Class.* New York: Macmillan.

Verba, Sidney, and Norman H. Nie. 1972. *Participation in America.* New York: Harper & Row.

Verba, Sidney, Norman H. Nie, and Jae-on Kim. 1978. *Participation and Equality: A Seven Nation Comparison.* Cambridge, UK: Cambridge University Press.

Verba, Sidney, Kay L. Schlozman, and H. E. Brady. 1995. *Voice and Equality: Civic Voluntarism in American Politics.* Cambridge, Mass.: Harvard University Press.

Vidich, Arthur J., and Joseph Bensman. 1968. *Small Town in Mass Society: Class, Power, and Religion in a Rural Community.* Rev. ed. Princeton, N.J.: Princeton University Press.

Vineyard, Sue. 1988. *Evaluating Volunteers, Programs, and Events.* Downers Grove, Ill.: Heritage Arts.

———. 1993. *Megatrends and Volunteerism: Mapping the Future of Volunteer Programs.* Downers Grove, Ill.: Heritage Arts.

———. 1996. *Best Practices in Workplace Employee Volunteer Programs.* Downers Grove, Ill.: Heritage Arts.

———. 2001. *Recognizing Volunteers and Paid Staff.* Darien, Ill.: Heritage Arts.

Vineyard, Sue, and Steve McCurley. 1989. *Resource Directory for Volunteer Programs.* Downers Grove, Ill.: VM Systems.

———. 1998. *Handling Problem Volunteers.* Downers Grove, Ill.: Heritage Arts.

———. 2001. *Best Practices for Volunteer Programs.* Darien, Ill.: Heritage Arts.

Vinitzky-Seroussi, Vered. 1998. *After Pomp and Circumstance: High School Reunion as an Autobiographical Occasion.* Chicago: University of Chicago Press.

Vinton, Linda. 1992. "Battered Women's Shelters and Older Women: The Florida Experience." *Journal of Family Violence* 7:63–72.

Von Hoffman, Alexander. 1994. *Local Attachments: The Making of an American Urban Neighborhood 1850–1920.* Baltimore: Johns Hopkins University Press.

———. 2003. *House by House, Block by Block: The Rebirth of America's Urban Neighborhoods.* New York: Oxford University Press.

Wade, Rahima C. 1997. *Community Service-Learning: A Guide to Including Service in the Public School Curriculum.* Albany: State University of New York Press.

Wainwright, Geoffrey. 1997. *Worship with One Accord.* New York: Oxford University Press.

Walkenhorst, Peter. 2001. *Building Philanthropic and Social Capital: The World of Community Foundations.* Gütersloh, Germany: Bertelsmann Foundation.

Walker, J. M. 1983. "Limits of Strategic Management in Voluntary Organizations." *Journal of Voluntary Action Research* 12(3):39–56.

Walker, Julia. 2005. *Nonprofit Essentials: The Capital Campaign.* Hoboken, N.J.: Wiley.

Bibliography

Wallenstein, Peter, and James R. Clyburn. 2003. "The Civil Rights Movement in the Urban Upper South." *Virginia Social Science Journal* 38:17–32.

Walter, Scott. 1996. "The 'Flawed Parent': A Reconsideration of Rousseau's *Emily* and Its Significance for Radical Education in the United States." *British Journal of Educational Studies* 44:260–274.

Ware, Alan. 2001. *Political Parties and Party Systems.* New York: Oxford University Press.

Ware, Kallistos. 1993. *The Orthodox Church.* New York: Penguin Books.

Warner, Carolyn M. 1997. "Political Parties and the Opportunity Costs of Patronage." *Party Politics* 3:533–548.

Warner, W. Lloyd, and Paul S. Lunt. 1941. *The Social Life of a Modern Community.* New Haven, Conn.: Yale University Press.

Warren, Chris R. 1997. *How to Compete and Cooperate at the Same Time.* Santa Fe, N.M.: Adolfo Street Publishers.

Warren, Mark E. 2001. *Democracy and Association.* Princeton, N.J.: Princeton University Press.

Warren, Mark R. 2001. *Dry Bones Rattling: Community Building to Revitalize Democracy.* Princeton, N.J.: Princeton University Press.

Warren, Nancy B. 2001. *Spiritual Economies: Female Monasticism in Later Medieval England.* Philadelphia: University of Pennsylvania Press.

Warren, Roland. 1967. "The Interorganizational Field as a Focus for Investigation." *Administrative Science Quarterly* 12:396–419.

Warwick, Mal, Ted Hart, and Nick Allen, eds. 2002. *The ePhilanthropyFoundation.org's Guide to Success Online.* 2nd ed. San Francisco: Jossey-Bass.

Warwick, Mal, and Stephen Hitchcock. 2002. *Ten Steps to Fundraising Success.* San Francisco: Jossey-Bass.

Washington, James M. 1986. *Frustrated Fellowship: The Black Baptist Quest for Social Power.* Macon, Ga.: Mercer.

Waterman, Robert H., Jr. 1990. *Adhocracy: The Power to Change.* New York: Norton.

Wearing, Stephen. 2001. *Volunteer Tourism: Experiences That Make a Difference.* Wallingford, Oxon, UK: CABI Publishing.

Weaver, Warren. 1967. *U.S. Philanthropic Foundations.* New York: Harper & Row.

Weber, Max. 1947. *The Theory of Social and Economic Organization.* Glencoe, Ill.: Free Press.

———. 1952. *The Protestant Ethic and the Spirit of Capitalism.* New York: Scribner.

———. 1958. *From Max Weber: Essays in Sociology,* trans. Hans H. Gerth and C. Wright Mills. New York: Oxford University Press.

Weeden, Curt. 1998. *Corporate Social Investing: The Breakthrough Strategy for Giving and Getting Corporate Contributions.* San Francisco: Berrett-Koehler Publishers.

Weinberg, Leonard, and Ami Pedahzur. 2003. *Political Parties and Terrorist Groups.* London: Routledge.

Weinstein, Jay A. 2005. *Social and Cultural Change: Social Science for a Dynamic World.* Lanham, N.J.: Rowman & Littlefield.

Weinstein, Lewis. 1993. *My Life at the Bar: Lawyer, Soldier, Teacher, and Pro Bono Activist.* Hanover, Mass.: Christopher Books.

Weisbrod, Burton A. 1977. *The Voluntary Nonprofit Sector: An Economic Analysis.* Lexington, Mass.: D. C. Heath.

———. 1988. *The Nonprofit Economy.* Cambridge, Mass.: Harvard University Press.

———. 1992. "Tax Policy toward Nonprofit Organizations: A Ten Country Survey." Pp. 29–50 in *The Nonprofit Sector in the Global Community: Voices from Many Nations,* ed. K. D. McCarthy, V. A. Hodgkinson, and R. A. Sumariwalla. San Francisco: Jossey-Bass.

———. 1997. "The Future of the Nonprofit Sector: Its Entwining with Private Enterprise and Government." *Journal of Policy Analysis and Management* 16(4): 541–555.

———, ed. 1998. *To Profit or Not to Profit: The Commercial Transformation of the Nonprofit Sector.* New York: Cambridge University Press.

Weiss, Carol H. 1972. *Evaluation Research: Methods of Assessing Program Effectiveness.* Englewood Cliffs, N.J.: Prentice Hall.

Weiss, Robert S. 1973. *Loneliness: The Experience of Emotional and Social Isolation.* Cambridge, Mass.: MIT Press.

Weitzman, Murray S., Nadine T. Jalandoni, Linda M. Lampkin, and Thomas H. Pollak. 2002. *The New Nonprofit Almanac and Desk Reference.* San Francisco: Jossey-Bass.

Wellock, Thomas R. 1997. "Stick It in L.A.! Community Control and Nuclear Power in California's Central Valley." *Journal of American History* 84:942–978.

Wellman, David T. 1995. *The Union Makes Us Strong.* New York: Cambridge University Press.

Wendroff, Alan L. 2004. *Special Events: Proven Strategies for Nonprofit Fundraising.* Hoboken, N.J.: Wiley.

Wendroff, Alan L., and Kay S. Grace. 2001. *High Impact Philanthropy.* New York: Wiley.

Wertheimer, Jack. 1987. *The American Synagogue.* New York: Cambridge University Press.

Werther, William B., and Evan M. Berman. 2001. *Third Sector Management: The Art of Managing Nonprofit Organizations.* Washington, D.C.: Georgetown University Press.

White, Barbara J., and Edward J. Madara, eds. 2002. *The Self-Help Group Sourcebook: Your Guide to Community and Online Support Groups.* Cedar Knoll, N.J.: Saint Clares Health Services.

White, Douglas E. 1998. *The Art of Planned Giving.* New York: Wiley.

———. 2001. "Why Do People Donate to Charity?" Pp. 347–360 in *The Nonprofit Handbook: Fund Raising,* 3rd ed., ed. James M. Greenfield. New York: Wiley.

White, Theodore H. 1973. *The Making of a President 1972.* New York: Bantam.

Whittaker, James K., and James Garbarino. 1983. *Social Support Networks: Informal Helping in the Human Services.* Hawthorne, N.Y.: Aldine.

Wholey, Joseph S., and Harry P. Hatry, eds. 2004. *Handbook of Practical Program Evaluation.* San Francisco: Jossey-Bass.

Whyte, William F., ed. 1990. *Participatory Action Research.* Thousand Oaks, Calif.: Sage.

Wiarda, Howard. 1993. *Civil Society: The American Model and Third World Development.* Boulder, Colo.: Westview Press.

———. 1997. *Corporatism and Comparative Politics: The Other Great Ism.* Armonk, N.Y.: M. E. Sharpe.

———. 2004. *Authoritarianism and Corporatism in Latin America—Revisited.* Gainesville: University Press of Florida.

Widmer, Candace H., Susan Houchin, National Center for Nonprofit Boards, and Nonprofit Sector Research Fund. 1999. *Governance of National Federated Organizations.* Washington, D.C.: National Center for Nonprofit Boards.

Wielhouwer, Peter W. 2000. "Releasing the Fetters: Parties and the Mobilization of the African-American Electorate." *Journal of Politics* 62:206–222.

Wilbur, Robert H. 2000. *The Complete Guide to Nonprofit Management.* 2nd ed. New York: Wiley.

Wilkinson, J. Harvie. 1997. *One Nation Indivisible: How Ethnic Separatism Threatens America.* Reading, MA: Addison-Wesley.

Wilkinson, Philip. 1999. *Illustrated Dictionary of Religions: Rituals, Beliefs, and Practices from around the World.* New York: DK Publications.

Wilkinson, Richard H. 2000. *The Complete Temples of Ancient Egypt.* New York: Thames & Hudson.

Williams, Peter W. 2002. *America's Religions: From Their Origins to the Twenty-first Century.* Urbana: University of Illinois Press.

Willsen, Jennifer S. 2003. *Alternatives to the Peace Corps: A Directory of Third World and U.S. Volunteer Opportunities.* Oakland, Calif.: Food First Books.

Wilson, Bryan R. 1970. *Religious Sects.* London: Weidenfield & Nicholson.

Wilson, Bryan R., and Jamie Cresswell, eds. 1999. *New Religious Movements.* New York: Routledge.

Wilson, Graham K. 1990. *Interest Groups.* Oxford, UK: Blackwell.

Wilson, J., H. Adams, and D. Carlson. 1993. "Cal-Pal: A County-Wide Volunteer Service Program." *Iowa Journal of School Social Work* 6(1/2):75–85.

Wilson, James Q. 1974. *Political Organizations.* New York: Basic Books.

Wilson, Marlene. 1976. *The Effective Management of Volunteer Programs.* Boulder, Colo.: Volunteer Management Associates.

———. 1983. *How to Mobilize Church Volunteers.* Minneapolis: Augsburg Publishing.

Wilson, Philip K. 2002. "Harry Laughlin's Eugenic Crusade to Control the 'Socially Inadequate' in Progressive Era America." *Patterns of Prejudice* 36:49–67.

Witcover, Jules. 2003. *Party of the People: A History of the Democrats.* New York: Random House.

Witmer, Judith T., and Carolyn S. Anderson. 1994. *How to Establish a High School Service Learning Program.* Alexandria, Va.: Association for Supervision and Curriculum Development.

Wittich, Bill. 2002. *Keep Those Volunteers Around.* Fullerton, Calif.: Knowledge Transfer Publishing.

———. 2003a. *Model Volunteer Handbook.* Fullerton, Calif.: Knowledge Transfer Publishing.

———. 2003b. *77 Ways to Recognize Volunteers.* Fullerton, Calif.: Knowledge Transfer Publishing.

———. 2003c. *77 Ways to Recruit Volunteers.* Fullerton, Calif.: Knowledge Transfer Publishing.

Wittrock, Bjorn. 2004. "The Making of Sweden." *Thesis Eleven* 77 (May):45–63.

Wittstock, Laura W., and Theatrice Williams. 1998. *Changing Communities, Changing Foundations: The Story of the Diversity Efforts of Twenty Community Foundations.* Minneapolis: Rainbow Research.

Wolf, Daniel R. 1991. *The Rebels: A Brotherhood of Outlaw Bikers.* Toronto: University of Toronto Press.

Wolf, Thomas. 1999. *Managing a Nonprofit Organization in the Twenty-first Century.* New York: Simon & Schuster.

Wolfe, Alan. 2001. "What Is Altruism?" Pp. 320–330 in *The Nature of the Nonprofit Sector,* ed. J. Steven Ott. Boulder, Colo.: Westview Press.

Wolfe, Joan L. 1991. *Making Things Happen: The Guide for Members of Voluntary Organizations.* Washington, D.C.: Island Press.

Wolfenden Committee. 1978. *The Future of Voluntary Organisations: Report of the Wolfenden Committee.* London: Croom Helm.

Wolff, Kurt H., ed. 1950. *The Sociology of Georg Simmel.* Glencoe, Ill.: Free Press.

Woliver, Laura R. 1993. *From Outrage to Action: The Politics of Grass-Roots Dissent.* Urbana: University of Illinois Press.

Wolozin, H. 1975. "The Economic Role and Value of Volunteer Work in the United States: An Explanatory Study." *Journal of Voluntary Action Research* 4:23–42.

Wood, Creston. 1988. "Securing Tax Exemption for Exempt Organizations." Pp. 4.1–4.25 in *The Nonprofit Organization Handbook,* 2nd ed., ed. Tracy D. Connors. New York: McGraw-Hill.

Wood, James L., and Maurice Jackson. 1982. *Social Movements.* Belmont, Calif.: Wadsworth.

Wood, John. 2003. "Hell's Angels and the Illusion of the Counterculture." *Journal of Popular Culture* 37:336–351.

Wood, Miriam M. 1996. *Nonprofit Boards and Leadership.* San Francisco: Jossey-Bass.

Wood, Peter. 2003. *Diversity: The Invention of a Concept.* San Francisco: Encounter Books.

Woycke, James. 2003. *Au Naturel: The History of Nudism in Canada.* Etobicoke, Ont.: Federation of Canadian Nudists.

Wouters, Mieke. 2001. "Ethnic Rights under Threat: The Black Peasant Movement against Armed Groups' Pressure in the Choco, Columbia." *Bulletin of Latin American Research* 20(4):498–519.

Wright, John R., and Bruce I. Oppenheimer. 2003. *Interest Groups and Congress.* New York: Longman.

Wuthnow, Robert. 1991a. *Acts of Compassion: Caring for Others and Helping Ourselves.* Princeton, N.J.: Princeton University Press.

———. 1991b. *Between States and Markets: The Voluntary Sector in Comparative Perspective.* Princeton, N.J.: Princeton University Press.

———. 1994. *Sharing the Journey: Support Groups and America's New Quest for Community.* New York: Free Press.

———. 1998. *Loose Connections.* Cambridge, Mass.: Harvard University Press.

———. 2004. *Saving America? Faith-Based Services and the Future of Civil Society.* Princeton, N.J.: Princeton University Press.

Wymer, Walter W., and Sridhar Samu, eds. 2003. *Nonprofit and Business Sector Collaboration.* New York: Best Business Books.

Yale, Robyn. 1995. *Developing Support Groups for Individuals with Early-Stage Alzheimer's Disease.* Baltimore: Health Professions Press.

Yamamoto, Tadashi, and Takayoshi Amenomori, eds. 1998. *The Nonprofit Sector in Japan.* New York: Manchester University Press.

Yankey, John A., and Carol K. Willen. 2004. "Strategic Alliances." Pp.254–273 in *The Jossey-Bass Handbook of Nonprofit Leadership and Management,* 2nd ed., ed. Robert D. Herman and Associates. San Francisco: Jossey-Bass.

Yinger, J. Milton. 1970. *The Scientific Study of Religion.* New York: Macmillan.

Young, David W. 1994. "Management Accounting." Pp. 444–484 in *The Jossey-Bass Handbook of Nonprofit Leadership and Management,* ed. Robert D. Herman and Associates. San Francisco: Jossey-Bass.

Young, Denis R. 1989. "Local Autonomy in a Franchise Age: Structural Change in National Voluntary Associations." *Nonprofit and Voluntary Sector Quarterly* 18:101–117.

Young, Dennis R., Stephen J. Finch, and Daniel Gonsiewski. 1977. *Foster Care and Nonprofit Agencies.* Lexington, Mass.: Lexington Books.

Young, Dennis R., Virginia A. Hodgkinson, and Robert M. Hollister. 1993. *Governing, Leading, and Managing Nonprofit Organizations.* San Francisco: Jossey-Bass.

Bibliography

Young, Joyce, John Swaigen, and Ken Wyman. 2002. *Fundraising for Nonprofit Groups*. 5th ed. Bellingham, Wash.: Self-Counsel Press.

Young, Ruth C., and Olaf F. Larson. 1965. "The Contribution of Voluntary Organizations to Community Service." *American Journal of Sociology* 71:178–186.

Yount, Christine. 1998. *Awesome Volunteers*. Loveland, Colo.: Group Publications.

Zablocki, B. 1981. *Alienation and Charisma: A Study of Contemporary Communes*. New York: Free Press.

Zack, Gerard M. 2003. *Fraud and Abuse in Nonprofit Organizations*. Hoboken, N.J.: Wiley.

Zagorin, Perez. 2003. *How the Idea of Religious Toleration Came to the West*. Princeton, N.J.: Princeton University Press.

Zakin, Susan. 1995. *Coyotes and Town Dogs: Earth First! and the Environmental Movement*. New York: Penguin Books.

Zald, Mayer N., and Roberta Ash. 1966. "Social Movement Organizations: Growth, Decay and Change." *Social Forces* 44(3):327–341.

Zald, Mayer N., and Patricia Denton. 1987. "Religious Groups as Crucibles of Social Movements." Pp. 161–184 in *Social Movements in an Organizational Society: Collected Essays*, ed. Mayer N. Zald and John D. McCarthy. New Brunswick, N.J.: Transaction Publishers.

Zald, Mayer N., and John D. McCarthy, eds. 1979. *The Dynamics of Social Movements*. Cambridge, Mass.: Winthrop.

———. 1987. "Resource Mobilization and Social Movements: A Partial Theory." Pp. 15–48 in *Social Movements in an Organizational Society: Collected Essays*, ed. Mayer N. Zald and John D. McCarthy. New Brunswick, N.J.: Transaction Publishers.

Zander, Alvin. 1993. *Making Boards Effective: The Dynamics of Nonprofit Governing Boards*. San Francisco: Jossey-Bass.

Zellner, William W. 1995. *Countercultures: A Sociological Analysis*. New York: St. Martin's Press.

Zellner, William W., and Marc Petrowsky, eds. 1998. *Sects, Cults, and Spiritual Communities*. Westport, Conn.: Praeger.

Zerubavel, Eviatar T. 1992. *Terra Cognita: The Mental Discovery of America*. New Brunswick, N.J.: Rutgers University Press.

Zieger, Robert H. 1995. *American Workers, American Unions*. 2nd ed. Baltimore: Johns Hopkins University Press.

Zimmerman, Marc A. 1995. "Psychological Empowerment: Issues and Illustrations." *American Journal of Community Psychology* 23:581–600.

Zipf, George K. 1949. *Human Behavior and the Principle of Least Effort: An Introduction to Human Ecology*. Cambridge, Mass: Addison-Wesley Press.

Zukowski, Linda M. 1998. *Fistfuls of Dollars: Fact and Fiction about Corporate Giving*. Redondo Beach, Calif.: EarthWrites.

Zurcher, Louis, and David A. Snow. 1990. "Collective Behavior: Social Movements." Pp. 447–482 in *Social Psychology: Sociological Perspectives*, ed. Morris Rosenberg and Ralph H. Turner. New Brunswick, N.J.: Transaction Publishers.

Index

Index

Index

Index

Index

David Horton Smith received his Ph.D. in Sociology from Harvard University (1965) and has spent most of his career as a professor in that field at Boston College, retiring in 2004. He is the founder of the Association for Research on Nonprofit Organizations and Voluntary Action (ARNOVA) and its journal. In 1993 he received the first ARNOVA Lifetime Achievement Award. His career-long central interest has been grassroots associations. His most recent book is *Grassroots Associations* (2000).

Robert A. Stebbins, FRSC, is Faculty Professor in the Department of Sociology, University of Calgary. He received his Ph.D. from the University of Minnesota (1964). He has written thirty-three books, including *Between Work and Leisure* and *Volunteering as Leisure/Leisure as Volunteering: An International Assessment,* as well as numerous articles and chapters. Stebbins is a Fellow of the Royal Society of Canada.

Michael A. Dover is Assistant Professor at Central Michigan University in the Department of Sociology, Anthropology, and Social Work. His voluntary action began in the anti-war, alternative press, and Chile solidarity movements from 1966 to 1974. In 1975, he entered social work, earning degrees at Adelphi and Columbia. He was co-convenor in 1985 of the Bertha Capen Reynolds Society (now the Social Welfare Action Alliance), a national organization of social work and human service activists. In 1991, he returned to Ann Arbor and earned a doctorate in social work and sociology (2003).